John Harris

The Great Commission

The Christian church constituted and charged to convey the gospel to the world

John Harris

The Great Commission
The Christian church constituted and charged to convey the gospel to the world

ISBN/EAN: 9783337285265

Printed in Europe, USA, Canada, Australia, Japan

Cover: Foto ©Lupo / pixelio.de

More available books at **www.hansebooks.com**

THE
GREAT COMMISSION:

OR,

THE CHRISTIAN CHURCH CONSTITUTED AND CHARGED TO
CONVEY THE GOSPEL TO THE WORLD

BY THE
REV. JOHN HARRIS, D.D.,
AUTHOR OF "MAMMON," "THE GREAT TEACHER," ETC

DAYTON, OHIO:
UNITED BRETHREN PUBLISHING HOUSE.
W. J. SHUEY, AGENT.
1886.

Contents.

	PAGE
INTRODUCTION	ix
PREFATORY NOTICE BY THE ADJUDICATORS	xiii
PREFACE	xvii

PART I.

THE MISSIONARY ENTERPRISE VIEWED GENERALLY IN ITS RELATION TO THE WORD OF GOD.

CHAPTER I.

THE SCRIPTURE THEORY OF CHRISTIAN INSTRUMENTALITY FOR THE CONVERSION OF THE WORLD STATED AND EXPLAINED.

I. Mutual dependence and influence the law of the universe. II. Its perversion by sin. III. Its restoration by Christ. IV. The plan of its operation in the Christian Church for the recovery of the world. 1. How it begins with the individual convert—2. Proceeds through him to the formation of a particular church—3. Leads to the formation of other churches, and unites the whole in one body—4. The Spirit preceding and pervading it to give it effect.

V. In this organization, every thing becomes an element of influence, congenial with the cross, and subordinate to it. Knowledge—Speech—Relationships—Property—Self-denial—Compassion—Perseverance in Christian activity—Prayer—Union...21

CHAPTER II.

THIS THEORY ILLUSTRATED AND ENFORCED FROM THE PRECEPTS AND EXAMPLES OF THE WORD OF GOD.

1. From the paternal character of the antediluvian economy—2. The migratory character of the Abrahamic—3. The national and stationary character of the Mosaic—4. The life and character of Christ—5. The agency of the Holy Spirit—6. The commands of Christ, direct or implied—7. The first missionary—8. The first missionary Church—9. The tenor of the Epistles—10. Forms part of a universal plan, which includes the agency of angels—11. And which devolves and accumulates all the moral influences of the Church from age to age..61

CHAPTER III.

ILLUSTRATED AND ENFORCED FROM PROPHECY.

1. Does prophecy afford any glimpses of the ultimate results of such instrumentality?—2. Will the final triumph of Christianity be in any way indebted to such agency?—3. Circumstances which now render this inquiry peculiarly important—4. Millenarianism (as popularly understood) unfriendly to missionary activity.
I. Millenarian doctrine at variance with some of the leading principles of Divine truth—1. With the fact that Divine commands imply the promise of aid and success—2. With the sincerity of the Divine character—3. With the Divine benignity—4. With the ordinary and wise reserve of Scripture—5. And is derogatory to the dispensation of the Spirit.
II Not warranted by prophecy. III. The enlargement of the Church resulting from Christian activity. IV. This view corroborated by every part of the word of God by which its correctness can be fairly tested. V. The whole harmonized with the foregoing parts, and applied 102

CONTENTS.

PART II.

THE BENEFITS OF THE MISSIONARY ENTERPRISE.

CHAPTER I.

THE HISTORY OF CHRISTIAN MISSIONS.

I. The state of the Church has varied in proportion as it has been faithful or otherwise to its missionary design. II. Progress of Christianity through the successive ages of the Christian era—1. Sixteenth century, or reformation within the Church—2. Seventeenth century, or period of missionary preparation and promise—3. Eighteenth century, or period of missionary association—4. Nineteenth century, or period of missionary enterprise. III Events which may be regarded as dividing the brief history of modern missions into epochs. IV. Statistical summary.......138

CHAPTER II.

ADVANTAGES OF THE MISSIONARY ENTERPRISE TO THE HEATHENS.

SECTION I.

TEMPORAL BENEFITS.

What it has done in this respect for the various nations of Christendom—1. Some islands owe their discovery to it—2. Wandering tribes localized—3. Taught useful arts and trades—4. Languages reduced to a written form—5. Education given—6. Laws and government instituted—7. Morality promoted—8. Checked depopulation and prevented extinction—9. Mediated between hostile tribes, and prevented sanguinary conflicts—10. Retrieved their slandered mental character—11. Protected the oppressed, liberated the enslaved—12. Various evils blotted out—13. Elevating effect on the character and social rank of woman; general views of temporal benefits; benefits unascertained greater still... 153

SECTION II.

RELIGIOUS BENEFITS.

1. Abolished idolatry—2. Imparted Christian instruction—3. Alleviated moral miseries—4. Instrumentally converted and saved many—5. Bibles; ordinances; churches—6. Accessions to the Church above..175

CHAPTER III.

THE REFLEX BENEFITS OF CHRISTIAN MISSIONS.

SECTION I.

TEMPORAL ADVANTAGES.

These afford a fine illustration of the remunerative influence of benevolence—1. Rendered great service to literature and science—2. Corrected and enlarged our views of the character and condition of man—3. Vindicated our own character in the eyes of the heathen—4. Preserved European life—5. Benefited our commerce—6. And shipping...183

SECTION II.

RELIGIOUS BENEFITS.

1. Broke up the prevailing monotony of the religious community—2. Enlivened the piety of Christians, and increased their happiness—3. Produced denominational emulation among them—4. Led to the formation of other institutions—5. Taught us that the cause of religion, abroad and at home, is one—6. Greatly enlarged our Christian views—7. Promoted sympathetic union of Christians—8. Increased pecuniary liberality—9. Awakened and cherished a spirit of prayer—10. Produced noble specimens of Christian character—11. Shown us the practicability of the missionary enterprise, and impressed us with our individual obligation to espouse it—12. Disarmed infidelity of its principal weapon—13. Promoted biblical study—increased the evidences of Christianity, and deepened our confidence in the divinity of its character and the certainty of its triumphs—14. Been the means of converting many of our countrymen abroad and at home—15. And, in various ways, eminently glorified God................................192

CHAPTER IV.

ARGUMENT DERIVED FROM THE BENEFITS OF CHRISTIAN MISSIONS FOR THE INCREASED ACTIVITY OF THE CHURCH.

I. Our missionary success fully proportioned to our efforts. II. Advantages have flowed from them which nothing else could have conferred. III. The history of modern missions illustrates every part of the theory of Christian influence. IV. Supplies a powerful motive to the increase of our missionary zeal 216

PART III.

ENCOURAGEMENTS OF CHRISTIANS TO PROSECUTE THE MISSIONARY ENTERPRISE.

I. Encouragement from the history of Christianity. II. Encouragement from the political aspect of the world. III. Encouragement from the moral state of the world. IV. Encouragement from the state of the Protestant churches. V. Encouragement from the word of God.
Connection with the preceding parts, and application of the whole. 231

PART IV

OBJECTIONS TO THE MISSIONARY ENTERPRISE.

I. The missionary enterprise unnecessary—the heathen safe. II. The missionary enterprise impracticable. III. Civilization should precede Christianity. IV. We have "heathen enough at home." V. We have not the necessary funds. VI. Of no avail, till Christians are united. VII. Of no avail, till the "personal reign" of Christ. VIII. The time is not yet come—" must not take God's work out of his hands," etc., etc.
Reflections 269

PART V.

THE WANTS OF THE CHRISTIAN CHURCH, AS A MISSIONARY SOCIETY, EXAMINED.

Found to consist, generally, in the want of entire devotedness to its office—1. More particularly in deep humility—2. In the due appreciation of the spiritual nature of its office—3. A clear conception and vivid conviction of the missionary constitution of the Christian Church—4. Missionary information should be more widely circulated, and more seriously pondered—5. A greater depth of personal piety—6. Holy wisdom to mark and improve the movements of Providence—7. Greater devotedness to the missionary object among ministers at home—8. Christian union—9. Greater pecuniary liberality—10. Missionary laymen—11. Energy and zeal—12. Prayer.
The whole applied to the enforcement of entire consecration........300

PART VI.

MOTIVES TO ENFORCE ENTIRE DEVOTEDNESS TO THE MISSIONARY ENTERPRISE.

1. To retrieve, if possible, the evil effects of past neglect—2. As the only alternative of partial hostility against Christ, at present—3 The state of the heathen requires it—4. The remarkable manner in which Providence is calling for it—5. Some have thus devoted themselves—6. It is only a devoted Church that is prepared to turn the characteristics of the age, change and transition, to a scriptural account—7. We are likely to impart our character to the future—8. Nothing done for Christ is lost—9. All things belong to him—10. The claim of redemption—11. The relative object of redemption—12. It would complete the honor of the gospel—13. Our regard for the glory of God requires it—14. And it would be the completion of human happiness.
Conclusion 348

Prefatory Notice

BY

THE ADJUDICATORS.

To the mind of the Christian philanthropist, no subject can possess a deeper interest than the state and prospects of the world in relation to the gospel of Christ: its *state*, as presenting, in the middle of the nineteenth century of the Christian era, so painfully mysterious an extent of ignorance, ungodliness, and misery: its *prospects*, as assured by the promises of the God of truth and mercy, of an approaching period of universal knowledge, love, purity, and happiness. Estimating the value of means by the value of the end to which they are subservient, the subject of *missions to the heathen*, for the subversion of false religions by the diffusion and Divine power of the true, cannot fail to hold a place preeminently high, in the minds of all who fear God, love the Saviour, and desire the good of their race.

Influenced by such convictions and feelings, "a few friends of the missionary enterprise in Scotland," connected with the Scottish Establishment, but modestly concealing their names, formed the purpose, between three and four years ago, of attempting the infusion of fresh spirit into the benevolent exertions of the Christian Church at large, for the speedier evangelization of the world, by inviting a "friendly competition" of talent and piety, in the production of a work less ephemeral than "the many excellent sermons, tracts, and pamphlets, which, during the last forty years, have appeared on the subject of missions to the heathen." With this view, these unknown philanthropists offered a prize of TWO HUNDRED GUINEAS for the best, and another prize of FIFTY GUINEAS for the second best Essay on THE DUTY, PRIVILEGE, AND ENCOURAGEMENT OF CHRISTIANS TO SEND THE GOSPEL OF SALVATION TO THE UNENLIGHTENED NATIONS OF THE EARTH. The competition was understood to be confined within the limits of the United Kingdom. The extension of it to America was subsequently suggested; but the suggestion, by whatever considerations recommended, came too late to admit of its being honorably adopted.

The proposals issued were commended to public notice and Christian interest by the signatures of three eminent ministers of the Established Church of Scotland—of whom one has since gone hence, to receive the reward of a faithful servant—the Rev. Dr. Chalmers, the late Rev. Dr. M'Gill, and the Rev. Dr. Duff. The Essays (with the usual precautions for the concealment of the writers' names) were to be submitted to the examination of *five adjudicators*, selected, on a principle of honorable liberality, from those bodies of Christians with which stood associated the principal Missionary Institutions—the two Established Churches of Scotland and England, the Wesleyan Methodists, the Independents, and the Baptists. *Forty-two* Essays were received, differing very widely indeed in character and claims, from some of an inferior order, rising, through higher degrees in the scale of merit, to a considerable number of sterling excellence. Between several of these the Adjudicators found no little difficulty in coming to a decision; nor did they ultimately arrive at perfect unanimity. The Essay which is now presented to the public, the production of the Rev. Dr. JOHN HARRIS, of Cheshunt College, was, after hesitation and correspondence, placed first by four Adjudicators out of the five; and, by the same majority, the second place was assigned to the Essay which has found for its claimant the Rev. RICHARD WINTER HAMILTON, of Leeds.

By one of the Adjudicators, the first place was given to a different Essay from either of these; which, also, in the judgment of more than one of the rest, competed strongly for the second, as a treatise of great excellence. In these circumstances, the Committee, desirous to give the cause every possible advantage, resolved on offering a distinct premium to its author—subsequently discovered to be the Rev. JOHN MACFARLANE, minister of the parish of Collessie, Fife; and, under their sanction, with the generous concurrence of the two successful competitors, and with the recommendation of such of the Adjudicators as felt themselves at liberty to give it, this Essay, too, will be published.

The Adjudicators, influenced in their decision by the sentiment, arrangement, style, and comprehensiveness of the Essays, and by their general adaptation to the avowed object of the projectors of the prize, have given that decision *in foro conscientiæ;* and they now leave it, so far as opportunity for judging is afforded, to the tribunal of public opinion. They consider it necessary, at the same time, to add, that, having selected the Essays which appeared to them the best, they are by no means to be understood as, either collectively or individually, testifying approval of every view or opinion of their respective authors.

An apology is due, especially to the Essayists, for the long, and what to them must have been the somewhat vexatious delay on the part of the Adjudicators, in delivering their decision. Such apology they deem it sufficient thus to offer, on behalf of themselves, and of the Committee, without attempting any detail of explanation, how satisfactory soever such detail might be rendered.

It now only remains that they breathe a united and fervent prayer for the success of this endeavor to advance the glory of God, and the happiness and salvation of men: a prayer in which they invite their fellow-Christians of every denomination to join—that the present Essay, as well as such others as may pass through the press, may, under the providence of the Divine Head of the Church, contribute to the further excitement of his people's zeal in this highest and best of causes; and so may accelerate the arrival of that happy period, when his own gracious and faithful assurance, confirmed with his oath, and pregnant with so vast an amount of blessing to mankind, shall obtain its full realization—"As surely as I live, all the earth shall be filled with my glory."

David Welsh
Ralph Wardlaw
Henry Melville.
Jabez Bunting.
Thos. S. Crisp.

Preface.

If the writer may be allowed to engage the attention of his readers for a moment, before they enter on the perusal of the following pages, his only aim in so doing will be to facilitate that perusal.

Of course, his first object in preparing this Essay has been to comply with the requirements of the advertisement, which has, indirectly at least, occasioned its existence. His compliance with these, however, has not prevented him from aiming at a point higher still; rather, it has formed the proper and natural ascent to it. That aim, he trusts, has imprinted its character, more or less visibly, on every portion of his work. He would briefly describe it as threefold; and endeavor to show that the Church of Christ is aggressive and missionary in its very constitution and design; its "field is the world;" that it is to look on the whole of this field as one, not regarding the claims of any particular portion as inimical to the interests of any other; but viewing the Divine command which obliges it to seek the salvation of any one individual, or the evangelization of any one country, as binding it to attempt the recovery of the whole world; but that, in order to the accomplishment of this high design, more is necessary than mere activity; that the entire consecration of all its resources is, for obvious reasons, made indispensable to success.

With this view, he has attempted to fill up the following outline. In the First Part, consisting of three chapters, his object has been to state and explain the Sripture theory of Christian instrumentality: to show, by a general examination of the Word of God, that this theory is there prescribed and made imperative; and that the same Divine authority predicts and promises its triumph in the conversion of the world. Thus, if the first chapter states the plan by which all the holy influences of the *past* should have been collected, multiplied, and combined, the second exhibits and enforces the obligation of the *present* to that entire consecration which the plan supposes; and the third engages that such consecration shall certainly issue in the *future* and universal erection of the kingdom of Christ. Having thus, in the First Part, viewed the Missionary Enterprise generally in its relations to the Word of God, the writer has proceeded, in the Second Part, to exhibit the *benefits* arising from Christian Missions, with the view of still further illustrating and enforcing their claims. This he has done in four chapters, the first of which contains an historical sketch of the diffusion of Christianity, and of the rise and progress of Modern Missions, with a statistical summary of their present state :* the second enumerates the leading temporal and spiritual benefits accruing to the heathen from Missionary operations: the third describes their reflex

---

* Perhaps the reader unacquainted with the fact ought to be informed that the "Evidence on the Aborigines," which is frequently appealed to in this part of the work, was given before a committee of the House of Commons, by the secretaries of the Church Missionary Society, the Wesleyan Missionary Society, and London Missionary Society, and by other competent witnesses.

advantages, temporal and spiritual; and the fourth shows that the history and effects of the Missionary Enterprise illustrate every view of the theory of Christian influence contained in the First Part, and supply a powerful inducement to the increase of missionary zeal. The Third Part exhibits the various sources of encouragement—historical and political, moral, ecclesiastical, and evangelical—which urge and animate Christians to advance in their missionary career. In the Fourth Part, he has endeavored to show that every objection to their course becomes, when rightly considered, an argument to redouble their efforts. But the Fifth Part ascertains the existence of a great defect—of the want of that entireness of consecration to their missionary office which is indispensable to complete success, and points out the various requisites which such consecration includes, and would infallibly supply; while the Sixth Part enforces the principal motives which should induce their entire devotedness to the great objects of the Missionary Enterprise.

Such, indeed, is the surpassing grandeur of the object of Christian missions, as to render any thing like justice to its merits impossible. Yet the writer feels humbled that the present contribution should fall so far short, even of his own conception, of what such a work might and ought to be. He is proportionally delighted, therefore, that since it was submitted for competent adjudication, so many able works on missions should have issued from the press as to render specification difficult; and especially that, besides having for its precursor the very seasonable and powerful production of the Rev. Dr. JOHN CAMPBELL, it should be accompanied, or speedily followed, by the publications of his well-known, able, and beloved friend, the Rev. R. W. HAMILTON, of Leeds; and of the Rev. JOHN MACFARLANE

Evident as it is that a crisis in the Missionary Enterprise

approaches—a crisis created partly by its successes abroad and by its reflex operation in calling into existence other societies at home, which divide with it the contributions of the faithful—his earnest prayer to God is, that this Essay, in connection with those of his Christian brethren referred to, may be among the means employed to convert that crisis into a blessing—the commencement of a new era of missionary prosperity.

CHESHUNT COLLEGE,
Feb. 12, 1842.

THE GREAT COMMISSION.

PART I.

THE MISSIONARY ENTERPRISE VIEWED IN ITS RELATION TO THE WORD OF GOD.

CHAPTER I.

THE SCRIPTURE THEORY OF CHRISTIAN INSTRUMENTALITY FOR THE EVANGELIZATION OF THE WORLD STATED AND EXPLAINED.

I. MUTUAL dependence and influence is the law of the universe. Look in whatever direction, and examine whatever object we may, we find nothing insulated and alone. From the globe we inhabit, which is one of a visible community of worlds, up to the great sidereal system, the whole of which is apparently moving together through space, and down to the minutest atom that floats in the air, all are bound together, and constantly acting on each other, by definite and universal laws. The body of the reader and the book which he is reading are held, by gravitation, in union with the remotest parts of the created system; while the material influences constantly transmitted from the most distant regions of space place them in physical contact with the universe.

In this literal dependence of every part of the material economy on every other part, we behold an image of the reciprocal action and mutual relation of all animated being. Here, each is connected with all, and the whole to God.

Here, in the absence of sin, we behold the sublime spectacle of the infinitely blessed God surrounded by distinct orders of sentient, happy beings; so various as to reach from the archangel down to the insect, yet so closely related, as parts of a mighty whole, that no single member can be detached and made independent of the rest; while the well-being of each is an ingredient in the happiness of the whole; and all, according to their respective natures, ascribe glory to Him, their centre and their source, by whom they are alike pervaded, and in whom they are all one.

That this interdependence, as far as it relates to the human family, is part of an original plan, is obvious. By creating, at first, one common father of the species, the Almighty designed that each individual should stand related to all the rest, and feel himself pledged to promote their happiness. By rendering us necessary to each other's welfare, he sought to train us up to an humble imitation of his own goodness, to make every hand and heart a consecrated channel for his love to flow in, and thus to find our own happiness in the happiness of others. In such a state, he who approached nearest to the pattern of the Divine Benevolence would necessarily have been the object of the greatest admiration; and as admiration leads, by a law of our nature, to imitation, men would have been always advancing towards higher and higher degrees of perfection. Inferior excellence being constantly drawn upwards by the strong moral attraction of that which was above it, a process of assimilation to the blessed God would have been perpetually going on, which would have rendered earth a copy of heaven.

The connection, then, subsisting between them would have been one, not merely of mutual dependence, but of reciprocal influence. And this moral influence it is which would have invested their mutual relation with so much importance. Could we have looked down upon them, we should have seen that every word uttered projected an influence: that every action performed drew after it a train of influence: that every relation sustained was a line along which was constantly transmitted a vital influence: that every individual was a centre ever radiating streams of living moral influence.

Could we have selected one such individual, and have investigated his moral history, we should have found that, from the first moment of his existence, his character went on daily and hourly streaming with more than electric fluid—with a subtle, penetrating element of moral influence: that, in whatever society he mingled, he left on their character, secret, perhaps, but not imperceptible traces that he had been among them: that his influence operated involuntarily; for though he might choose, in any given instance, what he would do, yet having done it, he could not choose what influence it should have: that it operated universally; never terminating on himself, but extending to all within his circle, emanating from each of these again as from a fresh centre, and thus transmitted on, in silent but certain effect, to the outermost circle of social existence: that it was indestructible, not a particle ever being lost, but the whole of it taken up into the general system of cause and effect, and always in operation somewhere. And thus we should have seen that, though he was apparently as isolated as a ship in the midst of the Atlantic, the waves which the motion of that ship generates from shore to shore were only an image of his ever-circling, widening, shoreless influence; and that the influence which thus blended and bound him up with the whole race, invisible and impalpable as it is, is yet the mightiest element of society—the element wielded by God himself.

But then, if such the relation and such the distinct influence of these holy, happy beings, their responsibility for the use of that influence would have been proportionate. The very fact that God had invested them with such influence would, without any verbal command, have been regarded by them as a sufficient expression of his will that they must use it to the utmost, and for his glory. They could not have lived to themselves if they would; for, from the moment they began to live, their influence necessarily linked them to the universe. And they would not if they could, for they would have found that living to God was usefulness, excellence, and happiness, all in one. They would have found that not more certainly is the order of the material world maintained by the action of matter upon matter, than the order of the moral world is by the action of mind upon mind. And under the hallowed influence of that reciprocal action, they would have been perpetually brightening and rising into the image of God.

How far the inhabitants of the celestial world would—on the hypothesis of man having retained his primal innocence—have influenced, by intercourse, the human character, admits of little more than conjecture. That He who has united distinct material worlds by indissoluble bonds, should leave two orders of holy intelligences, both of which had not only sprung from the same Fount of being, but acknowledged the same laws, and exhibited the same paternal image, to pursue their respective courses in perfect and unpassable separation from each other, is, to say the least, highly improbable. That the angelic "sons of God" took a deep and rejoicing interest in the creation of our world, is fact of Divine Revelation. And the scriptural history of the fall of man leaves us to infer that, if such of the angelic order as "kept not their first estate" had access to the human mind for purposes of evil, those of them who retained their original purity would not have been denied access of a similar kind for purposes of good. And thus the intelligent universe would have exhibited the sublime spectacle of distinct orders of holy beings, each composed of innumerable members, producing and receiving continual modifications of character by the mutual action of all its parts; and that modification assimilating them to the central and solar glory, on whom they were all alike dependent, and in whom they were all one.

II. But suppose—it might have been said—suppose that, by some dreadful possibility, *a principle of evil should obtain entrance into this all-related system.* If that entrance should be obtained, first, indeed, among the members of the human order, it is possible that the members of the angelic order, being less accessible to us than we are to them, might escape the contagion. But if it should obtain, first, in the higher order, how likely is it that it will descend and be communicated, by intercourse, to the family of man! In that event,—the very prospect and possibility of which appals,—the reciprocal influence of mind on mind, mightily efficacious as it is for good, may become equally efficacious for evil. One being may become the tempter of another. By the union of each with all, the moral poison may be taken up and circulated through the whole social system. The very first sin would be felt by all the race, and to the last moment of time. If any thing were then wanting to hasten and seal the self-destruction of the guilty community, it would be only the presence of some leading spirit who should be competent to organize and work its complicated agencies on a comprehensive plan. Should such a consummation arrive, how direful the results to those immediately involved, and how incalculable the effects on the universe at large!

Now, this hypothetical case is only a literal description of the history and actual condition of the world. At the time of the creation, a principle of evil was at large in the universe. Satan, together with an unknown multitude of associate rebels, having swerved from his allegiance to "the blessed and only Potentate," had been driven from the immediate presence of God, cut off from the loyal part of the creation, and doomed to be the prey of his own mighty depravity. Actuated by that universal law by which each being and principle seeks to conform all things to its own nature, and stimulated by implacable hatred against God, he came to efface from our world the Divine image, and to stamp his own on its breast instead. In the execution of this dreadful project he succeeded. By no employment of force, but by the simple action of mind on mind, through the medium of the senses, Satan prevailed on man to sin. As the first sinner was the first man, human nature was poisoned in its fountain. The first man is sinning still, in effect, in each of all his posterity. The first sin is thrilling still, and will vibrate on through the whole line of being, till it reaches the last of human kind. How closely compacted, how vitally interwoven, must be the system of our mutual dependence, and how mysteriously penetrating and pervading the principle of our reciprocal influence, when a single sin can thus distract and derange the whole!

Yet now it was that man first made the monstrous essay of living to himself. As if he had only to withdraw his allegiance from God in order to dissolve relations with the universe, selfishness now became the law of his sinful being. But such separation was impossible. Live to himself, in the sense of selfish appropriation, he might; but detach himself from the relations of dependence and influence he could not

Cease to be the centre of a hallowed influence he might; but cease to be the centre of all influence he could not. From the moment he ceased to be a universal good, he became a universal evil. Each act of selfishness is the infliction of a universal injury. And every successive sin awakens afresh the echoes of the original curse. Not only did our primary relations of mutual influence remain—the introduction of sin appears to have stimulated them into preternatural activity and power. Every man in effect became a Jeroboam—his life laid a train of evil for multitudes, and for ages to come. His infantine hand could open a floodgate of evil which the arm of Omnipotence alone could shut. His careless laugh could do more to counteract a moral principle than the proclamation of a law could do to enforce it. Though touching only one point in society, he could send an impulse of evil through the whole. While the thunders of Sinai soon died away to a whisper on the ear of the world, many a whisper of evil, as it passed from lip to lip, waxed louder and louder, till nations echoed with the sound, and distant ages received its reverberations as possessing all the authority of law.

Parental influences, blending with the first rudiments of infant being, tainted character in its very source. Familiar intercourse became one of the grand ordinances of mutual temptation and ruin. Relationships, calculated to circulate happiness through all the veins of the social system, were perverted by sin into so many channels of destruction. Tendencies and influences of evil, which had long been gathering, gradually assumed the definite and enduring form of civil government, and gave a character to nations; from which, again, as from so many centres, they propagated their effects through all the globe and for all time. Evil example, acquiring the despotic power of precedent and custom, showed itself stronger than any thing human which could be brought to counteract it; tended to displace every other power, and claimed to reign alone. In a word, the social principle, in all its forms, entered into the service of sin, and showed itself mightier for evil than for good. Thrones and temples, collecting the scattered elements of evil, concentrated, strengthened, and gave them back again to the world under the solemn names of law and religion. Yes, religion itself, or that at least which bore the name, lived only to aggravate the evil and to keep it in constant and destructive circulation. Satan became "the god of this world." Wherever he looked, the expanse was his own. Temptation in his hands had become a science, and sin was taught by rule. The world was for him one storehouse of evil—an armory, in which every object and event ranked as a weapon, and all were classed and kept ready for service. He beheld the complicated machinery of evil, which his mighty malignity had constructed, in full and efficient operation, and the whole resulting in a vast, organized, and consolidated empire.

But more: not only did the laws of our mutual influence remain—not only did sin stimulate them into fearful activity—they increased in power with each successive age. The mechanical philosophy informs us that, on the principle of the equality of action and reaction, no motion impressed by natural causes, or by human agency, is ever obliterated. No sound or sentiment, therefore, which has ever been uttered, is or can be lost. The pulsations of the air, which the utterance set in motion, continue in their effect to operate still; so that every sound or sentiment will be recoverable in the most distant ages. No deed has ever been performed without leaving behind it, on some part of the material universe, an indestructible witness to its existence. Had any one of all these sentiments and deeds never been uttered or performed, certain impressions would have been wanting from the material elements which they now contain; so that they form at this moment a minute and faithful record, to an eye capable of reading it, of all the eventful past. Their existing state is the complicated result of all the impressions produced on them from the commencement of time, and presents to the eye of Omniscience a vast book of remembrance, from whose unerring pages he could read forth at large the history of the world.

Just so, when the world had existed four thousand years, its moral condition was the exact result of the moral influences of all the past; for it had received the collected effect of the whole. Not only are all contemporaneous things mutually influenced and connected, but there is also a constant increase in the onward course and widening stream of influence from age to age. As every generation owes some part of its character to that which preceded it, so it imparts some portion of its own to that which follows it, and thus propagates the blended and augmented influences of itself and all its predecessors. And this shows the utter impossibility there was that man himself should ever remedy his depraved condition. By necessity of nature, it became worse and worse. Each age, in succession, inheriting the accumulated evils of the past, and adding to them something of its own, transmitted the whole to that which followed, and thus propelled the world in its downward course with an ever-augmenting force. While the air he breathed was only the record of the past, the moral atmosphere in which he moved, from the first moment of his existence to the last, was not merely the record, but the substance of the past; and, as such, it was one of the elements—a part of the material—out of which his character was necessarily formed. It was the atmosphere of a pest-house, and he entered it not merely to breathe the deadly infection of all who had preceded him there, but to add to it the infection of his own disease for all who came after him. So that, even then, when, compared with the unity and amity of heaven, mankind presented the aspect of mutual hostility and universal disorganization, it might most truly have been said, in the sense of relative influence, "No man liveth to himself:" every act of selfishness and sin is the infraction of a universal law, and as such the infliction of a universal evil.

III. What, then, is all lost? Is the benevolent design of God, in appointing the laws of our reciprocal dependence and influence, irretrievably defeated? Was the dreadful event of its perversion unforeseen and unprovided for? Has the chain of dependence, which unites us together, passed entirely into the hands of the destroyer, and is it henceforth to be used only for dragging mankind together to perdition? If not, *where is the remedy?* What can be the nature of that plan which, when all the influences of earth have been perverted to evil, can, without doing violence to any original principle, convert the whole into good? What can be the nature of that Being who, coming into the midst of a world where all men are laboring to live to themselves, can say, with a power which fulfils its own word, "No man liveth to himself?" Who can arrest a world that has broken away from its proper centre, and can return it to its appointed orbit?—who can stand in the midst of the great vortex of selfishness, and say to the mighty maelstrom, in the height and fury of its all-absorbing whirl, "Flow to the circumference;" and say it with an effect which can make it refund and float its choicest treasures to the ends of the earth: in a word, which can make men, who were their own centre and circumference, take Him for their centre, and for their circumference the universe? What can be the nature of such a Being, and where is he to be found?

"O the depth of the riches both of the wisdom and the knowledge of God!" Not only was the fearful catastrophe not unforeseen—the event demonstrated that mercy had only been waiting the moment of its occurrence, in order to unfold a plan which was evidently calculated on the certainty of that moment arriving—which took advantage of all its dreadful peculiarities—and of which every subsequent event in the Divine economy has been only a constituent part, and every age witnessed the progressive fulfilment. And still more: not only does the economy of our redemption propose to mitigate the destructive tendency of our influence on each other—it actually presses that influence into its own service; and proposes, by the agency of the Holy Spirit, to sanctify and employ it as the chosen instrumentality by which to expel from the earth the evils produced by its perversion; till every man shall once more have become what he was primarily formed to be—an agent of unmingled good to every other man, and the world be restored to God. Without repealing or deranging any of the original relations or existing arrangements of nature, though they had all been perverted into means of destruction, a plan is superinduced which proposes to turn all those relations and arrangements to the highest account, as the means of his recovery: to make the chain of our mutual dependence once more fast to the throne of God.

The seat of that plan was the bosom of God: the essence of that plan was, that the highest influence in the universe should be embodied and brought to bear on us: an influence emanating from Him who concentrates all the energies of the universe in himself, an influence streaming from the open heart of infinite love, should discharge its power on the heart of the world. The obstacle to that plan lay in the apparent impossibility of reconciling such benevolence with the known and necessary hostility of God against sin : of exercising such restorative influence on man, without relaxing general obligation, and thus diffusing a disorganizing influence through the universe at large. But the organ and agent of that plan came forth from his bosom, equal to all its conditions, and bent on its fulfilment. And the glory of that plan consists in this, that the greatest apparent obstacle was made the occasion of its greatest triumph; that the same act which made it consistent for God to be gracious to man, made it impossible for man, when duly acquainted and Divinely impressed with it, to resist its attractive and subduing power. Around that plan the purposes of mercy had from eternity revolved. Its earliest announcement in Eden, though only conveyed as an obscure intimation, touched every spring of hope in human nature, and left an ineffaceable moral impression on the mind of the world. The mere anticipation of that coming fact had the effect, for ages, wherever it was duly cherished, of transforming human hearts, and of bearing them on into the presence of God. And when at length the time for its fulfilment came, with the prospect of its grand results swelling and bursting his heart of love, it was that the Saviour uttered the sublime prediction, "Now shall the prince of this world be cast out; and I, if I be lifted up from the earth, will draw all men unto me." As if he had said, "The central power of the earth is a demon. I look for his throne, and find it in the midst of the world. There, where should have stood the throne of God, stands 'Satan's seat;' while in his hand are all the influences of earth, and at his feet all its prostrate homage. But there shall stand my cross. Casting *him* out, I will become the centre of the recovered world. Those human passions shall burn for me. Those countless idolaters shall bow to me. And all this will I do, not by force, but by influence alone. No single principle of human nature will I violate. Placing myself in harmony with them all, I will embody every element of influence, and engage every holy agency, in the universe. All evil influences have conspired: all good shall combine to oppose them. My benevolence can find employment for all. Man's depravity and danger require them all. None shall be absent. But chiefly thou, Eternal Spirit, my object requires that thou shouldst come to conduct and to give efficiency to the whole."

Thus the Saviour proposed to recover that principle of mutual dependence and influence by which sin was dragging the world to perdition, and to employ it as a golden chain for drawing all men to himself.

Now, could we stay to analyze the elements of the character and work of Christ, *as they relate to man,* we should find that each of them was studiously adapted to act on the human mind as an element of influence; and the more minutely we could examine them, the more should we see to admire in their exquisite adaptation and attractive power. Dignity is influence; and he demonstrated to our conviction that he was the Son of God. Identity of nature is influence; and he became "bone of our bone, and flesh of our flesh." Contiguity is influence; and he came and dwelt among us. Relationship is influence; and, so far from dissolving existing relationships, he actually instituted a new one—he became a man! Instead of moving away farther from us, as our guilt deserved, he came nearer: came, with all the fulness of the Godhead, to be one of ourselves: came to demonstrate before our eyes how much a God can love, a Saviour suffer, a Spirit effect, in order to our salvation. Character is influence: he saw that, as mind rules matter, character rules mind itself, draws other minds into sympathy with it, imparts new impulses to society, speaks with a voice heard by distant nations, and which goes down to future ages. He saw, therefore, that when his character should come to be truly known—known for his unconquerable devotedness to the cause of God and man, in having borne down, by a course of unexampled self-denial, the greatest obstacles in the universe, made his way from heaven, through the ranks of hell, into the midst of the world, and direct to a cross—known for his self-sacrificing benevolence, in having effected an unbroken descent, from heights of glory no wing can scale, to depths of humiliation no line can fathom—known for having presented to a world, which refused to live unto God, the amazing spectacle of a God living to it, turning his whole self into a sacrifice, compared with which nothing else would ever deserve the name—known for the richness of his gifts and the vastness of his design, as including the happiness without measure of numbers without calculation, and for ages without end—all who should experimentally "know the grace of our

Lord Jesus Christ" would be penetrated and possessed with the effect, and would compass sea and land to propagate the report.

He knew also that a Divine influence—the influence of the Spirit himself—would accompany and give it effect. He could foresee, indeed, that the recipients of his grace, moved by the Spirit of truth, would throw all their sanctified human influences into the work of preaching it. But even they who would glory in it the loudest, and or for it the most, would know but comparatively little of its excellence; whereas, the Infinite Spirit knows it perfectly: knows it as the basis of his own agency: knows the central place which the cross occupies, as the means of atonement, in the councils of God, the influence which it exerts on every part of the Divine government, and the glory which it is destined to shed over the universe; and the Saviour saw, therefore, that the Spirit would invest it with a power over the human mind corresponding with its value and supreme importance; and that so entirely would the whole economy be conducted from first to last by his agency, that it would be distinctly known as the dispensation of the Spirit.

True, indeed, what would influence the human mind was not the only thing, was not the first thing, which the Author of salvation had to provide. There was another mind to be consulted. There was the First, the Eternal Mind to be more than consulted—to be propitiated; for man had dared his judicial displeasure. Whatever adaptation, therefore, the gospel might seem to possess, it can contain no effectual remedy for man, unless it be in perfect harmony with that Mind. But to find that even he approves it; that he, who is himself the Infinite Reason, beholds in the satisfaction for sin which it provides a reason paramount to all law, a reason to which even justice bows, and before which it retires; that he who is himself absolute perfection should not only commend it as perfect in itself, but should actually employ it as his chosen instrument for restoring perfection to beings who had lost it; that all the laws of his moral government consent to it, and all the principles of his nature rejoice in it, is of itself sufficient to arm it with an arresting and attractive power. Now, the Saviour knew this: he knew that the cross, as the medium of forgiveness, is the direct product of the

Divine mind; that all the riches of the Divine nature are poured into it; that nothing in the treasury of the Divine resources would be deemed too costly to adorn it, in order to commend it to the world, and to insure its acceptance. He could not doubt, therefore, that the cross, which had moved God in his judicial capacity, will finally be made to move the world; that, as it is the centre round which the purposes of mercy revolve, so all the affections of man will be gathered about it also; that the very fact that God commends it would, when known, invest it with an unlimited sway over every renovated human heart. Yes, he had looked into the mind of man, and he saw that, debased and imbruted as sin had made us, there are still slumbering within us those great principles and powers originally meant to control our nature, and that he who should succeed in awakening them would obtain the mastery over the whole man. He saw that by suffering he should awaken its sympathies; that by suffering for us he should engage its gratitude; that by suffering for sin, which he hated—"bearing our sins in his own body on the tree"— he should be the means of awakening its astonishment and love; that by thus giving to it "a good hope," he should be moving the very first principle of moral power.

He was the maker of the mind, and knew all its mysterious laws and secret springs. That singular law which we call the principle of association, and which is to mind, in effect, what the law of attraction is to matter, drawing together ideas connected by common affinities, and repelling others having no such congeniality, was a law of his own appointment. And he saw how exquisitely the doctrine of the cross was adapted, resulting, as it does, from the first principles in the Divine nature, to touch and move the first principles in ours; and thus to become, through the agency of the Holy Spirit, a new principle of mental and moral association. But he knew that, besides this, the human mind was constituted for the reception and enthronement of one central and ruling idea—the idea of God; that that idea in its purity and vigor has been lost from the mind; that, in the absence of this primary principle, the mind is involved in moral confusion, and the passions perverted by an unlicensed association of ideas; and he saw that the cross, embodying, as it does, the essential compassion and love of God, was divinely calculated to restore order by obtaining ascendency, and to become the all-subordinating principle of the enlightened mind. Though we may not be able by an effort of our will to call up any one train of thought, we can, by the power of the will, select at pleasure any single thought in the succession, and dwell upon it with deep and prolonged attention; and he saw how eminently the cross is calculated to be that object; to rivet the attention and engross the affections of the renewed mind.

He saw that, as every truth, intellectual, moral, and spiritual, is invested by the God of truth with an influence and a power corresponding with its peculiar nature and its importance; and that as spiritual truths are above and beyond all others, as relating to the spiritual and loftiest part of our natures; so the great truth of the world's redemption—the very greatest for a sinful and ruined spirit—would only need to be proclaimed and put into Divine activity; to be brought by the Great Spirit into vital contact and combination with the heart of the world, in order to draw it with irresistible attraction to the Author of that truth. Mighty truths were extant before—truths which created other truths—which, wherever they were announced, quickened into activity the general mind, called forth the mental resources of a people, and went vibrating on through the universe. But a truth was wanting fitted to receive the great power of God—to be "the power of God unto the salvation" of all who should believe it—a truth which should animate all other truths—shed a flood of light and a stimulating influence on original but neglected obligations, and thus be the means of renovating the world. And the Saviour knew that his atoning sacrifice was that great conservative truth. He knew that, as no act terminates in itself, but tends to propagate an influence in obedience to its own laws, and commensurate with its own force—the event of his death for man's redemption—the greatest of all acts—greater than creation—greater than any which God has yet accomplished—would necessarily carry with it an influence greater than the influence flowing from any preceding acts, and therefore calculated, under the dispensation of the Spirit, to master and control the whole.

He saw that as no object in the universe exists alone—that as every thing is the centre of an influence which extends to all within its circle—so the cross, including as it would the means of exciting that love which is the very principle of all holy activity—complicated as it was with all interests of humanity, would become the centre of an influence, to which all other impulses would eventually yield obedience, and a centre of attraction around which all other objects would finally circulate—that the cross of Calvary would become the polar power of the spiritual world, to which every heart would tremble and turn.

He saw in the earnest expectation of the creature waiting for the manifestation of the sons of God, struggling to be delivered from the bondage of corruption into the glorious liberty of the children of God, joined with the Divine adaptation of the gospel to make that manifestation, and to effect that deliverance, a certain pledge of its universal triumph. "For we know that the whole creation groaneth and travaileth in pain together until now." But with how much deeper an emphasis may it be said that He knows it! To his omniscient eye the whole race was present. He marked the multitudes struggling against their fallen condition—carrying their desires beyond the limits of the present—yearning after a something undefined. Yes, he knew that his gospel is the hope of mankind—that every sigh and struggle of the whole creation is an act of homage to the salvation he brought, and a guaranty that all men shall eventually be drawn to him. And beyond this, he knew that so delighted was the Father with his work of mediation, that this redeemed world would be made his property, that the hearts of his people would be his at will, and all their influences his to wield at pleasure. He knew that "for this cause he was to die, and rise, and revive, that he might be Lord of the whole." And when, by anticipation, he heard them saying, "None of us liveth to himself: we are not our own : for us to live is Christ:" when, looking onwards, he saw the cross, in the hand of the Holy Spirit, attracting human hearts, combining human energies, turning every thing into influence, and all that influence into one channel, he exclaimed, "And I, if I be lifted up from the earth, will draw all men unto me."

For "the joy which was thus set before him," He—the Son of God—"endured the cross," as the sacrifice for the world. Into that act were put the heart of Christ, the love of God; and through it comes the mightiest influence of the

Holy Spirit. That cross is the shrine and medium of the whole. By becoming the instrument of human redemption, it acquires the right and the power to give motives to all actions, sanctions to all obligations, objects to all affections, a new nature to man, a new character to the world.

IV. Here, then, is the cross—here are the means for moving the world: where is the agency, or what is the plan for working the mighty engine? The Eternal Father has been moved by it to lift its author up far above all heavens: what is the mode by which, now, in his new and exalted capacity, he will draw the world in homage to his feet? So powerfully does its influence fall on the mind of God, as the means of moral compensation for sin, that he hath given all things into his hands: how is it to fall on the minds of men so as to induce them voluntarily to copy that Divine example? This is obviously the critical part of the great process. O, how important a theatre has earth become! Every eye in the universe is bent on it. Here is to be fought out the grand struggle of evil with good—of hell with heaven. Here the influence of the cross is to challenge and vanquish every other power: who is not anxious to know the plan of the contest?

This brings us to consider *the Scripture theory of Christian instrumentality for the conversion of the world.* The early triumphs of the gospel demonstrated that the influence of the cross was not left to find its way through the world as it could —to operate at random. The plan which provided the influence of the cross, provided, also, the method of its diffusion and propagation. And, on inspection, we shall find that plan so simple in its principle—so connected in its parts—so comprehensive in its outline—and so well adapted for efficiency and success, as to show that the wisdom which framed it was Divine; and that nothing but adherence to it is wanting in order to the conversion of the world.

We have already shown that, by the constitution of our nature, we are made to influence each other; that the perversion of that influence by sin is the great secret and means of the world's continued depravity; that, through the agency of the Holy Spirit, the doctrine of the cross is the antagonist principle, the counter influence by which sin is to be vanquished and man restored. We may expect, therefore, that the instrumentality to be employed in the service of the cross will consist of influence also. And, accordingly, human influence, deriving its efficacy from Heaven, is the specific instrumentality by which the gospel proposes to propagate its transforming effects.

But if so, it follows, of course, that such influence should be congenial with the character—the moral character—of the cross, and be produced by it, for this sufficient reason, that every other influence is, in truth, opposed to the gospel, and constitutes that which requires to be changed by it. The cross stands alone in the world. It does not find friends: it makes them. If it wants an agency, it has to create it. If the iron is to attract, it must itself be magnetized. And if the Saviour proposes to employ human instrumentality for drawing all men unto him, he has first to magnetize that agency at the cross, the great centre of moral attraction.

1. But how shall the gospel commence its operations on man—*individually* or *socially?* Civilization commonly begins with man in his social capacity, by giving laws to a community; expecting that they will gradually impart their appropriate influence to each of its individual members. But Christianity contemplates man, in the first place, *in his individual capacity;* for, besides the fact of his personal responsibility to God, his reception of it, as far as human authority is concerned, is perfectly voluntary. The gospel, therefore, proceeds on the supposition that only a single member of a whole community may embrace it; and, by addressing men at first in their individual capacity, it saves that single member; whereas, had his salvation been suspended on the will of the community, it would have been made impossible, owing to their rejection of the gospel: besides which, Christianity proceeds on the supposition so often realized, that it may only have a solitary agent to convey its message to a whole community; and that, in the midst of that community, he may long labor single-handed and alone. It begins with the individual, therefore, that it may advance to the society. In order to the cohesion and polarity of the globe, every atom of which it is composed is, in its separate capacity, possessed of polarity and attraction. And, in order to the ultimate evangelization of the world, the gospel operates, as it advances, on each of its component parts.

And here be it carefully remarked, that the doctrine of the

cross triumphs, not in the same way as other kinds of truth produce their results—by its mere fitness to convince the judgment, and approve itself to the mind. We believe, indeed, that the gospel has this fitness: that light is not more suited to the eye, than the entire system of evangelical truth is adapted to the original principles of human nature. And we believe that, owing to this inherent adaptation alone, the gospel can produce the mightiest civil and social results, without the aid of any special supernatural influence. And we believe that, because of this inherent adaptation, it is that God employs it to produce the great spiritual result of regeneration. But then we believe that in the production of this result, its mere adaptation alone would leave it quite impotent: that here it encounters a kind and a degree of resistance which renders a Divine agency indispensable: that here the influence of the Spirit comes into operation; and that on this account it is called the "power of God," because God alone renders it powerful to salvation. Hence, also, "faith" is termed "the gift of God." And God is represented as "opening the heart to receive the word." Still, the Spirit of God is pleased to produce the effect through the medium of the truth; and hence the Apostle Peter represents Christians as those who "have purified their souls in obeying the truth through the Spirit." Most impressively, too, is the same combination implied in the command of Christ "to hear what the Spirit saith," although he himself was the speaker; reminding us that this is emphatically the dispensation of the Third Person in the glorious Trinity: that every voice in the Church—even the voice of Christ himself—is in a sense subordinate to the Spirit, and can be heard with salutary effect only as the Spirit repeats it, and conveys it into the soul.

Now, in attempting to describe its transforming power on the human heart, it is somewhat disheartening to reflect that we are most likely addressing those to whom the subject has become comparatively trite, and almost every mode of presenting it perfectly familiar. The very facility with which the understanding apprehends our meaning, and the readiness with which the judgment admits it, allows no time for the sublime truth to settle down upon the heart. In order, therefore, to do any thing like justice to the subject, it is necessary that the individual supposed to be subjected to the influence in question should be taken, not from among ourselves, but from a region where the power and even the name of the gospel is unknown. Christianity is the only successful antagonist which sin has ever encountered: in order, therefore, to exhibit its influence fully, he should be taken from the darkness and distance of nature, where sin had operated on him unchecked, working out all its deadly effects, and reducing him to its dreadful purposes; and he should be brought, with all his depravity and guilt upon him, into the full light, and under the direct power, of the gospel.

Now, in this state, he is chiefly assailable at three points. Fortified in evil, as he may appear to be, there are yet three sides, so to speak, on which he may be approached, by the Spirit of truth, with irresistible effect—his immortality, his guilt, and his infinite danger. These are subjects relating to parts and principles of his nature which an abandoned world overlooks—it has little or nothing by which it can appeal to them if it would—and yet they lie at the very foundation of his constitution, so that whoever shall succeed in making him sensible of his immortality, in alarming his conscience to the danger to which all that immortality is exposed by sin, and then in delivering him from the whole, will necessarily acquire a master influence over his whole nature for ever. Now, the gospel does this. It does not affect a part of his nature merely. It does not operate superficially on the senses; nor convince his judgment, and leave his heart uninterested; nor move his passions merely, to the neglect of his judgment and his will. It goes in, and down, to the depths of his nature. It goes directly to move that which moves the whole man.

The world hides a man from himself—conceals from him the most important part of his nature. By shutting out the prospect of eternity, he loses sight of his immortality; and by constantly appealing to his senses, and thus keeping in exercise only the inferior parts of his nature, he tends to settle down into a mere creature of time. But the first effect, perhaps, which the gospel produces, is to reveal him to himself. But coming to him as a message from another world, he starts into a consciousness of his relation to that world; and by addressing itself to the spiritual part of his nature, he becomes sensible, however vaguely at first, that he is in some way related to the spiritual, the infinite, and the eternal. Now, it is obvious how this very first impression, by throwing open a part of the temple of his nature which had been hitherto shut up—the very sanctuary, containing the symbol of Divinity—prepares him to receive with deep effect every other communication which may come to him from the same quarter.

Not only does the world conceal from a man his spiritual and immortal nature, by allowing it to fall into disuse,—it tends also to merge the fact of his individual accountableness —his distinct personal responsibility. From living in society, and finding his interests and relations inseparably complicated with those of others, he comes to think of himself only as an undistinguishable part of a great whole. He loses himself in the crowd. But the gospel individualizes and detaches. It tells him of a law by which all the laws of society are themselves to be judged, but of which his life has been an unbroken violation—of a book in which his personal history is recorded moment by moment—of a Being who can disentangle and detach him from all his complicated relations, and assign to his every thought and word its precise character— and of a place and a punishment so exactly and necessarily resulting from his guilt, and proportioned to it, that he is the only being in the universe to whom they could be assigned. The only way, therefore, in which it can treat with him is in person. It lays its awakening and arresting hand on his personal conscience. It demands a personal interview—a conference in the centre of his nature. It brings forward his guilt into the strong light of distinct consciousness. Even if the gospel allowed him to act by another, his own conscience is now too deeply interested to permit it. All his faculties and powers seem collected into a point—the entire soul becomes conscience, and that conscience is against him—accuser, witness, and judge. As if the judgment had been set and the books opened, as if his personal case had been adjudged, his doom pronounced, and he himself suspended over the bottomless gulf, he feels that he is lost. His nature is now stirred to its depths, and his soul is one region of alarm. Mere *sympathy* now will receive his deep, deep gratitude: *deliverance* would secure his heart for ever. The Being who shall now arrive to his rescue will infallibly acquire an influence over the whole man, and may calculate on his allegiance for ever.

To ask if the world, or any person or power belonging to it, can extend the aid which the crisis demands, would be sheer impertinence. *That* is the very power which has brought on the crisis, and from which he requires to be rescued. So completely is he now detached from it in heart and hope, that he turns round and looks back on it with wonder at its infatuation, aversion for its sins, and yearning pity for its state. The cloud which threatens *him* with its bolt, impends also over *it*. What *must* he " do to be saved?"

In the absence of all the objects he has been accustomed to confide in, in the clear and open space which their withdrawment has left around him, behold the cross! All the forms of terror and ministers of justice which his sins had armed against him, blend and melt into a form of love dying for his rescue. The cross has received the lightnings of the impending cloud, and has painted upon it the bow of hope. To his anxious inquiry, "what he must do to be saved" the cross echoes back, *Be saved*, and every object around him joyfully repeats, *Be saved*. Then God *is* love! and the cross is the stupendous expedient by which he harmonizes that love with the rectitude of his government! Then the sinner need not perish! and this is the amazing means of his salvation! Had it ever been his lot to gaze on the appalling spectacle of an ordinary crucifixion, the sight would probably have left an image on his mind never to be effaced. Is it possible, then, that he can behold "Jesus Christ, evidently set forth crucified before his eyes:" that he can know the dignity of the sufferer, as God manifest in the flesh: can believe that he hates the sin as deeply as he loves the sinner: can reflect that the effect of his death is to be his own deliverance; and can look into the heart of this great mystery and find it to be *love*, without experiencing a change? If every word which he hears spoken even by a fellow-man leaves some impression on his mind, can he hear that he is saved, and believe that the voice which assures him of salvation is the voice of God, without feeling it thrill through every faculty of the soul? If every object and event he may witness produces some effect on his character, is it possi ble that the event which is to effect his whole being for ever—which for him shuts for ever the gate of hell, and throws open and fills with visions of glory the ample spaces of eternity, should produce only a transient and slender impression? Must he not, by necessity of nature, love him, without whom he would soon have had nothing in the universe to love, but have been eternally hateful even to himself? Must he not render obedience to him, without whom the chains of his slavery would soon have been riveted for ever? He waits not for a reply: he needs not a command. He is under the mastery of a principle which is its own law—a principle of boundless gratitude and love. The power of the cross has moved the primary forces of his nature—the mysterious springs of Hope and Fear, of Adoration and Love. The world has lost him. His heart is at the feet of Christ. He dates life and happiness from the transition. Henceforth he moves in a region of which the cross is the central object, and where the benignant and attractive influences which stream from it in all directions, hold him in willing and delighted allegiance.

Here, then, is the secret of that supreme influence which the gospel exercises over the man whom the world had debased and sin had ruined; and this is the line of truth along which the Spirit of God delights to operate. By acquainting him with its immortality, it, in effect, gives him a soul, and gives it on the threshold of a new and eternal world. By acquainting him with his responsibility and guilt, it calls his conscience from the dead; and by unveiling to him the mystery of the cross, by which that guilt is cancelled, and that immortality entitled to heaven, one overpowering sentiment subjects his whole nature to the authority of Christ. The Spirit has taken of the things of Christ, and has shown them to him with so transforming an effect, that he is "a new creature in Christ Jesus."

We are to suppose, then, that the gospel has, in this way, won its first convert; that the transforming effects, which the Saviour ascribed to his being lifted up from the earth, have taken place upon him. Here is a man imbued with the spirit of the cross, and ready to sacrifice life in its service—how is he to be employed? He is not to live to himself; for by the sentence of a law which has gone forth from the cross, he who lives to himself is not a Christian. He has not been "created anew in Christ Jesus" for mere self-enjoyment or idle show—that the act might terminate in itself. Every thing in nature exists for a purpose. Even the atom of the rock has its appointed place, and its definite end. Surely man—and, of all men, the Christian—is not exempt from this law! What, then, is his destiny?

Here is evidently a fitting agent for Christ to employ. No other being in the universe has the shadow of a claim to him, beyond that which his new proprietor may choose to grant. Every part and property of his nature, and every moment of his future existence, have been bought—paid for with "precious blood." And as the new interest to which he is pledged is opposed by every other, he cannot yield to any other claimant, even for a moment, without lending himself, during that moment, to a hostile party; so that he has no alternative but that of devoting himself unreservedly to Christ. Accordingly, the Saviour claims him for himself. From the moment he felt the power of the cross, his duty became definite, imperative, one. If every other member of the human family were abandoned to live without control—if the sun itself were abandoned to wander through infinite space—*his* course would yet be minutely prescribed. As if he alone held the great secret of the cross, and were consequently the most important being on the face of the earth, his every moment is charged with an appointed duty. As if he had been recalled from the state of death; yes, not merely as if he had been called out of nothingness into existence—not merely as if he had been selected and sent down from the ranks of the blessed above—but with stronger motives still, as if his guilty soul had been recalled from perdition, where the undying worm had found him, and the unquenchable flame had enwrapped him, and his dissolved body recalled from the dust of death—and as if he had literally come out of the tomb with Christ, and had received life and salvation together at the mouth of the sepulchre at the hand of Christ—all his new-found powers are to be held by him as a precious trust for the service of Christ. As if he had come forth from the sepulchre at first with life only; and as if his reason, knowledge, affections, speech, property, had there been restored to him separately, and in succession, with a distinct intimation accompanying each, that he received it back for Christ, he is to look on himself, henceforth, as a part of the cross, as taken up into the great designs of Christ—as bound up for life and death in his plans of mercy. His character is to be a reproduction of the character of Christ. The disinterestedness which appeared in Christ, is to reappear in him. The tenderness of Christ—his untold solicitude for human souls, is to live over again in his tones of entreaty, his wrestling prayer for their salvation. The blood of the cross itself is, in a sense, to stream forth again, in his tears of anguish, his voluntary and vicarious self-sacrifice to draw men to Christ. And if tempted to lend but a particle of his influence to any other claimant than Christ, his reply is at hand—"I am not my own, I am Christ's. He has put it out of my power to give him more than belongs to him, for he has purchased and challenges the whole through every moment of time; and out of my will to give him less, for, if I know any grief, it is that my all should so inadequately express my sense of obligation."

2. Now, all this necessarily invests the new convert with influence; and with influence of the same kind as that which instrumentally drew him to Christ—influence already felt, perhaps, in inferior degrees by many around him; and, accordingly, we are to suppose that, under God, he becomes the means of drawing some of these to Christ. Now, as union is strength, would it not be desirable that he and they should be organized into a society for the purpose of combining and diffusing their influence farther still? Here, then, is the next step in the theory of Christian influence—*the formation of individual Christians into a Church.* The *primary* design of a Church, indeed, is the spiritual benefit of the members composing it; that each might enjoy the assistance of all; that the Christian principles and graces of the whole community might be collected and concentrated into a focus, and each believer might stand at pleasure under its salutary and transforming influence; that scope might be afforded for the exercise of sympathy, and forbearance, and holy emulation; that each might feel his weakness supported, and his courage animated, by the presence of the whole—feel that, although he is "the least of all saints," he is a vital member of an organized body, allied to Christ, the living Head, and,

through Him, identified with all the excellence in the universe.

But the great ulterior object of forming them into a Church, is the increase of their usefulness to the world; and hence it is that every increase of their own prosperity is so much increase of their capacity for usefulness. In other words, in the formation and design of this Church, we behold that principle of mutual dependence and reciprocal influence, which sin had perverted into the means of the world's destruction, recovering its original value as the means of the world's regeneration; for here, "the communion of the saints," by heightening their piety, quickening their activity, and combining their resources, increases their fitness for the world's conversion.

As a Church, the mere circumstance of their separation from the world is, of itself, sufficient to attract attention. Their number invests them with comparative importance. Their formation into a visible society raises them into the rank of a distinct power. If we wish to render an object conspicuous, we detach it from surrounding objects, and place it apart; and if we wish to make it still more conspicuous, we increase it, multiply it to the utmost. The light of the sun is composed of particles inconceivably minute, which, taken separately, and placed at a distance from each other, would be lost in darkness; but, collected into that glorious orb, it attracts the eyes of ten thousand worlds, and becomes an image of the glory of God himself. Believers are to shine as lights in the world; but this end they answer best when their radiance is collected into the orb of a Christian Church.

As a Church, they are raised into an independence of the world; and thus furnish mankind with a standing representation of another world; of other laws than earth obeys; and of a higher order of enjoyment and power than man possesses, derived from a source superior to all created means. Its union to him, and oneness with him, make it independent of all the universe besides.

As a Church, they are to acquire and wield an influence of a character essentially distinct from that of all around, and incomparably superior to it. Whatever the moral state of the world may be, their fitness to improve it will depend, under God, on the breadth and distinctness of the line of demarcation which separates them from it, and on the perfection of contrast to the world which they exhibit. The world, for instance, is selfish, acts without reference to a supreme will, and constitutes itself the end of all it does. How important, then, that they should embody the self-sacrificing spirit of Christ! To do this by halves only, to study their own aggrandizement, or to live in comparative indolence and luxury, would be to symbolize with the world, and to confirm it in its besetting sin. But they are to exhibit that fiction of the world—a life of self-denial. By relinquishing all delights, all passions, all pursuits by which the world is engrossed and enslaved, and by going out of themselves, abandoning themselves, evincing a readiness to sacrifice life itself in the cause of Christ, they are to stand out in vivid contrast with the selfishness of the world, silently to condemn it, to proclaim a will higher than human, the responsibility of men to that will, and the supreme happiness of absolute conformity to it. And thus they are to prepare men to hear with effect of that sacrifice compared with which nothing else can ever deserve the name.

The world is sensual, supremely influenced by the visible and the present. The constancy and force with which the human body gravitates to the earth, is only an emblem of the manner in which the universal heart of man tends to the concerns and objects of the world. But the members of this new society are to come out from the world, and to "be separate;" "to love not the world, nor the things of the world;" "to set their affections on things above." The cross is to them the perpetual memorial of a nobler world, the representative of the most glorious being there, and the medium of constant communication with it. As if they were daily standing in the open portal of that celestial state, and surveying the glories within, they are to evince a decided superiority to all the objects of worldly pursuit. And as if they were empowered to take others with them there, and were only waiting here till they had succeeded, they are to move among them as men not of this world—angels partly on the wing.

Now, this twofold principle of worldly selfishness, or selfish sensuality, is the ruling principle of man and the essence of his guilt. How important, then, that the Christian Church should stand out from the world in bold and bright relief, as the representative of the pure and unworldly benevolence of the cross!

As a Church, the faithful are intrusted with means eminently calculated to affect and benefit the world around. They possess the ministry of reconciliation; and of what use is that but to "beseech men to be reconciled to God?" They are encouraged to pray, as a Church, by a promise of Divine success greater than any which is guaranteed to their separate and solitary requests. "If two of you shall agree on earth as touching any thing that they shall ask, it shall be done for them of my Father who is in heaven. For where two or three are gathered together in my name, there am I in the midst of them." We are assured that, in reclaiming the sinner, "the effectual fervent prayer" of even one of the faithful "availeth much." But here is a promise made to the united prayer of the Church, over and above that which is made to private devotion, and a power conferred on it greater than that which is promised to all its members praying separately.

As a Church, they have a special sphere of labor. However small the circle of Christian influence which each one separately filled before, from the moment they constitute a Church, the hand that so formed them may be regarded as drawing around them a circle which includes "the region round about." As a Church, they are now charged with a collective responsibility: all the souls within that circle are in a measure given into their hands. And hence all their means—the mite of the widow and the wealth of the affluent—the leisure of one and the learning of another—the ardor of the young, the wisdom of the aged, the resources of all—are to be combined and devoted to the object of saving them. Here, the motto of each is to be, "None of us liveth to himself:" each one is assigned a post of labor: the influence of each, by union with all, is made to be felt; and as often as others are added to them, they are to regard the circle as proportionally enlarged, and are again to fill it to the circumference with the influence of the cross.

3. In this way other Churches are supposed to be planted. Each of these becomes the centre of a new circumference. Every place to which its influence reaches is to be a point for extending it farther still. Bursting the limits of neigh-

borhood, and the confines of country, they are to carry the cross into other lands, there to rally around it other hearts, and thus to obtain the means of further conquests still. Now, if the influence of the first converts was augmented by collecting them into one compact society, would it not proportionally augment the influence of these several societies, if they were all sympathetically united, and visibly to coöperate as one Church? True, the obstacles are great, the sources of disunion and division many; but so much the greater the influence which would arise from the spectacle of their union. For in that event, their union would be their strength, not only by increasing their actual resources, but also by evincing to the world the surpassing power of that principle which could thus harmonize their jarring natures, and fuse all their hearts and interests into one.

Now, this, we know, is *the third step in the Scripture theory of Christian instrumentality for the conversion of the world.* So essential a part of the theory is this, that the Saviour more than commanded—he prayed for it; prayed for it at the foot of the cross; prayed for it there as a means of the world's conversion—"That they all may be one . . . . that the world may believe that thou hast sent me." The reason of their union as a whole, is one of the very reasons of their existence at all—the conversion of the world. Diversified as they are in mind, country, condition, age, one subject of emulation is to displace every other—who shall do most for the diffusion of that love which draws them to the cross, and which there binds them to each other? Zeal is to come from one part of the Church, to be directed by wisdom from another part. Here, agents of mercy are sent forth; and there, they are met by funds for their support. The conviction that in every enterprise of benevolence they carry with them the sympathies and prayers of the Church, keeps them, on the one hand, from the thought of declining, and puts them, on the other, on deeds of heroism in the cause of God which call forth the glad applauses of heaven. Such a union of love in a selfish world could not fail to arrest the public eye, and to assail and affect the public heart. But not long would the world be left to speculate and wonder about it. They would find that the Church had united for an object—that that object was *their* conversion—that they were actually beleaguered and assailed in every form, and on every side, by the united and irresistible forces of Christian love. Thus while, within itself, the Church presents the attractive and glorious spectacle of a universal feast of love; in relation to those without, it is to present one scene of spiritual enterprise and commerce, carried on for the advantage of the world at large, and visible to the universe. Convinced that such a union of love in a selfish world could be only resolved into a heavenly cause, mankind would be the more prepared to recognize the Divinity of the Saviour's claims, and gratefully to capitulate to his offered grace.

4. But now comes the last step—the crowning influence—that without which all the other parts of the theory are useless—*the effusion of the Holy Spirit upon the whole.* His presence, indeed, is, as has been already remarked, *essential*, and is taken for granted, in the renovation of each individual heart, and in the formation of every separate Church. In the scheme of salvation, every instrument and agent has its appropriate place, and its appointed order of succession. In that arrangement, the Spirit is the prime mover of the whole. But his full impartation is reserved for the combination of the whole. Mightily as that spectacle of Christian union is calculated to tell on the sinful influences of earth, as mightily is it to tell, in another respect, on the Divine influences of heaven. It is to draw down the very Source of influence himself. "For there is one body and one Spirit"—an entire body for an entire spirit. Having drawn them to one centre, and there united them in one object, that he might exhibit and employ them in one body, he is then to animate and inhabit them as the one soul of the whole. It is then to appear that their union is cemented, not only *by* him, but *for* him; for only let that union be complete, and forthwith he will be seen impelling the entire body of the faithful to one undivided effort for the conversion of the world—his sword the weapon they employ—his inspiration animating them to the fight—his unmeasured power, as the great missionary spirit of the Church, convincing the world of sin, and, as the glorifier of Jesus, crowning their instrumentality with complete success.

Here, then, we behold an answer to the question which we lately proposed—Where is the agency, and what is the plan, for drawing the world to the cross? Here is an agency organized expressly for this, and useful for nothing else. Here, if we briefly examine, we shall find that every element at work is an element of influence in harmony with the cross, and subordinate to it. The same agencies, which, in the world, operate against the cross, will here be found to operate for it; and other agencies, of which the world knows nothing, are here called into existence, and added to them.

Knowledge is a means of usefulness—"is power." "There is no power on earth," said the great man who originated that proverb, "which setteth up a throne or chair of state, in the spirits and souls of men, but knowledge." He who is the discoverer or sole possessor of a moral truth, has it in his power to exercise a sovereignty which approaches nearer than any other to the likeness of the Divine rule. Not only is he stronger than any other man, or than any given number of men, but stronger than all the race together. Now, the Christian has had disclosed to him the doctrine of the cross. His hand is on a lever which can move the world—on the lever which shall move it—and his hand is there that, instrumentally, he may attempt to move it. Moses, descending radiant from Divine communion in the mount; the high priest reäppearing from within the mysterious veil; Isaiah, fresh from the visions of the Lord, never returned to the waiting and breathless people with a burden so precious—a truth so great—as that which he holds. It is that from which all other truths derive their force: it comes, "not in word only, but in power:" it is, emphatically, "the power of God unto salvation to every one that believeth." It enables him to give back the world to God; and, by unveiling the Great Propitiation, to contribute towards giving back God to a world.

Speech is a means of influence. It is the great instrument for the interchange of thought and feeling. The thoughts of a community are by this means kept in perpetual circulation; and the long-cherished sentiment of a private individual is propagated till it acquires the force and universality of a law, and "sets on fire the whole course of nature." To say nothing of the power of public oratory, the simplest conversation has an effect on the minds of those who engage in it, regulated by laws as certain as those which direct the lightning in its course. So that never do we come out from such intercourse the same persons as we entered. The most casual remark lives for ever in its effects. There is not a word which has not a moral history. Hence the Satanic art of calling all evil things by harmless names; and hence it is, too, that every "idle word" which men utter, assumes a character so important, that it will be made a subject of inquest in the general judgment.

But the Christian is taught to regard the faculty of speech as a vehicle and means of grace. If the noblest use of his reason be to know God, the highest employment of his speech must be to impart that knowledge; and the highest knowledge of him which he can impart is surely that for which Christ himself assumed the power of human speech, and to the announcement of which he devoted it. In the Church, language is promoted into the grand ordinance of preaching Christ. Whoever his audience may be, the Christian is to "minister grace to the hearers." Even when he is not conversing on grace, his speech is to be "always with grace;" in harmony with his religious character, and favorable to a hallowed impression. Like the narrative and incidental parts of Scripture, it is to illustrate and subserve the sacred and saving tendency of the whole. In the salvation of the cross, the gospel has supplied him with a theme of which his heart is supposed to be full; and "he cannot but speak the things which he has heard and seen." Every man he meets is interested in it as deeply as himself. Every individual he addresses may be perishing through want of it. Every conversation he holds with others affords him an opportunity of introducing it. Every word he has to utter concerning it, is "good news." Unless he speak, they may die in ignorance of it; and he is held conditionally responsible for every word he might have uttered, but omitted; and for every soul that perishes through that neglect. "He believes, and, therefore, speaks." As if his lips had been touched with sacred fire, or sprinkled with consecrating blood, he is to stand in the midst of his circle as the oracle of the cross. His words are no longer his own: as if his were the tongue of Christ himself, or the only tongue on earth that could testify of the wonders of the cross, he is to regard himself as set apart to bear witness of Christ. And as it is his office, so is it to be his holy ambition, so to announce and make him known, that at the close of life, and even of each day of life, he may be able to say, as Christ himself appealed to the Father, and said, though in an inferior sense, "I have declared unto them thy name, and will declare it."

Relationship, whether natural or acquired, is a means of usefulness. The parent, for instance, possesses an influence over his offspring more powerful than the mightiest monarch ever swayed over his subjects. His voice is the first music they hear; his smiles their bliss; his authority, the image and substitute of the Divine authority. So absolute is the law which impels them to believe his every word, to imitate his every tone, gesture, and action, and to receive the ineffaceable impressions of his character, that his every movement drops a seed into the virgin soil of their hearts, to germinate there for eternity. His influence, by blending itself with their earliest conceptions, and incorporating with the very elements of their constitution, and by the constancy, subtlety, variety, and power of its operation, gives him a command over their character and destiny, which renders it the most appropriate emblem on earth of the influence of God himself.

Now, there is not a member of the human family who does not sustain some relation, original or acquired, public or private, permanent or temporary; nor is there any relation which does not invest the person sustaining it with some degree of influence. The particle of dust which we heedlessly tread beneath our foot, propagates its influence beyond the remotest planet, and is felt through all space. And though a man may be apparently standing on the outermost verge of the social system, he forms a vital link in the great chain of dependence which runs through the universe, linking man to man, age to age, and world to world. The connection, indeed, may not be visible to us to any great distance; yet does it exist as really as if he found himself standing in the centre of the universe, with visible lines of relation drawn from himself to every one of the congregated myriads; nor is it possible to detach him from the mighty whole. And— what is of importance to remark—not only is there no relation of life which does not invest the person sustaining it with some degree of influence, but which does not afford him the power of exerting an influence in it which no other being on earth possesses.

Here, then, is an important talent which the Christian is supposed to occupy for Christ. As if the relations which he sustains had been appointed now for the first time, and appointed expressly to give him a sphere of Christian influence, he is to hold them chiefly for Christ. And, indeed, for what but holy purposes were the primary and principal relations of life designed at first? For "did he not make one? yet had he the residue of the Spirit. And wherefore one? That he might seek a goodly seed." So that, in holding his relationships to Christ, the renewed man is but restoring them to the purpose from which sin has dissevered them. Is he a parent? "The promise is unto him and to his children." As he is related to the first Adam, they receive from him nothing but an inheritance of guilt, degradation, and death; but as related to the second, he is to aim to cut off the dreadful entail, and to train them to be sons and daughters of the Lord Almighty: as if they had been sent down to him in angel arms from heaven with a Divine command to train them for Christ. He is to radiate on them nothing but hallowed influence. Their first lispings are to be of Christ: their first imaginings of his love; and their earliest steps to his footstool. The influence of his Christian character is to surround them like the atmosphere of a temple: that, by being breathed and mingled with their earliest being, it may become an elementary part of their character. As if they had been sent to him expressly with a Divine charge to illustrate before the world the power and excellence of Christian influence, he is to set himself apart to the grand experiment of ascertaining the greatest amount of good which sanctified parental agency is calculated to effect: how completely it can sever and secure them from all counter agencies: how early it can affect them; and how devoted and useful it can render them as instruments for propagating the same influence among others. In this way he is to illustrate the tremendous operation of sin in having perverted a relationship meant for the transmission of nothing but good into a channel for the discharge of an ever-swelling flood of destruction; and the transcendent influence of the cross, which.

like the tree of Marah, tends to medicate its fatal bitterness, and to turn it into a stream of salvation.

But, whatever the relations which he sustains to others, he is to regard the influence resulting from it as a cord for drawing them to Christ. There is a sense, indeed, in which he stands related to the whole race. The cross vibrates to the sounds of human misery in every part of the earth, and his heart is to thrill in sympathy with it. As the representative of Christ, he is to regard himself as the centre of all that misery; but as his Christian duties lie around him in concentric circles, and as the first circle includes those most nearly related to him, nothing will excuse him for neglecting an inner for an outer, because a larger circle. In the day of final account, the first subject of inquiry, after that of his own personal piety, will relate to the salvation of the souls immediately around him. How came your wife, or child, or servant, to perish? is a question which cannot be met by a plea that he was achieving a distant good. He must not neglect the Christian welfare of his own household, then, even for the sublime occupation of evangelizing a nation. Nor need he: his duty in this case is coincident with his most enlarged ideas. For, by filling the sphere immediately around him first, he is multiplying his agencies for a wider and still wider range of usefulness. It is by entering into cohesive union with the particles immediately around it, that the atom becomes a component part of the rock, contributes something towards the stability of the everlasting hills, and towards the gravity of the great globe itself; and by erecting the cross in his own house, and converting his own house into a church, and that church into a centre of usefulness to the neighborhood, he is preparing to subserve most effectually the interests of the race at large.

Property is a means of influence. The material itself, indeed, of which money is made, is intrinsically worthless; yet having, by the general consent of society, been constituted the representative of all property, and, as such, the key to all the avenues of worldly enjoyment, it excites some of the strongest desires, and reflects some of the deepest emotions of the human breast. Its fluctuations are the tides of national fortune. It sways the heart of the world. Every piece of coin that passes through our hand, has been streaming with influence from the first moment it was put into circulation. It has a path through society, and a history of its own; rather, it belongs to the history of the world. Industry has toiled for it; enterprise has hazarded life for it; speculation has gambled for it; childhood has eyed it; poverty rejoiced over it; covetousness worshipped it: it has passed through the hands of profligacy, intemperance, and all the vices. How often has it been carried past the temple of God on its way to some shrine of Satan? how seldom been diverted from the service of sin? Could the history of all the wealth of antiquity be given, what should we hear, but, substantially, the history of the ancient world itself—of its sensual pleasures, its projects of ambition, its sanguinary wars, polluting temples, and national oppressions. How great the opportunity, then, which the Christian possesses of glorifying God in this department alone! While others are sullenly appropriating every thing to themselves, as if God had ceased to reign, and even to exist, he is to consecrate and offer up his substance, before their eyes, as an oblation to his glory, and thus daily to vindicate his claims. While they are idolizing money, and making it the common object of their trust, he is to strike at its very throne, and to awaken them from the dream of its omnipotence, by showing that its highest value arises from its subserviency to the purposes of the gospel. He may not possess much; but he is to look on himself as entrusted with what he does possess partly for the purpose of disparaging it before the world. Its influence depends, not on its amount, but on the way in which he employs it; and by casting his "two mites" into the temple treasury, he may at once be publicly vindicating the outraged supremacy of the "blessed God," and asserting the claims of "the glorious gospel," and constraining men, more than by a thousand arguments, to bow to its divinity.

Self-denial is a means of useful influence. So unearthly a quality is this, that no man can fully and consistently exhibit it without exposing himself, perhaps for years, to the suspicion of assuming it for some sinister object in the distance. But does not this very incredulity, arising from the extreme rareness of true self-denial, hold out to him the promise of proportionate influence hereafter, should he live long enough to vanquish that incredulity, and to enjoy the reaction of opinion in his favor? His self-denial, indeed, is meantime furnishing him with all those means of benevolence which self-indulgence would have lavished on itself; and these, by increasing his usefulness, are augmenting his influence. But the influence which he acquires, by this increase of actual means, is as nothing compared with that which he obtains by the fact—when it comes to be known—that he denies himself in order to obtain it. The amount which he saves may be only an additional mite; but the fact that he habitually denies himself in order to obtain it as a means of doing good, will ultimately invest him with a greater moral influence than the stranger to self-denial, though the giver of thousands, can ever possess.

Now, Christianity is a system of self-denial, and the Church is supposed to be its home. How can it be otherwise? Its centre is a cross. This is at once the secret of its influence to attract, and the means of its power to save. Having felt that attraction and experienced that power, the Christian is to extend its influence by exhibiting in his own life the image of the cross. Were it possible for him to live in worldly self-indulgence, he would be doing all in his power, not only to stop the influence of the cross from extending beyond himself, but to efface from the memory of a world too willing to forget, that Christianity had ever a cross. The only evidence on which the world will believe that Christ was voluntarily crucified for its redemption is, that the Christian be seen, in the true spirit of his Lord, voluntarily, and, in a sense, vicariously, denying himself, in the work of diffusing the blessings of that redemption.

As the representative of the cross, then, the Church is charged with a responsibility which requires the principle of self-denial to pervade the whole of its instrumentality, and to become the law of its beneficence.

Compassion is a means of useful influence. Even one of its tones has often opened the heart, when the rack could not open the lips; and in the Christian Church it is supposed to reign. The cross is the utterance of Divine compassion, and the Church collected around it is a proof of its power. The compassion which bled on the cross here beats in the hearts of all its members. They know the wretchedness of sin into which the world has sunk—look forwards to the end of its course—hear already its doom pronounced—see the pit open to receive it—and hear, by anticipation, its hopeless cries for deliverance. And the deep anxiety which they feel to "snatch the firebrands from the flames," and to quench them in the blood of the cross, imparts a depth of tenderness to their tones, an earnestness of solicitude to their manner, and a combination and energy to their efforts, which give them a power over the mind beyond that of the most original truths unfeelingly delivered, or the stern authority of law itself.

Persevering activity in the attainment of a useful or benevolent object is another means of usefulness. It is by perseverance that the small stream of the mountain, a thousand leagues from the parent sea, conquers intervening obstacles, wears itself a channel, swells to a river, traverses continents, gives names to countries, assigns boundaries to empires, and becomes celebrated in history. And by patiently persevering, with his face and step always direct towards his object, a single individual will acquire an amount of influence and success, in reference to that object, which a multitude, pursuing it only by convulsive starts, would fail to obtain. The multitude itself, gradually awed into respect for his steady, onward course, will come at length to clear a space, and make way for his advance. And though for years his cause may not appear to be attended with any success, an event, unexpected perhaps, will at length disclose that there never was a moment in which he was not exciting the silent admiration of some, and preparing numbers to fall into his train, and to yield themselves up entirely to his influence.

Now, the Christian has motives to patient perseverance in promoting the knowledge of Christ which no other object can inspire, no other man can know. The persisting energy which built the mountain pyramids of Egypt—which reared the Chinese wall—by which Alexander conquered the old world—Columbus discovered the new—and Newton elaborated the system of the universe, had trifles for its objects, compared with the aim of Christian instrumentality to save the world. But besides the infinite importance of his object, engaging, as it has, the *Divine* perseverance from eternity, there never was a moment in the life of Christ, his Great Exemplar, which was not directly or indirectly made subordinate to it: there is not a moment in which the command is suspended, "Be not weary in well-doing," "Be always abounding in the work of the Lord." So that, unless it can be shown that the perishing world ever pauses in its cry for deliverance, or that the destroyer ever pauses in working the great system of destruction, the Christian can know no moment in which it is permitted him to pause in his peculiar vocation. The termination of one duty is to be only a signal for the commencement of another; his life is to be one continuous act of obedience. Every day returns charged with an amount of obligation proportioned to his utmost means of usefulness. His utmost powers are to be constrained into the service, till, by the force of habit, his perseverance becomes invincible. He is to live under the ever-present conviction that he has one thing to do, and that he is in danger of dying before it is done: cheered on by the assurance that every act adds a ray to the radiance of that crown which he hopes to lay at his Saviour's feet, and tends to secure the perseverance of others when he himself shall have gone to receive it.

And this reminds us that the great designs of the Christian are entailed; for the Church on earth, though mortal in its members, as a community is undying. History informs us of some governments which, having formed schemes of national aggrandizement too vast to be accomplished within "the hour-glass of one man's life," have devolved the prosecution of them, as a sacred duty, on those who came after them. The Christian Church is to exhibit the sublime spectacle of an unearthly government, embarked in an enterprise of mercy for all time. Its members are "commanded to make it known to their children, that the generation to come might know it, even the children who should be born: who should arise and declare it to their children." And as time rolls on, the only change which this spiritual government is to exhibit is that which necessarily arises, under God, from persevering fidelity to its original design—extended domains, and a nearer approach to universal conquest. "For the greatness of the kingdom under the whole heaven shall be given to the people of the saints of the Most High."

Prayer is influence. Appeals, entreaties, and petitions, between man and man, move the affairs of this world; but in the Church they move Heaven. All those other things which we have described as exercising influence, become spiritually useful only by that power which descends in answer to prayer. Other means may be influential, but the amount of their influence is calculable, bearing a proportion to the power employed; but prayer, by engaging a Divine power, sets all calculation at defiance. Other means may be good—but what must *that* be, the effect of which is to bring down Goodness himself?—and yet here the entire Church is supposed to be in daily, unceasing, impassioned entreaty for the Spirit to "convince the world of sin."

Union is a means of usefulness. And here it is supposed to be universal, visible, Divine. As to each individual; here is the union of the whole man—all his principles and passions combined—no part of his nature wanting—no part shedding a counter-influence—the whole man bound and braced up for one purpose, as if devoted to the grand experiment of ascertaining how much a single human agent can effect in the cause of Christ. Here is the union of a number of these in a particular Church—in which none is inactive—each has his post—all act in concert—the whole blent into a single power, and putting forth an undivided effort to draw the world around them to Christ. Here is the union of all these distinct societies in one collective body—bringing together agencies the most distant—harmonizing materials once the most discordant —blending hearts naturally the most selfish, in bands more tender than those of kindred, and so sympathetic that the emotion of one thrills through them all—a union which economizes and combines all the energies and passions of sanctified humanity—which, collecting all the scattered agencies of good that earth contains, organizes them into a vast engine whose entire power is to be brought to bear for the conversion of the world. And then, not merely in addition to, but infinitely more than all, here is the union of Divine influence with the whole—heaven come down to earth—the powers of the future world imparted to the present—the Spirit himself, in a sense, incarnate—pervading his body, the Church—investing it with unearthly power—and employing it as the organ of an almighty influence for recovering the world to Christ.

Such, then, is an outline of the Scripture theory of that

agency by which Christ proposes to reclaim the world. Can we forbear to admire the simplicity of its principle? It is simply the law of reciprocal influence, baptized in the blood of the cross, and endued with the energy of the Holy Spirit. All in God that can influence is brought to bear, through the cross, on all in man that can be influenced, and the whole of that is then put into requisition by the Spirit to influence others. If this theory were realized, could we question its efficiency? Of all who are brought within its scope, each of them is prepared to say, "None of us liveth to himself;" and what but the expansion of that sentiment is necessary to fill the world with the influence of the cross? Could we doubt its ultimate and universal triumph? What, when the Spirit himself had come down to work the entire system? What, when the Church withheld nothing that could influence, and the Spirit withheld nothing that could crown that influence with success? If even the secret tear of an obscure penitent on earth creates a sensation among the seraphim, the "travail" of such an agency for the salvation of the world would carry with it the sympathies of the whole universe. God would bless it; and "all the ends of the earth would fear him."

CHAPTER II.

THE THEORY OF CHRISTIAN INSTRUMENTALITY FOR THE CONVERSION OF THE WORLD ILLUSTRATED AND ENFORCED FROM THE WORD OF GOD.

If it be true that the Christian Church is thus constructed expressly to embody and diffuse the influence of the cross—and if its full efficiency for this end depends, under God, on the entireness of its consecration to this office—we may take it for granted that this truth will not only bear to be subjected to certain appropriate tests, but that all the results of such an examination can only tend to illustrate its importance, and to enforce its practical application.

If the economy of Christian influence be more than a temporary expedient to meet an emergency—if it form a part of an original plan—may we not expect to find, for instance, that he who "sees the end from the beginning," and who so often sketches an outline of the future in the events of the present or the past, has indicated his purpose in the dispensations which preceded it? Accordingly, we find that, from the moment when the first promise was announced, the instrumentality employed to impart it was calculated to give it the widest diffusion and the greatest effect.

I. During the long lapse of years prior to the flood, this instrumentality was *domestic*, or *patriarchal*. By creating one common father of the species, making him the depositary of the first communication from heaven, and prolonging his life to nearly a thousand years, the Almighty may be regarded as making the wisest and most gracious arrangement for the welfare of his fallen posterity. For in each and all of the myriads to which they had multiplied, Adam would only behold the multiplications of himself, and would therefore be supposed to feel a father's yearning solicitude for their recovery to God. And even as late as " in the days of Noe," the comparative recency of the fall, and its immediate results, by rendering these results so much the more impressive and personally interesting; the small amount and the simplicity of the revelation which had then been made, by rendering it so much the easier to be remembered and imparted; the universal prevalence of the same language, by rendering it so much the easier to diffuse that knowledge universally; and the continued longevity of man, by enabling one party to speak with the authority and tenderness of a parent, disposing the other to listen with the docility and faith of children, and giving to each a family interest in the religious welfare of all—afforded facilities for diffusing the knowledge of God, which strikingly evinced his readiness to save, and loudly called on all to inculcate and exhibit that faith by which Abel "obtained witness that he was righteous," and Enoch "had this testimony, that he pleased God."

II. The patriarchal dispensation, subsequent to the deluge, was *migratory.* By calling, and "preaching the gospel to Abraham"*—removing him from province to province through a protracted life—investing him with importance in the eyes of the nations among whom he sojourned—sending his posterity into Egypt, and keeping them there for ages as a marked and distinct people—leading them out by miracle—conducting them slowly and circuitously to Canaan as an entire "Church"—by these means, not only did the Almighty render the truth migratory, and afford every nation which it visited an opportunity of learning it, he may also be regarded as intimating the aggressive and missionary character of his future Church, and the entireness with which it should unite and consecrate all its resources to accomplish its march through the world.

III. The Mosaic dispensation was *national and stationary.* Yet, differing as it did in this respect from the preceding, it contained every prerequisite for answering its end as a local witness for God, and for proving a universal blessing. It was first a focus in which all the rays of revelation met, that it might next be a centre whence the light of truth should radiate and pour forth in all directions over the face of the earth. Nothing was omitted from its character and constitu-

---

*Gal. iii. 8.

tion calculated to promote this gracious design. Its early history was a history of miracles, to excite the attention and draw to itself the eyes of the wonder-loving world; its ritual was splendid and unique; its members were distinguished in character from those of every other people on the face of the earth; its creed or testimony was eminently adapted to the existing state of the world, for it proclaimed a God and promised a Saviour; its members possessed a deep personal interest in the truth of the testimony they gave; and, what was especially important, its geographical position was central.* That large portion of the earth, whose waters flow into the Mediterranean, is the grand historical portion of the world as known to the ancients. Judea was situated in the midst of it, like the sun in the centre of the solar system. Placed at the top of the Mediterranean, it was, during each successive monarchy, always within sight of the nations; and its temple-fires, like the Pharos of the world, were always flinging their warning light across the gross darkness of heathenism, protesting against idolatry, proclaiming the one living and true God, inviting the nations to come and worship before him, and foretelling the advent of One whose light should enlighten the world. The very sight of its temple was prophetic; placed on the summit of Zion, it foretold that "it shall come to pass in the last days, that the mountain of the Lord's house shall be established in the top of the mountains, and it shall be exalted above the hills, and all nations shall flow unto it."

And thus, though the Jewish economy was essentially national and stationary, yet so far from being exclusive, it was studiously adapted to bless the entire race. Its history attested an omnipresent Providence. Its moral laws were of universal obligation. Its sacrifices proclaimed the Divine placability, and said, "Look unto me, and be ye saved, all ye ends of the earth." The name selected and inscribed on his temple by God himself, harmonized with this unlimited invitation of mercy: "My house shall be called a house of prayer for all people: it shall proclaim that I am now on my throne giving audience to the world." And with this gracious design the prayers of his worshippers concurred: "Let the people praise thee, O God, let all the people praise thee; and

---

* Ezek. v. 5.

let the whole earth be filled with his glory." While the spirit of its evangelical prophecies looked forward to the sublime spectacle of a world in prayer, and sang, " O thou that hearest prayer, to thee shall all flesh come."

To this high and holy office of blessing the world the Jewish Church was devoted by God, with all the entireness of consecration belonging to their own temple: " This people have I formed for myself: they shall show forth my praise." They constituted his chosen representatives to an apostate world. And how could they represent his existence and spirituality but by maintaining their own existence entirely distinct from the idolatrous nations around, and exhibiting a character for excellence incomparably above them? How could they exhibit to mankind an image of the amplitude of the Divine benevolence but by becoming the priests and intercessors of the revolted world, and by entreating that he would hasten the advent of Him in whom all the nations of the earth were to be blessed? As certainly as they failed to answer their end, by losing sight of the lofty relative intention of their office, so surely, by keeping that gracious intention in view, and devoting themselves to the exalted task of answering it, would they have become the spiritual benefactors of the world.

The institution of the Christian Church, then, the union of all its parts, and the consecration of all its powers, for the spiritual recovery of the world, is no new thing in the earth. The Jewish economy, in which every act of a nation was prescribed, from which nothing was excluded as insignificant, by which every thing was exalted into religion, and the whole combined into a useful instrumentality, was its ancient, appropriate, and luminous type. Nor will the Christian Church answer the sublime purpose of its institution in relation to the world, unless it recognizes in the entire consecration of the Jewish Church a type of its own, and devotes itself to the work of blessing mankind with an entireness, spirituality, and zeal, as much superior to what was to be expected from the Jews, as the character of its redemption is superior to the mere temporal deliverance from Egypt. Alas! that we should be so much more ready to recognize in their rescue a type of our own, than to discern the intended emblem of that relative devotedness which God requires in the perfect consecration of their temple, and the studied adaptation of their entire economy to instruct and benefit mankind.

IV. But if even the preliminary dispensation thus clearly intimated what would be the lofty and benevolent character of the Christian Church, may we not much more expect to find that character embodied in *the life of its Incarnate Founder?* Accordingly, the character of Christ will be found not merely to illustrate his new dispensation, but to form at once its type, its origin, and its glory. His Church is to be simply the expansion of his character. So that, were each of its members to emulate a Paul in devotedness and zeal, and all of them to be united in a body as entire as the person of Christ himself, they would be only and inadequately exemplifying the character of their Lord. "For their sakes," said he, "I sanctify myself"—I devote myself entirely to the work of human redemption. In pursuance of this voluntary engagement he withdrew himself, as we have seen in the preceding chapter, from the glories of heaven, and set himself apart to the sorrows of earth, and to the sufferings of a vicarious death. Though he saw, as from a height, the whole array of duty and trial which awaited him, the only emotion he evinced at the sight was a holy impatience to reach the cross which stood at the end of his path—a self-consuming ardor to be baptized with that baptism of blood. Though all the fullness and fire of the passions dwelt in him, never did he waste a single feeling, but devoted the whole as a consecrated fuel for offering up the great sacrifice in which his life was consumed, and by which the world might be saved. And why did he this? Not merely to impart a benevolent spirit to his dispensation, though this is one of its sublime results. But as the reason of that benevolent spirit is to be sought for in his character, so the reasons of his character are to be sought for in a sphere higher than this world, and in a period prior to the commencement of time. "To the intent that now unto the principalities and powers in heavenly places might be known, by the Church, the manifold wisdom of God, according to the eternal purpose which he purposed in Christ Jesus our Lord."* The reasons of his mediatorial character are to be found in that eternal purpose which appointed him

---

* Eph. iii. 10, 11.

to the office of embodying before the eyes of the universe the glory of the Divine benevolence in the salvation of man. Charged with this exalted office, he came forth and stood before the world as the visible representative of the invisible God. "He that hath seen me," said he, "hath seen the Father also." "Henceforth ye know the Father, and have seen him." "I and my Father are one." Possessed with the infinite magnitude of the task he had undertaken, nothing could for a moment divert his eye from it: every action and item of his life was referable to this, and subsidiary to it. As far as consistent with the laws of mediation, he was content to conceal himself, to merge his own claims, that he might occupy the whole of our field of vision with the love of God. He goes even beyond this: "Therefore doth my Father love me," saith he, "because I lay down my life for the sheep:" in other words, "My Father loves you with a love so unbounded, that he even loves me the more for dying to redeem you. He so loves you, that whatever facilitates the expression of his love receives an expression of his Divine esteem. By sustaining your liabilities, by surrendering my life as an equivalent for your transgressions, and thus vindicating his law from all appearance of connivance at sin, I am setting his compassion at liberty: I am removing a restraint from his love which threatened to hold it in eternal suspense: I am enabling his grace to act, to save whom it will; and for thus concurring in his benevolent purpose, and opening an ample channel for the tide of his love to flow in, the Father loves me: I receive such additional expressions of his complacency, that, though ineffably beloved from eternity, he may be said to have had added infinite delight to infinite." Thus unreservedly did the Saviour lay himself out even to the death, to aggrandize our conceptions of the grace of God.

And how could it be otherwise? Reposing, as he had from eternity, in the bosom of that infinite love which he had come to earth to represent; mingling, as he had, in its all-comprehending counsels; knowing, as he did, its infinite treasures accumulated from eternity, he knew that no representation within the limits of possibility could adequately impress us with its vastness: how, then, could he be satisfied with doing less than the uttermost which humanity, sustained by Divinity, could effect, in order to express it? A love whose sacrifices might be numbered and measured could not adequately express a "love which passeth knowledge;" therefore it was that he withheld nothing, but "gave *himself* for us." Could less than the deep "travail of his soul" have represented the pulsations and throes of infinite compassion? Therefore it was, that, "being in an agony, he sweat as it were great drops of blood falling to the ground"—that he "endured the cross, despising the shame." True it is, that, knowing as we do the grace of our Lord Jesus Christ, we may well be filled with astonishment at its amazing riches; but equally true is it that, knowing as he did the infinite extent of the love of God which he had engaged to represent, he felt that nothing less than such a display of grace could sufficiently express it—that even when all the infinite capability of his nature was in stress, nothing that he might say or suffer could possibly exaggerate our conceptions of the grace of God.

Now, be it remembered, that, having thus embodied the love of the Father, he has devolved it on his people to multiply the copies of his character in their own lives. "As thou hast made me thy messenger to the world, I have made them my messengers to the world."* They have now to do instrumentally for Christ what he did efficaciously and really for the Father; to represent his benevolence to the world. In making them partakers of his grace, he not only intends their own salvation, he intends the salvation of others by their instrumentality: he intends that they should go forth from his presence as messengers, conveying to the world the cheering intelligence, that he is still sitting on his throne of mercy, waiting to be gracious; and that they should spare no effort or sacrifice which may be necessary in order to proclaim the fact universally. He says to them, in effect, You have given yourselves to me, and I give you to the world—give you as my representatives. Look on yourselves as dedicated to this office, as I, in another and a higher sense, was appointed to represent the gracious character of God.

Hence, partly, the mighty obligations they are under to

---

* John xvii. 18. Dr. Campbell's translation, only substituting "messenger" for "apostle."

task their utmost powers for the diffusion of his gospel. For if it was necessary that he should turn all his infinite nature into grace—that he should dissolve into a fountain of healing mercy, for the recovery of the world, in order to do justice to the love of God, is it less necessary that their natures should be turned into tenderness and love, in order to furnish the world with an idea of his grace? A very small portion of the ocean might suffice to represent a river; but will less than the Amazon suffice to represent the ocean? And are our powers so capacious, our natures so exalted, that less than the consecration of the whole should be able to convey an idea of his grace? So vast were his conceptions of the love of God, that he attempted not to describe it—he contented himself with saying, that "God so loved us;" and aimed rather to express its indescribable amount in godlike deeds. And did he fall so far short of the great reality—was his representation of it so scant and meagre that we can imitate it without sacrifice or effort? It is true, his example can never be equalled, for it embodies infinite goodness; but with so much the greater force does it oblige us in our humble measure to attempt the imitation. Having *died* for the good of man, the least he is entitled to expect is, that we should *live* for the same benevolent object. To save the world was his vocation, his supreme and single object—so that never do we so much resemble him as when we make it our *business* and *calling* to carry out his gracious design. Yes, as far as religion is practical and relative to others, he has made benevolence its life and essence; not merely a part of the Christian's character, but the character itself.

V. The fact that the followers of Christ are appointed to be the channels and representatives of his grace to the world, supposes that they are called, prepared, and aided by *an agency from on high*. Accordingly, he promised them that the loss of his visible presence should be amply compensated by the advent of "another Comforter, who should abide with them for ever." May we not expect, then, that the Scripture theory of Christian instrumentality will receive abundant confirmation from the nature of his dispensation, and the doctrine of his influence? Let us seek the answer—where alone it can be found—in the word of God.

What, for instance, is the history of his first impartation in the Christian Church? No sooner had the Saviour ascended his mediatorial throne, than the Spirit came down, as he had promised—came like a rushing, mighty wind, filling the whole house where the disciples were assembled, filling each heart, filling the whole Church — came with a copiousness and power, as if his influences had for ages been pent up and under restraint, and now rejoiced in being able to pour themselves out over the Church and the world.

And what was the immediate effect of that event? Thousands were instantly converted; the sword of the Spirit seemed newly edged with power; and, bathed in the lightnings of heaven, smote and subdued multitudes at once.

Was the sphere of his agency to be limited to any particular country or province? His field was the world. "He shall convince the world of sin." What was the instrumentality which for this purpose he was to employ? What, but the instrumentality of those to whom his power was promised, and on whom his influence rested? By whose feet but theirs was he to carry the gospel "among all nations?" By whose lips but theirs was he to "convince the world of sin?" By whose hand but theirs was he to wield that weapon of celestial truth, which, because it is the only weapon he employs, is called the very "sword of the Spirit?"

Hence some of them he specially selected and appointed to particular spheres of labor. Many of them he miraculously endowed for the office. All of them found, that wherever they went in his name, he "caused them to triumph."

But if the world was to be converted by their instrumentality, would he not require and incline them all to tax their resources to the utmost, compatible with other incumbent claims? He did so. One interest prevailed. One subject of emulation swallowed up every other — who should approach nearest to the likeness of Christ—who should do most for the enlargement of his reign. "The multitude of them that believed were of one heart and of one soul;" the spirit of Christ animated the whole community, and every particular pulse beat in concert with it.

What, then, was the effect of his agency through the instrumentality of the Church? The gospel went flying abroad to the ends of the earth. New territories, for a time, were daily added to the domains of the Church. Her converts were seen flocking to her from all directions, like clouds of doves to their windows; and, among the wonders of that period, one was to see some of her bitterest persecutors become her champions and her martyrs.

And what was the great design of the Spirit in all this? How remarkable and emphatic the language of Christ in reply! "He shall not speak of himself." "He shall testify of me." "He shall glorify me." As the Saviour came to glorify the Father by the demonstration of his infinite love, so the Spirit came to glorify Christ by exhibiting and carrying that demonstration home, through the Church, to the heart of the world. But what must be *His* estimate of the work of Christ, that he should thus, in a sense, be content to be silent concerning himself, in order that the world might resound with nothing but the claims of Christ; conceal his only splendors, that the eye of the world might rest, undisturbed, on Christ alone? And who can compute the enormous guilt of those by whose instrumentality his infinite propensions to exhibit the glory of Christ might be carried into effect, but who give that instrumentality to other objects, and thus unutterably "grieve the Holy Spirit of God?"

Possibly, however, the promise of the Spirit to convert the world, it may be said, was not meant for all time, but only, or chiefly, for the first ages of the Church. So far from this, the gift of the Holy Spirit is the great *promise* of the Christian dispensation: "Ask, and ye shall receive." The *law* of the dispensation on the subject is this: "Every one that asketh receiveth"—a law which establishes the certain and permanent connection between asking for the influence of the Spirit and obtaining it. While the Sacred Scriptures, public worship, a standing ministry—all the means of grace—what are these but the great *ordinances* of the dispensation, appointed as so many channels to receive the living waters of prophetic vision, and to convey them into all the world? And the great unfulfilled *prophecy* of the dispensation is, "I will pour out my Spirit upon all flesh." Till this prediction is fulfilled, and the world convinced of sin, the promise of the Spirit to accomplish the work may be regarded as repeated to every believer, through every hour of time.

Now, as the fitness of the Holy Spirit to be the agent of Christ consists in his due appreciation of the claims of Christ, and in his perfect sympathy with the design of Christ to save the world, so the fitness of the Church, as the instrument of the Spirit, can only consist in its sympathy with the Spirit in converting the world and glorifying Christ. Did Christ travail in soul for the redemption of the world? Then the fitness of the Spirit as his representative consists in an infinite travail of compassion for the application of that redemption; and never, till "Zion travails" for the same object, can she expect to "bring forth." Did Christ devote the entire fulness of his nature to the salvation of man? Then the fitness of the Spirit to be the steward of all that fulness of grace, consists in his readiness to administer the whole to the perishing race; and never till the Church is in readiness, by entire devotedness, to convey it into all the world, is it prepared to do justice to the office and agency of the Holy Spirit. Did Christ appoint the Christian ministry, and the various means of grace, as the channels for conveying his gospel to every creature? Then the suitableness of the Spirit to carry out this intention must consist in his readiness to replenish these channels with heavenly influences, till the earth be filled with the glory of the Lord; and never till the Church has multiplied these channels sufficiently to realize this grand consummation, will it adequately sympathize with the office of the Spirit, or satisfy his infinite desire for the glory of Christ.

Hence the importance of each believer individually, and of the Church collectively, being "filled with the Spirit." So lofty is his estimate of the claims of Christ, and so perfect his sympathy with him in the great object of the world's recovery, that he requires every member, agency, and influence of the entire Church to unite to the utmost in enforcing the one and realizing the other. The absence of a single means which might have been employed, is not only to rob the world of that promised influence of the Spirit which might have accompanied its presence—it is to proclaim to the unthinking world that he is not entirely devoted to the glory of Christ, and thus to cast a shade of grievous dishonor on the dispensation of the Spirit.

VI. But if the theory of Christian influence contained in the preceding chapter be scriptural, we may expect to find not only that it is thus in harmony with other truths, and deducible from independent doctrines, but that *it stands out on the inspired page with all the particularity and boldness of a distinct command, and all the authority of apostolic practice.* Nor are we disappointed.

The mission of Christ from the throne of heaven to the altar of the cross, contains in it the spring and principle of every other mission from that cross to the ends of the earth. By dignifying us with his own love, and allying himself to our nature, he proposes every other human being as a magnificent object of affection to the whole species. By requiring us to forgive even our enemies, he would have it impressed on us that we owe to every man a debt of affection which is never discharged. By sending forth the seventy to proclaim the kingdom of God through Judea, he taught that the piety of his people is to be diffusive, and was training his Church for that bolder flight which should eventually sweep the horizon of the world. In order to enlarge the sphere of Christian beneficence to the utmost, he annihilates the ancient distinction between neighbor and enemy; teaches us to regard every man as our neighbor who needs our aid: to look on our field as the world. Taking us from that small circle which our selfishness prescribes, he conducts us to a mount of vision, from which all the territorial lines and artificial distinctions of society are no longer visible, and where the living landscape presents us with the view of one vast community of immortal beings, claiming the same distinguished origin, involved in a common danger, invited to one grand deliverance, and passing together into the unseen state. By teaching us there to pray, "Thy kingdom come, thy will be done on earth, as it is done in heaven," he would open before us the prospect of unbounded progression and improvement, inspirit us to enter on a career of emulation with angels, to despair of nothing, to hope for every thing in the moral advancement of the world, and to call in at every step the almighty agency of God. By simply commanding us to do unto others as we would they should do unto us, he lays a principle of relative duty so broad and deep, that, if rightly built on, it would sustain a pyramid of benevolent and heroic deeds whose top should reach unto heaven; and by leading us to the throne of God, and teaching us to pray that earth may be assimilated to heaven, he reminds us that our means of doing good are never exhausted, since we are empowered at every step to touch and set in motion the almighty agency of God.

But if the glorious object of this prayer is to be realized, if the harvest of the world is to be gathered into the garner of his Church, where are the reapers? "Pray ye, therefore, the Lord of the harvest," saith he, "that he would send forth more laborers into his harvest."

But not only will reapers be necessary; so vast is the sphere of labor, that agencies of every kind will find scope for operation; and, as every follower of Christ can do something, *not* to do it would evince indifference to his claims, and would, in moral effect, be ranging themselves against him. "He," therefore, saith Christ, "that is not with me is against me;" a sentence which at once divides mankind into two classes, denouncing the absence of activity in any of his professed followers, and ranking it with positive hostility against him.

For the same reason, however, that every member of his Church is to be employed in his service, it follows, of course, that every means of influence which each possesses should be employed also, and employed to the utmost. Accordingly, he not only startles the indolent, by the inquiry, "Why stand ye here all the day idle?" and by the command, "Work while it is day, for the night cometh wherein no man can work;" but our life in his hands is converted into a lamp, which, like the virgins in the parable, we are to keep bright and burning; and into a stewardship, concerning every item of which we are to render him finally a faithful account. Our "every word," our "pound," our various endowments, whatever they may be, are so many talents which he expects us to multiply by constant use. He will not require the possessor of two talents to account for three, but neither will he permit him to account for one only. The very fact that he possesses two, constitutes his call and his obligation to employ them; nor is he at liberty to set any limits to his endeavors short of those which his means and opportunities prescribe. And, as Christian influence multiplies itself by use, he is held responsible not only for the right employment of his two talents, but for the other two, which that employment would have added to them. To deny himself for Christ is his daily obligation; but to show him how entirely he is the property of Christ, he is required to hold life itself in subordination to the Christian cause, and to surrender it to martyrdom whenever the welfare of that cause may require. "He that loseth his life for my sake shall find it."

Having made it imperative on every individual disciple to consecrate his entire influence, from the moment of his conversion, to the diffusion of the gospel, the Saviour made it equally binding on them all to *unite* for the same object. By calling them "brethren," he would remind his followers that they form a brotherhood. Of all "the sheep which should hear his voice," he declared, "there shall be one fold and one shepherd." In the exercise of his high prerogative as the lawgiver of his Church, the only new command which he issued to its members was, "that ye love one another." That they might have a pattern which should move as well as teach, he proposes to them his own example, by adding, "as I have loved you, that ye love one another." To bind them together still more effectually, he made their affection to each other the badge of their discipleship to him: "By this shall all men know that ye are my disciples, if ye have love one to another." And, as if to render the obligation irresistible, he lifted up his eyes to heaven, and, as in the very presence of the cross, entreated "that they all may be one;" adding, as the great reason of the whole, "that the world may believe that thou hast sent me." At this practical and ultimate design of their unity he had glanced, indeed, at the commencement of his public ministry; describing his people as "the salt of the earth," and "the light of the world." For as, in the former capacity, they are to suspend, by their holy and combined activity, the tendency of the world to a state of general dissolution, so, in the latter, they are placed to catch the radiance of his throne, and to transmit it to a world immersed in the shadow of death. Not only are they kindled in their respective orbits to irradiate the gloom immediately around, but as a Church they are to unite and constitute "the light of the world." And thus, from his opening discourse to his closing prayer, he constantly kept in view the combination of his people for the recovery of the world.

For the same end he predicted and promised the mission of the Spirit. So candidly and explicitly had he described the trials of their office, that such a promise was necessary, if only for their encouragement. Having, therefore, taken them to an eminence, and shown them the vast confederacy of evil arrayed against them, he reminded them that they were to fight in fellowship with all the children of light: that more than angels would mingle in their ranks: that the Eternal Spirit himself, arming their weakness with his might, would advance with them to the work, and convince the world of sin.

And when at length "the hour had come," when the Son of man, having been lifted up from the earth, proceeded to put into motion the instrumentality which he had arranged for drawing all men unto him, as if he had been sitting on the circle of the heavens, and surveying all the possibilities and events that could occur down to the close of time, he answers the objections to this design before they are uttered, anticipates wants before they arise, and provides against dangers before they threaten. Was it necessary, for instance, that he should first legislate on the subject? "Go," said he— and he was standing but one step from the throne of heaven— "Go into all the world, and preach the gospel to every creature." Still, plain as this command might at first appear, the duty which it enjoins is so novel, and the project which it contemplates so vast, that doubts are likely to arise as to its import and obligation: he repeats it, therefore, again and again: repeats it in other forms, as an old prediction that must be fulfilled, and as a new injunction: "Then opened he their understandings, that they might understand the Scriptures, and said unto them, Thus it is written, and thus it behooved Christ to suffer and to rise from the dead the third day, and that repentance and remission of sins should be preached in his name among all nations, beginning at Jerusalem. And ye are witnesses of these things." If they are to enter on their office at once, peculiar and even miraculous qualifications are necessary. "Ye shall receive power from on high," said he, "after that the Holy Ghost is come upon you; and ye shall be witnesses unto me, both in Jerusalem and in all Judea, and in Samaria, and unto the uttermost parts of the earth." But peculiar dangers will assail them: "All power is mine," said he. "Go, and you shall move under the shield of Omnipotence." "Lo! I am with you alway, even to the end of the world." Thus, making the most comprehensive provision, and taking the whole responsibility of success on himself, his last word to his witnesses was, "Go;" his last act was to bless and dismiss them to their work; and the last impression he left on their minds was, that they held in trust the conveyance of his gospel to all mankind.

And, as this was the last indication of his will on earth, we know how his first act in heaven corresponded with it. The Eternal Spirit himself came down—came expressly to testify of Christ—came to be the Great Missionary Spirit of the Church, to "convince the world of sin." We know how the apostles began at Jerusalem, when three thousand souls received their testimony. We know how their hesitation to quit Jerusalem and Judea was gradually overcome—how a Paul was added, like a new missionary element infused into their spirit—and we can conceive how they must have felt, as if, in the terms of his new commission to be a witness to the Gentiles, their own original commission had been renewed and reënforced. We know how they were divinely allured farther and farther from Jerusalem; how vision after vision drew them on to invade the neighboring territories of idolatry; and how, at length, when even a Paul evinced a reluctance to pass the last limit of Jewish restriction, when even he scrupled to leave the confines of Asia, a vision was seen far back in the western regions of idolatry—a Macedonian suppliant—the emblem of Europe—saying, "Come over and help us." Bursting that last enclosure, the outermost circle of restriction, he was not disobedient to the heavenly vision; and the Church found itself fully committed to its lofty office of traversing the world.

And now, we might have thought, the Saviour has surely made it sufficiently apparent that his people are to be his messengers to the world. Nothing more can be necessary to show that this great object enters into the very design and principle of his Church. But not so thought the Saviour himself. Once more does he come forth, and reiterate the truth. When we might have supposed that his voice would be heard no more, once again does he come forth, and break the silence of the Church; and the subject on which he speaks is the missionary character of that Church. Not that it had lost sight of its office. His servants were carrying their testimony in all directions. But, as if the angel having the everlasting gospel did not yet speed on his way fast enough to satisfy the yearnings of infinite compassion, or as if he feared that angel would stop ere the whole earth, the last creature, had heard the gospel testimony, he came forth personally, and announced, "The Spirit and the bride say, Come; and let him that heareth say, Come; and let him that is athirst come; and whosoever will, let him come and take of the water of life freely."

Here is the summing up of all his arrangements and commands for the diffusion of the gospel. Having opened the fountain of eternal life in the midst of the desert world—the Spirit—the Church—every member of that Church—every power of every member, even if he can only utter the exclamation, Come, are all to be combined and devoted to the grand object of inviting the perishing world to partake. Every one that hears the call is to transmit it farther still—there is no point at which it may stop—a chain of living voices is to be carried round the globe in every direction, till the earth grows vocal with the sound of the Church inviting men to Christ.

Thus, if the last act of Christ on earth was to make the world the heirs of his grace, his first act in heaven proclaimed that he required all the benevolent agency of his Church to be put into full activity, in order to do justice to the purposes of his love; and as this is his last recorded command, the postscript of the Bible, he would have it impressed on the mind of the universal Church, in every age, with all the freshness and force of a parting injunction.

VII. If the preceding exposition of the will of Christ concerning the missionary character of his Church be correct, we may expect to find a further illustration of that will in *recorded sentiments and "acts of the apostles" and "primitive churches."*

Let us look at the great missionary of the Christian Church—the apostle of the Gentiles. It is admitted, indeed, that he had been specially designated to the office; but by this circumstance he is so far from ceasing to be an example, that the Head of the Church may be regarded as saying, "For this purpose, partly, have I called and employed him, and placed his history on record, that my people may possess in him a model of the missionary character for all succeeding times."

It is admitted, also, that Christians generally, and even Christian ministers, are not called to the literal imitation of his missionary career. At the same time, it is meant that they should more than admire it—that they should imbibe and imitate its entire spirit. The same principle of loyalty to Christ and love to man they must possess; and from that same principle must they rise superior to selfish indulgence, and be able to appeal to their self-sacrificing piety that for them "to live is Christ."

The apostle could do this; and it was the sole secret of his heroic devotedness and missionary enterprise. In the ear of the selfish and the worldly, the language doubtless sounds extravagant and absurd. In the ear of God, and indeed of every enlightened being, it is only the language of sobriety and wisdom. It was dictated by no mere momentary impulse of zeal, but was the result of a sober calculation frequently repeated, and of enlightened principle gradually matured. There was a time when, in common with the world, he regarded life as superlatively valuable; but he now looked on it as comparatively insignificant, for he had found an object of unspeakably greater importance. Others might copy the example of their fellow-men, but he had risen to the high and holy ambition of copying the example of incarnate perfection, of God manifest in the flesh. Others might waste their precious time in ease, and sloth, and worldly indulgence; but he aspired to enter into the counsels of Heaven, to become a co-worker together with God, and instrumentally to mingle in the operations of Almighty love in renewing and blessing a world of apostate but immortal beings. Others might content themselves with the praise of men, with the good opinion of creatures perishing like themselves; but he aspired to the high distinction of pleasing God—of being received and welcomed into the presence of the Supreme, with the sentence, "Well done, good and faithful servant." Others might be satisfied with their own personal salvation, but, feeling that he had a Saviour for the world, he panted to go everywhere, claiming that world for Christ—panted to "present every man perfect in Christ Jesus"—"travailed in birth" for the regeneration of the human race.

Hence the secret of his self-denial—"I am made all things

to all men, *if by any means I might save some.*" Hence, too, the spring of his Christian zeal—"*If by any means I may provoke* to emulation them who are my flesh, *and might save some of them.*" This was the reason of his prudence and vigilance—" I please all men in all things, not seeking mine own profit, but the profit of many, *that they may be saved.*" And hence, too, his joy in suffering—" It is for your consolation *and salvation.*" This was the object at which he aimed, and which filled the whole sphere of his vision; comparatively speaking, he saw nothing else. Ease might offer him indulgence; wealth might display her bribes; pleasure might exhibit her charms; but these had lost their power to tempt; to him they had become objects of supreme indifference. Persecution might bring out and spread in his path a fearful array of scourges, and chains, and axes—all the instruments and apparatus of torture and death. But he looked at the cross, and, beholding the Son of God suspended there, he armed himself "likewise with the same mind." He looked around; and he saw the assembled Church of Christ urging him, for the glory of the cross, for the sake of perishing humanity, to go forwards. He listened, and heard the whole creation groaning to be delivered. He looked above; and he saw "a great cloud of witnesses" bending with intense interest from their blessed seats; and beyond and above them all, he saw the throne of the Lamb and him that sat on it; and in his hand a glorious crown of life; and he saw that it was extended toward him; and thus sustained, he could point to all the instruments of torture, and exclaim, " None of these things move me, neither count I my life dear unto myself, so that I might finish my course with joy, and the ministry which I have received of the Lord Jesus to testify of the gospel of the grace of God." And thus impelled, again and again he led the van of the army of the cross, stormed the very strongholds of idolatry and sin, proclaimed the name of his sovereign Lord " where Satan's seat" was, planted the standard of the cross in the very citadel of the foe, till his progress from place to place was to be traced, not indeed by blood—or if so, by no blood but his own, for he was covered with the scars of the Christian conflict—but with the fall of idol temples, the plantation of Christian Churches, the trophies of ransomed human souls, and with the song of the Christian warrior, exulting, "Now thanks be unto God, who always causeth us to triumph in every place." And yet, in all this heroic devotedness and self-consuming zeal, was he exceeding his obligations—doing any thing more than carrying out principles to their legitimate application—living to Christ? Did he ever utter a word which implied that he considered himself an exception to what others should be? that no one was bound to be so zealous for Christ as he was—that a lower standard of benevolence was sufficient for them? On the contrary, how humbly did he account himself less than the least of all saints, how uniformly did he speak of himself only as one of a number constrained and borne onwards by the love of Christ, and how earnestly did he say to all, "Be ye followers of me, even as I also am of Christ."

VIII. Now, if such be an exemplification of what, in spirit and principle at least, each individual convert should be, let us next glance at the illustration of that missionary spirit and principle *as exhibited in the conduct of a primitive Church.* The Church at Jerusalem was denominational, consisting exclusively of converted Jews. The Church at Antioch, including as it did all believers, irrespective of their nation, was the first Catholic Christian Church—"Now there were in the Church that was at Antioch certain prophets and teachers: as Barnabas, and Simeon that was called Niger, and Lucius of Cyrene, and Manaen, who had been brought up with Herod the tetrarch, and Saul. As they ministered to the Lord, and fasted, the Holy Ghost said, Separate me Barnabas and Saul for the work whereunto I have called them."* Deeply impressed with their individual responsibility, different members of the Antiochian Church had already made certain unconnected efforts for the diffusion of the gospel. Grateful in the last degree for their own salvation, and encouraged by the conversion of the Roman Cornelius, they could not but speak of the things which they had seen and heard—"And the hand of the Lord was with them, and a great number believed and turned to the Lord."†

But the time had now arrived when they were to attempt

---

* Acts xiii. 1, 2.   † Acts xi. 21.

a united and systematic effort for the same object. It was not likely that such piety, wisdom, and zeal, could long commune together without making a combined movement. One, we may suppose, would insist on the evident *design* of a Christian Church to extend the gospel: another, on the authoritative *will of Christ*: a third, on the *depraved condition of the heathen*; and a fourth, on the instances in which they themselves had seen the gospel prove "the power of God unto salvation;" while all would acknowledge the importance of a more direct, vigorous, and sustained effort than had yet been made for enlarging the kingdom of Christ. "But who is sufficient for these things?" Agents must be selected—a sphere of labor appointed them—and their hands sustained by the prayers, and, if need be, by the contributions, of the disciples remaining at home—for this is to be a mission of the Church. Conscious of their own incompetence, and anxious to take no step which God has not encouraged, they wait together before him by prayer and fasting.

"And as they ministered to the Lord, and fasted, the Holy Ghost said, Separate unto me Barnabas and Saul for the work whereunto I have called them." Here we see the Church whose members had been the most zealous, *individually*, for the extension of the faith, honored to be the first missionary society for the conversion of the heathen. While from the Divine designation of the two most distinguished members and ministers of that Church to be the first missionaries, we learn, that Christians will never evince that they estimate the missionary office as God does, till they select for it the choicest instrumentality which the churches contain.

"And when they had fasted and prayed, and laid their hands on them, they sent them away." Directed, probably, to their particular scene of labor, by the same Divine authority which had nominated them to the work, Barnabas and Paul proceeded to Seleucia, the nearest port, and sailed at once to the isle of Cyprus. Paul had already gratified the instinctive longing of the young convert, to benefit those first to whom he is most nearly related, by preaching the gospel in his native Cilicia. And now Barnabas enjoys the same sacred gratification, by preaching salvation in his native

Cyprus. Thus it is that the gospel recognizes all the natural and social relations of life, and teaches us that in seeking to evangelize a distant region, we are not to overlook the prior claims of our family, neighborhood, and native land.

Crossing to Peninsular Asia, Paul and Barnabas prosecuted their mission by traversing Pamphylia, Pisidia, and Lycaonia, till they touched on the borders of Cilicia, where Paul had already published the gospel. In this way, the whole of the intermediate country between their two native places resounded with the preaching of Christ crucified. In establishing this chain of Christian posts from point to point, they proposed to make it the base of a future mission into the region beyond. And here we find the apostle, on a subsequent occasion, enlarging the sphere of his labor by preaching in the remoter regions of Phrygia, Galatia, and Mysia. An apt illustration, this, of the expansive power of the gospel; of the manner in which it enlarges the circle of its beneficent operation; and in which the Christian Church should ever be meditating further conquests for Christ, and preparing for the final occupation of the entire globe.

Having touched the boundary of Cilicia, Paul and Barnabas retraced their steps, revisited the Churches which they had planted, and then "returned to Antioch, from whence they had been recommended to the grace of God for the work which they fulfilled. And when they were come, and had gathered the Church together, they rehearsed all that God had done with them, and how he had opened the door of faith unto the Gentiles."* Regarding themselves as the representatives of the Church which had sent them forth, and still retaining their communion with it, they take it for granted that all its members will feel the liveliest interest in the results of their mission. In the same way should every thing connected with the progress of the gospel in heathen lands now thrill through the heart of the Church at home, and be regarded as a subject of deep personal interest by each of its members.

The Church at Antioch was now surrounded, as far as its position would permit, with the wide field of its missionary

---

* Acts xiv. 26, 27.

operations. In whatever direction it might look, it had the hallowed satisfaction of beholding the fruits of its labor stretch away to a remote circumference—an image of the manner in which every particular Church, and in which the whole collective Church of Christ, should sit in the centre of a widely-extended missionary domain, filled to the verge with the influence of the cross, and thus prepared to enlarge and extend its circle till it embraces the world.

For what is there in all this piety and zeal which is not equally obligatory on the Churches of the present day? What had the Lord of the Church done for the Christians at Antioch, which he has not equalled, and, in some providential respects, even exceeded, for us? "Compassion moved them;" but is heathenism less depraving, or sin less destructive, or hell less fearful, now, than then? "Zeal for the glory of Christ incited them;" but are we less indebted to redeeming love than they? We do not hope for less than eternal life, and did they expect more? "The Spirit of God impelled and directed them;" but it was in answer to earnest, united, and persevering prayer; and is the throne of grace less accessible to us than it was to them? or the promise which encouraged them to repair to it repealed—"Ask, and ye shall receive?" And is not the same Spirit saying to every Church, by the voice of Scripture, and the movements of Providence, as distinctly as to the Church at Antioch, "Separate unto me your Paul and your Barnabas. Select your holiest, ablest men; cultivate their mind and piety to the utmost; and set them apart to the missionary office?" "A Paul and a Barnabas were among *them*, and if we could command such agents—if we could select even an Eliot or a Swartz—we would strain every effort to send them forth; but there are few, or none, such among us." Yes, there are; or, if not, there might be. "Who, then, is Paul, and who is Apollos, but ministers by whom ye believed, even as the Lord gave to every man?" By the grace of God they were what they were; and, by the same grace, their distinguished excellences can be reproduced and repeated in every Church. Only let not Christians expect their agents to be apostles, in order that they themselves may sit at home in indolence—only let them expect that their agents will be their *representatives*, and nothing more—only let them look for a Barnabas in a

Church worthy of a Barnabas, and look for him by earnest and united prayer to God—and they will find the Spirit of God raising up an agency as suitable for the present day as that of Paul and Barnabas for apostolic days.

IX. If we now proceed to examine *the inspired epistles to the Churches*, we shall find that, as the missionary character of the Apostle Paul is only an exemplification of what, in spirit and principle, every other Christian should be, so the missionary conduct of the Church at Antioch is only a model for all other Christian Churches.

The Churches at Ephesus and Colosse are exhorted to be fervent, incessant, and united, in prayer for the wide and successful propagation of the gospel. For well the apostle knew that the zeal for Christ, which led them to become suppliants for that object at the throne of grace, would lead them, while there, to inquire, "Lord, what wilt thou have us *to do?*"— that, so far from there expiring, it would there rather be fanned and fed, and rise into a flame, into which property, influence, life itself, if necessary, would be offered up as an oblation to his glory.

The Philippian Christians were to shine as lights, exalted to irradiate the surrounding gloom, "holding out the word of life."

To the Christians at Galatia, the apostolic injunction is, "As ye have opportunity, do good unto all men;" language which laid under tribute every moment of their time, and every energy of their renewed nature, for the good of the world.

In his Epistle to the Romans, the calling and conversion of the heathen world is a subject of constant recurrence. "But how shall they call on him in whom they have not believed? and how shall they believe in him of whom they have not heard? and how shall they hear without a preacher? and how shall they preach except they be sent?"* Leaving it to be inferred, that if the proclamation of the gospel be necessary to the salvation of the world, the greater the number of heralds employed, the greater the number of conversions which, by the agency of the Spirit, would ensue; and, consequently, the greater the obligation of every Christian community to pray

---

* Rom. x. 13, 14.

the Lord of the Church to raise up and send forth from among them the greatest number of missionaries which their resources can supply.

The members of the Church at Thessalonica "became ensamples to all that believe in Macedonia and Achaia; for from them sounded out the word of the Lord."* Not only was the report of their conversion circulated by others through all the neighboring districts, but they themselves followed that report with as loud a call to those regions as they could raise, to "turn to God from dumb idols, to serve the living and true God."

While to the Church at Corinth the apostle writes, "We are come as far as to you also in preaching the gospel of Christ, . . . having hope, when your faith is increased, that we shall be enlarged by you . . . abundantly, to preach the gospel in the regions beyond you."† Already had he hastened from province to province, "weeping over the wreck of immortal souls," and leaving behind him, wherever he had been, monuments of the power of the gospel to save. But, much as he rejoiced in this, the vast circuit which he had already filled with the sound of salvation could not limit his desires or his labors. There were "regions beyond;" regions which were still immersed in the shadow of death; and the weight of their misery rested on his soul. If he reposed a moment, therefore, it was only to gather strength for his onward course. If he remained a short time with a Church already formed, it was only that their flame might supply him with the means of kindling another light in the distance. If he rejoiced in his success at Corinth, it was chiefly as it enabled him abundantly to enlarge the sphere of his labors in "the regions beyond." He takes it for granted that the members of a Church have "a claim to the exclusive enjoyment of the Christian ministry only until they have reached a certain maturity in religious" attainments; but that, from that moment, they are equally bound with himself to extend the knowledge of Christ into "the regions beyond." All their resources are to be taxed for the enlargement of his

---

* 1 Thess. i. 7, 8.
† 2 Cor. x. 14–16. See an excellent discourse on this text in the Works of the Rev. Richard Watson, vol. iii.

kingdom. Circle beyond circle of benevolent effort is to be described by the Christian Church, till the earth is encompassed in the vast embrace of mercy.

And has the missionary enterprise diminished, by the lapse of time, either in its obligation on the Church, or in its magnificence? St. Paul is still exhorting "that supplications, prayers, and intercessions be made for all men;" and declaring that "this is good and acceptable in the sight of God our Saviour, who will have all men to be saved, and to come to the knowledge of the truth."* St. James is still announcing to the Church, "Let him know, that he who converteth the sinner from the error of his way,"—let him ponder the mighty truth—let him publish it through the Church as a proclamation from the throne of God to inflame the zeal of others—"let him know, that he shall save a soul from death."† What an inducement to the united Church to attempt the stupendous object of saving a world from death! The Apostle Peter is still affirming that the existence of the world continues, because God is "long-suffering to us-ward, not willing that any should perish, but that all should come to repentance."‡ And St. John is testifying that "the Father sent the Son to be the Saviour of the world;"§ and leaving us to draw the startling inference, that if "he who seeth his brother have need, and shutteth up his bowels of compassion from him, is a murderer," the Christian Church can wash its hands from the crimson guilt of murdering the souls of the heathen only by making the mightiest effort of which it is capable for their salvation.

X. But if it be true that this theory was prefigured by former dispensations; that it was substantially realized in the person of Christ; that it is called for by the office and agency of the Holy Spirit; that our Lord prescribed it; and that his primitive Churches either practically exemplified it, or were authoritatively exhorted to do so, might we not venture to suggest that most probably a scheme so wide in its sweep is even more comprehensive still? Knowing, as we do, that God acts by general laws—laws which include in their range worlds as well as atoms, and systems as well as worlds—may we not

---

* 1 Tim. ii. 1, 3, 4. ‡ 2 Peter iii. 9.
† James v. 20. § 1 John iv. 14.

suggest that a principle which unites and lays under tribute all the sanctified influences of earth, adds to them also the influences of heaven? Revelation decides that this is the fact; that as there is but one object in the universe at which to aim, so there is but one plan on which it is pursued, and one being by whom it is conducted, the Lord Jesus Christ.

From the moment—if we may be allowed to employ the language of time in speaking of things which acknowledge no date—from the moment when the Eternal Father determined to create, and to exhibit his glory and impart his fulness to his intelligent creation, a scheme of mediation became indispensable. The Son of God, as the only adequate representative of his person, and medium of his fulness, became indispensable to that mediatorial scheme. And from the moment he began to fulfil its conditions, and realize its designs, he became, by right and by appointment, the centre of the whole. "For by him were all things created, that are in heaven, and that are in earth, visible and invisible, whether they be thrones, or dominions, or principalities, or powers: all things were created by him and for him; and he is before all things, and by him all things consist. And he is the head of the body, the Church; who is the beginning, the first-born from the dead: that in all things he might have the preëminence. For it pleased the Father that in him should all fulness dwell; and having made peace through the blood of his cross, by him to reconcile all things unto himself; by him, I say, whether they be things in earth or things in heaven." And from that moment he acquired the right and the power to lay all the agencies and influences of this vast system of existences, economies, and constitutions, as it revolved around him, under tribute, in order to maintain the union, dependency, and order of all its parts to each other, and of the whole to himself. To withhold this tribute in the least degree is to derange the entire plan. Should such derangement occur even in the remotest part of the system, every other part and being belonging to it would sympathize with the shock, and feel himself personally aggrieved. Should it be announced, as the supreme will, that the offending party be reclaimed and saved, every order of being, every rank, each individual, would feel himself bound to task his energies to the utmost, as far as they could be made available, and to combine them with all the rest, in a grand endeavor to reclaim and restore the offender to the place and the happiness which he had lost. Even if some of those orders, owing to the difference of their nature, should not be able to minister *directly* to his recovery, they would take the liveliest interest in every stage of the process, and never rest till it was brought to a happy conclusion; while every being of his own order would feel himself bound, by the particular obligation of kindred, as well as by the general obligation of loyalty to Christ, to unite in an untiring endeavor for his recovery.

Now, who does not recognize in this representation a sketch of what has actually taken place? Not an individual merely, but an entire race, has broken the law which bound it up with all the orders in the mediatorial government of Christ. The integrity of the universe, as a union of different intelligent orders under one head, is destroyed. But by virtue of an eternal purpose, that integrity is to be restored: they are again to be "gathered together in one." The disclosure of this sublime "purpose which God had purposed in himself," stirred the entire universe of holy beings; and for its execution every agency it contains is not only put into motion, but into actual requisition. The whole, animated and united by this one design, move towards the scene of revolt. The Mediator himself descends into the midst, carrying with him the intensest sympathies, if not also the actual presence, of all the beings who retain their first estate. For one of them to have withheld his sympathy, or to have evinced that less than his entire nature was interested, and held ready for the occasion, would have been to inflict the shock of a new revolt, if not even to create a pause in the onward movement of mercy. But "he was seen of angels." In the whole of his progress from the throne to the cross, they may be said to have formed one unbroken and undeviating procession. He advanced to Calvary with all the lovers of mercy, the friends of man, the servants of God, in his train. In the sacrifice which he there presented, they beheld the means of mediation made visible to the universe, and complete for eternity. There they saw the *doctrine*, of which they had ever been enjoying the advantage, and the *fact*, or means, of which it had never entered into their minds to conceive, meet and become one. In its aspect toward God, as a fact, they saw mercy answering the claims of justice with an infinite compensation; and in its aspect towards man, as a doctrine, they saw both unite in appealing to the heart of the world, and establishing an infinite claim on its grateful and instant return.

They themselves, indeed, are personally benefited in a great variety of ways by the advent and death of Christ. "To the principalities and powers in heavenly places are made known by [means of] the Church the manifold wisdom of God." But on account of its remedial aspect on man it is that they chiefly prize it. They know that the race among whom the altar of atonement is erected, is the race whom it chiefly concerns; and their perfect sympathy with its gracious intention makes them conscious of a holy impatience to see that intention fully realized. Reasons, indeed, sufficient to prevent their repining, forbid them from presenting themselves visibly in the Church, or carrying the gospel audibly to the world; but not the less ardently do they burn to see this done by those on whom it devolves. Does not the first tear of the penitent create a sensation of joy through all their adoring ranks? As if to show the identity of their interests and ours, was not an angel employed to dictate that last portion of Scripture which discloses the vicissitudes of the Church to the end of time?* Have they not been heard rehearsing for the day when they will have to lead the anthem of the blessed, and celebrate the triumph of the mediatorial scheme in our recovery? In fine, "are they not all ministering spirits, sent forth to minister to them who shall be heirs of salvation?" and when the success of the gospel provokes the hostility of the world, is it not theirs to sound the trumpets and to discharge the vials of judgment? and are not all their ministries combined, as far as compatible with the laws of their economy, for advancing the progress of the gospel?† and would they not denounce the highest intelligences among them, who should withhold a single ministration which was due to this object, as a traitor to the cause of mercy? And if it is ever permitted them to offer a petition, must it not be one which prays, "Thy kingdom come, thy will be done on earth as it is in heaven?"—one which shows they are travailing in birth for the conversion of the world, and panting to

---

* Rev. xxii. 16.   † Acts v. 20: Rev. xiv. 16.

see the Church on earth as devoted to its office as the Church in heaven, and both coöperating together for this great consummation?

Had it been permitted to angels to occupy the place of man in the administration of the gospel, would whole regions have been now sitting in darkness and in the shadow of death? would not each of them have resembled him who was seen in vision flying with the everlasting gospel through the midst of heaven? Or were they now to be permitted by God, and authorized by the Church, to prescribe its duties and to dispose of its resources, would not a revolution be speedily effected in its state which would say to numbers who are now slumbering at home, "Go, stand, and speak unto the people [in the distant temples of idolatry] all the words of this life;" and which would put them in possession of the means of going? Or were it permitted them even to address us on the subject, what could the import of their language be, but an urgent exhortation to diffuse the knowledge of that mediation by which they and we are made one? "Brethren in Christ," they would say—for in him "the whole family in heaven and earth is named"—"you have been brought back into order and harmony with the universe: how can you live for any other object than that of aiming to add others to your number? When we saw you restored to the circle from which you had been lost, we exulted in the event; for not only did we behold you, by anticipation, occupying your appointed place in heaven—we saw your appointed place in the Church on earth; saw that you were called to occupy it as agents for Christ, and knew the happy consequences which would ensue from your required devotedness to its duties. Not more certainly is the throne of every believer prepared in heaven, than his appropriate place is prescribed on earth. In the system to which you now belong, every being, from the loftiest archangel to the lowliest saint, has his course assigned, and every holy act its appointed effect. You 'have come to an innumerable company of angels.' But the only object in which you and we can practically sympathize and unite is in the enlargement of the kingdom of Christ, and the celebration of his glory. In every thing which relates to this, so truly are we one, that never can you put forth the least effort for its furtherance, but the act thrills through all our principalities and powers, and carries with it all our sympathies. So distinctly do we see the design of Christ in calling you to occupy a place among the agents of his mediation; so evident is the adaptation of his Church to collect all such agencies as they arise, and to combine them with those already in operation; and so evident the certainty with which the whole is calculated instrumentally to repair the effects of sin and restore the harmony of the universe, that we beseech you, by the new fellowship to which you are admitted, and by our gathering together in him, that you do the will of God on earth as unitedly and devoutly as we your co-workers are doing it in heaven. From the higher ground we occupy, we can survey the fearful consequences of your neglect in all their aspects, bearings, and dimensions—the glory lost to God, the happiness lost to yourselves and to us, and the immortal spirits which you are allowing to pass into misery in unbroken procession, unwarned, and unsaved—consequences so fearful, that, were the exchange permitted, gladly would we resign our heavenly places to you, that we might discharge your trust, wield your influence, and win the honors which are offered to you in drawing men to Christ. So eager are we to behold the completion of the mediatorial scheme, as it relates to the recovery of man—to gaze on the Only-Begotten of the Father on the throne of the universe, encircled by the thrones and dominions, principalities and powers, of heaven, and by the number which no one can number, saved from the earth—all radiant with his glory, living in his smiles, and joined in his praise—and so fully are we possessed with the conviction that the entire consecration and union of all your sanctified instrumentality are essential to bring it to pass, that we adjure you, by the glory which shall then be revealed, that you 'henceforth live, not unto yourselves, but unto Him who died for you and rose again.' All in heaven is ready for the great consummation: each angel, as an agent of Providence, is at his post—each vial of judgment waits to be discharged on your foes. He in whom we both are one is on his throne, 'from henceforth expecting' the glorious issue. What other mediatorial wonders may await the disclosures of eternity we know not; but as if the restoration of man were only the first in a series of wonders—as if infinite plans were held in abeyance—the happiness of unknown worlds were kept in suspense till this be complete, unite all your influence in a great endeavor to make good our announcement at the advent of Christ, 'Glory to God in the highest, on earth peace and good-will towards man.'"

Now this, in effect, is the language in which the hierarchy of heaven may be regarded as perpetually stimulating the apathy, and urging the efforts, of the redeemed on earth. To the eye of faith they stand revealed, and are ever present, as a great cloud of witnesses. Never are they absent from our midst, either actually mingling their agencies with ours, or through the medium of our faith shedding a practical influence on our conduct; and thus, in the mediatorial economy, all the sanctified influences of heaven and earth are combined in the prosecution of its saving design. The chain of relationship and mutual influence passes not only from hand to hand through the Church militant, but through "all the family in heaven and earth," holding the entire community in union for the good of the world.

XI. But, further, this economy not only unites all the diversified influences which it includes into one agency—it also combines all their accumulations from age to age, and seeks to devolve the whole entire on each successive generation in the Church; so that we of the present day are living under the collected influences of all the past, and moving under an impulsive power greater than that of any preceding age.

The analogy of this truth indeed runs through all nature;* and the moral influence of national history furnishes perhaps its best illustration. A people rich in the wealth of ancestral worth possess strong incentives perpetually urging them to noble deeds. To this cause much of Roman greatness is ascribed. "The Roman citizens adorned the vestibules of their dwellings with the images of their ancestors; so that the faces of the patriot, the warrior, and the philosopher, were ever present to remind them of their exploits, and to stimulate them to imitation. The design was crowned with success. The virtue of one generation was transferred by the magic of example into several; and heroism was propagated

---

* See Bishop Butler's Analogy, Part ii., Chap. iv.

through the commonwealth." "Among no other nation," says Schlegel, in his Philosophy of History, "did historical recollections, even of the remotest antiquity, exert such a powerful influence on life, or strike so deep a root in the minds of men." But, surely, (if it be allowed to bring sacred history into the comparison,) the Jewish nation must be regarded as forming a grand exception. According to apostolic authority, the "advantage of the Jew was much every way, but chiefly that unto them were committed the oracles of God." That which distinguished them far above all the nations of the earth was, that, from the time of their settlement in Judea, they lived and moved under the direct influence of their miraculous history; while one design of the temple appears to have been, that, by making it the shrine of their most ancient and sacred relics, and the visible abode of religion, that influence might constantly act on them with ever-augmented force. If it be true that the man is little to be envied who could walk "indifferent and unmoved over any ground which has been dignified by wisdom, bravery, and virtue—whose patriotism would not gain force upon the plain of Marathon, or whose piety would not grow warmer among the ruins of Iona—that to abstract the mind from local emotion would be impossible if it were endeavored, and would be foolish if it were possible," how deep and lasting the impression calculated to be produced on a people who had to walk daily amidst the solemn and gorgeous magnificence of an ancient economy adjusted and adorned by the immediate hand of Deity! As if inhabiting the sacred enclosure of the temple itself, they were addressed perpetually by solemn voices from the past, and called on from every side by influences accumulated from the creation of the world. So deep was the effect produced on them—though, alas! a perverted one—that ages on ages of suffering have not been able to efface, nor hardly to impair it.

Now, all the wealth of moral influence which belonged to that dispensation has been poured into the treasury of the Christian Church. We "have come unto Mount Sion." It is not lost, but transferred, accumulated, and put into wide circulation. True, the temple is gone—its most sacred things have disappeared—the economy itself is abolished—the very nation scattered to the winds of heaven—but all its proper and mighty influence still exists. Nothing that belonged to it existed for itself. Every judgment that made it awful looked on beyond its own time, and is frowning still. "All these things happened unto them for ensamples; and they are written for our admonition, upon whom the ends of the world are come." Each of its prophets spoke less for his own time than for ours; so that for us he is prophesying still, "Not unto themselves but unto us they did minister the things which are now reported unto you by them that have preached the gospel unto you with the Holy Ghost sent down from heaven; which things the angels desire to look into." Every event which distinguished it is still in actual operation, diffusing the elements of other events, and propagating its influence somewhere. And where shall we look for that influence, but within the limits of the Christian Church? The Bible is the true conductor of all the holy influences the world has contained since the dawn of creation. From it the Jewish Church received, in a concentrated form, all that had distinguished the preceding economies, from the giving of the first promise to its own establishment in Judea. Not even the holiest of all its members would have been what he was, had Enoch never " walked with God," or had the Bible omitted to record the fact. In that Church, therefore, it may be truly said, Abel, though dead, was ever speaking; and "Enoch, the seventh from Adam," was ever prophesying of the coming of the Lord. There, the patriarchs came and lived again for their posterity. There, the rod of Aaron was ever blooming; the manna ever fresh;* the rod of Moses ever working and repeating its wonders. There Sinai reared its awful head, and from its thundering top the law was ever demanding for God the heart of the world, and demanding from every man the love of all the rest.

In the same sense the Bible has now discharged all the accumulated moral influences of the last economy into the present. The cross has received and transmitted the whole. Here, in effect, the temple of Jerusalem still stands. Though in a literal respect not one stone of that sacred pile remains upon another, in the hallowed influence which it sheds over the Church of God it still lifts up its awful front—its fires

---

* Heb. ix. 4.

still burn—its victims still bleed—its day of atonement still returns—its sanctity is still calling on the Church for its entire consecration. We behold these objects now—we shall see them in eternity. All the great events and solemn transactions of the Old Testament may be regarded as having taken place in the Christian Church. Here, in the ministry of the gospel, they do come and occur again. Here its miracles are still convincing, and its angelic messengers still appearing. Here Moses is still teaching self-renunciation, by wishing himself "blotted out from the book of life" for the good of others; and David leading the intercessions of the Church for the salvation of the ends of the earth; and the prophets still "testifying of the sufferings of Christ and the glory that should follow."

And, what is more, here they are all present at once. Truths and events which for the Jewish Church were scattered thinly over a long tract of time, are here collected to a point and made operative at once. Ages, with the men who made them memorable—and dispensations, with all the miraculous facts and sublime disclosures which distinguished them, pass in quick and close succession before our eyes; and we feel ourselves standing under the eye and influence of the whole.

And, more even than this, there is reason to believe that great as was the influence which that economy was calculated to exercise during its actual existence, that influence has gone on gathering strength with each successive age, and is incalculably mightier at this moment for us than for those who lived in its immediate presence. Not only do all its parts act on us at once, they act on us also in their highest and noblest form. For us it is all meaning and spirit, emancipated principle, and active power. Liberated from its former restraints, brought into the light of a more spiritual economy, and allowed free scope in the ampler sphere of the Christian Church, its power is greater now than during its actual reign on Zion. As it was typical, it was temporary—formed for, and acting upon, "the time then present;" but as it embodied evangelical and immortal principles, it was far in advance of its time, and destined to act chiefly on the future. Who will not admit that the character of the Psalmist, for instance, is exercising much greater moral power now than when he was alive? Who does not feel that his prayers for the universal diffusion of the truth, and the splendid visions of prophecy in which those aspirations were seen realized, have not yet attained their proper place of power? that they have all along been struggling to reach it; that they are only as yet beginning to produce their legitimate effect; and that with every successive year that effect, under God, is likely to increase? What manner of persons ought we to be to whom all this rich inheritance has descended!

But together with all this influence from the former economy, there blends a mightier influence peculiar to the present, a power so irresistible, that wherever it has had "free course" it has swept away the thrones of idolatry, changed the aspect of society, and left its impress on every object it has touched. Ours is the CROSS—the great power of God—not only absorbing and concentrating all the influences of the past, but charged with a new power direct from God—containing in its bosom all the springs of benevolence the world will ever know; an energy of expansive goodness capable of replenishing the universe with light and love. Here God is seen enriching the world with a gift which leaves it nothing to dread, or to ask for more. Here Christ is seen taking the world to his heart—seizing our nature as it trembles over the bottomless gulf—assuming it into union with his own—taking our place under the descending stroke of justice, and suffering in our stead. Before our eyes "Jesus Christ is here evidently set forth crucified amongst us." Here the Infinite Spirit himself descends from the heights of his everlasting dwelling-place, as a rushing mighty wind, and the cries of penitence are heard around. Here angels, drawn from heaven, bend to gaze, and labor to comprehend the mystery of incarnate love. Apostles come to lose themselves in wonder, and exclaim, "Herein is love;" and to surcharge their hearts with a benevolence which impels them to the ends of the earth, testifying that "the Father hath sent the Son to be the Saviour of the world." Here the bigotry of the Synagogue, the doubts of the Academy, and the pride of the Portico, are seen kneeling around, and humbled in the dust. And here he who was the fit representative of them all, comes to smite on his breast, and say, "God forbid that I should henceforth glory save in the cross of our Lord Jesus Christ," and hastens away to fill the nations with the report of its glories, and to call on all who believed it to help him onwards to the regions beyond.

If the influence of promises comparatively vague in their meaning, and indefinitely distant in their fulfilment, could produce, under God, the martyr-piety of Abel, the dauntless fidelity of Enoch, the persevering obedience of Noah, the missionary pilgrimage of Abraham, and the self-sacrificing zeal of Moses; if the comparatively feeble influences of the Jewish dispensation could create, under God, those splendid constellations of excellence which glow and burn in the eleventh chapter to the Hebrews, who shall set limits to that moral greatness and Christian devotedness which the mightier influences of the gospel should produce? To know that, in practical effect, a whole economy has existed for us, that is, for the Church of which we are members—that for us its heroes lived, and its martyrs died—to know that for us that economy of a thousand years was at last dismissed, as for us it had at first been called into being, leaving to us all its rich accumulations of inspired wisdom, godlike example, and moral wealth—this, alone, should surely be sufficient to teach us the greatness of living for the future, and to kindle in our hearts the unquenchable desire of transmitting the great inheritance to those who succeed us, not merely unimpaired, but augmented by the influence of our own devotedness.

But to know that that which displaced that economy was the personal advent, the visible humiliation, the actual sacrifice of the Son of God—that the eternal Father should have so loved us as to give from his bosom "the express image of his person"—should surely come on us with an effect which should leave us no power but that of obedience—no wish but that of multiplying our means of serving him a thousand-fold. "He that spared not his own Son, but delivered him up for us all, how shall he not with him also," asks the apostle, "freely give us all things?" Might he not, with equal conclusiveness, have inquired, How shall *we* not for him also freely give him all things? Before that gift could have been bestowed, the ocean of the Divine benevolence must have been stirred in all its unfathomable depths: should the shallow stream of our gratitude be only rippled on the surface? Of all his infinite resources, he freely gave the *sum:* of the mite like penury of our nature, shall we return him only a part? To know that he who was rich should for our sakes have become poor—that the Second Person in the mysterious Godhead should have personally descended to our rescue—descended from one depth of humiliation to another, till a cross arrested his farther descent, and made it impossible for Divine condescension itself to stoop lower—this is knowledge which, as it has moved all heaven, should surely be sufficient to move and agitate all earth. To hear that event succeeded by the sounds and signs of another advent—the advent of the Holy Spirit, as the converter and sanctifier of human souls—to find that thus each of the three Persons in the awful and mysterious Godhead is infinitely interested in our recovery—that there has actually been disclosed, in consequence, a new bond of their ineffable union in the fact of their coöperation for that recovery—and that so intently is the compassion of the Triune God set on the object, that no truth is left untaught, no miracle of mercy unperformed, no angel or agency unemployed, no part of the universe unmoved, no perfection of the Divine nature unconcerned, no aspect of the Divine character unexhibited, which is in the least essential to its accomplishment—surely this should leave no portion of the Church at rest, no means within its farthest reach untaxed for the attainment of the same end.

To find that this is clearly the Divine *design:* that Christ, as the Head of the Church on earth, authoritatively requires that each individual Christian surrender himself and live supremely for the conversion of others; that these unite into particular societies for the conversion of greater numbers still; that all these societies, in every land, combine in sympathy and purpose for the salvation of the entire race; to find that, as the President of the universe, having "all power in heaven and on earth," he commands and combines the sympathies and instrumentality of the Church in heaven with that of the Church on earth—assigning to angels the time and the place for their agency in providence, concurring with the movements of his kingdom of grace; and to find that in the same mediatorial capacity he even adds the presence and the renewing power of the Holy Spirit himself—surely this should leave no Christian unemployed, no Church unrelated, no agency we could invoke in earth or heaven to be absent from our combined endeavor to carry it into effect. And to find that this design is as *practicable* as it is *obligatory;* to hear other Christians avowing their readiness to be messengers or martyrs—honored or "accursed," any thing or nothing —so that they might be instrumental in promoting it; to see Churches selecting and sending out such men to carry the gospel onwards—other Churches emulating their example; to find that each convert, as he comes into the Church, is expected to proceed to his post and to commence his service, and that each Church, as it comes into being, is expected to enter into the general fellowship, and to help forward the common object of the whole; to see that the success of one Church is rejoiced in as the triumph of all, and that, if they suspend their song of praise for a while, it is only to read over again the command which first sent them forth, "Go into all the world and preach the gospel to every creature"—to prostrate themselves in prayer for that aid which the Spirit alone can impart, and which furnishes them with renewed occasion for louder triumphs still—this is a spectacle which should surely leave no other question on the lips of the individual Christian than, "Where is my post, and what shall I do?" and no other law for the Church universal than that of entire consecration.

Now, this was the prayer of Christ, not for the apostles only, "but for them also," he adds, "who shall believe on me through their word; that they all may be one, . . . that the world may believe that thou hast sent me." Finding themselves acted on by hallowed and benevolent influences from every quarter, and, from the remotest period of the Church, surrounded by lofty examples of Christian devotedness, and ever standing in the presence of his wondrous cross, he prayed that they might feel themselves impelled to make his consecration the model and motive of their own, that God might be glorified, and man be saved.

Be it remembered, also, as we shall hereafter have occasion to show, that there is a sense in which we of the present day sustain the accumulated responsibility of the eighteen centuries which have revolved since that prayer was uttered. In each succeeding age "the truth" to which it refers has, through the promised agency of the Holy Spirit, been exercising its consecrating influence, and instrumentally creating eminent examples of conscientiousness which treated no duty as unwelcome, and which evaded no obligation—of fidelity which spared no sin, nor allowed any iniquity, however splendid and powerful, to pass unrebuked—of courage which cowered before no danger, and shrank from no conflict—of enlarged benevolence which knew no limits to its plans, and toils, and travels for the welfare of man—of Christian self-abandonment, which swore eternal devotedness to Christ, though in the presence of the flames which were kindled for its martyrdom—and of love for man, which, even in those flames, wept over the misery of the world, and agonized in prayer for its recovery. These examples are not lost, though their memory is not embalmed in the volume of inspiration; their influence has been really added to that of patriarchs and prophets, of apostles and primitive saints. Whether we are conscious of its stimulating power or not, we are all at this moment reaping its advantage, and are consequently standing under the weight of an increased responsibility.

And to this, as the next chapter is intended to evince, is also to be added the influence acting on us from the prophetic disclosures of the future. The torch which the hand of prophecy holds up, throws its beams onwards to the consummation of all things. By this light we catch glimpses of noble examples yet to arise, and of glories yet to dawn. Many are seen running to and fro with the message of salvation—the Spirit poured out from on high to give it success—multitudes flocking to embrace it—angels discharging destruction on its foes—mountainous obstacles rolled from its path—nations walking in its light—heaven and earth celebrating its triumphs—and Christ encircled by his redeemed myriads, and receiving the homage of the universe. One of the obvious intentions of these disclosures is, that, by the certain prospect they afford of ultimate success, the Church may be encouraged to act out its Divine design, and to throw all its sanctified energies into the object of the world's recovery. This is the effect which they have had on many of its members in every age. "Having seen them afar off," and caught their inspiration, the martyr for Christ has embraced the block; the minister has startled the slumbering Church; the missionary has gone forth to awake the slumbering world; the saint, like David, has poured out as his latest prayer, "Blessed be his holy name for ever and ever, and let the whole earth be filled with his glory;" and the Church has echoed with the response of thousands, adding, "Amen, and amen!" And for us the light of prophecy still burns, that on us it may produce the same effects.

And who is sufficient for these things? "We are placed, as it were, in the middle of a scheme, not a fixed but a progressive one." The character of the economy under which our lot is cast is, in this respect, unity in progress—unity with all the past, in progress for all the future. Upon our heads, the relations, influences, and consequent responsibilities of all the past meet and rest, and to us the ends of the earth, the remotest generations of time, and all the holy beings and interests in the universe, are looking for corresponding fidelity and zeal. Whoever may deem it necessary to form plans of independent action, we are surely exempted from the necessity; for we ourselves form parts of a mediatorial plan, whose provisions prepared a place for us, and bespoke the entire activity and influence of our whole nature, even before we came into existence; so that the only solicitude left for us is, how best we may satisfy its high requirements. Boast who may of extensive relations and influence, this plan connects us with every being and agency the past has known, and places in our hands lines of interminable relation and influence with all the universal and endless future. Tremble who may under a sense of responsibility, "upon us the ends of the world are come." Our very position consecrates us to the loftiest service, loads us with the weightiest obligation, surrounds us with anxious eyes and cries of solicitude from every quarter of the Divine dominions. For the Church to be faithful now, is to save the world. Now, if ever, "the weak should be as David, and David as an angel of the Lord." Now, if ever, prayer should wrestle, liberality should bring forth its richest offering, its final mite, the Church should unite and clothe itself with zeal. For now, if ever, crowns may be gained, and kingdoms won, and a world, in the crisis of its danger, be saved, crowns to be cast at the feet of Christ, kingdoms of which he is rightful Lord, and a world from which he is destined to derive his richest revenue of praise for ever.

CHAPTER III.

CHRISTIAN INSTRUMENTALITY FOR THE EVANGELIZATION OF THE WORLD ILLUSTRATED AND ENFORCED FROM PROPHECY.

If such be the theory of Christian instrumentality, if its place in the Divine administration be so definite, its obligations so solemn, and its capabilities, under God, so great, we may reasonably expect that in a book so abounding with prophetic disclosures as the Bible, some glimpses, at least, will be afforded us of its ultimate results.

That the kingdom of Christ is not to be always limited and depressed, is clearly affirmed and universally admitted. For, as it has been justly remarked, "The prophecies respecting the kingdom of the Messiah, its extension and duration, and the happiness of his innumerable subjects, are in a much greater proportion than those which describe his humiliation to sufferings, and his dreadful death."* The isles are to wait for his law, the ends of the earth are to fear him, all nations are to be blessed in him, the heathen are to become his inheritance, and the uttermost parts of the earth his possession; for the mouth of the Lord hath spoken it.

Inspired by the kindling influence of such a prospect, the Christian Church has, in every age, sung of a millennium: a period during which all the authorities of earth are to take law and life from the lips of Christ; all nations to be enrolled among his subjects; all flesh to come before him; and all his enemies to be placed beneath his feet.

But if the Bible be thus the prophet of hope, and if the loftiest strains of those who believe it be of a glory yet to come, it becomes proportionably important to inquire whether

---
* Rev. J. P. Smith, D. D.

it deigns any disclosures *concerning the means which are to lead to it:* whether the universal triumph of the gospel is to be achieved, for example, by the noiseless and gradually augmented instrumentality of the Christian Church, accompanied by the energizing influence of the Holy Spirit; whether it is to be effected in a manner quite irrespective of such instrumentality, and calculated to disparage it before the eyes of the universe as misplaced and officious; or whether the grand consummation shall be realized by a middle course, which, while it will be always demanding, employing, and absorbing all the sanctified resources of the Christian Church, will yet leave room for the marked, and frequent, and direct interference of Heaven, and which will render such interposition indispensable to final and complete success.

This, indeed, has been a subject of the deepest interest to the Church in every age. For as her heralds have gone forth to proclaim the gospel, and her martyrs have poured out their blood to seal its truth, which of their bosoms did not swell with the ennobling thought which fired the bosom of Latimer in Smithfield: that they were assisting to enkindle a light which should never be extinguished—that their devotedness would be in some way connected with the eventual triumph of the cross, and be made subservient to it? In proportion, however, as the time of the end approaches, the question as to the relation which sanctified human instrumentality bears to it acquires additional interest. A thousand signs are supposed to prognosticate that the end draweth nigh; and each of them awakens the inquiry anew, "What is the relation which the sanctified agency of Christians sustains to it? Is their benevolent activity essential, in the order of means, to the latter-day glory? or does the tenor of prophecy indicate that, so far from contributing aught to its arrival and its splendor, they should rather 'stand still, and see the salvation of the Lord?'"

Still more important does this inquiry become in proportion as Christians, awakening to what they regard as the voice of duty, multiply their institutions, and enlarge the sphere of their activity, animated by the hope that their humble endeavors shall certainly be crowned with success. Who that surveys the wide field of missionary effort in the present day, and marks the "note of preparation" for still greater activity, can feel indifferent to the inquiry, whether or not it is to lead to any valuable result? Who does not perceive that on the answer to this inquiry depends, if not the very continuance of our activity, much, at least, of the cheerfulness of our obedience, and the degree of our devotedness? And who does not perceive that if the glory of the millennium is to burst on the world quite irrespective of Christian instrumentality, to urge such instrumentality as the appointed means of hastening that period is to indulge in delusion for the present, and to prepare mortification for the future?

But should there be those in the Church of any consideration or influence, whose views of prophecy induce them to depreciate, if not even to deprecate, the high attempt which aims at the conversion of the world, it becomes a step of the first importance to inquire into the authority of such views, and, if found unscriptural, to obviate their paralyzing effect. We are aware, indeed, that among those who, for the sake of distinction, are called millenarians, there are to be found divines of considerable reputation, and Christians of the highest sanctity. And equally aware are we that under the generic name of millenarianism is included a great diversity of opinions as to the *order of the events* immediately preceding the millennium, and the *kind of means* which will be made contributory to it; that it does not necessarily disparage the benevolent endeavors of the present day, nor seek to discourage them by constantly harping on their ultimate failure; but that many of those who hold it profess to derive from it motives to increased diligence in the cause of God. And, accordingly, some of them, we are aware, number among the liberal and active supporters of our religious institutions. Still, however, we cannot but suspect that in *many* of such instances we are indebted for what they do, rather to the very natural desire of recommending their peculiar views to others than to the views themselves: that their conduct is, in this particular, better than their creed: that it is the triumph of their piety over their opinions; and that, as a vehicle put into rapid motion will continue to advance for a while by its own momentum, after the power which first propelled it is withdrawn, their present activity is the result of principles which date anterior to their peculiar views of prophecy. Our warrant for this fear is to be found in the fact that of those who, prior to their adoption of millenarianism, "did run well," and who even subsequently continued for a while to move in the same direction, are now acting, in reference to the diffusion of the gospel, as if a prophet had been deputed to say to them, "Your strength is to sit still."

That such must be the necessary effect of all views of the future which tend to show that the endeavors of the present will prove abortive, is evident. Hope is the parent of all activity. We ourselves "are saved by hope;" and we shall attempt instrumentally to save others only as we are animated by the same principle. To be doomed to labor without hope, has been mythologically represented as one of the punishments of the lost. To expect, then, that the same efforts will be made where failure is certain as where success is anticipated, is to overlook a fundamental principle of human nature.

To say that "duty is ours and events are God's," and that therefore we are to advance, whatever the result may be, is to forget the important fact, that, in the case before us, the "events," according to the millenarian, are no longer God's, for he is supposed to have clearly foretold them. This proverbial saying, therefore, has no application here. As long as the result of a course of duty is doubtful only, hope and fear alternate; nor would it be possible for fear entirely to prevail, without bringing the mind to the full and fatal pause of despair. But in the question under consideration, we are not supposed to be left in a state of uncertainty as to the issue of our endeavors, but to be distinctly apprised that they will end in defeat. And the known and inevitable tendency of such a state of mind is (with certain exceptions of the kind we have noticed) to produce relative inaction; for if the members of the Christian Church were to be now divided into those who are strenuous in the cause of missions, and those who are comparatively inert, where should we expect to find the latter but among those who are postponing the moral improvement of the world to the second coming of Christ; and who, relying on the sufficiency of that *future miracle*, anticipate little or no advantage from the use of *present means?* Nor would our expectation, it is to be feared, be disappointed.

On a question, then, involving nothing less than the movements and hopes of the Christian Church in relation to the world, and the practical aspect of prophecy toward each, it is important that we should distinctly state what it is we object to in others, and what are the views and expectations which, from a consideration of prophecy, we ourselves are led to entertain.

With the minor points of controversy in the pre-millennial creed, we have at present nothing to do; nor even with the great question of the "personal advent." From more than a cursory survey of prophecy, the writer is free to admit that the hope of those who anticipate that the happy reign of piety on earth will be attained by the peaceful and uninterrupted progress of the means at present employed, and by these alone, is unwarranted by Scripture.

The cause of Christ, as now conducted, is no doubt destined to sustain many a severe encounter and disheartening reverse. And even his coming*—the advent of his power, in strange providences and at critical junctures—may again and again be necessary, in order to turn the battle at the gate, and to crown it with success. But that which we strenuously oppose is the practical inference too generally drawn from the pre-millennial creed, and which operates, as we think, both to the dishonor of the prophetic Scriptures, and to the discouragement of Christian activity—namely, that because a mighty conflict may await the Christian Church, and because the marked interposition of Christ may be necessary to terminate that struggle, and to take actual and entire possession of the earth, therefore but little real good is to be expected from the most devoted endeavors of the Church at present. And that which we hope to substantiate is, first, that such an inference is at variance with some of the admitted principles and necessary deductions of Divine revelation ; secondly, that it is not warranted by prophecy itself ; but, thirdly, that the very reverse is the doctrine of the prophetic Scriptures, and, fourthly, is found to be in perfect harmony with every other part of the word of God, by which its correctness can be properly tested.

---

* The παρουσία, or "coming of Christ," is referred to various *providential* events by some of those, even, who believe that it relates preëminently to a personal pre-millennial advent.

The prosecution of this inquiry will, if we do not greatly mistake, disclose the important facts, that whatever conflicts may hereafter ensue between the Church and the world, will be provoked chiefly by the success of the gospel, and that whatever judgments the earth may yet be called to witness, they will only concur with the power of the gospel, like the miracles of the primitive Church, to enlarge the domains of the Christian faith; so that those very predictions which are too often made to depress the hopes and dishearten the zeal of the Church, will be found calculated, when rightly understood, to animate its activity as with the blast of a trumpet. It will then be our aim, in concluding the chapter, to harmonize the whole with the chapters which have gone before; and to show the bearing of the entire Part on the consecration of the Church for the conversion of the world.

I. "Every single text of prophecy," remarks Bishop Horsley, "is to be considered as part of an entire system, and to be understood in that sense which may best connect it with the whole." Extending still farther the application of this valuable rule of prophetic exposition, we may add, that the entire scheme of prophecy itself is to be regarded as a part of the great system of revelation, and to be understood in that sense which may best harmonize with every other part.

1. Now, if there be a principle in Scripture to be relied on, surely it is this, that the Divine injunction of any relative duty implies a promise of the Divine assistance requisite to its performance, and of success proportioned to the degree in which we avail ourselves of that assistance. In illustration of this position, it will be sufficient to quote the familiar passage, "Train up a child in the way he should go; and when he is old, he will not depart from it." Nor does this language, or the large class of scriptures to which it belongs, imply any thing more than that the moral department of the Divine government is conducted on a plan equally with the natural or physical; that, in the world of mind as well as of matter, certain causes produce certain effects. The effects, indeed, may not result precisely in accordance with human calculations. As in the ministry of Christ, they may be long delayed, and even apparently be made frustrate. But though "he was despised and rejected of men," the same chapter which foretold his rejection adds, "He shall see of the tra-

vail of his soul, and shall be satisfied;" and every subsequent age has witnessed its gradual fulfilment. This constancy of connection, indeed, between means and ends—between causes and effects—seems essential to the character of a wise and gracious government, as well as to furnish some of the motives necessary to obedience; especially, too, as it still reserves to its Divine Sovereign the right of exceeding his promises in whatever way he pleases.

But, according to the views of many of those of whom we are speaking, here is a grand exception to the uniformity of the Divine procedure. Yes, in the very last act, the closing scene of the great drama of Providence—where, if apparent irregularity had previously obtained, we should rather have looked for the explanation and coincidence of the whole—even here, forsooth, the universe is to witness the disruption of a principle which had previously maintained the stability of a rock: a great gulf is to open and yawn between means and ends. For though the commands of God had pointed to a particular issue—the conversion of the world; and though the hopes and endeavors of his people had, in dependence on his gracious aid, travelled in the same direction, it is then to appear that they had never tended to realize it, and that a stupendous miracle alone can prevent the dreadful result. Thus the prophecies of Scripture are made to clash with its commands.

2. Equally at variance does such an interpretation appear with the unimpeachable sincerity of the Divine character. The substance of all the relative commands which God has enjoined is this, "Evangelize the world;" and the substance of all his promises corresponds with it—"The world shall be evangelized." In obedience to this command, and animated by this promise, his Church is beginning to address itself more seriously than ever to its great vocation. But while it is allowed that the command which enjoins this duty, and the promise which inspires this hope, stand out so clearly on the sacred page that he who runs may read, it is contended by the party in question that a third class of Sacred Scripture comes to light; more occult, it may be, in meaning, and requiring very prolonged and careful consideration; but the practical result of which is, that obedience to the command will prove all but fruitless for the end proposed, and that the hope of

personal success inspired by the promise is almost entirely unfounded. As if a king should forward to the commander of his forces positive orders to engage the foe, accompanied with assurances of certain triumph, but should interline the dispatches with a secret writing in cipher, which required to be held to the fire and laboriously studied in order to be understood, and the inference to be drawn from which was, that the campaign would end in all but entire defeat, and that the victory promised would ensue in a manner quite irrespective of his conflicts. Such a communication would throw at least a deep shade on the sincerity of him who sent it.

3. Nor does such an interpretation seem less to impugn the benignity of the Divine character. Instead of taking it for granted that we should be enamored of duty for its own sake alone, he evinces the kindest consideration for our fallen condition by accompanying his commands with appropriate promises and blessings: graciously alluring us to cultivate the tree by engaging that its fruits shall be our own. The Saviour himself was not called to suffer without enjoying the sustaining prospect of its glorious results. On the lofty moral elevation of the cross, the triumphs of his gospel, through all the ages of time, passed in review before him; and " for the joy which was thus set before him, he endured the cross, despising the shame."

But on the hypothesis in question, his followers are required to labor and suffer, not only without the hope of consequent usefulness, but even in the clear foresight of comparative failure. Now to expect that we should be as active in our efforts to evangelize the world in the face of this foreseen defeat as we should be in the prospect of success, is, to say the least, at variance with that benignity by which we are accustomed to regard the Divine requirements as ordinarily distinguished.

4. It may properly be objected, also, that the hypothesis which makes prophecy disclose the comparative failure of a course of conduct which the command of God has yet made obligatory, is at variance with that wise reserve of Scripture concerning such events of the future as involve the freedom of human action. While some of the prophecies predictive of happy results are so constructed as to encourage the obedience of those whom they chiefly concern, and others pre-

dictive of evil are calculated to produce repentance, and while they thus denote the benignity of their Author, by furnishing motives to holiness, there is none which, if rightly interpreted, can be regarded as furnishing a single motive of a contrary nature. But according to the views we are opposing, here is a large class of prophecies the tendency of which is to dishearten obedience by depriving it prospectively of its appropriate results; thus interfering with that probationary freedom of action which a concealment of the future would have left undisturbed.

5. Besides which, the views in question appear highly derogatory to the present economy as the dispensation of the Spirit, and to the ordinance of preaching as the medium of his operation. "Glorious things are spoken" in prophecy of the results which should signalize the impartation of the Spirit. If Isaiah, for instance, be asked how long the spiritual desolation of his people, as at present exhibited, will continue, he replies,* "Until the Spirit be poured upon us from on high; then shall the wilderness be a fruitful field, and the fruitful field be esteemed a forest." If we inquire of the Lord, at the hand of Ezekiel, by what agency the Jews are to be finally converted, and made eminent in the earth, the reply is substantially the same :† "Neither will I hide my face any more from them; for I have poured out my Spirit upon the house of Israel, saith the Lord God." In the prophecy of Joel the promise of the Spirit takes a still wider range: "For it shall come to pass in the last days, saith God, I will pour out of my Spirit upon all flesh."‡ Gentiles as well as Jews are included in its comprehensive embrace; for, says the Apostle Paul, when quoting a part of the prediction,§ "There is no difference between the Jew and the Greek; for the same Lord over all is rich unto all that call upon him. For whosoever shall call upon the name of the Lord shall be saved."

Here, then, is a series of predictions importing that during the last days|| spiritual transformations of the most glorious

---

* Chap. xxxii. 15; see also Zech. iv. 6.　　† Chap. xxxix. 29.
‡ Chap. ii. 28, as quoted Acts ii. 17.　　§ Rom. x. 12, 13.
|| The phrase אחרית הימים, LXX. ἐν ταῖς ἐσχάταις ἡμέραις, originally and properly denoted *future times.* But as the coming of the Mes-

and comprehensive nature shall result from the impartation of the Holy Spirit. From the day of Pentecost down to the present, the Spirit has effected these transformations chiefly through the preaching of the gospel. Even on that memorable day, the "signs and wonders" which attended his effusion only *prepared* the way for the pungent address of the Apostle Peter. It was "*when they heard this,*" that the arrows of the Lord took effect in three thousand hearts. Miraculous phenomena may be employed to engage the requisite attention for a messenger from God, and adequately to attest the Divinity of his message, and may even disarm unbelief, and enlist the judgment on the side of the truth; but when the heart is to be pierced and subdued, the "*message*" itself is "the sword of the Spirit." Whence we may infer that in all subsequent times, whatever miraculous means may be subordinately employed, his renewing influence will be exerted principally through the same instrumentality. And as the Church has not yet witnessed any thing answering to the fulfilment of these predictions, as an untouched ocean of spiritual influence is yet contained in them, we are to conclude that, great as the triumphs of the gospel at times have been already, a period is impending when we shall see far greater things than these. So that any views which cast but a passing shade on that happy prospect, or which transfer the honor of effecting them to any other department of the Divine government, must be regarded as disparaging to the dispensation of the Spirit, and to the Divine appointment of the diffusion of the gospel as the medium of his influence.

II. But instead of multiplying objections to a view which may prove on investigation to have no foundation in Scripture, let us, secondly, inquire whether it can produce any direct warrant from the word of God.

In applying the predictions of the Old Testament to the present economy, our first care should be to select those only which cannot possibly have found their accomplishment in the restoration of the Jews from the Babylonish captivity.

siah was, for the Jew, the most glorious event in all the future, the phrase came to be appropriated to the period of his advent and reign. Accordingly, in the New Testament—for example, in Acts ii. 17, Heb. i. 2, 1 Peter i. 20—it is employed to denote the times *ever since the first coming of Christ.*

Now, confining our attention to a few of such only, we find that the predictions relative to the enlargement of the kingdom of Christ may be arranged in reference to the question before us, *i. e.*, as to the means of that enlargement, into five classes.

1. The first class consists of those predictions which simply announce the final evangelization of the earth: such are Ps. xxii. 27, Hab. ii. 14, and Mal. i. 11. But as this class is silent, except by inference, concerning both the agent and means by which the end predicted will be attained, they leave us to pursue our inquiry in other quarters.

2. A second class describes the agent, but is silent concerning the means. Looking forward to the final union of Israel and Judah, the Almighty promises, "Moreover, I will make a covenant of peace with them; it shall be an everlasting covenant with them; and I will place them and multiply them, and will set my sanctuary in the midst of them for evermore. My tabernacle also shall be with them: yea, I will be their God, and they shall be my people."* Here, the hand engaged is Divine, while the means to be employed are apparently omitted. But even supposing that the nature of those means could in no instance be inferred from a consideration of the context, we should be as much warranted in concluding that the changes predicted would be accomplished by human instrumentality, as any other party would be in advocating a purely miraculous fulfilment. Spiritual transformations are in Scripture ascribed to God when they are effected by such means, as directly as if they were effected without them; and for this simple reason, that the efficient cause of the change is exclusively Divine. "So, then, neither is he that planteth any thing, neither he that watereth; but God that giveth the increase." Still, then, we are left to look farther for a description of the means by which the world is to be planted and watered for the Divine "increase."

3. Now, the millenarian supposes that he has found these in a third class of Sacred Scriptures, which foretells a series of judgments and preternatural events, to be followed by permanent and universal blessedness. The existence of such a

---

* Ezek. xxxvii. 26, 27

class we not only readily, but joyfully, admit. But here it is obvious to remark that such providential occurrences have no moral adaptation whatever to renovate the minds of men; "for, if they believe not Moses and the prophets, neither will they believe, though one rose from the dead." All that such dispensations are appointed to effect is, as we have already remarked, to prepare the way, under the overruling guidance of God, for the wider diffusion of the gospel. When the river of living water, deepening and widening in its onward course, has reached some Alps or Andes, which threaten to arrest for ever its healing progress, Omnipotence will then say to the mountainous obstacle, "Be thou removed, and be thou cast into the sea," and onward the tide of life shall flow. So that the most stupendous events of Providence must be regarded, even when they are charged with the greatest results, as only secondary and subordinate to the spiritual influences of the truth.

Allowing, then, for the sake of the argument, that all the momentous events which are supposed by many to be now impending are actually at hand, surely they are not to be spoken of by the Christian in terms of gloom and deprecation. If they are to "turn out rather to the furtherance of the gospel," we ought to hail *them* with welcome, and the *Church* with congratulations. Let us not be told, for instance, with looks of solicitude, that the honor of converting the world is not designed for us, but is reserved for the restored and enlightened Jews. Even admitting that it is so, it is enough for us to know that success is not, meanwhile, withheld from Gentile Christians; but that our usefulness is in the full proportion of our endeavors; and that we have scriptural reason to believe it will continue to be so. And if, besides this cheering fact, we can be certified that, great as our success is, the spiritual triumphs of a coming day, and of another people, will be incomparably greater, we "therein do rejoice, yea, and will rejoice." Could we now be assured that in India, for example, "a nation had been born in a day;" that great numbers of its converts were going "everywhere, preaching the word;" and that, wherever they preached, more than the triumphs of apostolic days were the result, would not our "joy be as the joy of harvest?" and if ever the period should come when a similar report shall be true of the Jewish people, will our transports be less? "Would to God that all the Lord's people were prophets!" and would to God that they were so at once! "For in Christ Jesus there is neither Greek nor Jew." The joy of one would be the joy of all.

But, says the millenarian, the period of which you speak will be introduced by appalling judgments. And in what age of the world, we ask, was the progress of religion ever unattended by such visitations? Were the ancient Israelites restored from their Chaldean exile, and the temple rebuilt, without changing the fortunes of the political world? Did the unity of the Roman empire, at the commencement of Christianity, provide for the easier circulation of the gospel through the civilized world? But how many a fair and populous province was subjugated in order to that unity! Did God design to bring the uncivilized world, soon after, under the influence of the gospel? The end was gained by the northern invasion, and the consequent breaking up of the Roman empire. And be it remembered, that these are events which, though described by us with a stroke of the pen, filled the eye of the prophet with a vision of broken thrones, and his ear with the shriek of expiring nations; events which, when they occurred, threw the earth into political convulsions, and the history of which might be easily expanded into blood-stained volumes. Nor have the last fifty years fallen short, in eventful interest, of any equal period, perhaps, since time began.

In the sacred calendar of prophecy we may suppose these years to have been marked with peculiar signs. Europe—the world—has been in a state of volcanic activity. Yet stand with Daniel on the bank of the river Ulai, and you will see that all these events belong to a series which know no pause. Stand with the seer of the Apocalypse "in the isle which is called Patmos," and you will see that, from the very first age of Christianity, seal after seal has been opened, trumpet after trumpet sounded, and vial after vial poured out without intermission; that if there has been "silence in heaven about the space of half an hour," it has been only the profound silence which precedes the bursting of a scene of stupendous interest. Speak not, then, as if the Almighty were about to clothe himself with judgment, and to arise out of his place now, for the first time. The solemn events which are yet to transpire belong to a series which began in Eden. Like the pillar of cloud and of fire, they only indicate the continued presence of Him who, having accompanied the march of his cause through all the ages of past time, is graciously pledged to vindicate, sustain, and facilitate its progress through all the future; and who thus furnishes his people with motives to increased activity, and inspires them with the hope of success.

But, says the millenarian, the events which impend are charged with unexampled judgments; they contain the very dregs of the vials of wrath. Still, we reply, they are only events which harmonize with the progress of the gospel and the wants of the world; and which show that providence and grace are but two departments of the same universal government. For in what are these judgments to consist? In the subversion of the Mohammedan empire? in the destruction of the man of sin? in the overthrow of Antichrist, Mohammedan, Papal, and Infidel? in the purgation of Christendom? And is this a consummation which the Christian should dread? Is this a prospect which should paralyze our activity, or depress our expectations of usefulness? Has the empire of imposture been so innoxious in its influence that we shall be tender of its termination? Has the mystic Babylon been so sparing of the blood of the saints, and so true to the interests of the Church, that we should deprecate the descent of the angel who is to "lighten the earth with his glory," while he cries "mightily with a loud voice, Babylon the great is fallen, is fallen?" Is the pouring out of the seventh vial on the air, the seat of Satan's empire, a prospect to fill us with apprehension? True, the accomplishment of these events may ask a larger theatre, and the arm of Providence may take a wider sweep, than has hitherto been deemed requisite. For who can expect that forms of evil, nursed in conflict, and which have attained the growth of centuries, will yield the final contest, and retire to the pit whence they issued, without a struggle? and what if that contest should enlist, on one side or the other, the ardent sympathies of all creation? if the earth should be cleared of every minor interest till this is decided—what if the battle of Armageddon be fought? What should it show but that the world was at length completely aroused from that moral torpor in which it has ever slumbered, and to awake it from which had often been the earnest endeavor of the Church? and what if, on the eve of that conflict, the armies of the living God should find that He on whose "head are many crowns," who "hath on his vesture and on his thigh a name written, King of kings and Lord of lords," had led forth the armies of heaven, "on white horses, clothed in fine linen, white and clean," and that they were actually mingling with their martial ranks, and already shouting of victory? what could be the issue, but glorious triumph? What, but an ample, godlike answer to the prayers of ten thousand times ten thousand saints—to the cries and throes of the whole creation, till then groaning and travailing in pain together? And is this a prospect to be spoken of in terms of gloom and sadness? Ask we how Heaven regards it? The vision has for ages filled it with Alleluias—"And the four-and-twenty elders," saith John, "and the four living creatures, fell down and worshipped God, that sat upon the throne, saying, Amen: Alleluia. And a voice came out of the throne, saying, Praise our God, all ye his servants, and ye that fear him, both small and great. And I heard as it were the voice of a great multitude, and as the voice of many waters, and as the voice of mighty thunderings, saying, Alleluia; for the Lord God Omnipotent reigneth."*

III. Still, the millenarian may add, Does not the very necessity for such a conflict, together with the character of the parties, and the numbers who will join it, indicate that the previous diffusion of the gospel will have proved, in its spiritual results, a comparative failure? This, we are aware, is your inference. But against such a conclusion, we propose to adduce a fourth class of Sacred Scriptures which clearly predicts that the diffusion of the word of God shall be attended with the most glorious results.

4. And here we might first refer to certain prophecies which foretell that even during an era of great judgments—in one of the very crises of the world's tribulations—the evangelization and salvation of mankind, so far from being arrested, shall proceed in triumph. "For when thy judg-

---

* Rev. xix. 4-6.

ments are in the earth," saith the prophet Isaiah, "the inhabitants of the world will learn righteousness:" thy heaviest inflictions will subserve thy purposes of mercy in the salvation of mankind.

But let us rather direct our attention to a small selection of those prophecies which describe the future enlargement of the Church as the result of Christian teaching.

"And it shall come to pass in the last days, that the mountain of Jehovah's house shall be established in the top [or, as the chief] of the mountains, and shall be exalted above the hills; and all the nations shall flow unto it. Yea, many people shall go and say, Come, and let us go up to the mountain of Jehovah, to the house of the God of Jacob; that he may teach us his ways, and that we may walk in his paths. For out of Zion shall go forth the law, and the word of Jehovah from Jerusalem. And he shall arbitrate between the nations, and dispense justice to many people; so that they shall beat their swords into ploughshares, and their spears into pruning-knives: nation shall not lift up the sword against nation, neither shall they learn war any more."* Here the Church is represented as being central and accessible to the entire race, and as capable of receiving and accommodating a worshipping world as the temple on Zion had been to the tribes of Israel. And the points to be particularly remarked are, that, of the nations thronging to it, the great mass has been influenced by the exhortation, " Come, and let us go up to the mountain of Jehovah;" and that the reason which moves the world towards this central point is, that "out of Zion shall go forth the law, and the word of Jehovah from Jerusalem"—that, through the appointed instrumentality of the gospel, they hope to be made wise unto salvation; while the result of that Divine teaching upon the great society of the nations is to be, the utter abolition of war, the cultivation of the arts of peace, and the recognition of the Divine authority as universal and supreme.

On another occasion,† the prophet, having described the peace and happiness to be enjoyed under the reign of the Messiah, in a strain surpassing the sublimest notes in which the classical poets celebrate the return to the golden age, adds,

---

* Isaiah ii. 2–4. This passage, with slight verbal differences, is found also in Micah iv. 1–3. † Chapter xi. 9.

in explanation of the glorious change, "For the earth shall be full of the knowledge* of Jehovah, as the waters cover the sea." The universal diffusion of that knowledge, which "is life eternal," is assigned as the cause of the happy transformation.

Now, if to these bright anticipations it should be objected, that they will not be realized till after the calling and conversion of the Jews, and by their instrumentality, we might content ourselves with replying that the question pending relates not to the specific personal agency by which these prophecies will be fulfilled, (though, even granting that the honor is reserved for the Jewish nation, the objector should remember that, according to his own supposition, the Jew will then have become a Christian, and his people an integral portion of the Christian Church,) but to the kind of instrumentality by which the world is to be evangelized. We will, however, proceed to show that the preaching of the gospel is to be made conducive to the conversion of the Jews themselves. "In that day," saith God, "will I raise up the tabernacle of David that is fallen, and repair the breaches thereof; and I will raise up its ruins, and I will build it as in the days of old: that they may possess the remnant of Edom, and of all the heathen upon whom my name is called, saith the Lord that doeth this."† Now, that this prediction relates partly to the conversion of the Jews, we have the authority of St. James: (Acts xv. 15–17:) "And to this agree the words of the prophets; as it is written,"‡ and forthwith proceeds to quote this prophecy from Amos; evidently taking it for granted that the ministry of the gospel would be the means employed by God for rebuilding the promised tabernacle—for that ministry was the only instrumentality which had then been appointed and employed for the purpose§—and only cites

---

* דֵּעָה אֶת יְהוָה, a verbal noun, construed as an infinitive; and, as such, denoting the mind as the *seat* of the knowledge, and the *activity* of the mind in relation to it.
† Amos ix. 11, 12.
‡ The quotation is not made literally either from the Hebrew or from the Septuagint, which also differs from the Hebrew, though only in letters of similar form. But this slight difference in no respect affects the question before us.
§ Acts ii. 37; xv. 7, 14.

the prophecy to show that it was clearly the Divine design that the Gentiles thus converted should be incorporated in the same Church with the Jews.

That the vision of the valley of dry bones relates ultimately to times yet future, may be seen by a glance either at the context preceding or following.* And it can hardly be necessary to show how strongly confirmatory that vision is of the point before us. When the prophet had surveyed the dreary Golgotha, and beheld, in the withered fragments of mortality with which it was filled, what was, and what would be, the hopeless condition of his people, he was commanded to prophesy upon these dry bones, and to say unto them, "O, ye dry bones, hear the word of the Lord." And, having delivered to them that word, consisting of a promise of life and salvation, he is next commanded to prophesy to the wind, and to say, "Thus saith the Lord God, Come from the four winds, O breath, and breathe upon these slain, that they may live." In other words, having preached to the politically and spiritually dead the glad tidings of deliverance, and invoked on them the vital influence of the Spirit, a moral resurrection ensued which filled the valley with life and activity. It follows, then, that the same instrumentality will be made conducive to the conversion of the Jews which will be employed with success for the conversion of the Gentiles—the ministry of the gospel of Christ.

Accordingly, we might specify predictions which contemplate the conversion of Jews and Gentiles alike, through this ministry, and which thus unequivocally foretell the coming salvation of the world. Such is the prediction to which we have already alluded for another purpose in the book of Amos. As quoted by the Apostle James, (Acts xv. 16 and 17,) it evidently imports that the tabernacle of David is to be rebuilt expressly, "that the residue of men might seek the Lord." By the tabernacle of David can only be intended the Christian Church; for what other tabernacle had *then* begun to be reared? and yet the apostle speaks of the fact stated by Peter that "some time before God had chosen" him as the instrument by whose "mouth the Gentiles should hear the word of the gospel and believe," as a convincing proof that the pro-

---

* Ezek. xxxvi. 24–28; and xxxvii. 14.

mised rebuilding of the spiritual fabric was commenced. And this Church, he adds, is evidently instituted for the reception and salvation both of Jews and Gentiles. But in what conceivable manner can the Church of Christ answer this high design, if not by the continued diffusion of the same blessed gospel to Jews and Gentiles alike?

Such, too, is the tenor of the new covenant: (Jer. xxxi. 31–34:) "Behold the days come, saith the Lord, that I will make a new covenant with the house of Israel, and with the house of Judah: not according to the covenant that I made with their fathers in the day that I took them by the hand to bring them out of the land of Egypt; which my covenant they brake, although I was a husband unto them, saith the Lord. But this shall be the covenant that I will make with the house of Israel: after those days, saith the Lord, I will put my law in their inward parts, and write it in their hearts, and will be their God, and they shall be my people; and they shall teach no more, every man his neighbor, and every man his brother, saying, Know the Lord; for they shall all know me, from the least of them unto the greatest of them, saith the Lord; for I will forgive their iniquity, and I will remember their sin no more." On the authority of the Apostle Paul, (Heb. viii. 8–13,) we learn that this new covenant is the dispensation of the gospel. The houses of Israel and Judah, therefore, to whom this dispensation is sent, cannot be supposed to be literally and exclusively the lineal descendants of Abraham, but his spiritual offspring; for it is the peculiar glory of the gospel that, in contradistinction from the national and limited economy of the Jews, it bears an aspect of benignity equally to all mankind. Nor will any one contend that until the gospel is known universally, it will ever cease to be the duty of Christians to say to all around them, "Know the Lord;" or that we have any reason to expect that the Bible will ever be superseded by a miraculous dispensation which shall flash Divine illumination on the mind, and thus raise mankind above the use of means. The import of the prediction appears to be simply this, that when the reproach of indolence shall have been wiped away from the Church, and every man shall have said to his neighbor. "Know the Lord," the reproach of ignorance shall be wiped away from the world; for the Spirit of God will so graciously and universally bless the means employed as to render *their continuance comparatively unnecessary*. So widely will the Church, aided by the providential interpositions of her exalted Lord, have diffused the knowledge of salvation, and so abundantly will the great renewing Spirit have crowned it with success, that efforts to diffuse it farther will be superseded; "for I will forgive their iniquity, and I will remember their sin no more." This amnesty from Heaven having been universally preached and received, "the earth shall be filled with the knowledge of the glory of Jehovah, as the waters cover the sea."

5. The allusions which we have made to the agency of the Holy Spirit, in the preceding paragraph, remind us of another class of predictions, in which the renovation of the world is ascribed prospectively to his transforming influence. We have just seen that the new covenant, which engages to impart the saving knowledge of God, is the gospel of Christ, and that, consequently, the promise knows no limitation of place or people. But, on comparing this prediction with a parallel prophecy, in Ezekiel xxxvi. 25–27, which declares, "Then will I sprinkle clean water upon you, and ye shall be clean; and I will put my Spirit within you, and cause you to walk in my statutes," we learn that the agent employed to carry into effect the gracious purposes of the Christian economy is the Holy Spirit. If the house of Israel is to experience a spiritual resurrection, it is because the Spirit, whose emblem is the wind, will descend on the moral Golgotha, and replenish it with spiritual life. If the wilderness of the Church is to be a fruitful field, and the fruitful field to be counted for a forest, it is not until the Spirit be poured upon us from on high. If the world is to be convinced of sin, the Spirit alone is appointed and adequate to the office. But the only medium through which he operates in the discharge of his office is that of the truth; on which account he is designated, by Christ himself, "the Spirit of truth." The gospel is the only weapon he employs in his aggressions on the territories of darkness, and hence it is called "the sword of the Spirit." And when, by the successful employment of that instrument, he shall have convinced the world of sin, and have become the great animating spirit of mankind, that which he has promised to write on the general heart is, the "laws" of

God, and the "ways" in which he will cause them to walk are, in his "statutes." So that when at length he shall be poured out upon all flesh, and when, as the one soul of the whole, he shall have led them to crown the Saviour "Lord of all," it will be found that no moral conquest has ever been achieved but by the agency of the Spirit, and that in achieving it, no weapon has ever been directly employed but the gospel: that, from first to last, the sword of the Spirit was never laid aside.

Now, we think it will be found that under one or other of these five classes, every prophecy relative to the kingdom of Christ on earth may find an appropriate place. Whence it appears to follow, that, though its progress to the universality and glory which await it may be attended by a series of providential judgments, *that* progress will be made, and that ultimate glory attained, by the diffusion of the gospel directed and made efficient by the agency of the Holy Spirit. Let us "not, then, be moved away from the hope of the gospel," and expect that judgments and providential occurrences are to produce effects which are promised only to the diffusion of the word of God. That judgments will accompany and pioneer its march through the earth, as they ever have done, we freely admit. But they are not to be regarded as forming an order of means distinct from the gospel economy, and superior to it. They wait on its steps. So vast is that economy in its sweep and design, that it includes and appropriates every kind of agency; presses into its service, as we saw in the preceding chapter, the angel of wrath, as well as employs the angel of mercy; and lays under tribute all the revolutions of time, and all the dispensations of Providence. In those events, then, which may lead others to say, "Lo, here is Christ," or, "Lo, there is Christ;" and which may thus distract attention from present duty, and awaken hopes never to be realized, we are to recognize only a call to greater diligence, and to remember that if we would apply them to their proper purpose, we must study to render them subservient to the diffusion of the gospel.

We admit, also, that, at times, the progress of the kingdom of Christ may be too slow for our impatience, and may seem to postpone its consummation to a hopeless distance. But let us remember that he can afford to wait. Had he any occasion to doubt the issue, he might be induced at times to precipitate the end. But "he seeth the end from the beginning"—sees it so clearly, and awaits it so confidently, that his patience emphatically announces the efficiency of his government.

And not only do impending judgments call for the diligence of the Church, and proclaim the efficiency of the Divine administration—they indicate also the surpassing claims of that dispensation on whose account they are to be made to impend. Had the final sufficiency of the gospel economy been doubtful, we may warrantably suppose that many of the Divine disclosures of coming terrors would have been graciously withheld. Their unreserved disclosure is a certain pledge of its constant progress and eventual triumph. The eye of faith can only behold, in the awful pomp and grandeur of the future, the indication of its greatness and the celebration of its triumphs.

IV. Now, if the conclusion to which we have come be scriptural, we may take it for granted that it will bear to be subjected to certain appropriate tests; and that the result of such an ordeal can only tend to illustrate and confirm the truth.

1. If it be a doctrine of prophecy that the diffusion of the gospel is to be the grand instrument in the hand of God for the conversion of the world, may we not expect that other departments of Holy Scripture will be found to contain allusions and statements corroborative of the doctrine? May we not expect, for example, that the apostles have left on record some indications, however incidental, that they interpreted ancient prophecy in the manner supposed? Accordingly, we find that such indications actually exist. The application which St. James makes of the prophecy of Amos, to which attention has already been called, is precisely on this principle, and might properly be regarded as supplying the legitimate key to all those figurative predictions of the gospel dispensation which employ language drawn from the Jewish economy. Had Isaiah predicted that Christ should "be given for a light to the Gentiles?" "Lo, we turn to the Gentiles," said Paul and Barnabas, "for so hath the Lord commanded us, saying, I have set thee to be a light of the Gentiles, that thou shouldest be for salvation to the ends of

the earth."* Whence we learn, first, that they inferred the prophecy was to be fulfilled, and the world to be enlightened, by the publication of the gospel, for this was the only instrumentality they employed. And, secondly, that so coincident in their view was the spirit of the prophecy with the spirit of the apostolic commission, that they regarded the prediction as equivalent in meaning to a Divine *command* to preach the gospel.

Had the prophet Joel announced that during the "last days whosoever shall call upon the name of the Lord shall be saved?" "How then shall they call upon him in whom they have not believed?" inquires the Apostle Paul;† "and how shall they believe in him of whom they have not heard? and how shall they hear without a preacher? and how shall they preach except they be sent?" By putting the necessity of preaching the gospel in this interrogatory form, he would impress us in the most emphatic manner that there is no other conceivable instrumentality by which the Gentiles *can* be saved.

And had "the voice of him that crieth in the wilderness" announced, "All flesh is grass, and all the goodliness thereof is as the flower of the field: . . . the grass withereth, the flower fadeth, but the word of our God shall stand for ever?" "This is the word," says the Apostle Peter,‡ "which by the gospel is preached unto you;" plainly implying that, in opposition to the instability of all things human, the dispensation of the gospel is to last for ever; and that, in defiance of all the hostility of earth, it is to continue as the great and only principle of the world's regeneration. Were it possible that the present economy should be suspended or terminated before the world is saved, all hope of human recovery would perish. Man would behold the only rock on which his hope can anchor, sink in a shoreless and tempestuous sea. For amidst the ceaseless whirl and disappearance of every thing around him, the only ground of hope for the future which God himself has supplied consists, according to this apostle, in the sufficiency and perpetuity of the gospel of Christ.

2. May we not expect to find that the cheering anticipation of a world reclaimed by the sanctified diffusion of the

---

* Acts xiii. 46, 47.   † Rom. x. 14, 15.   ‡ 1 Peter i. 24, 25.

gospel would lead "holy men of God" to give utterance to corresponding desires in prayer? The expectation is not disappointed. The Psalmist prayed,* "That thy way may be known upon earth, and thy saving health among all nations:" that the healing influence of Divine revelation, like a heavenly current of vital air, might sweep over the spiritual sickness of the world, and impart to it health, and vigor, and happiness. And as he regarded the knowledge of God as the only remedy of the world's misery, so he appears to have taken it for granted that the prosperity of the Church would be marked by the diffusion of that knowledge, and that such diffusion would be attended with the most happy results. "God shall bless us," he adds, "and all the ends of the earth shall fear him:" the leaven of his grace shall work from his Church outwards till the entire mass of humanity be leavened: his kingdom shall extend on every side till it embraces the world. But the language of Christ himself on this subject is conclusive.† "When he saw the multitudes, he was moved with compassion on them, because they fainted, and were scattered abroad, as sheep having no shepherd. Then saith he to his disciples, The harvest truly is plenteous, but the laborers are few; pray ye therefore the Lord of the harvest, that he will send forth laborers into his harvest." That this was not a duty binding only on those immediately addressed is evident, for the reason of the command is laid in the destitute condition of the multitudes. As long, therefore, as it is true that any portion of mankind are perishing "as sheep having no shepherd," it will continue to be the duty of Christians to pray that shepherds may be provided for them. And as long as any disproportion remains between the vast harvest of souls to be gathered into the garner of Christ and the number of laborers employed, it will ever be imperative on the Church to repeat the cry for an increase of Christian instrumentality. The language of Christ thus plainly implies that the harvest of the world is to be reaped by the agency of his people; and that in proportion as that agency is increased under his superintendence, will be the extent of harvest saved.

And still more to the purpose, if possible, is the language

---

* Psalm lxvii † Matt. ix. 36-38.

of Christ in his intercessory prayer: "Neither pray I for these alone, but for them also who shall believe on me through their word; that they all may be one—that the world may believe that thou hast sent me;" leaving us to the necessary inference, first, that the only way in which the Church is to look for additions, is by men being brought to believe the gospel; for if any are to be converted otherwise, for such the Saviour did not pray. And, secondly, that as often as such additions are made, they are to unite with the great body of the faithful for the conversion of others, and thus to proceed till the world is saved.

3. May we not expect, further, that if the kingdom of Christ on earth is to be set up by means of his dependent but devoted subjects, the result will be attained gradually as opposed to suddenly; and that, in order to correct and guide our expectations, scriptural intimations will be afforded that progressiveness will be one of the characteristics of the work? Analogy, indeed, might lead us to expect this; for progress is one of the distinctive features of all the Divine operations in nature and providence. But here, where the agency to be employed is human, it appears unavoidable. For the eminent piety of the individual Christian, and the union and devotedness of the collective Church—the twofold element of instrumental fitness requisite for the conversion of mankind—can only result from a prolonged course of Divine discipline. Accordingly, the various imagery under which the dissemination of Christianity is represented in the word of God, is remarkable for the uniform manner in which it preserves this characteristic of progressiveness. If Ezekiel beheld it in the living stream which flowed from the sanctuary, he saw that stream deepen and widen in its onward course, till "the waters were risen, waters to swim in, a river that could not be passed over." If Daniel was instructed to recognize, in "a stone cut out without hands," an emblem of the kingdom of Christ, the mysterious manner in which it became enlarged, and occupied province after province, till it "filled the whole earth," strikingly represented the growth of that spiritual empire which is destined to "break in pieces and consume all" hostile power, and to "stand for ever." If the Sovereign himself of that kingdom selects appropriate emblems of its progress, he finds them in the growth of the mus-

tard-seed, and in the diffusive influence of the leaven. Not, indeed, that in its progress to perfection it will be entirely exempted from external shocks. Like the earthly empires which it is destined finally to absorb, its affairs may often approach a crisis which may appear to threaten its existence. But, true to the emblems by which our Lord represents it, its history will eventually exhibit the threefold characteristic, of original insignificance, constant though often imperceptible progress, crowned with ultimate greatness and universal power.

4. But what appropriate test of the truth of the doctrine can we look for in Scripture without readily finding it? Is it an express command on the subject? We possess it in the final command of Christ to his servants, to "preach the gospel to every creature." Is it a promise of Divine assistance and success in obeying this command? We have it in the promise which accompanies it, "Lo, I am with you alway, even unto the end of the world;" for the context implies and requires a promise, not so much of protection in danger, as of success in the accomplishment of the object proposed; so that the command and promise combined may be regarded as the great missionary charter of the Church for all time; securing to his devoted servants, in every age, a measure of success proportioned to their zeal for his glory.

V. It remains, then, in the next place, that we harmonize the whole with the chapters which have gone before. And here our course is too obvious to be mistaken. For, if the object of the first chapter was to unfold that Scripture theory of influence by which Christian is to be united to Christian, and Church to Church, and the whole to be subordinated to the agency of the Holy Spirit for the recovery of the world, we have seen that prophecy points to the same comprehensive arrangement for the same exalted issue. Indeed, that sublime prophecy of Christ which may be regarded as the sum of the whole of unfulfilled prediction relative to his kingdom on earth—"And I, if I be lifted up from the earth, will draw all men unto me"—may be regarded also as the sum of the theory of spiritual instrumentality. For not only does it predict the manner of man's recovery, by the attracting and saving influence of the cross, but it obviously implies that all the influences of the Church are to be subordinated to that central power, till all the agencies and powers of earth are entirely in unison with it. And if the object of the second chapter was to show that the whole tenor of Scripture command and example on the subject, and the entire constitution of the mediatorial economy, including all holy power in heaven and earth, form but one loud practical call on Christians to unreserved consecration, we have seen that prophecy is only the voice of that future which is included in the same economy, chiming in with the voice of the past and the present, and calling louder still for the same consecration.

Are we tempted to apprehend, for instance, that the Christian Church exhausted its energies in its first days, and can never again expect to see them repeated? Prophecy points us aloft to an emblem of the present, and, behold, an angel comes speeding through the vault of heaven, having the everlasting gospel to preach to all the dwellers on earth—telling us of facilities for its propagation yet to appear, of resources in the Church yet to be developed, and of unexampled triumphs in the world yet to be won. Do we entertain a fear that the hostility of the world will cloud our prospect and arrest our progress? In the visions of prophecy we behold another mighty angel casting a millstone into the sea, and crying, "Thus Babylon is fallen, is fallen;" and another drying up the Euphrates of Mohammedan power; and another binding Apollyon himself in the chain of God's decrees, and casting him down into his own pit. The mountain full of horses and chariots of fire round about Elisha, which bursts on the opened eyes of his servant, is tameness itself compared with the vision of the future to which prophecy points the Church—all heaven marshalled, and occupied in removing every conceivable obstacle to the free and universal diffusion of the gospel of Christ.

At no period of the past, probably, could our eyes have been opened to the reality of supernatural agency in the Church, without beholding the sublime spectacle of "the angels of God ascending and descending" in its service, or arrayed in its defence. But, as if the active share they have hitherto taken in its affairs were as nothing when compared with that which devolves on them during "the time of the end," the successive scenes of Apocalyptic vision are crowded with their numbers and distinguished by their agency. Is it that, as that time approaches its close, and events rush to their final result, they will take a more intense interest in the issue? Or is it that the ranks of the Church triumphant will be allowed to draw nearer to those of the Church militant, and more frequently to mingle and make common cause, preparatory to their complete and everlasting juncture in heaven? However this may be, should not the prophetic vision of their winged activity and flaming zeal kindle the fire of a holy and consuming emulation in the Church below? "A great nation," it was lately said by a high political authority, "a great nation cannot have a little war." The Church of Christ is militant; and, considering the object of its contest, the character of its spiritual allies and resources, the divinity of its Leader, and the grandeur of its destiny, it absorbs all the spiritual and created greatness of the universe; and should it be satisfied with a little war? Should not every blast of the Apocalyptic trumpet ring through the Church as a summons to universal action? and every soldier of the Christian army demean himself as if an angel fought at his side, and infinite issues were waiting the result? Do we ask to look beyond the conflict, and see its final results? They have been seen; and the eyes that gazed on them, though closing in death, beamed and brightened with the reflected glory. They have been sung; and they who sang them may be regarded as having lived for this as for their highest earthly end; and while they sang, angels have hushed the music of their harps to listen to the strain. And still it is the office of prophecy to point out these results to the eye of faith. But what is the form in which we would see them? for "in the visions of the Lord" they have been made to assume every hue of beauty, every character of greatness, every aspect of glory. Is it that of a stone instinct with life, and growing as it rolls, by an invisible power, till it fills the earth? Prophecy conducts us to an elevation where we behold that mystic stone in motion. Already has it attained the magnitude of a mountain, and attracts the eyes of the nations. Now it moves, and all things vibrate at its approach. Now it is arrested by an obstacle which appears insuperable; but still its base expands, and its head towers higher. Again it moves, and the obstacle that opposed it is "ground to powder." Onward it rolls through islands and continents, scattering from its sides the seeds and fertility of a new creation, and pouring from its bosom the streams of the water of life. It touches another province, and is resisted on the very shores. But vain is the opposition. After the pause of a moment, the falling of idols and shrines announces that it is again in motion. Even while we have been describing its progress, it has continued to swell and enlarge. Like the Andes to South America, it is seen from every quarter; and, with the light of an unsetting sun resting on its summit, and the nations collecting at its foot, it forms the only object of true sublimity the earth contains.

Is it a temple? Now, it is only in the course of erection; and we find ourselves standing amidst the apparent confusion of the surrounding materials; while many of the laborers are away, preparing the "living stones;" and the great majority of the race are bowing at idolatrous shrines, and worshipping an unknown God. But prophecy takes us to a mount of vision, and, lo! the stupendous fabric, ample as the earth, silently rising toward heaven: the pediment placed on the columns, the edifice crowned with its dome, and all nations flowing unto it! And while we are looking, they suddenly recover from their breathless admiration of its magnitude, proportions, and glories, to burst forth into that anthem of praise with which the universe and eternity are destined to resound.

Is it the achievement of a conquest, and the erection of a kingdom? "The God of heaven shall set up a kingdom which shall never be destroyed." When we read the history of an earthly power, we are constrained to admire the march of events by which it attains to national greatness. As its population multiplies and its boundaries enlarge, battles are fought and victories won. Its times of excitement develop greatness of character, and that greatness of character impresses its image on the times. But how effectually is all this glory eclipsed when brought into contrast with the progress of the kingdom of Christ! Here the field is the world, while every object in it is a weapon, every being it contains is in action, and every issue depending is eternal. In this strife already kingdoms have been subverted, and generations have been engaged! Who does not pant to gain a height whence he can look down and survey its progress? To such a point does prophecy conduct us. Even while we look, the charge is sounded, and the onset made. Far and wide the conflict rages. Banner after banner joins the foe: tribe after tribe comes "up to the help of the Lord, to the help of the Lord against the mighty." Victory seems to alternate from side to side. Now the soldiers of the cross give way, "as when a standard-bearer fainteth;" and now raise a shout of joy as they plant their standard on some fallen fortress of Satan. Here "the Captain of salvation" sends them unexpected support; and there "his right hand teaches him terrible things." Leading them on from "conquering to conquer," opposition gradually slackens: "the armies of the aliens" are put to flight, or yield themselves willing captives. The earth with joy receives her King; and his kingdom of righteousness, peace, and joy embraces the world.

Is the aspect under which we would look on the results of spiritual agency that of a new creation? "He that sat upon the throne said, Behold, I make all things new." Even now the Spirit is moving on the face of the human chaos. Fiat after fiat goes forth; and what light breaks in on the darkness of ages! what mighty masses of humanity are uplifting themselves in solemn majesty, like primitive mountains rising from the deep! what more than verdant beauty clothes the moral landscape! how gloriously dawns the Sabbath of the world! Where now is the midnight gloom of ignorance and idolatry? the desolations and misery attendant on sin? We look, and listen; but no reign of darkness, no habitation of cruelty, no sound of anguish remains! The will of God *is* done on earth, as it is done in heaven! The nations own no other law; and hence their aspect is that of a happy family. The Church aims at no other end; and hence all her members are invested with the garments of salvation and the robes of praise. The world is bathed in the light of peace, and purity, and love. Inanimate nature itself partakes of the general joy. To the eye of renewed man it exhibits a beauty unknown before, and to his ear it brings lessons of surpassing wisdom. Trees wave with gladness, and the floods clap their hands: the light of the moon is as the light of the sun, and the light of the sun is sevenfold. Over that scene, the morning stars sing together, and the sons of God shout for joy; while the Divine Creator himself complacently beholds it, and proclaims it good.

Or, finally, would we contemplate the result of the whole in heaven? Then must we take up a position from which we can behold the closing scenes of time, and the opening grandeurs of eternity: the coming of Christ, the pomp and ministry of his attendant angels, the resurrection of the dead, the awful solemnities of the judgment-day. With the prophet of Patmos, we must mark the numbers of those who go away into everlasting life, and learn their songs: we must try to estimate their joy when they cast their crowns at the feet of infinite love, and to multiply its amount by the ages of eternity.

True, these are visions; but they are visions painted by the hand of God: dear in every age to the Church of God: gazed on in death by the Son of God. Yes, then they were brought and set before him; and such was the joy with which they filled him, that he endured the cross, despising the shame. He saw that stone advance; that temple rise; that kingdom come; that new creation dawn; that beatitude of the redeemed in heaven—his grace the theme of every tongue, his glory the object of every eye. He saw of the travail of his soul, and was *satisfied*—*his* soul was satisfied. Even *in the hour of its travail* it was satisfied. What an unlimited vision of happiness must it have been—happiness not bounded by time, but filling the expanse of eternity! His prophetic eye, even then, caught a view of the infinite result in heaven. His ear caught the far-distant shout of his redeemed and glorified Church, singing, " Worthy is the Lamb that was slain!" And if we would do justice to our office as instruments for the salvation of the world, if we would catch the true inspiration of our work, we, too, must often cross, as he did, the threshold of eternity, transport ourselves ten thousand ages hence into the blessedness of heaven, and behold the fruits of our instrumentality there, still adding new joy to angels, and new tides of glory around the throne of God and of the Lamb.

What other practical purpose, indeed, can these prophetic disclosures, at present, answer? Or to what higher end can they be applied? If the progress of the gospel, and its happy results, assume the appearance of a mountain ever moving onward, and ever growing as it moves, displacing or crushing every obstacle, and filling the whole earth with its presence— what does it say to our inactivity, but that we must advance along with it, or be annihilated by it? And what does it say to our fears of opposition and failure, but that we may give them all to the wind? If, for the same end, a temple rises whose courts include a worshipping world, and whose incense of praise perfumes the universe, what is the language in which it addresses us but that of David in the prospect of erecting its ancient type: "And who then is willing to consecrate his service this day unto the Lord?" If the Church appear in conflict with the world, and triumphant over it, why are we allowed to look on the stirring scene but that we may catch the ardor of the Christian hero? may mark how certainly every one that is not for Christ is against him—how necessarily inactivity in his cause produces the effect and receives the punishment of positive hostility? may be excited to endure hardship, and to aspire to the glorious deeds of good soldiers of Jesus Christ? If the splendors of a new creation burst on our view, why is it but that we may feel a pang of solicitude for the groans and travails of the old? Why, but that we may remember that we are living during the workdays of the mighty process; and that He who commanded the light to shine out of darkness hath issued the fiat to us, "Let *your* light shine before men: go into all the world and diffuse it?" Each stage of the material creation was wisely adapted to prepare the way for that which succeeded. All its unfinished parts reciprocated their influence, pointed to that which was to follow, and craved and tended to a perfect whole. Light was given to the sun to be dispensed; and he fulfilled the law of his being, and thus prepared the way for other and higher beings. Had he been endowed with intelligence and responsible power, and had he, in the exercise of that power, retracted his beams, and refused to shine, how enormous the guilt, how fearful the result! In the process of the new creation, the darkness has passed away, and the light of salvation has come—light in the presence of which all material splendor is eclipsed and disappears. That light has been given to us in a sense which justifies its Author in saying, "Ye are the light of the world;" and given to us with a solemn charge that we so dispense it as that the world may rejoice in its beams. To withhold our light, then, is to contract guilt of a magnitude never to be computed. Or if, while we are asking, "What shall the end of these things be?" we are answered by the sight of numbers without number, waving their victorious palms, and by the voices of all these, joined by the hosts of the unfallen, in one stupendous concert of praise—who does not hear, above this "sound of many waters," the voice which says, "Be thou faithful unto death, and I will give thee a crown of life?" "They that be wise shall shine as the brightness of the firmament, and they that turn many to righteousness as the stars for ever and ever?"

And is this the lofty practical purpose of prophecy? And are these our inducements to proceed in the diffusion of the gospel? Then ought they not to be felt by us at this moment with as much freshness and force as if they had opened on us now for the first time? Suppose this were literally the fact. Had prophetic visions, like those we have considered, never as yet been vouchsafed to us: had the Christian Church commenced its missionary operations simply in obedience to what it supposed to be the unuttered will of God: had it assembled by its representatives to consult on the propriety of continuing those operations: had a spirit of indolence or despondency seized it, and a disposition to wait for some Divine intimation before it advanced any farther: had it wrestled in prayer for such an intimation; and if, while its members were thus "with one accord in one place," there had suddenly come "a sound from heaven as of a rushing mighty wind," filling all the place: had Isaiah come and sung the glory of the latter days: had Daniel shown them the kingdom of the Messiah enlarging and absorbing all earthly power: had John recounted the scenes of Patmos; and had He who sent his angel there to interpret them, again appeared, commanding them to hasten away with his gospel into all the world, promising to be always with them, and assuring them of "floods" of spiritual influence yet to be poured out upon all flesh—whose zeal would not kindle and burn? Whose purpose would not catch a measure of Divine greatness? Whose lips would not be ready to exclaim, "Here am I, send me?" As if such a vision had just transpired, let us aim to realize its inspiring motives; and every Christian will be transformed, in effect, into a prophet, "crying, Prepare ye the way of the Lord, make his paths straight."

Thus, if the first chapter explains the Scripture theory of Christian instrumentality, the second prescribes and makes it imperative; and the third predicts and promises its triumph, in promoting the conversion of the world. If the first chapter states the plan by which all the holy influences of the past should have been collected, multiplied, and combined, the second exhibits and enforces the obligation of the present to that entire consecration which the plan supposes, and the third engages that such consecration shall certainly issue in the erection of the kingdom of Christ. And one passage of Scripture there is, which, if we mistake not, virtually includes and practically applies the whole. That passage we have already quoted as the Divine postscript of the sacred volume. "And the Spirit and the bride say, Come. And let him that heareth say, Come. And let him that is athirst come. And whosoever will, let him take the water of life freely." Here are at once the plan by which every holy agency is combined and put in requisition for the recovery of man: the summons of the Lord of the Church himself for every new agency, as it comes into being, to join in the great object for which the plan exists; and—considering the position which the verse occupies as among the closing words of the Revelation—the practical application of all unfulfilled prophecy respecting that object. Taking the verse in connection with its contexts, its practical power becomes even more emphatic. "'I, Jesus, have sent mine angel to testify unto you these things in the Churches. I am the Root and the Offspring of David, and the bright and morning Star.' And as my person unites the wide extremes of divinity and humanity, my office invests me with all power in heaven and on earth, and my purposes of mercy require that angels, as well as men, should be employed in my service. Accordingly, one of them has been sent to instruct the Churches in those mysteries of Providence whose accomplishment is to reach to the end of time. And now I myself appear, to close the prophecy, as I came to open it. Hear, then, the conclusion of the whole matter. I have opened a fountain of life for the perishing world. The Spirit and the Church—God, angels, and holy men—are combined in urging the world to *come*. And as often as a single soul is prevailed on to obey the call, he is to consider himself bound, even though he can but feebly lift up his voice, and say, 'Come,' to unite with all who are already employed in publishing my invitations of mercy; for whosoever will is welcome to partake. Such is, simply, my final will; such the practical application of all the predictions which my angel has now testified to the Churches; and such the sum of all that Scripture testifies on the subject, and of the means by which I propose to draw all men unto me. I testify, therefore, that if any man shall alter the words of the book of this prophecy, so as to disturb the legitimate and practical application which I thus finally and authoritatively give to them, I will visit him with signal marks of my most awful displeasure."

How glorious the object which induces the Saviour to address his Church—the salvation of the world! How simple the method by which he proposes to accomplish it! How fearful his sacred jealousy that nothing should be said or done to impair its efficiency! How strong the certainty implied in that jealousy that his end will be finally gained! And how loud the summons of the whole to every Christian, and every Christian Church, to unite and call the world to *come!* If all the orders of the Church triumphant were permitted audibly to address the world, but were restricted to a single word, that word would be *come*. If all the invitations of the gospel, travailing as they do with the burden of infinite compassion, could be condensed and uttered in a single word, that word would be *come*. But the Church of the day is the only organ through which that word can be uttered; so that were all its duties in reference to the world to be expressed in a single term, it would be to utter the invitation, *come;* and if, in uttering it, all its tongues were to become vocal, and each of its members could pour into it all the passionate and holy emotion the heart of man has ever known, it would only be approaching the emphasis with which the invitation should be uttered. As if the Church of the present day, then, had to retrieve the silence of all the past, and as if it had only a word in which to retrieve that silence, and a moment in which to utter that word, let it call, beseech, adjure the world to *come;* and the Spirit himself would speak in its tones with an infinite energy; and then, to the sublime announcement of Christ, "Behold, I come quickly," the Church would be prepared to respond with joy, "Amen, even so, come, Lord Jesus."

PART II.

THE CLAIMS OF THE MISSIONARY ENTERPRISE ARISING FROM THE BENEFITS WHICH HAVE ATTENDED IT.

CHAPTER I.

THE HISTORY OF CHRISTIAN MISSIONS.

Now, if it be true that the Christian Church is thus constructed expressly to embody and diffuse the influence of the cross, and if its full efficiency for this end depends, under God, on the entireness of its consecration to this office, we may expect to find that every page of its history illustrates and corroborates this truth.

I. No law of nature can be obeyed without advantage to him who obeys it; nor be violated without avenging itself, and vindicating its authority. The same is true of the laws of the Christian Church. And, accordingly, it might easily be shown, by an induction of *the great facts of its history*, that in every age it has flourished or declined in proportion as it has fulfilled this primary object of its constitution.

Need we repeat, for instance, that the period of its first and greatest activity was the season of its greatest prosperity? that it expanded without the aid of any of man's favorite instrumentality, learning, eloquence, wealth, or arms? that it achieved its triumphs in the face of all these? that its progress from place to place was marked by the fall of idol temples, and the substitution of Christian sanctuaries? and that God caused it to triumph in every place? And why all this, but because the Church was acting in character, and fulfilling its office, as the representative of the cross to the world? Had we witnessed the devotedness of its first days—subject though it was, even then, to many and grievous deductions—had we heard only of its early history and triumphant progress from land to land, how naturally might we inquire the date when the gospel completed a universal conquest: at what precise period it was that India embraced the faith of Christ: how long it was before China was evangelized: whether there was not a year of jubilee on earth, when the gospel had been preached to the last of the heathens, and in what year the festival occurred. Alas for the Church that these inquiries should sound so strange! and alas for the world!

Need we remind the reader that the decline of Christian devotedness was the decline of Christian prosperity? We might, indeed, have inferred that such would be the result from the known constitution of the Christian Church: that if its relative efficiency depends on its entire consecration, the slightest diversion of its influence would be so much given to the very power which it was called into existence expressly to counteract; and that if that influence should come to be so diverted to any considerable amount, the efficiency of the Church would be comparatively destroyed, and itself be in danger of being vanquished by the counter influence of the world. And this, we repeat, is, substantially, the history of its long decline and fall. Physiologists inform us that life radiates, or acts from the centre outwards; and that on ceasing to expand, it ceases to exist. And history affirms that nations flourish only while they continue to enlarge their bounds: that the tide of national prosperity no sooner ceases to flow than it begins to ebb. Whether these statements be founded in truth or not, they may find at least an obvious analogy in the history of the Church. From the moment it lost sight of its expansive character, it began to lose ground to the world. The strength which should have been spent in conflict with foes without was exhausted in fierce contentions within. When it ought to have been the almoner of God to the world, it became the great extortioner, absorbing the wealth of the nations. When it ought to have been the channel of the water of life to the world, it became a stagnant reservoir, in which the very element of life corrupted and bred "all monstrous, all prodigious things." When it ought to have been the birthplace of souls, it was the grave of piety, so that in order to live it was necessary to leave it. And at the moment when it should have been giving law to public opinion, and have attained the mastery of the world, it was actually in alliance with it—the willing and accomplished agent of its vilest purposes.

But as every departure of the Church from its missionary design is sure to be avenged, so we may expect that every return to that character will be Divinely acknowledged and blessed. Had we no facts at hand to prove this, the injunctions which our Lord gave to the seven Asiatic Churches to repeat their first works, and his promises of prosperity if they did so, would lead us to infer it; the uniformity of the Divine procedure would warrant us to expect it; the very return itself, implying as it would a Divine influence, would be a proof of it. But facts *are* at hand. The history of the Roman Catholic Church demonstrates that even every apparent return to first principles has been, in so far, a return to outward prosperity: that, as Machiavel remarks, the kingdom of the hierarchy would have been sooner at an end, if the reputation of the friars for poverty and activity had not borne out the scandal of the excesses and inactivity of those above them: that no sooner have symptoms of returning vigor appeared in one part of that Church, than all the vital properties which it still contained have moved off in that particular direction: that, as if conscious of owing its continued existence to the working parts of its body, it has recently (in 1814) repealed the order of Clement XIV., which restrained the aggressive activity of the Jesuits, and is already exulting in the ecclesiastical benefits arising from the change. And while facts demonstrate that activity will keep alive even a corrupt system, the history of every Protestant Christian Church in Christendom, during the last fifty years, clearly proves that every return to spiritual devotedness is, in so far, a return to Divine prosperity. If we ascertain the measure of holy activity in any Church, we have ascertained the measure of its internal prosperity; so that a person might at any time safely say, Tell me which branch of the Christian Church is the most scripturally active and aggressive in its spirit, and I will tell you which is the most prosperous.

Before we proceed, however, to examine and exhibit the

advantages accruing to the Christian Church from its recent resumption, in part, of its original design, it will be proper to furnish a brief chronological sketch of the steps by which it has reached its present activity; as well as a general survey of modern missionary labors. Thus prepared, we shall be the better qualified to enumerate and estimate the benefits with which those labors have been attended, both in subserving the temporal welfare of men, and in promoting the higher objects and interests of the Church. After which we shall endeavor to connect the whole with the preceding Part, and practically to apply it, by showing that our success has been fully proportioned to our efforts: that advantages have flowed from our returning activity which nothing else could have conferred: that the one design of God, in conferring that success, is to animate and redouble those efforts; leaving us to infer that a full return in faith and prayer to the aggressive design of the Christian Church would be a full return to its first prosperity.

II. It is not till the eighteenth century that the era of Protestant missions can be said to have commenced. Not indeed that the missionary spirit had slumbered in the Church from the apostolic age till then. *Every intermediate century had witnessed the diffusion of, at least, nominal Christianity.* Although as early as the *third** century the original impulse given to the progress of the gospel had evidently declined, in the *fourth* we find Christianity existing in Persia: become general in Armenia,† where it had been introduced as early, probably, as the second century: carried from Armenia into Iberia: rapidly spreading throughout Ethiopia, whither it had been conveyed by Frumentius; and published, about the year 350, by Theophilus, at the instance of Constantine, in

---

* About the middle of the *second* century, we find Churches in *Gaul*, at Lyons and Vienne. (Euseb. Hist. Eccl., b. v. chap. 1.) In *Africa*, Carthage was the chief seat of the new religion; where, according to Tertullian, (Apologet., chap. 37,) its professors were so numerous, that to extirpate them would be to decimate Carthage. In the East, at the same early period, Christianity was planted at Edessa. And about the year 190, according to Eusebius, (b. v., chap. 10,) Pantænus went from Alexandria to proclaim the gospel in India.

† An alphabet and a translation of the Bible were introduced by Miesrob, about 410.

the south of Arabia In 314, we find bishops from England present at the council of Arelate. How much earlier the gospel had entered Britain, it is impossible to state.* Probably, as Giesoler† suggests, it was brought from Gaul early in the second century. Through the instrumentality of Ulphilas, the Visigoths now embraced Christianity; and to him they were indebted also for an alphabet and a translation of the Bible. The Goths had probably received the gospel in the century preceding; for in the early part of this century we find a Gothic bishop at the council of Nice.

The *fifth* century was signalized by the nominal conversion of several of the German nations. In 432, Patricius, a Scotsman, induced the Irish to embrace Christianity. And in 496, the Franks assumed the Christian name, and induced the Alemanni to follow their example. In the *sixth* century, Christianity was professedly embraced by many of the barbarous nations bordering on the Euxine Sea, and was more widely diffused among the Gauls. From about the year 565 to 599, the Irish monk Columban labored with considerable success among the Picts;‡ and in 596, Augustin succeeded in converting Ethelbert to the profession of the Christian faith; whose example was immediately followed by his Anglo-Saxon subjects in Kent, and soon after by the other Anglo-Saxon kings of England.

Ecclesiastical missionaries from England, Scotland, and Ireland, carried the gospel, in the *seventh* century, to Batavia, Belgium, and several of the German nations. Traces of its extensive propagation, by the Nestorian Christians of Syria, Persia, and India, are also to be found, at this period, in the remotest regions of Asia; and, if the *Monumentum Syro-Synicum* is genuine, it obtained a footing in China about the year 636. Tartary, parts of Germany, Friesland, and Saxony, were the principal additions to the domains of Christendom

---

* Those who would assign to the event an apostolic date, have little ground except their own wishes. That the Apostle Paul visited England, rests on the *ipse dixit* of Jerome, a Latin father of the fourth century.

† Vol. i. § 37. The authorities for the statements above, when the works are not specified, are derived from the Ecclesiastical Histories by Mosheim, Gieseler, and Neander

‡ Bede. Eccl. Hist., b iii. chap 4.

in the *eighth* century. In the *ninth*, Denmark and Sweden, Bulgaria and Moravia, professed subjection to the faith, as well as parts of Slavonia* and of Russia. From Moravia, the gospel was carried into Bohemia. In the *tenth* century, the rays of Christian light began to enter Poland; in Hungary, Christianity was made the national religion by a royal decree; and in Norway—where it had been first introduced from England—it was imposed by the severest measures. From Norway it was carried into Iceland, the Faro and Shetland Islands, and even to Greenland.

The *eleventh* century saw Christianity established as the national religion of Russia, and records its wider diffusion in the East. Conquest and conversion had now come to mean nearly the same thing; and hence, in the *twelfth* century, the political subjugation of Pomerania was followed by its nominal subjection to the Christian faith; the island of Ruegen, long the stronghold of heathenism, was subdued, and its inhabitants baptized; and the conquered Fins were compelled to submit to the same rite. The nominal Church was still further enlarged, in the *thirteenth* century, by the forced submission of Prussia, Livonia, and many of the northern provinces; as well as by the recovery of portions of the Saracenic territories in Spain. The *fourteenth* century was marked by the professed conversion of the Lithuanians, one of the last of the heathen nations of Europe which embraced Christianity; while the *fifteenth* was indelibly stained by the forced subjection of parts of the newly-discovered hemisphere. Towards the middle of the *sixteenth* century, Ignatius Loyola founded the order of the Jesuits; one of whose grand objects was the propagation of Christianity among heathens and infidels by means of missionaries. Accordingly, the missions of the Jesuits form an important part of the history of their society. Xavier led the way into India and Japan; and, within a very short period, the agents of this formidable body spread over South America, and penetrated into almost every part of Asia.†

---

* Cyril of Thessalonica, and his brother Methodius, invented the Slavic alphabet, and translated the Bible, and some Greek and Latin authors, into the Slavic tongue. Balbini Miscell., part i.

† Concerning other papal missionary institutions, it may be suffi-

It is historically true, indeed, that many of the agents employed, from century to century, in this wide diffusion of the gospel, were men whose wisdom, piety, and zeal, would have adorned the apostolic age ; but it is notoriously known that its principal instrumentality consisted of worldly policy and martial power ;* and consequently that its immediate results were only territorial aggrandizement and nominal submission. Accordingly, as many of these conquests had been made by the sword, by the sword many of them were subsequently lost. Civilization itself, at one period, suffered a decline. Ages of darkness rolled over the Church; until Christendom, so far from being in a capacity to convert the world, stood itself in the most urgent need of substantial conversion.

That glorious change, of which the signs and means had long been gathering, was the great event of the century of which we are now speaking. But, essential as the renovation of the Church was to the conversion of the world, the direct effect of the Reformation, properly so called, was confined to the Church itself. Indeed, so far from immediately benefiting the world, its primary force was soon exhausted within even a small circle of Christendom. Nor has the line of demarcation between Protestantism and Popery been materially moved during the two hundred and fifty years which have since elapsed.

The *seventeenth* century was an age of *missionary preparation and promise*. The close of the preceding century, indeed, had witnessed the first attempt, on the part of Protestant Christians, to make a descent on heathenism. The distinguished honor of making it belongs to the Swiss. For,

---

cient here to notice the College *de propaganda fide*, founded at Rome in 1622, by Gregory XV., and soon enriched with ample resources. Another college—*pro fide propaganda*—founded in 1627, by Urban VIII., and very munificently endowed, appears to have been merged, in 1641, in the preceding institution. In 1663, Louis XIV. instituted the *Congregation of Priests of the Foreign Missions;* while an ecclesiastical association founded the Parisian seminary for the missions abroad ; and the apostolical vicars of these societies were soon found in Siam, Tonquin, Cochin-China, Persia, etc.

* This has been ably shown, as far at least as the latter part of the period referred to is concerned, by the Rev. Dr. John Campbell, in his late excellent Treatise on "Maritime Discovery and Christian Missions."

In 1556, fourteen missionaries were sent by the Church of Geneva to plant the Christian faith in the newly-discovered regions of South America.* In 1559, a missionary was sent into Lapland, by the celebrated Gustavus Vasa, King of Sweden. Early in the seventeenth century, the Dutch, having obtained possession of Ceylon, attempted to convert the natives to the Christian faith. About the same time, many of the Nonconformists, who had settled in New England, began to attempt the conversion of the aborigines. Mayhew, in 1643, and the laborious Eliot, in 1646, devoted themselves to this apostolic service. In 1649, during the Protectorate of Cromwell, was incorporated, by act of Parliament, the "Society for the Propagation of the Gospel in New England." In 1660 the society was dissolved; but, on urgent application, was soon restored; and the celebrated Robert Boyle was appointed its first governor. The zeal of this distinguished individual for the diffusion of the gospel in India and America, and among the native Welsh and Irish; his munificent donations for the translations of the Sacred Scriptures into Malay and Arabic, Welsh and Irish, and of Eliot's Bible into the Massachusetts Indian language; as well as for the distribution of *Grotius de Veritate Christianæ Religionis;* and, lastly, his legacy of £5400 for the propagation of Christianity among the heathens, entitle him to distinct attention. In 1698 was instituted the "Society for promoting Christian Knowledge;" whose objects comprise, to a certain extent, the labors of missionaries. Its missions, chiefly in the East, are subsequently associated with such names as Ziegenbalg, Gericke, and Swartz. And besides these incipient efforts to diffuse the gospel, glowing sentiments on the subject are to be found scattered through the sermons and epistolary correspondence of the age, which show that many a Christian heart was laboring and swelling with the desire of greater things than these. Still the century closed with witnessing little more than individual and unsustained endeavors. Had they been all suddenly arrested, only a very feeble call would have been made for their resumption. Like the repeated flights of the dove of the deluge, they served to show that there was

---

* Picteti Orat. de Trophæis Christi *in* Fabricii Lux Salutaris Evangelii, etc., p. 586.

shut up within the ark of the Church a principle of activity impatient to be free, and which promised, when opportunity served, to traverse the globe.

The *eighteenth* century began to fulfil that promise, and may be denominated *the age of missionary association.* In 1701, the "Society for the Propagation of the Gospel in Foreign Parts" was chartered; having in view exclusively the benefit of our plantations and colonial possessions. In 1705, Frederic the Fourth, King of Denmark, was induced, by one of his chaplains, to send two missionaries to Tranquebar, on the coast of Coromandel. One of these, Ziegenbalg, may be considered almost as the parent of the Eastern missions. The Society in Scotland for "Propagating Christian Knowledge" was instituted at Edinburgh in 1709. The philosophic Dr. Berkeley, then Dean of Derry, published his noble proposal for the erection of a college in the Bermudas, with a view to the conversion of the American Indians; a plan in the prosecution of which he displayed a degree of self-denial, generosity, and devotedness, rarely equalled. The persevering Egede sailed from Bergen, in 1721, for the coast of Greenland. Influenced partly by seeing at Copenhagen two Greenlanders who had been baptized by Egede, the persecuted Moravians commenced a mission to the same country in 1741. To their everlasting honor, and to the deep disgrace of the rest of the Christian community, it is to be remembered, that when they sent out their first missionaries, their entire congregation did not exceed six hundred persons, and that of these the greater part were suffering exiles. Yet so noble and extensive were the exertions which they made for the evangelization of the heathen, and so abundantly were their unostentatious endeavors blessed by the great Head of the Church, that within the short period of ten years their heralds had proclaimed salvation in Greenland, St. Croix, Surinam, and Rio de Berbice; to the Indians of North America, and to the negroes of South Carolina; in Lapland, Tartary, and Algiers; in Guinea, the Cape of Good Hope, and Ceylon.

Brainerd entered the field of missionary labor in 1743. In the year 1784, at a Baptist Association held at Nottingham, it was determined that one hour on the first Monday evening of every month should be devoted to solemn and special intercession for the revival of genuine religion, and for the extension of the kingdom of Christ throughout the world; hence the origin of Monthly Missionary Prayer-meetings. Wesleyan Methodism, being strictly missionary in its character, extended its operations to the West Indies in 1786. The "Baptist Missionary Society" was organized in 1792. The "London Missionary Society," on the principle of embracing all denominations, arose in 1795. The year following, the "Edinburgh Missionary Society" was instituted. And in 1801 arose the "Church Missionary Society."

From this brief outline, the progress of Christian association for missionary purposes during the last century is obvious. Not only were societies organized to send forth and to sustain the missionary of the cross, but, unlike several preceding organizations, they were instituted for this object alone. While, among the happiest signs which accompanied their formation, it may be remarked, that missionary information began to be regularly circulated in periodicals; that sermons began to be addressed to large and interested audiences, exclusively on the obligations of Christians to diffuse the gospel; that the people generally responded to the call by their willing contributions; and, especially, that thousands of them met at stated times to implore the influence of the Holy Spirit on the new field of missionary labor: signs which indicated the approach of yet further association, and of greater enterprise, for the recovery of man.

The missionary character which will belong to the *nineteenth* century remains to be seen; for one half of its sands have not yet run out. Were we required, however, to give a descriptive name to that portion of it which has elapsed, we should unhesitatingly denominate it the age of general Christian association for the *missionary enterprise*. The union of Christians for this great object has yet to become universal; but the interest felt in it now, compared numerically with that which existed at the close of the last century, may be said to be general. The object could not be suddenly withdrawn from the Christian world now, without occasioning a sensation of dismay which would thrill through the entire community, and which would raise the cry of tens of thousands for its return. Its presence has taken the rank of a new power: and its absence would be felt as a great general want.

The correctness of this representation will be seen from a

further enumeration of the societies which the missionary enterprise has originated. The "Glasgow Missionary Society" commenced its operations soon after the establishment of the London Society. In 1808 was organized the "Society for promoting Christianity among the Jews." In 1816, a Missionary Seminary was established at Basle; the interest in which continuing to increase till 1821, the "German Missionary Society" was then formed, or, as it is sometimes called, the "Evangelical Missionary Society." In 1816, also, was formed the "General Baptist Missionary Society," in distinction from that of the particular Baptist body of 1792. As early as 1799 a missionary spirit was awakened in various parts of Germany; in consequence of which, first Elberfield, and then Barmen, originated societies for the contribution of funds to missionary and kindred institutions. In 1828, these societies united, and having been since joined by the societies of Cologne and Wesel, they together form the "Rhenish Missionary Society." About this time, also, the "Netherland Missionary Society" commenced operations, and was associated with the name of the enterprising Gutzlaff. And in 1822 was organized the "French Protestant Missionary Society." Nor should it be omitted, that the claims of the heathen to Christian instruction have so far attracted the attention of the society of Friends, that they have commenced a solitary mission to Western Africa.

The Missionary Societies of America demand distinct regard. The land of the Mayhews and of Eliot, of Brainerd and of Sergeant, could never be entirely lost to the cause of Missions while their names continued to be revered, and their journals to be read. It was not, however, till the inspiring accounts of a Carey, a Vanderkemp, and a Buchanan, had been extensively circulated, that American piety became divinely awakened to its claims. With that awakening, the names of Mills, Judson, and their coadjutors, stand vitally connected. On these youthful students in divinity, the missionary spirit had eminently rested; and, having presented a memorial on the subject of Missions to the General Association of the Ministers of Massachusetts in 1810, the "American Board of Commissioners for Foreign Missions" was formed the same year; and in the year following sailed the first mission sent from America to any foreign heathen land. In 1814 was formed the "American Baptist Board of Foreign Missions." The "American Methodist Episcopal Missionary Society" followed in 1819. In the year ensuing, the "Domestic and Foreign Missionary Society of the Protestant Episcopal Church in the United States" commenced its operations, and in 1831 the Presbyterian Church instituted the "Western Foreign Missionary Society."

III. Now, in marking the principal circumstances which have accompanied this rapid accumulation of missionary organization within the last forty years, and which may be said to divide its brief history into important epochs, we may notice,—

1. The formation of the Tract Society in 1799, and the origin of the Bible Society in 1804—institutions which have proved the right arm of missionary activity, and increased its means of usefulness to a very considerable extent. 2. An important era for missions arrived when the fact was practically and openly admitted, that no sect or denomination of Christians can sustain a reputation for Christian consistency without laboring to extend the gospel to pagan lands. 3. The accession of the American Churches to the missionary enterprise was another and a glorious stage in its progress. 4. But if the adhesion of Christians to this object, in their denominations and larger divisions, was important, equally important was it to be able to announce that the missionary spirit had descended to the individual members of the particular churches and congregations of which these denominations are composed, and had created for itself a deep, general, and permanent interest in the mass. 5. The formation of branch and auxiliary societies, by which the cause of missions becomes located among a people, draws them gradually within the circle of its action, and lays all the piety which may exist among them under contribution for its advancement, is to be marked as another leading event. 6. The conviction which has now generally obtained that the missionary service deserves the consecration of the greatest talent, and the most marked wisdom and piety, which the Churches can supply, is a distinct indication of another stage in the progress which that service is making in public opinion, and is full of promise as to the character of its future agency. 7. Another era in its history was the employment of native agency, and the project of in-

stituting colleges abroad with an ultimate view to the education of that agency for more efficient service. If we are not intending to furnish the nations with an adequate supply of stated preaching from our own land, and for generations to come, the heathen must be rendered independent of Christendom for their religious instructors as soon as possible. And in no other way can this be done than by taking the necessary steps for raising up a native ministerial agency. 8. And another important step in the progress of missions is the conviction which is beginning to obtain, not only that the Christian Church must be brought to look more closely and practically at the object of evangelizing the earth, but that for this end it must act on a system. The more vast its projects, the greater the necessity of a fixedness of design, and a steady adaptation of means to the end. On this principle it is that an American Missionary Society has lately presented the outline of a plan for its own operations, the filling up of which, under the Divine sanction, will plant four or five hundred stations in the more eligible parts of Africa and Asia, as well as thirty or forty theological seminaries, and require about twelve hundred ordained missionaries, and three hundred laymen, as physicians, printers, and teachers. Thus the most enlarged desires are beginning to assume that distinctness of plan which is essential to their wise and steady prosecution.

IV. The following table [p. 151] contains a statistical survey of our principal missionary societies, arranged alphabetically,* and of their present operations. Other societies exist of a strictly missionary character; but they are not here introduced, not because they are not equally meritorious with those named, but because they do not directly contemplate the conversion of the heathen. Such are the Colonial Missionary Society; the European Society for aiding the Diffusion of Evangelical Christianity on the Continent of Europe; and the Society for the Promotion of Female Education in the East.

From this survey, and from other inquiries made by the writer, but to which the replies have not been sufficiently definite to justify insertion, it will be seen that there exist at

---

* Where a dotted line occurs in the table, it denotes that the results under that head, if there are any, have not been ascertained.

THE HISTORY OF CHRISTIAN MISSIONS.

Names.	Day of Formation.	Countries occupied.	Central or Principal Stations.	Ordained Missionaries.	Native Teachers.	Members, or Communicants.	Schools.	Scholars.	Printing Establishments.	Translations.	Colleges.	Year.	Receipts.
American Board of Foreign Missions	1810	Africa, Asia, India Archipelago, N. Pacific, and N. A. Indians	86	140	138	19,742	524	24,529	15	In 23 languages	1	1841	£48,492.. $235,189
American Baptist Board, etc.	1814	Burmah, Siam, China, Hindoostan, W. Africa, etc., Europe, Am. Ind.	80	46	102	2,931	44	872	6	Scriptures, Tracts, etc.		1841	17,723.. 85,960
American Episcopal	1820	Greece, Crete, Constantinople, China, W. Africa, Texas	12	11	17					Scriptures, Tracts, etc.		1841	6,291.. 30,514
Amer. Ep. Methodists	1819	Africa, Brazil, Buenos Ayres, Texas, Oregon, N. A. Indians	99 In ten ch's, etc							New Testament, Tracts, Hymns	1	1841	$25,020.. 121,350
American Presbyterian	1831	Africa, China, Siam, Am. Indians, Texas, W. India	11	23	8					Scriptures, etc., into forty languages		1841	10,37.. 49,649
Baptist	1792	India, Africa, West Indies, etc.	137*	72	127	30,000	180	18,000	2	Scriptures and Tracts into fifteen languages	1	1841	26,656.. 159,261
Baptist (General)	1816	India	7	11	6		2			Scriptures and Tracts into five languages		1841	1,600.. 7,760
Church (of England)	1801	Africa, the East, and America	97	103	946	4,603	696	35,396	3	Scriptures and Tracts into fifteen languages	2	1841	101,576.. 492,643
Church (of Scotland)	1829	India	4	3	11		12					1841	7,000.. 33,950
French Protestants	1822											1840	2,436.. 11,814
German Evangelical	1821											1836	4,325.. 21,946
London	1795	India, West Indies, South Africa, South Sea Islands, etc.	387	163	528	11,485		4,222	15	Scriptures, Tracts, etc.	1	1841	80,100.. 388,485
Propagation of the Gospel	1701	India, Africa, Australia, etc.	287	245		1,897	12					1841	78,651.. 381,457
Rhenish	1825	Jamaica	5	5	6			2,000				1841	4,740.. 22,990
Scottish	1796	West Indies, N. and S. Labrador, Greenland, and S. Africa	56	5		17,606		6,070		Scriptures, etc., into six languages		1841	2,965.. 13,604
United Brethren (or Moravians)	1741‡			256†						Scriptures, etc., into fourteen languages		1841	10,651.. 51,657
Wesleyan†	1817	Europe, the East, Africa, and N. America	26	367	2,361	84,234	300	56,819	7			1841	90,182.. 437,382

* The very unequal results exhibited under the head of "Principal Stations," show that the phrase is differently understood by different societies; some adopting the principle of centralization much more generally than others. The exact number ordained not known.

† This includes the wives of missionaries.

‡ Commenced missionary operations in 1728.

§ This embraces both foreign and domestic missions.

[☞] Since the foregoing statistics were published, there has been a gratifying increase in the results of missionary enterprise. See Introduction.—T. O. B.

present, in Britain and America, about* fourteen missionary societies, of which seven may be denominated first-rate: the remaining seven, were they blended into one, would not much more than equal a single society of the former class.

That the annual income of these societies amounts to about £505,000; of which about £400,000 are contributed by British Christians, and the remainder by the Christians of America.

That the number of missionaries at present in the field of labor is about fifteen hundred; and that these missionaries occupy about twelve hundred principal or central stations.

That at these stations are to be found, in subordinate co-operation with the ordained missionaries from Britain and America, about five thousand native and other salaried teachers, catechists, readers, helpers, and assistants of various kinds, engaged in the offices of education and religious instruction. That about fifty of these stations have printing establishments.

And that all the missions, combined, exhibit about 180,000 converts in Christian communion; and about 200,000 children and adults belonging to their schools.

The only remark which it would here be in place to add is, that these results have been attained gradually: that, taking the collected reports of all the missionary societies for any given year, they will be found to exhibit an advance on the reports of the year preceding, leaving us to indulge the hope that by the same blessing by which they have been progressively brought to their present state of enlargement, they will continue to report an annual increase of resources, activity, and usefulness, for an indefinite number of years to come. The practical benefits arising from missionary labors will next become the subject of distinct consideration.

---

* Of course, these figures claim to be regarded only as an approximation to the truth. Even the income of one society, as compared with that of another, is to be understood with this qualification, that one society includes in its general accounts the pecuniary support which it receives for a particular field of labor, for the prosecution of which, perhaps, another Christian denomination maintains a distinct society. In this summary the three continental societies are omitted.

CHAPTER II.

ADVANTAGES RESULTING TO THE HEATHEN FROM THE MISSIONARY ENTERPRISE.

SECTION 1.

TEMPORAL BENEFITS.

At the commencement of the preceding chapter we remarked, that such are the gracious arrangements and promises of God, that every return of the Church to its missionary design entitles it to hope for corresponding prosperity. Having taken a general survey of the manner in which Christians have recently resumed their missionary vocation, we are the better prepared to look after the expected results of their activity.

And here, the first fact which meets us on opening the inquiry is, that, independently of the direct and spiritual benefits at which we aimed, a host of minor but magnificent temporal advantages have been gained, and which alone would have amply repaid all the cost of the missionary effort. This is as if, in attempting to estimate the benefits of the Saviour's mission, a contemporaneous inquirer, who had only heard of him as a Teacher sent from God, and had only thought of spiritual results, should have had to make his way to those results through the thronging and grateful ranks of those who had been healed, and who insisted on presenting themselves first, as a part of the fruits of that mission. And, indeed, what was the character of Christ, but the character of his dispensation? and what was the design of his Divine mission, but that it should be the source and type of all the good attending the march of his gospel through the earth?

Accordingly, we find, that even where Christianity has, for obvious reasons, produced but slender spiritual results, the inferior benefits which it has scattered have rendered its progress through the nations as traceable as the overflowing of the Nile is by the rich deposit and consequent fertility which it leaves behind.* This is a well-known subject of devout exultation in many of the inspired epistles. The apologies of the Fathers prove it; and the records of profane history, unintentionally, but abundantly, confirm it. Every city which the gospel visited presents itself in proof of its corrective influence; and every nation we enumerated in the preceding chapter, stands forward as a witness to the same effect. It produced charity even in Judea, humility at Athens, chastity at Corinth, and humanity at Rome—cleansing her imperial amphitheatre of human blood, and evincing that her boasted civilization had been only a splendid barbarism. Softened by its influence, the Armenian, says Jerome, lays down his quiver, the Huns learn to sing the praise of God, the coldness of Scythia is warmed by the glow of faith, and the armies of the Goths carry about tents for Churches.† Theodosius and Justinian took much of their codes from its inspired lips; and thus the gospel may be said to have read laws to the Visigoths and Burgundians, the Franks and Saxons, Lombards and Sicilians. On the Irish, as well as on many other nations, it bestowed a written language, and made Ireland, for centuries, the university of Europe. It raised the German barbarian into a man; and elevated the wandering hordes of the Saxons, Marchomani, and Bohemians, into civilized communities. It approached the Dane, and he forgot his piratical habits; and the Swede and the Norwegian stayed within their own boundaries, and ceased to be a general terror. It called the Russians, Silesians, and Poles, to take rank among the nations; won the Livonians and Portuguese from their idols; and taught the Lithuanians a worship superior to that of reptiles, or of the sun.

Virtue went out of it in every age, and wherever it came. The Roman empire was rushing to ruin : the gospel arrested its descent, and broke its fall. Nearly all the nations of

---

* *Vide* Ryan's Effects of Religion on Mankind, *passim*.
† Epist. lvii.

Europe which we have named, were sitting at a feast on human flesh, or immolating human victims to their gods: it called them away from the horrid repast, and extinguished their unholy fires. The northern invasion poured a new world of barbarism over Christian lands: the spirit of Christianity brooded over the chaotic mass, and gradually gave to it the forms of civilized life. Where it could not sheathe the sword of war, it at least humanized the dreadful art. It found the servant a slave, and broke his chains. It found the poor—the mass of mankind—trampled under foot; and it taught them to stand erect, by addressing whatever is Divine in their degraded nature. It found woman—one half of the species—in the dust; and it extended its protecting arm to her weakness, and raised, and placed her by the side of man. Sickly infancy, and infirm old age, were cast out to perish: it passed by, and bade them live; preparing for each a home, and becoming the tender nurse of both.

Yes, Christianity found the heathen world without a single house of mercy.* Search the Byzantine Chronicles, and the pages of Publius Victor; and, though the one describes all the public edifices of ancient Constantinople, and the other of ancient Rome, not a word is to be found in either of a charitable institution. Search the ancient marbles in your museums; descend and ransack the graves of Herculaneum and Pompeii; and question the many travellers who have visited the ruined cities of Greece and Rome; and see if, amidst all the splendid remains of statues and amphitheatres, baths and granaries, temples, aqueducts, and palaces, mausoleums, columns, and triumphal arches, a single fragment or inscription can be found " telling us that it belonged to a refuge for human want, or for the alleviation of human misery." The first voluntary and public collection ever known to have been made in the heathen world for a charitable object, was made by the Churches of Macedonia, for

---

* There is ground to believe that the provision by some of the Greek states for those wounded, and for the children of those slain in battle, flowed from martial policy alone; and that the *Valetudinarium* of the Romans was only an infirmary for the sick servants and slaves of a great family. *Si quis sauciatus in opere noxam ceperit, in valetudinarium deducatur.*—Col. xi. 1. Conf. Sen. Epist. 27.

the poor saints in Jerusalem. The first individual known to have built a hospital for the poor was a Christian widow. Search the lexicons for interpreting the ancient Greek authors, and you will not find even the *names* which divine Christianity wanted, by which to designate her houses of charity—she had to invent them. Language had never been called on to embody such conceptions of mercy. All the asylums of the earth belong to her.

And be it remembered, that Christianity has accomplished much of this under circumstances the most unfriendly to success. As yet it has had but a very limited influence even in what are denominated Christian countries. But yet, while bleeding herself at a thousand pores, she has saved whole tribes from extermination, and comparatively stanched the flow of human blood. Though a prisoner herself, and walking in chains, she has yet gone through the nations, proclaiming liberty to the captive, and the opening of the prison to them that are bound. Even when Popery had converted her creed into a libel on her name, it yet contained truths which eclipsed the wisdom of Greece, and which consigned the mythology of Rome to the amusement and ridicule of childhood. Even there, where her character was most misunderstood, so high had she raised the standard of morals, that Socrates, the boast of Greece, would have been deemed impure; and Titus, the darling of Rome and of mankind, would have been denounced as a monster of cruelty. When disfigured to a degree which would have made it difficult for her great apostle to have recognized her, yet, like him, she went about "as poor, yet making many rich, as having nothing, and yet possessing all things." Herself the victim of universal selfishness, she yet left on every shore which she visited everlasting monuments that she had been there, in the hospitals and edifices of charity which lifted up their heads, and in the emollient influences which stole over the heart of society.

We are warranted in affirming, then, that, as far as the temporal welfare of man is concerned, the history of the past demonstrates that even the worst form of Christianity is preferable to the very best form which heathenism ever knew. Who has not heard, for instance, of the atrocities which men called Christians committed in her abused name in South

America? Yet even there, though her pretended priesthood was an army, and though they hewed their path with the sword, her humanizing influence was quickly felt. No longer are wives buried with their deceased husbands in Congo; nor do the aborigines of Florida quench the supposed thirst of their idol in human blood. At Metamba they no longer put the sick to death; nor sacrifice human victims at funerals in Angola. No longer do the inhabitants of New Spain offer the hearts of men in sacrifice, nor drown their children in a lake to keep company with the idol supposed to reside within it.

But why do we speak of other lands? Britain itself owes every thing, under God, to the influence of the gospel. The cruelties of Rome did not humanize, nor the northern superstitions enlighten us. The missionary who first trod our shores found himself standing in the very temple of Druidism. And wherever he turned, he heard the din of its noisy festivals, saw the obscenity of its lascivious rites, and beheld its animal and human victims. But Christianity had marked the island for its own. And although its lofty purposes are yet far from being worked out on us, from that eventful moment to the present, the various parts of the social system have been rising together. Even when most at rest, its influence has been silently penetrating the depths of society. When most enfeebled and corrupted itself, its authority has been checking the progress of social corruption, rendering law more protective, and power more righteous. When most disguised and repressed, its wisdom has been modifying our philosophy, and teaching a loftier system of its own. A Howard, sounding and circumnavigating the ocean of human misery, is only an obedient agent of its philanthropy. A Clarkson and a Wilberforce have only given utterance to its tender and righteous appeals for the slave. A Raikes, a Bell, and a Lancaster, have simply remembered its long-neglected injunction, "Suffer little children to come unto me." While all its Sabbaths, Bibles, and direct evangelical ministrations, are only the appropriate instrumentality by which it has ever been seeking to become the power of God to our salvation, and preparing us for the office to which Providence is now distinctly calling us, to be the Christian ministers and missionaries of mankind

To have predicted, then, at the commencement of modern missions, that the diffusion of the gospel would be attended with the diffusion of, at least, temporal good, would only have been making the past the prophet of the future. Let us proceed to inquire how far such a prediction would have been verified by actual results.

1. Judging from the costly price at which civilized nations have purchased distinction, it would seem that it is no small advantage *to be known*. Now, there are some tribes of the human family which are indebted to Christian missions for their discovery. The first vessel known to have visited the islands of Mitiaro, Mauke, and Rarotonga, was steered by a missionary of the cross; while other islands, though discovered, had not been visited, or, though visited, had remained almost entirely unknown, until sought out by Christian perseverance and compassion; so that, hereafter, when they shall have acquired historical importance, they will have to record that they were called from their original obscurity by the servants of Him who came to seek and to save that which was lost.

2 As the primary object of the Christian missionary is to bring the heathens, to whom he is sent, under the influence of the gospel, it is important that, if they have been accustomed to roam from place to place, they should *renounce their wandering habits, and adopt a settled abode*. And, hence, one of the first and necessary consequences of a desire to hear a "man of God" is, a disposition to locate themselves in his vicinity. This is the first step of their transition from a horde of the wilderness to a civilized community. But this has been the almost uniform effect of the introduction of the gospel among such a people. Who does not here think of the dwellings of Nonanetum rising around Eliot in the wilderness? of the twelve Indian villages of Zeisberger? of Brainerd's Indians coming from the far-off forks of the Delaware to his beloved Crossweeksung; killing a supply of deer that they might be able to listen to him for days together without interruption; and then "building themselves little cottages" up to "his own door?" and of the Esquimaux coming from Okkak, as far as to the Moravian settlement at Hopedale? "where," said the missionary, "our congregations are blooming like a beautiful rose." Not more certainly was

the erection of the tabernacle in the wilderness a signal for the Israelites to pitch their tents around it, than the successful introduction of the gospel among a roving and uncivilized tribe has led to their settlement. The North American Indian emerging from his filthy wigwam, the Greenlander leaving his burrow in the snow—compared with which the den of the bear itself is inoffensive—and the Hottentot coming in from the bush, have alike proceeded to prepare for themselves comfortable abodes. The New Zealander may be seen making bricks, and the South Sea Islander burning lime, for the erection of a house. "The traveller through the Cherokee settlements," says the Report of the Methodist Episcopal Mission in America for 1835, "observing cottages erected, regular towns building, farms cultivated, the Sabbath regularly kept, and almost an entire change in the character and pursuits of the people, is ready to ask with surprise, 'Whence this mighty change?' Our only answer is, Such is the effect of the gospel. Here is a nation at our door, our neighbors, of late remarkable for their ferocity and ignorance, now giving the most striking evidence of the utility of missionary exertions."

And "instead of their [the South Sea Islanders] little contemptible huts along the sea-beach, there will be seen a neat settlement, with a large chapel in the centre, capable of containing one or two thousand people; a school-house on the one side, and the chief's or the missionary's house on the other, and a range of white cottages, a mile or two long, peeping at you from under the splendid banana trees, or the breadfruit groves; so that their comfort is increased, and their character is elevated."*

3. But when the wanderers of the wilderness or of the plain become localized, their erection of permanent dwellings supposes many a previous step of instruction and improvement; their new condition entails on them wants which they never knew before; and labor becomes necessary in order to supply them. Accordingly, *all the more useful among the arts and trades of civilized life* are to be found accompanying the progress of the gospel. In the schools of Sierra

---

* Evidence on the Aborigines, before a Committee of the House of Commons in 1833–35, p. 307.

Leone, the girls are taught to spin cotton, and the boys to weave.* Even the New Hollander may be seen ploughing and reaping for the missionary, and planting corn, melons, and pumpkins for himself.† The journal of a missionary catechist at New Zealand records his daily superintendence of the natives while occupied in the various labors of the blacksmith's shop, of house-building, and of the plough. The testimony of Lieutenant Stockenstrom, lieutenant-governor of the eastern division of the Cape of Good Hope, imported, that the land at Kat river was cultivated, "to the astonishment of everybody who visited it, in proportion to the strength and means of the Hottentots."‡ "At the station where I live," said the head of the Moravian Missionary Institution in South Africa, "one half of the population subsists by working at mechanical arts—cutlers, smiths, joiners, turners, masons, carpenters, shoemakers, tailors, and so on."§ "We have ploughing, wagonmakers, and shoemakers, and other tradesmen amongst us," said Andrew Stoffel, a Hottentot; "we can make all those things except a watch and a coach."‖ The following is a concise enumeration of the useful arts, the animals, and the vegetable productions, which have been introduced by the missionaries into the various stations they have occupied in the South Seas:

USEFUL ARTS.	VEGETABLE PRODUCTIONS.	ANIMALS.
Smith's work.	A variety of valuable esculents.	Goats.
House-building.		Sheep.
Ship-building.	Pumpkins, melons, sweet potatoes, etc., etc.	Horses.
Lime-burning.		Asses.
Turning.	Oranges, lemons, and limes.	Cattle, etc.
Sofa, chair, and bedstead-making.		Pigs, into several islands.
Growth and manufacture of tobacco.	Pine-apples.	Turkeys.
	Custard-apples.	
	Coffee.	Geese.
Sugar-boiling.	Cotton.	Ducks, etc.
Printing.	Indigo.	Fowls.¶

4. When the missionary has thus put a newly-reclaimed people in the way of providing for their immediate wants, it

---

* Evidence on the Aborigines, p. 89.
† Idem, p. 110. ‡ Idem, p. 353. § Idem, p. 355. ‖ Idem, p. 360.
¶ Williams's Missionary Enterprise, pp. 578, 579.

might be supposed that the next step would be to devote every
moment of their leisure, which could be spared from their
religious instruction, to their mental education. Having
taught them the alphabet of civilization, the alphabet of their
own language would seem naturally to follow. But perhaps
the language is without an alphabet. In many instances, the
*modern missionary, like an Ulphilas, a Patricius, and a
Cyril of earlier times, has given to the people a written language.* From the time when the "Indian Evangelist" reduced the Massachusetts Indian language* to form, in 1660,
down to the present day, when the New Zealander, the Caffre,
and the Rarotongian, are just beginning to learn the written
signs of their respective tongues, this is a benefit which the
Christian missionary has often conferred. With scarcely any
aid besides that which they derive from the oral and uncertain explanations of the natives, the missionaries of a single
American society have constructed the framework of at least
seven languages from the foundation; forming the alphabet,
determining the orthography, arranging the grammar, and
presenting the whole in a written form; and, where circumstances have required, other societies have been proportionally
useful in conferring on the heathen the same benefit. Qualified missionaries are employed at the present time in reducing
to a written form the Australian, Foulah, Mandingo, and
other languages. In this way, Christian missions are incidentally laying the foundation for all the literature which the
millions of these various nations may ever possess. Besides
which, the treasures contained in the Hebrew, Greek, Latin,
French, German, and English languages, are in the process
of transmission into all the written and unwritten tongues
which our missionaries employ.

5. The next step in the civilizing process *is education.* As
the missionary does not address the heathen in his own name,
but in the name of God, and as the book containing the will
of God is made ready to their hands, what more natural than
a mutual anxiety that they should be able to consult it? Accordingly, as soon as possible, every mission opens its infant,
youth, and adult schools; and the natives generally both hasten

---

* Of which Mather said that the words looked as if they had been
growing ever since the confusion of Babel.

to it themselves, and send their children. About two hundred thousand children and adults are now receiving instruction through the agency of missionaries; perhaps nearly an equal number have already enjoyed it. Here may be seen the infant learner, who, but for the timely interposition of the Christian missionary, would have been immolated, as all his brothers and sisters had been; and there may be seen the hand that would have done it, tracing the alphabet. Here, the parent is seen learning of his child; and there, the female is seen imparting instruction, where, once, her presence would have been deemed pollution, and have incurred her destruction. Who does not prospectively recognize in many of those youthful pupils the future instructor of other tribes, and the missionary to distant lands? Who does not see in many of those schools the promise of theological seminaries, and the germ of future colleges? And in the press, with which many of them are connected, who does not recognize the sure prevention of a return to barbarism, and the foundation of national cultivation and of future mental greatness?

6. Education tends, in a variety of ways, to create a demand for *the institution of laws.* By teaching them to read, a people obtain a knowledge of the customs and advantages of law in civilized lands: by enlightening their minds, such knowledge shows them the evils which they have suffered from the want of law: by quickening their moral nature, it awakens a craving after a rule to walk by; and, by thus humanizing them, it prepares them to conform to the law enacted. Hence the missionary, as their only adviser and friend, is often called on to become, in effect, their lawgiver. The Cherokees of North America,* and the Caffres of the Little Namaquas, have their respective codes.† The Sandwich Islands recognize the authority of law. Formerly, in the Island of Rarotonga, "the king, when a thief was caught upon his premises, would have him cut up, and portions of his body hung in different parts of the farm on which the depredation had been committed. But when Christianity was embraced by them, they saw immediately that such sanguinary proceedings were inconsistent with the benign spirit of the gospel, and they inquired of us what would be done in Eng-

---

* Evidence on the Aborigines, p. 51. † Idem, p. 157

land, and what was consistent with the Christian profession We informed them that there were judges in England, and all such offences were tried regularly, and particular punishments awarded. They immediately said, 'Will it not be well for us to have the same?' and, after months' and months' consultation with them, and explaining those things to them, a very simple code was drawn up."* The Tahitians have also a simple, explicit, and wholesome code of laws, as the result of their imbibing the principles of Christianity. This code of laws is printed and circulated among them, understood by all, and acknowledged by all as the supreme rule of action for all classes in their civil and social relations. The laws have been productive of great benefits;† and of these benefits all the Society Islands are more or less partakers. To the practical working of these laws, impartial and ample testimony has been borne as to "one of the greatest temporal blessings they have derived from the introduction of Christianity."‡ By making the New Testament the basis of their civil enactments, they have placed their government under the Divine protection, and laid a foundation for lasting national prosperity.

7. To say that the gospel has *erected a standard of morality* among those of whom we are speaking, is only to state what is clearly implied in the paragraph preceding; for it is not until men are becoming a law unto themselves, that they begin to think of enacting rules for their own conduct, or for that of others. To say that they have been rendered moral, compared with their idolatrous fellow-countrymen, would be to fall far short of the truth: in many respects their example is a loud lecture on morality to the civilized Briton. Not in vain has the Bible said to the Sandwich Islanders, "Thou shalt not commit adultery." Having enacted a law in 1825 prohibiting the sins which violate that law, and having extended it to foreign visitors as well as to themselves, "the rage of the former, who came in the ships in the autumn of the year, was such that they could scarcely be restrained from acts of the most violent outrage." "Once," write the missionaries, "we thought a single couple would be exposed

---

* Evidence on the Aborigines, p. 300.
† Idem, p. 180. ‡ Idem, p. 182

to insult from the natives: now the natives are a defence from lawless foreigners, to whose violence we are all exposed."* Not in vain has the gospel said to the New Zealander, " Let him that stole, steal no more." " Ten years ago, a person scarcely dared to lay a tool down, as it was almost sure to be stolen : now, locks and bolts are but little used, and but little needed; working tools are safe, although lying in all directions."† Not in vain for the Hottentot and the Tahitian has the Bible denounced drunkenness. The former has petitioned from Kat river that no canteens might be allowed in the settlement: the latter has enacted a law which prohibits trade with ships which come for the purpose of introducing ardent spirits; and, indeed, the Island of Porapora is the only one that retains the use of ardent spirits in the whole of the Tahitian and Society Island group.‡ The Honorable Justice Burton informed Doctor Philip, of the Cape of Good Hope, after a circuit tour, that he had made three journeys over the colony as a circuit judge : that, during these circuits, he had had nine hundred cases before him, and that only two of these cases were connected with Hottentots who belong to missionary institutions, and that neither of them was an aggravated case. On a comparison of the population at the missionary stations with that of the rest of the colony which was under the jurisdiction of the circuit court, the fact stated by the Judge marked the proportion of the crimes as one to thirty-five.§

8. If, in some instances, heathen tribes are indebted to Christian missionaries for their discovery, in still more, probably, have they been *saved, by the same agency, from extinction*. A competent witness testifies, in his " Evidence on the Aborigines,"|| that " wherever the gospel has not been introduced among the Indians of Upper Canada, there the process by which the diminution of their numbers is effected is steadily going on; but wherever Christianity has been established, there a check has been opposed to the process of destruction; and on the older stations, among the tribes that have been the greatest length of time under the influence of

---

* Evidence on the Aborigines, pp. 42–44. † Idem, p. 119.
‡ Idem, pp. 351, 301, 276.
§ Tract Society publication. || Page 145.

Christian principles, there the proportion has begun somewhat to increase." The missionary establishments have "unquestionably done much good," said Major Dundas,* "in bringing together, and in keeping together, the wrecks of the Hottentot nation." The depopulation of the Sandwich and South Sea Islands, since the time of their discovery by Captain Cook, is truly fearful. His estimate of the number of the inhabitants was probably much too high; but, within the memory of the missionaries, the prevalence of wars of extermination, of infanticide, and the introduction of European diseases and vices, had reduced the population of some of the islands from thousands to hundreds, and of others from hundreds to tens. But the Christian missionary "stood between the dead and the living, and the plague was stayed." Since Christianity has prevailed among the people, there has been a reaction: the population is supposed to have increased about one-fourth. Thus the gospel came between them and annihilation.†

9. Missionaries frequently *act the part of mediators between chiefs and tribes at variance*, and have thus been the means of arresting many a sanguinary conflict, and of reconciling the parties to each other. On some of these occasions they volunteer their mediation, bring the hostile chiefs together, and continue to exert their peaceful influence till a friendship is effected. But so well is their peace-making character known, and so highly is it esteemed, even by those natives who have not embraced Christianity, that they are often sent for to interpose; and, generally, from the moment they come between the parties at issue, the breach is considered to be as good as healed. Even when the hostile ranks have been confronted, with thousands on a side, ready at a word to rush in savage and deadly encounter, the missionary has pitched his tent of peace between, and, for days together, has gone from tribe to tribe, and from chief to chief, till they came to a resolution of peace.‡

10. But, if the Christian missionary confers a benefit on heathen tribes in preventing wars of extermination, and saving them from extinction, still more does he serve them, accord-

---

* Evidence on the Aborigines, p. 347. † Idem, pp. 51, 292.
‡ Missionary Enterprises, p. 457; and Evidence on the Aborigines, pp 15, 211-218.

ing to the ordinary mode of calculation, by *rescuing their mental character from undeserved ignominy, and restoring them to the rank of our common humanity.* A false philosophy, while complacently monopolizing all the genuine philanthropy to be found in the world, has yet most strangely evinced its philanthropy by consigning a large proportion of the species to neglect and extermination, as irreclaimably degenerate and savage. The advocates of such a philosophy, while affecting this superiority over their brother savage, must have forgotten that those very airs are among the certain marks of an imperfect civilization: that they are shared by every untutored tribe on the face of the earth; and that there was a time, in the history of Britain, when the ancestors of these very philosophers were deemed by similar philosophers at Rome to be too stupid even for slaves—when Cicero could advise his friend Atticus not to obtain his slaves from Britain, " because they are so stupid, and utterly incapable of being taught, that they are unfit to form a part of the household of Atticus." But that which the gospel effected for us, its modern missionaries are accomplishing, under God, for the slandered heathen of the present day. The Moravian missionaries soon discovered, when the gospel began to affect the Greenlander, that his previous condition had been one, not of hopeless stupidity, but of utter ignorance: that in proportion as the influence of grace prevailed on his heart, his torpid mind awoke and came forth: that the dawning of spiritual light, like the return of the sun after the one long night of his own winter, ended both his brutishness and his vice, and gave him a mind and a heart together.* The Hottentot, through all his varieties, is found as eager for instruction, and as capable of cultivation, as the European himself.†
The liberated negro child at Sierra Leone is soon found worthy of being prepared to become a native teacher; while the enslaved adult negroes have abundantly proved their equality, at least, to those who have held them in bondage.
"Your missionaries have determined that: they have dived into that mine from which we were often told no valuable ore or precious stone could be extracted; and they have brought

---

* Carne's Lives of Eminent Missionaries, vol. i., p. 247.
† Evidence on the Aborigines, pp. 350–353: also, p. 104.

up the gem of an immortal spirit, flashing with the light of intellect, and glowing with the hues of Christian graces."* Even the native children of New Holland, placed by common consent in the lowest grade of humanity, are found in no degree inferior in intellect, or ability to learn, to children in general in an English school.† How mighty must that influence be which can thus disinter the mental faculties, and quicken into quivering sensibility what appeared to be a mass of unconscious brutality! And how beneficent that agency which takes whole tribes and nations, whom a worldly philosophy had struck out from the family of man, and exalts them, through grace, into the family of God!

11. Christian missions have proved eminently beneficial in affording *protection to the oppressed, and in procuring liberty for the enslaved.* At some stations, the mere presence of the missionary has proved a salutary check on the lawless barbarities which Europeans had been accustomed to commit on the aborigines. At others, he has obtained magisterial interference in behalf of the oppressed, and has secured their rights in defiance of their cruel taskmasters. In one place, he has guarded against the danger of domestic slavery by inducing the natives themselves to prohibit it by law. In another, he may be seen hastening with presents to ransom captives taken in war. While in other instances, the influence of that gospel which he has preached has induced the converted natives voluntarily to break the chain of their slaves, and to let them go free.‡

But the great triumphs of Christian missions, in ameliorating the state of the slave colonies, and liberating the slave, have yet to be recorded. No one acquainted with the history of negro emancipation will for a moment question that these happy results were hastened and effected by Providence, through the moral influence of Christian missions. The ordinance issued at the Cape, in 1828, by the provisions of which the Hottentots and other free persons of color within the colony were placed on a civil and political equality with the white colonists, was the undeniable effect of missionary perse-

---

* Rev. R. Watson on the Religious Instruction of the Slaves.
† Evidence on the Aborigines, p. 107.
‡ Evidence on the Aborigines, pp. 5–21, 30–35, 157, 238, 247. Missionary Enterprises, p. 325.

verance and fidelity. The publication of "Researches in South Africa," and the proclamation of this African bill of rights—this Magna Charta of the Hottentot nation—stand together in the relation of cause and effect.

The great Act which enacted that, "from the first of August, 1834, slavery be utterly and for ever abolished throughout the British colonies, plantations, and possessions abroad," was doubtless the result, chiefly, of missionary influence. By bringing to light the real condition of the slave—his brutal ignorance and heart-rending wrongs—the religious part of the community had long been preparing for some great movement in his behalf. By the frantic and murderous violence with which some of the planters assailed the men who were engaged in his instruction, the people of England were ultimately aroused to petition Parliament for the overthrow of the system. And by the influence of the compassion thus awakened, and which stopped not to count the ransom for suffering humanity, the nation generously cast twenty millions at the feet of the slaveholder, as the price of the negroes' deliverance. Thus humanity triumphed through religion, and religion through her missionaries. Nor have their services in the cause of the negro been less important since the Act of Emancipation took effect. On the recorded testimony of colonial governors, we learn, that to their invaluable influence partly it is to be ascribed that the colonies have been brought so safely as they have through the successive stages of the critical transition. And from what we know of the past, we may confidently add, that not only have their known character and activity, as the friend of the negro, tended to check his distrust and impatience, and to inspire him with confidence, but that the same causes have equally tended to secure for him, what otherwise he would not speedily have obtained, the unperverted operation of the Act which treats him as "a man and a brother."*

12. But colonial slavery is only one of a long catalogue of evils which Christianity has blotted out by the hand of her missionaries. If *the tapu*, one of the chief obstacles to New Zealand civilization, has been abolished, it is to be ascribed entirely, under God, to "the agency of missionaries."† If

---

[* See Introduction.—T. O. S.]
† Evidence on the Aborigines, p. 218.

habitual idleness, one of the most prolific evils of savage life, has been extensively replaced by honest industry, the change has been effected entirely by the new wants and habits which Christianity has created, and by missionary instruction in the arts of civilization. If an order in Council has been issued for the suppression of the pilgrim tax in India, it was obtained by the expression of Christian opinion in this country, and that opinion was sustained and made active by the representation of our missionaries there. If a cannibal would now be sought for in vain, or an altar stained with the blood of human sacrifices, throughout nearly the whole nation of Polynesian Asiatics, the glory of the happy change redounds entirely to the influence of the gospel. If the fearful trade of the "infant-killer" has ceased to exist throughout the same vast region, and if the Ganges no longer receives its accustomed number of new-born babes, it is because the gospel is going through the world restoring a heart to the human bosom. If the Indian suttee no longer receives its annual holocaust of 30,000 widows, it is because its unholy fires have been dimmed, and all but extinguished, by the rising of the Sun of righteousness. If Brahminism is rapidly falling into discredit, and the cruelties and immolations practiced in honor of the Indian Moloch greatly diminished, Christianity has been mainly instrumental in producing the change. In a word, if populous islands and regions of the earth have been lately wrested from the empire of idolatry, and brought under the happy influence of an enlightened civilization, the change has been effected by the blessing of God on the diffusion of the gospel.

13. Among the most distinguished benefits accruing to the heathen world from Christian missions—so distinguished that we deem it worthy of separate notice—is their elevating effect on *the moral character and social rank of woman*. Wherever our missionaries have gone, they have found that degradation is the condition of the sex, and insult and suffering its reward. Of the Chinese women, Gutzlaff writes, they are the slaves and concubines of their masters, live and die in ignorance, and every attempt to raise themselves above the rank assigned them is regarded as impious arrogance.* As might be expected, suicide is a refuge to which thousands of these igno-

---

* Preface to Voyages, p. xxiv.

rant idolaters fly.* And a large proportion of their new-born female children is destroyed. Even in Pekin, the residence of the emperor, about 4000 are annually murdered;† and to ask a man of any distinction whether he has daughters, is a mark of great rudeness.‡ The condition of the Hindoo women is, if possible, worse. "Any thing," says Bishop Heber,§ "is thought good enough for them; and the roughest words, the poorest garments, the scantiest alms, the most degrading labor, and the hardest blows, are generally their portion." And yet China and India alone are at this moment holding two hundred millions of immortal beings in this abject condition! If there are those who can account for the entailed slavery of the negro race only by resolving it into a Divine malediction, where is the curse recorded which can account for the social slavery and wretchedness of one half of the human race? For be it remembered that Divine Christianity is the only system which denounces the enormity. Mohammedanism adds its authority to that of Hindooism and Budhism, in excluding woman, by system, from instruction, and in pronouncing her soulless and irreclaimably wicked. But if such be the verdict of civilized heathenism, what may we expect to be her doom in uncivilized lands? To be prohibited from certain kinds of food which are reserved for the men and the gods, and from dwelling under the same roof with their tyrannical masters, are among the lighter parts of their fate. Well might the female barbarian of North America look on the coming of Eliot as that of an angel.‖ Well might the Caffres denominate a missionary "the shield of woman."¶ While every other system makes her the butt of their cruel shafts, the effect of the gospel is to provide her with a shield. By exalting marriage, and denouncing licentiousness in all its forms, it provides for her the honorable relation of a wife, and the comforts of a home. By discountenancing polygamy, it dries up unnumbered sources of domestic discord, and challenges for her the undivided affections of her husband. By extinguishing infanticide, and inculcating the parental duties,

---

* Abeel's Appeal to Christian Ladies.
† Abeel. ‡ Gutzlaff.
§ Twenty-fourth Report of B. and F. S. S., p. 39.
‖ Carne, vol. i., p. 19.
¶ Evidence on the Aborigines, p. 323.

it multiplies the ties of conjugal endearment, and increases her importance to the welfare of her family. And by developing her mind, and exalting her character, it adds respect to domestic love, and renders her influence useful and lasting. All this Christianity has done. Ten thousand happy Polynesian, African, and negro homes attest it. And the operations of the "Society for promoting Female Education in China, India, and the East," are calculated, by the Divine blessing, to increase their number.

Now, that the benefits which we have enumerated are among the results of Christian missions, is become an established and familiar fact. To ask for any vouchers of the truth of our representation, beyond those which we have given, would betray ignorance of the passing events of the day, and an anxiety for something more and other than the truth. "These things have not been done in a corner." The narratives of impartial witnesses have recorded them. A succession of officers in the army and navy have borne spontaneous testimony to them. They are registered in colonial reports, and taken for granted in government dispatches. Our commerce wafts us to them; and the reclaimed idolaters themselves have come amongst us, as the representatives of their fellow-countrymen, to exhibit in their own persons the value of the missionary enterprise. Even the anti-supernaturalist, who regards their conversion as the natural result of their contact with missionary morality and intelligence, does not hesitate to ascribe it to missionary instrumentality. So important an element of civilization has that agency become, that the continental literati and savans—the Balbis and Kieffers, the Jouffroys, Remusats, and Klaproths —regard it with admiration. So conspicuous are its triumphs, that Rome itself, in the spirit of envy or emulation, is essaying to achieve the same with her enchantments. And so demonstrable and valuable is its practical bearing on the temporal welfare of man, that the highest municipal body in the kingdom has given it aid; " not as forming a precedent to assist merely religious missions, nor as preferring any sect or party, but to be an extraordinary donation for *promoting the great cause of civilization, and the moral improvement of our common species;*" while the inquiries of our legislature, in seeking "Evidence on the Aborigines," have established the fact, that Christian missionaries are the great agents of civilization, and rank amongst the most distinguished benefactors of mankind.

The social and moral advantages, then, which the missionary enterprise has conferred on the heathen, are before the world. And had the good which it has imparted terminated here, who does not feel that it would have amply repaid the cost and toil with which they have been attended? What vast tracts has it rescued from barbarism, and with what creations of benevolence has it clothed them! How many thousands, whom ignorance and selfishness had branded as the leavings and refuse of the species, if not actually akin to the beasts that perish, are at this moment rising under its fostering care; ascribing their enfranchisement, under God, to its benign interposition; taking encouragement from its smiles to assume the port and bearing of men; and, by their acts and aspirations, retrieving the character and dignity of the slandered human form! When did literature accomplish so much for nations destitute of a written language? or education pierce and light up so large and dense a mass of human ignorance? When did humanity save so many lives, or cause so many sanguinary "wars to cease?" How many a sorrow has it soothed; how many an injury arrested; how many an asylum has it reared, amidst scenes of wretchedness and oppression, for the orphan, the outcast, and the sufferer! When did liberty ever rejoice in a greater triumph than that which missionary instrumentality has been the means of achieving? or civilization find so many sons of the wilderness learning her arts, and agriculture, and commerce? or law receive so much voluntary homage from those who but yesterday were strangers to the name? By erecting a standard of morality, how vast the amount of crime which it has been the means of preventing! By asserting the claims of degraded woman, how powerful an instrument of social regeneration is it preparing for the future! And by doing all this by the principle and power of all moral order and excellence—the gospel of Christ—how large a portion of the world's chaos has it restored to light and harmony and peace!

Had human philosophy effected such results as these—or only a thousandth part of them—how soon would her image be set up, and what multitudes would fall down and worship!

By leaving a single esculent on an island, Kotzebue plumed himself with the assurance of having secured its ultimate civilization.

But great as are the benefits which we have enumerated, and most of which can, in a sense, be seen, and measured, and handled, we venture to affirm that those which are at present comparatively impalpable and undeveloped are greater still. The unseen is far greater than that which appears. The missionary has been planting the earth with principles; and these are of as much greater value than the visible benefits which they have already produced, as the tree is more valuable than its first year's fruit. The tradesman may take stock and calculate his pecuniary affairs to a fraction; the astronomer may count the stars; and the chemist weigh the invisible element of air; but he who in the strength of God conveys a great truth to a distant region, or puts into motion a divine principle, has performed a work of which futurity alone can disclose the results. At no one former period could either of our missionary societies have attempted to "number Israel," to reduce to figures either the geographical extent or the practical results of its influence, without having soon received, in the cheering events which followed, a distinct but gracious rebuke. How erroneous the calculation which should have set down the first fifteen years of fruitless missionary labor in Greenland, or the sixteen in Tahiti, or the twenty in New Zealand, as years of entire failure! when, in truth, the glorious scene which then ensued was simply that which God was pleased to make the result of all that had preceded—the explosion, by the Divine hand, of a train which had been lengthening and enlarging during every moment of all those years. So that, were the whole field of missions to be suddenly vacated, and all its moral machinery at once withdrawn, we confidently believe that the amount of temporal good, arising from what has been done, will be much greater twenty years hence than it is at present.

Who can say, for instance, to what extent the entire fabric of idolatry is undermined? remembering the fact that the Sandwich Islands abandoned their gods at the mere rumor of Tahiti's conversion, and before a Christian missionary had approached them; although that report had to be borne across the waters nearly three thousand miles. Who can walk to the circumference of the moral circle of which a missionary station is the centre, and say, here its useful influence will be exhausted? For the gospel moralizes even when it does not convert; and where it does not so much as induce the abandonment of idolatry. It checks unnumbered evils, unveils the deformity of vice, restores the lost influence of shame, and thus gradually diminishes crime, and raises the moral tone of society: even the hemlock and the nightshade grow less rankly where the sun shines. Who can calculate the effect of emancipation in the West Indies on the servile population of the Union? "The sympathies between the colonial inhabitants of the two regions," says an American authority, "must become more and more extensive. No legal enactments, no armed cordon around Florida, can prevent it. News of the progress of human freedom will fly faster than civil proclamations. Human sympathies cannot be blocked up by negotiations, nor by ships of war. Rumors of this sort will fly on the winds of heaven."*

This, too, is the prospective view to be taken of that munificent gift, by which the nation charmed the dragon slavery from its victims. True, its immediate purpose may, in some respects, have partially failed; but not one of all its higher ends. Twenty millions of enactments against slavery would not have made a return to that enormity so impossible as that gift has done. Twice twenty million hearts beat quicker in the cause of humanity than ever. More than that number of benevolent impulses have been sent thrilling through all the departments of social improvement. We meant it for our country—it has touched the heart of the world. We meant it to take full and final effect on a day at hand—it will operate till the last day. We meant it for a given number of slaves— in an important sense, it has bought the freedom of mankind. And thus nothing good is lost. The feeblest act for God, not by any inherent strength of its own, but by being linked on to some great principle of the Divine government, is carried on through all time, and, for aught we know, through all worlds.

And who does not foresee that, owing materially to missionary influence, the whole system of British colonization, as far as it affects the aborigines, is likely to be essentially improved?

[* See Introduction.—T. O. S.]

By exposing the fact that for ages we have been imitating the Spanish and the Portuguese in the worst parts of their policy, and in the blackest features of their national character; that while we have been priding ourselves on our superior humanity and civilization, we have been laying whole regions desolate, and consigning entire tribes to destruction, Christian missions have aroused the national indignation, and thus taken the first step towards remedying the evil. While, by pointing out the only legitimate method of colonization; by perseveringly imploring, and, through the public voice, demanding, in the name of outraged justice and humanity, that this method shall be adopted; and by continuing to report every fresh violation of it, they are powerfully tending, under God, to base our future intercourse with the aborigines on righteousness and peace, and thus to promote, on a most extended scale, the temporal welfare of myriads of mankind.

SECTION II.

THE RELIGIOUS BENEFITS AND SPIRITUAL RESULTS OF CHRISTIAN MISSIONS AMONG THE HEATHEN.

GREAT as are the social and moral blessings which Christian missions have been the means of imparting to heathen lands, they have only, in a sense, been imparted incidentally, by aiming at greater things than these. The great design of Christ in coming into the world was to erect his cross, and the supreme object of his missionary is instrumentally to dispense its blessings—blessings as much superior to those which relate only to the present, as the nature and duration of the undying soul surpass the body which enshrines it. While he rejoices, therefore, in being made the medium of imparting temporal benefits, he values them chiefly as the signs and the means of yet greater good. He remembers that, important as they may be in the class of blessings to which they belong, they are only accidental to religion—the dust of that diamond which constitutes her crowning gift— the shed blossoms of that tree of life of which his office is to dispense the immortal fruit.

In enumerating the benefits glanced at in the last section, then, we have only been ascending the steps of that temple which it is the design of the missionary enterprise to erect. And although it is allowed us to sing our "song of degrees" as we ascend them, our great business is within. Here angels join us, and mingle their joy with the grateful tears of myriads of reclaimed penitents. Here the Redeemer himself sees of the travail of his soul, and is satisfied.

1. But in order that we may be the better prepared to estimate this spiritual result, let us begin with the first religious benefits of Christian missions, *in effecting an extensive abolition of idolatry*. If there existed a region on the face of the earth where, in defiance of the law which commands, "Thou shalt have no other gods before me," the Divine Lawgiver himself were forgotten, and demons placed on his throne; where the moral darkness had for ages been deepening and concealing abominations, till diabolical ingenuity itself had exhausted its hideous devices; and where a cloud stored with the bolts of Divine displeasure had been consequently collecting and impending, ready every moment to discharge a tempest of destruction, would he not be an instrument of immense good who should hold up a light in the midst of that darkness, by which the deluded worshippers should see that they had been sacrificing to devils, not to God, and before which those demons should fly? Such regions there are. The entire empire of polytheism is a realm of diabolical dominion. It assembles its votaries only to blaspheme the name of God; erects its temple only to attract the lightning of the impending cloud on their devoted heads; calls them around its altars only that in the very act of supposed atonement they may complete their guilt; and gives them a pretended revelation only "that they should believe a lie." And such an angel of mercy is the Christian missionary. To say nothing, at present, of the decline of idolatry in India, and of the conversion of some of the tribes of Africa and North America, where now, we ask, is the idolatry which lately revelled in the Sandwich, the Marquesan, the Paumotu, the Tahitian and Society, the Austral, the Hervey, the Navigators, the Friendly Islands, and New Zealand, and in all the smaller islands in their respective vicinities? Idolatry still reigns in Western Polynesia, and still steeps its

victims in blood and guilt: what benevolent power has swept the curse from Eastern Polynesia? The missionary of the cross has been there, proclaiming that "there is one God, and one Mediator between God and man, the man Christ Jesus" —and about ninety islands have "cast their idols to the moles and to the bats," and about four hundred thousand idolaters have become the professed worshippers of the only living and true God. We admit, indeed, that the mere abandonment of idolatry is very remote from scriptural conversion to God. But if the inspired history exhibits the Almighty in one continued contest with idolatry, is it nothing to find, though it be only about the fifteen hundredth part of his infatuated foes lay down their arms, and virtually acknowledge their guilt? If the mere casting out of a demon was a benefit to the dispossessed which called for his ardent and lasting gratitude, is it nothing for whole demoniac communities to have the fiend of idolatry, whose name is Legion, cast out of the body politic, and to be now found "clothed, and in their right mind?" The renunciation of a false religion is at least one step towards the adoption of the true one.

2. If we knew of a region where the sun of knowledge—if ever it shone there—set long ages ago; where the absence of truth has not merely left the mind vacant, but in actual possession of destructive errors, like a deserted mansion, converted into a den for robbers and murderers; and where truth is not only lost to man, and fatal error is in full possession, but where man is actually lost to the truth—lost to the power of even intellectually apprehending it when first presented to his mind; and if there existed a process by which that darkness could be pierced, those errors exploded, and this power restored, would not he be a great benefactor who should attempt and conduct it to a successful issue? That region is heathenism; that process is education; and that benefactor the Christian missionary. Visit, in thought, the two hundred thousand youthful and adult scholars sitting at his feet to receive instruction, and imagine what all those immortal beings would have been if left to themselves. A considerable number would doubtless have been destroyed in infancy, had he not gone to their rescue; while, for the rest, the past would have been all a fable, the future a blank, and

12

the present would have been spent in a perpetual conflict whether the fiend or the brute should predominate in their nature. Does the reader deeply commiserate such a condition? Let him remember that the depth of his compassion is a measure, however inadequate, for estimating the value of that process which enables them to emerge out of it. Let him observe, further, as the process advances, how the faculties recover their proper pliability, how the understanding rejoices in the power of apprehending truth, and reason gradually resumes its throne, and even the countenance itself is humanized, "losing the wild and vacant stare of the savage" in the mild and intelligent expression of the reasonable being; and let him remember that the pleasure which he experiences in marking the transformation is another measure by which to estimate the value of missionary effort.

Let him not suppose, however, that he has all the evidence of its value before him till he has ascertained the importance attached to it by the recipients themselves: till he has marked the adult barbarian indignant at his own slowness of comprehension; till he has seen the negro parent patiently submitting to be taught by his own children;[*] and the New Zealander establishing schools in his own villages, under the direction of native youths;[†] till he has beheld the fierce warrior of a hundred battles presiding at the examination of the children of his people, and has seen amidst the beaming looks of the parents who had spared their children, and the tearful countenances of those who had immolated theirs, some venerable chieftain rise, and, with impassioned look and manner, exclaim, "Let me speak: I must speak! O that I had known that the gospel was coming! O that I had known that these blessings were in store for us; then I should have saved my children, and they would have been among this happy group, repeating these precious truths; but, alas! I destroyed them all, and now I have not one left;" then, cursing the gods which they had formerly worshipped, and adding, with a flood of tears, "It was you that infused this savage disposition into us; and now I shall die childless, although I have been the father of nineteen children. O that some one had seized my

---

[*] Evidence on the Aborigines, p. 105   [†] Idem, p. 249.

murderous hand, and had told me, The gospel of salvation is coming to our shores!"* And even then let the reader remember, that in estimating the value of missionary instruction, the chief element is wanting, unless he could foresee the number who will go forth from enjoying it, "wise unto salvation."

3. If there existed a region where the mind of millions, heaving and surging like the laboring ocean, was ever seeking rest and finding none, would not he be conferring on it an incomparable good who should instrumentally allay its perturbations, and minister to its enlightened repose? Such a region is to be found wherever the terrors of superstition prevail. How dense must be that moral darkness which is only comparable to the shadow of death! What must be the state of that mind which could realize its conception of the invisible powers only in the forms of idols so monstrously distorted and horrible as to shock the imagination! How intense must be that anguish of soul which can impel men to lacerate their flesh, and inflict agonies of self-torture! which can burst the sacred bonds of humanity, and offer a brother-man in sacrifice! or which can even suppress the still more sacred feelings of the mother, and induce her to immolate her infant child! Then what must be the amount of obligation conferred on the victims of such a reign of terror by him who takes into the midst of them an infallible remedy for the whole! And yet the Christian missionary does this. He goes to tell the dupes of imposture of essential truth; to tell the infanticide mother that she may save her offspring, and may press them to her heart; and the devotee of the Ganges of the washing of regeneration, and the renewing of the Holy Ghost; and the self-torturing votary of cruelty that the name of God is Love; and the self-immolating worshippers of Juggernaut of the sacrifice offered once for all, and of the blood which cleanseth from all sin. Whether the heathen avail themselves of the proffered good or not, he takes into the midst of them light which can dissipate the gross darkness of ages, unveils a propitiation which expiates the guilt of a world, and the offer of a peace which reflects the cloudless tranquillity of heaven itself.

---

* Missionary Enterprises, p. 564.

4. Nor does his usefulness stop even here. At this point it assumes its loftiest character, and only begins to produce its noblest results. An agency there is which can not only take these blessings into the midst of a heathen tribe, but which can then dispose that tribe to receive them; and by that agency the Christian missionary is actually accompanied. A change there is which new-creates the soul; and of that change he is the honored instrument. Pointing to a hundred and eighty thousand Christian converts, he can say, "Ye were darkness, but now are ye light in the Lord." Name the most depraved and degraded of the species, and pointing to those converts he can say, "Such were some of you; but ye are washed, but ye are sanctified, but ye are justified, in the name of the Lord Jesus, and by the Spirit of our God." Do we speak of "the vision of dry bones" as a scene typical of a great spiritual triumph? Here is, at least, "an exceeding great army" raised from the dead by the same renewing power, and whose spiritual change is worthy of being classed with the most stupendous miracles of grace. Do we point to the three thousand converts of the Pentecost, and pray for a similar triumph of the converting Spirit? Here are, numerically at least, the fruits of the Pentecostal scene fifty times repeated.

5. If we knew of a volume, parts of which were prepared for converts such as those we have described, and the whole of which, written by the finger of God, was calculated to reflect light, and love, and glory around them; if we knew of a day on which they could statedly assemble together to worship God, and associate in spirit with the seraphim around the throne, and enjoy a foretaste of the Sabbath above; and if there existed a society instituted by Christ, enjoying his perpetual presence, and designed expressly to train them up for the perfect society of the blessed, would not he who should be the means of putting them in possession of all this do more than confer on them the wealth of a world? Such a volume there is, and with incalculable toil the missionary has prepared and placed it in their hands; and as they bend over the sacred page, or press it to their hearts, the language which beams in their eye, and escapes from their lips, is, "Lord, to whom shall we go but unto thee? thou hast the words of eternal life!" Such a day there is; and as it

dawns with all the hallowed tranquillity of the first Sabbath, ten thousand dwellings, once the habitations of cruelty, resound with the morning hymn of praise; and as its sacred hours advance, a number greater than "the number of them that are sealed," "of all nations, and kindreds, and people, and tongues," may be seen assembled "before the throne" of grace, and "before the Lamb," worshipping God "in the beauty of holiness,". and "crying, Salvation unto our God, who sitteth upon the throne, and unto the Lamb." And such a Divine society there is; and to all those worshippers the Christian missionary can say, "Ye are come unto Mount Sion; . . . . to the general assembly and Church of the firstborn, which are written in heaven." Upwards of a thousand particular Churches, belonging to the great community of the faithful, are at this moment to be found in heathen lands. In each of these, truths are statedly proclaimed, and ordinances administered, which the wise and the holy of former times panted and prayed in vain to enjoy; and on which infinite wisdom and grace have expended their most precious resources. So richly worthy of God are they in their constitution and design, that did even the least of them all exist alone in the earth, it would form a study for angels, from which they might "learn the manifold wisdom of God." So important and precious are they in the estimation of Christ, that while he is represented as only extending his sceptre and dispatching his messengers to other parts of his dominions, he himself "walks in the midst of his Churches." And, consequently, so ennobling are they in their practical influence, that every act, and privilege, and law, by which they are distinguished, tends directly to prepare their members for the loftier worship of the beatified Church above.

6. And this reminds us that the bright and ultimate results of Christian missions are nowhere to be found on earth. They are to be looked for in heaven. Could we actually traverse every part of the wide field of missionary labor of which we have spoken, and could we compute the value of its spiritual fruits with the accuracy of the angel who measured the ancient temple with a golden reed, vast as the total would be, it would only furnish us with the first figure of the mighty reckoning which the subject requires. In order to estimate their value aright, we must stand where the seer of

the Apocalypse did, and command a view of heaven. For be it remembered, that since the modern missionary enterprise commenced, heaven has been constantly receiving accessions from its triumphant labors. And be it observed further, that could the number of these be counted, and be added to the missionary converts now on their way to the hill of God, still, in order to calculate the mighty sum of good, we should require to know the trains of usefulness which they have been enabled to lay for all the future. But what do we attempt? Even then the computation would be only commenced. Were the last Christian missionary sent forth, and the last missionary proclamation of mercy delivered, the spiritual good already effected or commenced by such instrumentality is infinitely beyond the reach of numbers. Empty, weak, worthless as it is in itself, the Holy Spirit of God has been pleased to employ it as a means by which guilt which might destroy a world has been cancelled; iron chains of sin have been burst asunder; misery, second only to that of hell, has given place to the peace of God; hearts, stored with pollution, made habitations of God; where "Satan's seat" was, happy communities have been formed; large tracts of the earth have been blessed by it; and heaven has been deriving from it some of the richest trophies of redeeming grace. It is important as the salvation of myriads; precious as the blood of Christ; immeasurable as the joys of heaven; incalculable as the revolutions of eternity. The mind which at first put it into motion can alone compute the value of its results. If an apostle felt constrained to "give thanks to God always" for the converts of a single Church; if the fact that at Thessalonica a small number had been "turned from idols to serve the living and true God," called forth the perpetual thanksgiving of one who had labored in the missionary field more than all his contemporaries, what should be the amount of our gratitude on beholding our surpassing success, and recollecting how little we have done individually to achieve it? "Not unto us, O God, not unto us, but unto thy name be all the glory."

CHAPTER III.

THE REFLEX BENEFITS OF CHRISTIAN MISSIONS.

SECTION I.

TEMPORAL BENEFITS.

ONE of the most benevolent arrangements of the Divine government is to be found in the fact that no one can impart, or even attempt to impart a benefit, without himself being benefited. "He that watereth, shall himself also be watered." This is not to be regarded so much in the light of a promise, as of a law of the Divine administration—a law by which the streams of beneficence are kept, like the waters of the ocean, in perpetual circulation, so that they are sure, sooner or later, to revisit their source; and a law, therefore, of which the great Author is himself the sublime illustration. And one of the brightest exemplifications of this law, in modern times, is to be found in the reflex influence of Christian missions. In proof of this, we may begin by calling attention to a class of benefits which even the most sanguine and far-sighted friends of the missionary enterprise hardly contemplated at first— *the temporal advantages which it returns to the people with whom it originates.* Had one of its more calculating and sagacious friends ventured at the outset to prophesy such effects, the intimation would have been likely to excite greater contempt, if possible, from the world, than even the expected spiritual result; and even some of the Church would have been ready to say, "If the Lord would make windows in heaven, might this thing be." Yet such is the imposing magnitude to which this class of its results has now attained, that men who care for no other or higher benefit, acknowledge that this alone would amply repay the effort by which it is gained.

1. As one of the lowest, but very important advantages of Christian missions, we might name *the services which they have rendered to literature and science*. Geographical and statistical information, to a very large amount, has been furnished by the missionaries respecting Western Africa.* The Christian Researches of Buchanan in India, and of Jowett in the Mediterranean, Syria, and the Holy Land; the journals of Heber; the biographies of Martyn, Hall, Turner, Thomason, Brown, and others; the periodical accounts of the Serampore brethren; and the voluminous reports of several of the missionary institutions, are of great value to the historian and the naturalist. The Travels of Tyerman and Bennett; of Gutzlaff in China; and of Smith and Dwight through Georgia, Armenia, etc.; the Polynesian Researches of Ellis, and Heartley's Researches in Greece and the Levant; Gobat's Abyssinian Journal; Williams's Missionary Enterprises in the South Sea Islands; Medhurst's China; and the invaluable volume of "Evidence on the Aborigines," are books whose attractions of subject and style have secured them an admission into the library of the philosopher as well as of the Christian. Geography, geology, natural history, philology, and ethnography—the science which classifies nations according to their languages†—have been greatly enriched by them. "Numerous materials," says Balbi,‡ "for the comparison of languages, have been collected at various times during the last three hundred years. In this field, along with many other very useful laborers, the ministers of Christianity have occupied the first rank. To the zeal of the Moravian, Baptist, and other Protestant missionaries, as well as to the

---

* See the Life of S. J. Mills; the eleven volumes of the African Repository; the London Missionary Register; and Reports of the African Institution.

† Or, more strictly, the science which has for its object to classify nations.

‡ Preliminary Discourse prefixed to the Atlas Ethnographique, Paris, 1826

members of Bible Societies* of all Christian sects, ethnography owes its acquaintance with so many nations hitherto unknown in India and other regions of Asia, in various parts of America and Oceanica, along with the translation, in whole or in part, of the Bible, in more than a hundred different languages."

In philology especially, the contributions of the missionaries have been distinguished. By correcting prevailing errors respecting linguistic affinities;† by bringing to light some of the choicest literary treasures of antiquity;‡ by their valuable translations from the languages of the East;§ by reducing many of the unwritten languages of the earth to order and intelligible classification;|| and by the patient and laborious preparation of English and foreign dictionaries and grammars,¶ they have laid the philologist under permanent obligation. Accordingly, not only has commerce been indebted to them, and an embassy employed them,** but even learned societies†† call in their aid, and accord their grateful

---

* The British and Foreign Bible Society has printed the Bible in nearly two hundred languages and dialects.

† Rev. Mr. Lieder, of the Church Missionary Society, seems to have determined that the Berber language of North Africa has no resemblance to that spoken by the Berberi of Nubia, as supposed by Balbi and others. His investigations throw great light on the languages spoken in Nubia.

‡ The German Missionary Society entertains the hope that its missionaries at Shoosha will soon succeed in publishing that most precious relic of the Armenian Church, their earliest translation of the Bible, dating from the fourth century. [*A hope since disappointed, by the expulsion of the missionaries.*]

§ Mr. Thomson is understood to have engaged to translate, for the Oriental Translation Society, some original works from the language of the Bugis, or principal nation of Celebes.

|| See the chapter preceding.

¶ Here Morrison—the Johnson of Christian lexicographers—stands conspicuous. Klaproth, in a detailed critique on his Chinese and English Dictionary, in the *Allgemeine Litteratur Zeitung*, places it beside "the great lexicon of the immortal Meninski." Montucci goes much beyond this praise. M. Abel Remusat, Davis, and Huttman, pronounce on it the highest eulogy.

** Dr. Morrison, in the suite of Lord Amherst, and Chinese interpreter to the British commission at Canton; in which office he was succeeded by Gutzlaff.

†† The Oriental Translation Society. See above.

thanks;* while the leading critics and journalists record their praises,† and the graver encyclopædist‡ registers the activity of their labors for the information of posterity.§

2. Christian missions have *corrected and enlarged our views of the character and condition of man.* In vain would it now be for a Rousseau to repeat his foolish fancies concerning the perfections of the savage man, and the happiness of the savage life, and quite unnecessary that a Forster should gravely adduce evidence to the contrary,‖ a Ferguson honor them with a philosophical investigation,¶ or a Burke expose them to ridicule.** The universal degradation and misery of unreclaimed man, even of that boast of a false philosophy, the North American Indian, has, chiefly by the circulation of missionary information, become a fact as fully accredited as that of his existence. In vain would it now be for a certain class of Europeans to paint in glowing colors, as they once did, the virtue of Asiatic pagans, and to eulogize their mythology as the most perfect system of morality which ever demanded the homage of the heart. That spell of falsehood Buchanan broke, by the exhibition of Juggernaut and his horrors. And if there was not in so old and well-examined a thing as human nature any new principle of evil to be brought to light, missionary disclosures have at least shown some of its known evil principles operating in the mild Hindoo, "with such an absoluteness of possessive power, and displaying this disposition in such wantonly versatile, extravagant, and monstrous effects, as to surpass all our previous

---

* At a meeting of the Oriental Translation Society, in London, June 23d, 1832, a vote of thanks to this effect to the American mission in Ceylon, proposed by Sir A. Johnston, and seconded by Sir W. Ouseley, was unanimously carried.

† "These authors," says the Foreign Quarterly Review, No. 28, referring to Marsden, Raffles, and Crawford, "have been followed, and, at least, in practical acquaintance with the languages of the Eastern islands, surpassed, by several of the English missionaries."

‡ See Balbi.

§ In the American Biblical Repository for January, 1836, there is an article on the subject of the above paragraph, replete with information, to which the author gratefully acknowledges his obligations.

‖ Observations, etc., by J. R. Forster, LL. D., 1778.

¶ View of Society.

** Vindication of Natural Society

imaginations and measures of possibility."* And, on the other hand—for the same persons who profess to regard the perfection of one class of pagans as all but inimitable, can, with singular versatility, pronounce another class irreclaimable—in vain would they now refuse the claims and rights of humanity to any portion of the species. "Ten years ago," says the report† for 1820 of an American missionary society, "the aborigines of our country were regarded by this great community, with the exception of here and there an individual, as an utterly intractable race, never to be brought within the pale of civilized society, but doomed by unalterable destiny to melt away and become extinct; and a spirit of vengeance and of extermination was breathed out against them in many parts of our land. Now, the whole nation is moved by a very different spirit." The missionary experiment has determined that there is no form of humanity, however lost to civilization, which cannot be restored to it; or however sunk in the brute, which cannot be raised, recovered, and taught to hold communion with the skies.

And almost equally in vain will it soon be for the disciples of the French naturalist to continue to deny the origin of the race in a single pair. "God has made of one blood all nations of men to dwell on the face of the earth." In this doctrine of a common nature, and the consequent closeness of relationship among all the branches of the human family, is laid the foundation of all the social affections and duties. Whatever tends to confirm this doctrine, therefore, must be pronounced of vital importance. Now, the philological labors of the Christian missionary are serving to simplify that process which goes to show that all the known languages of the earth are but dialects of one now most probably lost.‡ Besides which, the identity of effect which the preaching of the gospel universally produces, contributes new and satisfactory species of evidence of the identity of the origin of all man-

---

* Foster's incomparable Missionary Discourse, or profound Treatise, bound up with his Essay on Popular Ignorance, p. 422.

† The Eleventh Annual Report of the American Board of Commissioners for Foreign Missions.

‡ The French Academy, after long research and deliberation, have given to this view their decided approbation; so also Schlegel and other distinguished scholars.

kind. When we see how Christ was "followed by the Greek, though a founder of none of his sects; is revered by the Brahmin, though preached to him by men of the fisherman's caste; worshipped by the red man of Canada, though belonging to the hated pale race; we cannot but consider him as destined to break down all distinction of color, and shape, and countenance, and habits, and to form in himself the type of unity to which are referable all the sons of Adam, and to give us, in the possibility of this moral convergence, the strongest proof that the human species, however varied, is essentially one."*

3. But not only has the Christian missionary contributed to correct and enlarge our views of the distant branches of the human family—in numerous instances he has been the means of *correcting and elevating their views of our character*. Numerous and substantial services have accrued to the European from this source, especially in the islands of the Pacific. The single illustration we shall cite, however, has its scene in semi-civilized India. "Do not send to me any of your agents," said Hyder Ali, in his messages to the council at Madras, "for I do not trust their words or treaties; but, if you wish me to listen to your proposals, send to me the missionary Swartz, of whose character I hear so much from every one—him I will receive and trust." And in his letter to the Marquis Cornwallis, General Fullarton writes, "On our second march, we were visited by the Rev. Mr. Swartz, whom your Lordship and the Board requested to proceed to Seringapatam, as a faithful mediator between Tippoo and the Commissioners. The knowledge and integrity of this irreproachable missionary *have retrieved the character of Europeans from imputations of general depravity.*"†

4. To a very considerable extent, *Christian missions have been instrumental also in the preservation of European life*. On the capitulation of Cuddalore, in 1782, the influence and efforts of Gericke were the means of saving numbers from the fangs of Hyder, and from all the accumulated miseries which he heaped on his victims.‡

"When Bishop Johannes de Watteville was on a visitation

---

* Wiseman's Lectures, vol. i. p. 257.
† See Gutzlaff on this subject, Voyages, p. 58.
‡ Smith and Choules's History of Missions, vol. i. p. 81.

of the negro congregations in the Danish West India islands, the governor pointed to the church of the missionaries, and remarked that it was the principal fortress, and considered by him as the great safeguard of the island. He added, that before it was built, he had not ventured to sleep a night out of the fortress on his plantation; but now he had no fear; for even if there was a conspiracy among the slaves, the Christian slaves were sure to hear of and to discover it."*

But on this important though incidental service rendered by Christian missions, the "Evidence on the Aborigines" abounds with illustrations. When, in consequence of unprovoked injuries inflicted by whalers and others, the natives have determined to seize, in blind retaliation, on the next European vessel that touches their shores, the missionary has often succeeded in dissuading them from the execution of their fatal purpose.† Disputes which could have ended only in personal conflicts between European crews and native tribes, have been terminated amicably by missionary mediation.‡ And even when a conflict of mutual destruction has actually occurred, the missionary station—as in the late insurrection of the Caffres—has been a city of refuge to the fugitive European. Not only were their own lives saved, but, owing to the influence which they possessed, they were the means of preserving several of the traders.§

5. This reminds us that *commerce itself is under no small obligations to missionary influence.* In vain were all the attempts of the colonial government to establish a commercial intercourse with the Caffre tribes, until the Christian missionary had gained a footing amongst them.|| But not only does he now form a connecting link in the chain of civilization between the colonies and the Caffres and other tribes¶—by the introduction of the plough, he is likely to be the means of turning the attention of the aborigines from pastoral to agricultural pursuits; in consequence of which their cattle will no longer prove a source of irritation and conflict with the frontier colonists,** and a much narrower compass of land will be sufficient for their comfortable support.††

---

* Ryan's Effects of Religion on Mankind, p. 229.
† Evidence on the Aborigines, pp. 47, 48, 285.
‡ Idem, p. 207.   § Idem, p. 344. || Idem, p. 339.
¶ Idem, p. 346.   ** Idem, p. 155.   †† Idem, p. 93.

New Zealand is unquestionably the key to India, on the one hand, as the Cape of Good Hope is on the other. And if, as events increasingly indicate, a wise policy should require our government to enter into a friendly treaty with that country, the measure would be greatly facilitated, if not entirely owing, to the favorable predisposition created in our behalf by missionary influence.*

Up to a very recent period, the South Sea Islands were, in a commercial point of view, a complete blank; but now they are made to contribute to our wants, and to take off our manufactures to a considerable extent.† Sugar is cultivated, and taken in native-built vessels to the colony of New South Wales;‡ and more arrowroot has been brought from thence to England in one year, than had been imported for nearly twenty previous years.§ Between two and three hundred thousand of the natives are now wearing European clothing, and using European implements and articles, who a few years ago knew nothing of our manufactures.‖

6. *The shipping of our country, too, derives as much advantage from Christian missions* as its commerce. This will appear if it be recollected that intercourse between Europeans and the untaught islanders of the Pacific is always dangerous, and has often proved fatal. The adventurous Magellan fell at the Ladrone Islands; Captain Cook was barbarously murdered at the Sandwich group; the ship *Venus* was taken at Tahiti; M. de Langle and his companions were killed at the Samoas; the *Port au Prince* was seized at Lefuga; and the crew of the *Boyd* were massacred at New Zealand. And now, at all these islands, with the exception of the Ladrones, there are missionary stations, where between two and three hundred vessels annually resort; the crews of which look forward with delight to the hour when the anchor shall be dropped in the tranquil lagoon, and they shall find a generous welcome and a temporary home. Here, at the smallest possible expense, the captains can obtain a supply of fresh meat and provisions, refit their vessels, and recruit their crews.¶

---

* Idem, p. 85.
† Idem, p. 314; and Howitt's Colonization and Christianity, pp. 440, 441. ‡ Evidence on the Aborigines, p. 179.
§ Idem, p. 180. ‖ Idem, p. 311.
¶ Williams's Missionary Enterprises, pp. 584, 585.

Formerly, also, when a wreck occurred, the natives hastened to plunder and murder, or reserved those who escaped from the sea for sacrifices. Witness the unhappy sufferers of the Charles Eaton, and the still more recent massacre of Captain Fraser and his crew on the coast of New Holland. But now, wherever Christianity has been introduced, the occurrence of a wreck is the signal for the exercise of the kindest feelings towards the sufferers themselves, and of the greatest zeal for the protection of their property. The Falcon, the Sir Charles Price, and several other vessels, have been cast away at or near such stations; and not only have the captains and others attested that "not a nail was lost," and that all the attention was given to their personal comfort which kindness could bestow, but thousands of pounds have been transmitted to England and America as the proceeds arising from the sale of property saved on such occasions by native activity and zeal.* Thus many a Christian missionary is, in effect, a British consul of the most unexpensive and efficient kind; and his congregation a society for the protection of British lives and property. While the missionary enterprise itself, by finding new havens at the antipodes for our fleets, opening new channels for our commerce, and everywhere multiplying the friends of our country, is eminently conducive to the prosperity of its temporal interests.

Such, we repeat, is the imposing magnitude to which this class of its results has now attained, that men who care not for any other or higher benefit, acknowledge that this alone would amply repay the efforts by which it has been gained But though the benefits we have now specified possess all the importance attached to them; and though they are among the first to catch the eye in a survey like the present, we conceive that there are others of the same class of greater moment still. In closing our estimate of the temporal good accruing to the heathens from Christian missions, we remarked on the surpassing value of the services which they have rendered to negro emancipation, and to general colonization. And in concluding this brief account of their reflex temporal effects on ourselves, we cannot but avow our belief that their

---

* Evidence on the Aborigines, p. 183; and Williams's speech before the Common Council.

chief national value will hereafter be found to have consisted in the influence which they have shed on the same great objects. The full and distinct proof of this would doubtless require a large induction of historical facts. We will only ask, however, Where now are the possessions of that kingdom, whose armies and governors, with savage cruelty, exterminated the Caribs, the Mexicans, and the children of the sun? In whose hands are the Floridas, Mexico, Darien, Terra Firma, Buenos Ayres, Paraguay, Chili, Peru, and California? But if there be any truth in the doctrine of Divine retribution, or any thing fearful in the Divine displeasure, then every one admitting the guilt of slavery and the criminal spirit of our colonial conduct, will instantly grant that the missionary enterprise, by powerfully tending to abolish the former, and to ameliorate the latter, has instrumentally averted a great national curse, and has proved a proportionate national blessing. The magnitude of the blessing, indeed, is unknown; for its moral influence will continue to extend through every coming generation of mankind, and its value to increase with every moment of time.*

SECTION II.

THE REFLEX SPIRITUAL BENEFITS OF CHRISTIAN MISSIONS.

BEFORE the distant regions of the earth are likely to be turned to the knowledge of the truth, says Douglas in his Advancement of Society, England herself will be evangelized in the act of evangelizing other nations. Whatever may be thought of this remark, we would venture to ask, if the sole object of Christian activity within the last fifty years had been the advancement of religion in our own land, in what other way could it have been better promoted than it has been by sending the gospel abroad? In other words, had the same amount of money and effort which the missionary object has absorbed, been devoted to the diffusion of the gospel at home, is there any reason to believe that our country would have reaped greater spiritual benefit than it is now enjoying by the

[* See Introduction.—T. O. S.]

reflex influence of Christian missions? The particulars following will furnish materials for a correct reply.

1. It is not for us to say at what moment, or in what mind, the heavenly purpose arose which God has graciously made the occasion of modern missionary instrumentality. Even were the circumstances submitted to our investigation, they would probably present a web of mutual influence far too complicated for us to unravel. To the eye of God, however, such a mind, and such a moment, are doubtless present. The conception of the purpose was an era in the history of the Christian Church, comparable only with the Reformation itself. And not less eventful to the *moral* condition of the world at large was the moment which saw its birth, than the hour in which Columbus determined to give a new world to the old, to their *temporal* concerns. And here, be it remarked, that He who hath made it "more blessed to give than to receive," began to bless the giver even before he could begin to impart—in the very act of intending and arranging to give. The mere announcement of the project was a blessing. *If only by helping to break up the monotony which extensively prevailed in the religious services and topics of the day*, it rendered a service to the Church which those who are accustomed to the variety of the present time can scarcely estimate.

2. The striking manner in which the missionary enterprise *enlivened the piety, and increased the happiness*, of those who first espoused it, may be illustrated best by the following quotations: "There was a period of my ministry," said the devoted Andrew Fuller to a friend, "marked by the most pointed systematic effort to comfort my serious people; but the more I tried to comfort them, the more they complained of doubts and darkness. . . . I knew not what to do, nor what to think, for I had done my best to comfort the mourners in Zion. At this time it pleased God to direct my attention to the claims of the perishing heathen in India; I felt that we had been living for ourselves, and not caring for their souls. I spoke as I felt. My serious people wondered and wept over their past inattention to the subject. They began to talk about a Baptist mission. The females especially began to collect money for the spread of the gospel. We met and prayed for the heathen; met and considered

what could be done amongst ourselves for them; met and did what we could. And, whilst all this was going on, the lamentations ceased. The sad became cheerful, and the desponding calm. No one complained of a want of comfort. And I, instead of having to study how to comfort my flock, was myself comforted by them. They were drawn out of themselves. Sir, that was the real secret. God blessed them while they tried to be a blessing."

"After the departure of our brethren"—the first Baptist missionaries to India—says the brief narrative of the Baptist mission,* "we had time for reflection. In reviewing the events of a few preceding months, we were much impressed. The thought of having done something towards enlarging the boundaries of our Saviour's kingdom, and of rescuing poor heathens and Mohammedans from under Satan's yoke, rejoiced our hearts. We were glad also to see the people of God offering so willingly; some leaving their country, others pouring in their property, and all uniting in prayers to Heaven for a blessing. A new bond of union was formed between distant ministers and churches. Some, who had backslidden from God, were restored; and others, who had long been poring over their unfruitfulness, and questioning the reality of their personal religion, having their attention directed to Christ and his kingdom, lost their fears, and found that peace which in other pursuits they had sought in vain. In short, our hearts were enlarged; and if no other good had arisen from the undertaking than the effect produced upon our own minds, and the minds of Christians in our own country, it was more than equal to the expense."†

3. The benefit of Christian activity became general; for the missionary spirit, *seizing in steady succession the various sections of the Christian community, quickened them all into emulation.* The movement of one department was a signal for the movement of every other. And long before the last tribe of our British Israel had unfurled its banners and followed the van, the Churches of America, excited by our example, gave "note of preparation," and took the field. In

---

* Second Report of the Southern Board [American] of Foreign Missions.
† Smith and Choules's History of Missions, vol. i., p. 189.

equally quick succession, their tribes came "forth to the help of the Lord," and were soon seen "provoking one another to love and to good works." Nor, indeed, has the hallowed provocation on either side of the Atlantic been confined, subsequently, to its own hemisphere. The identity of our object has given us a reciprocity of influence which places each separate portion of our respective communities under the impulse of the whole; so that a movement made by one is almost instantly felt by all. What an illustration has the working of our missionary institutions thus created, of the incalculable value and power of Christian influence!

4. Nor was the institution of one missionary society a signal for the establishment of other societies of the same kind, merely. The Spirit of God had moved upon the face of the ecclesiastical waters, and each succeeding period was distinguished by creations of its own. Like a true scion from the life-giving tree of prophetic vision, "which bare twelve manner of fruits," the missionary enterprise soon found itself *the stock of various kindred institutions.* While, judging from the subsequent renovation of some other societies of a prior existence, it has had the effect of fertilizing and improving institutions which it has not originated. So that, pointing at many of our associations and efforts for the distribution of Bibles and tracts; for the establishment of Sunday-schools, and the advancement of village evangelization, we may ask, Which of these did not receive either its existence, or its impulse, from the missionary enterprise?

5. And thus we have been gradually regaining the long-forgotten but invaluable conviction, *that the cause of religion at home and abroad is one.* If Christian missions have taught us, on the one hand, that the same principles which prompt us to train up our children in the fear of God, and to seek the salvation of those immediately around us, impel to evangelical efforts for the benefit of every portion of the human race, and that to attempt to separate living piety from expansive beneficence is almost as vain as it is unscriptural, by bringing to light new and fearful scenes of foreign destitution, and by thus arousing attention and quickening our Christian sensibilities, they have been the means, on the other, of preparing us to feel a livelier interest in the claims of home. Evils to which we had become resigned, because they were

continually before our eyes, and which escaped our animadversion almost as much as if they formed an inseparable part of the course of nature, have consequently been not only deplored, but successfully assailed. The reasons which are assigned for sending the gospel abroad, are felt to acquire augmented force when applied to the wants of the perishing at home. Besides which, the efforts which are made abroad are found to demand more than an equal effort at home to supply their expenditure. While this improvement at home, demanding a wider sphere than the country which gave it birth, is transferred to the unlimited range of missionary labor; and thus the infant-school of yesterday has its counterpart to-day in the glens of Africa, the Australian wilderness, and the islands of the Pacific; and what is gained for humanity in any one spot, is found not to impoverish any other, but to be gained for humanity throughout the world.*

6. By this and similar means, *the views of the Christian Church have been greatly enlarged.* The missionary enterprise could have been conceived only on the top of Pisgah. It refuses to entertain any design less than the amelioration of the species. Taking it for granted that every true interest is universal, it consults, as it prosecutes its march, the map of the world. Its appropriate type is an angel flying through the midst of heaven.

Even the discovery of a new continent, and the enlargement of the universe by the invention of the telescope, gave an impulse to Europe, the force of which is still felt, and still carrying us forward. And should the objects and prospects of the missionary enterprise produce impressions less powerful or sublime? So lofty is the mount of contemplation to which it conducts us, so boundless the prospect which it there stretches before us, and so completely does it familiarize our minds with the vast designs of God, and the ample plans of his providence, that our purposes may well seem to enlarge greatly beyond the proportion of our means. The statesman, who plans only to preserve the balance of empire, and whose scheme embraces an age beyond his own, is praised for the reach and comprehensiveness of his views. But what are the purposes formed, and the ends aimed at, by the friends

---

* Douglas's Advancement of Society, etc., p. 216.

of missions? They lie in a sphere so lofty, that the ambition of the warrior has never reached it, and require so ample a scope, that the policy of the statesman would be spent in it and lost. Their field is the world; and their aim is to carry the torch of truth into the shadow of death; to prepare the savage for society, and to give society a sure foundation; to rescue the slave from his chains, and to welcome him to the liberty of the gospel; to hush the discord of war, and to restore the various branches of the human race to each other by restoring them to God; and to see all the crowns of the world at the feet of Christ. These are their daily thoughts, their most familiar designs. If true greatness ennobles whatever it touches, must not the missionary enterprise tend to dignify all who voluntarily come under its influence? By employing us as its agents, it has involved us in the mightiest conflict which the universe ever saw, and has invested us with its own exalted character. It has given to the prayer, "Thy kingdom come," a sublimity in ten thousand eyes, which would otherwise have been blind to its grandeur. And twice ten thousand who, but for it, would most likely have been immured at this moment within their little denominational enclosure, and complaining, like Elijah, of their supposed isolation, are exhorting each other in the glowing language of Isaiah, and saying, "Lift up thine eyes round about and see: all they gather themselves together, they come to thee; thy sons come from afar, and thy daughters are nursed at thy side. Then thou shalt see and flow together, and thine heart shall fear and be enlarged; because the abundance of the sea shall be converted unto thee, the forces of the Gentiles shall come unto thee."

7. But such Christian enlargement of spirit *leads to the sympathetic union of all who become conscious of its expanding influence.* True, it must be deplored with deep humiliation before God that the cementing tendency of Christian missions has of late years met with lamentable interruptions. In the midst of those very interruptions, however, the missionary spirit, by often triumphing over them, has been the means of exemplifying the surpassing power of genuine piety, and of furnishing the strongest ground to hope for their final and utter removal. Forgetting their scruples and their preferences, the friends of missions have at times been seen accord-

ing their hearty support of the glorious gospel, by whomsoever diffused. With a happy inconsistency, they have hailed the missionary successes of others, and have thus crossed the denominational line of separation, and seized the fruits which belong to a season of visible union. While, by every prayer they have breathed for missionary efforts, they have been virtually affirming and consecrating this catholic principle, that it is becoming and scriptural to aid the diffusion of the gospel abroad, whoever the Christian agents may be; and to aid them in the mightiest of all forms, by invoking in their behalf the blessing of God.

But besides affirming this great principle of Christian sympathy, under circumstances the most adverse to more visible and entire union, the missionary enterprise has been extensively the means, under God, of preventing many a rupture which would otherwise have occurred, and of strengthening many a bond of attachment which would else have been burst asunder. As a fine illustration, we quote the following extract from the Report* of an American missionary society: "The whole business of forming these Boards [of Foreign Missions] was conducted in all three of the Synods with entire unanimity, and was felt by all to have exerted on these bodies, and on the cause of religion as they are related to it, a most happy influence. In the Synod of South Carolina and Georgia, the business was concluded by the unanimous adoption of the following resolution: 'Resolved, That this Synod acknowledge with gratitude the goodness of God, in bringing before them the great subject of foreign missions, and in directing them to a unanimous and blessed result.'" And a member of the Synod, a pastor of one of its most important churches, speaks of the influence of these proceedings as follows, in a letter to one of the secretaries: "This Synod has been by it saved from disunion and discord. It has been harmonized and united. It has been melted down into one mass. It has now one soul, and breathes one sentiment—to live, not for ourselves, or our own sectional interests, but for the conversion of the world. Such a happy, holy, rejoicing, and blessed meeting of Synod has never, according to the

---

* Twenty-fifth Annual Report of the American Board of Commissioners for Foreign Missions, 1834, pp. 80, 81.

opinion of the eldest members, been witnessed and enjoyed. There were dark and portentous clouds hanging over it. Every mind was filled with apprehension. Each feared to ask the sentiment of his brother. But the clouds are dispersed and gone. Our fears are changed into joys, and we parted from each other in the warmest interchange of brotherly affection. And all is attributable—and, by a solemn recorded resolution of the Synod, is ascribed—to the discussion of the missionary subject, and engagement in the missionary cause. The scene which occurred when we all stood up, after uniting in prayer, to adopt the whole constitution, was overpowering. There were few dry eyes, even of those unused to tears. There were frequent and loud sobbings. There was the solemnity of eternity. There was the cool intrepidity of a band of soldiers, preparing for a charge upon the citadel of an armed and enraged enemy. After adopting the constitution, we sang the missionary hymn, when it seemed that heaven heard the sound, and earth responded with a glad 'Amen.'"

8. But the same missionary enlargement of spirit which tends to unite all who partake of it into one sympathetic brotherhood, has also *led to the willing consecration of their property*. Such was the boundless benevolence of Christ, that "for the joy set before him," and which consisted partly in the prospect of human salvation, he "endured the cross, despising the shame." Was it, then, to be wondered at if his professed followers should so far share in his benevolence as to contribute a portion of their property for an object for which he gave "his own self?" Accordingly, the widow has been seen casting into the mission treasury of her penury, and the rich man of his abundance; and though the scale of Christian liberality is still far below the standard of the gospel, yet how much lower would it have been, humanly speaking, but for the ennobling influence of Christian missions! How many have been led to abandon the notion that we may allowably hoard up our property while we live, if we will only make a religious bequest of a certain proportion of it at death! Strange as it would have appeared to us all a few years ago, and strange as it seems even now to those who are behind their age, Christians can be found whose religious charities considerably exceed a tenth of their income. Mil-

lions have been contributed to Christian missions, a large proportion of which would otherwise have been given to "the lust of the flesh, and the lust of the eyes, and the pride of life." And the number is increasing of those who are ready to add to their other offerings upon the altar, themselves and their children.

In three respects especially has the missionary enterprise produced a most salutary effect on Christian liberality. It has shown that, like every other disposition, benevolence is strengthened by exercise; for in proportion as information concerning heathen wretchedness and Christian obligation to alleviate it has been circulated, every increased demand for Christian charity has been regularly met with an increased supply. 2. It has led many who gave from impulse only to contribute from principle, and on a system; and has thus given to charity the character of a holy philosophy. 3. And it has produced an auspicious dissatisfaction with the highest scale of liberality hitherto attained, and awakened a conviction that the pecuniary resources of a Church adequately alive to its obligations would, under the Divine administration of Him who multiplied a morsel into a feast for five thousand, prove indefinite and inexhaustible.

9. Nor has the missionary enterprise less directly *tended to awaken and cherish a spirit of prayer*. We have already spoken of the period when monthly missionary meetings for prayer were commenced as an era in the history of Christian missions; and though every division of the Christian community may not have formally adopted the same course, there is no portion perhaps which has not in consequence been favorably influenced; certainly none which the missionary spirit has not quickened into increased devotion. Owing to the same cause, how much greater a prominence has been given to the doctrine of Divine influence, and how much more deeply have thousands felt their dependence upon it! How many a public meeting has solemnly resolved to the effect, "That, recognizing their dependence on the gracious agency of the Holy Spirit for all success in labors for saving the heathen, and the indispensable importance of fervent and importunate supplication to Almighty God for this purpose," Christians should be exhorted and excited to increased intercession! And how many an instance of private devotion has

ensued, unknown to man, but witnessed by angels, and recorded in heaven, in which such resolutions have been carried into effect "with strong crying and tears!" Indeed, what is now the one ardent, all-comprehending desire of the holiest portion of the Christian Church but this, "Let the whole earth be filled with his glory?"—a desire which, in the eye of God, is equally a prayer, whether it be "uttered or unexpressed;" so that it may be regarded as always ascending; a desire which gives birth in every heart that cherishes it to a thousand kindred desires, each of which brings down the Divine blessing, not on the missionary enterprise alone, but on the entire field of Christian activity; and a desire which, as it cannot be urged in prayer without being fulfilled, so it cannot be fulfilled without multiplying the number of Christian suppliants, and thus filling the Church with intercessors for the world. "O Thou that hearest prayer, unto thee shall all flesh come."

10. *What noble specimens of Christian character has the missionary enterprise given to the Church and to the world!* The enterprise itself is a pure creation of Christianity. It is a combination, not of the worldly and selfish to advance their own peculiar interests; not of the powerful and the wealthy to tyrannize over the poor and the helpless; but an association of the great and the good, of the aged pastor, the ardent missionary, and the young disciple—of all that is excellent in the Christian Church; an association in which the wealth of the affluent, the tongue of the learned, the prayer of the poor, and the mite of the widow, are combined and engaged to give the gospel to all the tribes and nations of the earth.

But among the friends and agents of this unworldly confederation there are some whose character shines with peculiar lustre. Here female piety has recovered and displayed anew the glory which it won when it wept at the cross, and was early at the sepulchre. Here offerings more costly than those of the "sweet spices" of the sepulchre have been presented by the Christian Marys of modern times. Here many a mother, whom the world knows not, has, in the depth of her own heart, like the mother of Mills,[*] dedicated her offspring to a post of distant labor. What Spartan mother of

---

[*] Smith and Choules's History of Missions, vol. ii., p. 234.

old, when buckling on the armor of her son, and bidding him, as she gave him his shield, "either to bring it back, or to be brought back upon it," can compare with the widowed mother of Lyman, when she replied to the intelligence that her son had been murdered by the cannibal Battas, "I bless God, who gave me such a son to go to the heathen, and I never felt so strongly as I do at this moment the desire that some others of my sons may become missionaries also, and may go and preach salvation to those savage men who have drunk the blood of my son."* What ancient Hebrew women, receiving "their dead raised to life again," surpassed the self-denying faith of the widowed mother who could say of a son to whom herself and her seven children were beginning to look for support, "Let him go: God will provide for me and my babes. And who am I, that I should be thus honored to have a son a missionary to the heathen?" and who, when that son had labored successfully in India, and had died, could say of a second, who aspired to walk in the footsteps of his brother, "Let William follow Joseph, though it be to India, and an early grave?"† Here the accomplished and highly intellectual female may be seen meekly, yet firmly, devoting herself to a distant and arduous career: vying with the hero in his defiance of dangers, and with the martyr in the endurance of them. If self-devotion deserve our applause, who can present a stronger claim than Harriet Newell? If the heroic endurance of suffering is to be embalmed in the memory, who deserves a brighter memorial than Anne Hazeltine Judson?

But to speak of all the examples of moral greatness associated with the missionary enterprise, is to speak of a number which "the time would fail me to tell." Who does not think of those men of the western wilderness who first taught us in modern times *how* the savage is to be reclaimed? Who does not think of the Moravian heroes of Greenland and Labrador in the north; of the early mission to Tranquebar in the east; and of those who first toiled and fell in Africa, south? and who can think of them without feeling that, under God, they and their successors have served, and saved the character of, the Christian Church?

To admire self-devotion and noble daring in theory only is

---

* Holt's Missionary Anecdotes, p. 260.   † Idem, p. 262.

cheap virtue; and yet, prior to the rise of missions, but few Christians were doing more than this. If the rising offspring of religious parents would read of wasting privations endured, of dangers braved and vanquished, and of conflicts attempted and achieved—the most attractive topics for the young—they had to seek them in the pages of the enterprising merchant, the soldier, or the scientific traveller. To practice self-denial which should be repaid only by conscience, to think of beneficence without fame, to do any thing more than admire the disinterested zeal of the reformers, confessors, and missionaries of former times, would have been deemed not less impracticable by the Church, generally, than irrational by the world. Now, to the men who have been raised up by God in the service of modern missions we are greatly indebted for the termination of this guilty delusion. They have shown that the Church need not be tame and uninteresting in its character; that the world need not be allowed to monopolize all that is fascinating in youthful eyes; that real greatness need not be suspended in the clouds, and admired as a rainbow, but that it may be brought down and embodied in actual life. Who does not feel that their example has instrumentally created in the Church the atmosphere of a nobler piety, and that we are living under its influence?

The lowest benefit they have conferred is, that they have robbed the apathetic of their plea; so that, till the voice of history shall be dumb, wherever an effort shall be made to invade the kingdom of darkness, their example will be present to silence the objection that, though the theory is good, it is impossible to put it in practice. There is virtue even in their memory. It imposes a restraint on the worldliness of thousands. As their professed admirers, we feel ourselves bound not to fall too glaringly below their standard of excellence.

But if they are only preventing some from falling below a certain point, they are exciting numbers to rise. And who does not recognize the wisdom of God in appointing that some of the pioneers in the modern missionary field should have been giants in holy daring and strength, and, as such, fitted to be exemplars to all who came after them in the same career? In the vocabulary of the Church, their names have become synonyms for every species of active excellence.

Eliot, Zeisberger, and Brainerd, are but other names for indefatigable labor and enterprise, and self-consuming ardor. We think of Swartz, and the might of character. The accomplished youth, panting to live for Christ in distant lands, but derided as a visionary, thinks of Martyn, and takes courage. Pious and disinterested poverty reads of Carey, and emerges from its humble cell to perform labors which excite the devout thanksgiving of the Church. Faith looks at the origin and early history of the Moravian mission, and, undismayed by the scantiness of her human resources, girds up the loins of her mind, and addresses herself to her task afresh. Their biography is creating for the Church a literature of its own. Their example is reproducing itself in a second race. To the influence of Brainerd the Church is chiefly indebted, under God, for the labors of a Milne. The pious father gives their names to his sons, as a title of excellence, and an incitement to attain it. Their zeal for God has kindled a fire at which numbers daily are lighting their torch. And thus, in various ways, have they given ardor to holy activity, and multiplied the power of truth; while the Church below unites with the Church above in "glorifying God in them."

11. Owing to some of the particulars last enumerated it is that the Christian Church has been gradually awakened to the practicability of the missionary enterprise, and to *the conviction that it is the duty of all its members to espouse it.* The rising children of the Church may regard this duty as so self-evident that it could never have been doubted. They are to be assured, however, that its practical admission is but of recent date, and that their fathers in Christ had first to be convinced of it themselves, and then laboriously to convince others. They are to be assured that it was but as yesterday that Christians generally were regarding the enormous abominations of paganism with a kind of submissive awe, as if they had been inevitable conditions of humanity; or, if they thought of their ultimate removal, it was expected only as the result of a miraculous intervention which it was almost presumptuous in them to urge, and in prospect of which it became them rather to "stand still and see the salvation of God." Meanwhile, the heathen were perishing through their neglect. He who had laid all their powers under tribute for the service, was "walking in the midst" of them, and repeat-

ing, " Go into all the world, preach my gospel to every creature;" and the guilt of centuries of disobedience, accumulated at their door, was daily and hourly rising higher. Who, then, can duly estimate the magnitude of the benefit conferred on the Church by that instrumentality by which it has been aroused to attempt the salvation of those heathen, to obey that high command, and, at least, to prevent that mountain of guilt from rising higher? Yet such is the nature of the benefit conferred by the missionary enterprise. Not only has it been the means of creating lofty specimens of individual Christian character—it has given a new character to the collective Church. The knowledge which it has circulated even in the most retired parts of the country, and among the lowest ranks of society, concerning the state of the heathen, has moved the compassion of the faithful generally. By the enforcement of scriptural obligation on the subject, it has made them all feel, in different degrees, that every one can do something. By the organization of auxiliary societies, it has excited and engaged the aid of the humblest, and seeks to engage the coöperation of all. By the noble examples of self-consecration which it has placed before the Church, numbers have been led to inquire whether or not they are living as they ought for the conversion of the world. While, with each returning year, the sentiment of a thousand resolutions proposed at public meetings, and responded to by twice ten thousand hearts, is substantially this—"that more must be done." In this way the Church is becoming more than ever militant and aggressive. The spirit of missions is felt to be the true spirit of the gospel. The noblest ambition is aroused,— the ambition of turning the world's darkness into an empire of light and peace.

12. But by conferring this benefit on the Church, and directing its attention to the state of the world, the missionary enterprise has been gradually *reducing the strongholds of infidelity*, and "taking from it the arms wherein it trusted." As far as the assaults of this monster evil have been made, at any time, against the grounds of our faith, Christians have only themselves to thank. That the world should voluntarily lay aside its hostility to holiness, do whatever the Church may, is not to be expected; but that hostility is divisible into

two kinds—that which is directed against Christianity, and that which is aimed at its professors. And what Christian would not rather that it should be levelled at his own character, than at that of the gospel, or of his ever-blessed Lord? And who does not perceive, judging from the history of the Church, that Christians may generally choose which shall be the object of the world's attack—the gospel or its professors? Let them take the field, act on the aggressive, carry their arms into the enemies' country, and we hear scarcely a word against the truth of the gospel: we give the world no leisure to indulge in speculative skepticism; it finds enough to do in stigmatizing our character as hypocrites, enthusiasts, and fanatics. But let us quit the field, shut ourselves up in self-indulgence within the walls of the Church, and the world will advance, as an earthly army in similar circumstances would do, and will sap and mine our defences as the only means of reaching and destroying us. Our indolence, in that case, leaves it nothing else to do.

Now the effect of modern missions, on the tactics of infidelity, illustrates the truth of these remarks. Where now is the infidelity of Spinoza and the Pantheists; of Bayle and academic doubts; of Voltaire and ridicule; of Hume, Gibbon, and Rousseau? Since the missionary enterprise commenced, it has almost entirely changed its ground and its weapons. Was it one of its favorite objections that the apathy of Christians for the heathen demonstrated that they did not believe their own book? Every additional missionary that goes forth is assisting to convert that objection, from a weapon of attack, into a means of Christian defence. Was the extreme limitation of Christendom, as compared with the world at large, another of the objections on which it relied? Every new region reclaimed from idolatry, and every additional Church planted in heathen lands, blunt the edge of this objection. After pointing with scorn at the contracted limits of Christendom, did it then pour ridicule on Christians for attempting to enlarge those bounds? But this could have arisen only from the supposed impotence of the gospel by which they proposed to effect the change. So conspicuous, however, have been the triumphs of the cross, in many of the most hopeless parts of the heathen world, that even the magicians of worldly philosophy themselves begin to acknowledge that "this is the finger of God," and to despair of ever being able to "do the same with their enchantments."

13. But besides assisting to disarm infidelity, the missionary enterprise has eminently *promoted the cause of biblical study, augmented the evidences of Christianity, and proportionally increased our confidence in the divinity of its character, and in the certainty of its ultimate triumphs.* If sacred science be distributed into the critical or verbal, the devout or practical, and the scientific or theological, the cultivation of the first of these may be considered as laudably characteristic of the present day. Now, whatever advantage may accrue from this source to the cause of truth in general, must be ascribed, partly, if not chiefly, to the influence of Christian missions. For by creating a demand for the circulation of the Holy Scriptures in heathen lands, and by securing their translation into many of the languages of the earth, it has, in conjunction with the Bible Society, necessarily led to the unprecedented cultivation of this important branch of sacred study. And even as to the other departments, which we have specified, the influence of missions has conferred on the Church a greater benefit than all the theological polemics of the last century; for if it has not confuted any heresy, it has rendered perhaps a still more important service, in causing some to be practically extinguished and forgotten. While, by the new demands which it has devolved on the Church, and the new relations which we find ourselves called to sustain, the entire Bible has come to assume a comparatively missionary character. Not merely single verses, but whole masses of truth, have acquired a meaning and an importance in our eyes, before unknown.

The missionary enterprise has contributed in various ways to *illustrate the divinity of the gospel.* It assumes that men are everywhere the same—guilty and depraved. But who could be aware of the fact except "the God of the whole earth?" When the gospel was written, vast regions of the earth remained to be explored, and populous countries to be discovered. How, then, could the writers of the gospel have accurately described the character of men in unknown lands, if they had not "spoken as they were moved by the Holy Ghost?" Infidelity has often essayed to prove that the depravity of man admits of large exceptions; that in some states of society he is innocent; and that nothing but the discovery of a new people was wanting to demonstrate the truth of its theory. Who, then, could sketch a likeness of man, which men of all times and tongues should recognize as their own, but He who "knew what was in man?" By the same means, *the universal adaptation of the gospel has received the most striking additional proof.* Not only have missionaries in India been charged by the natives with forging its faithful delineations of heathenism after their arrival in that country, but when it has filled the soul with a sense of guilt approaching to agony, and which nothing human could allay, it has further demonstrated its divinity by saying, "Peace, be still, and there was a great calm." How often has the convert from heathenism acknowledged, like Cupido, the well-known Hottentot, that, while listening to the gospel for the first time, he was compelled involuntarily to exclaim, "This is the truth : that is what I want!" At the bare announcement of the words, "The blood of Jesus Christ, his Son, cleanseth us from all sin," the devotee walking on spikes to atone for his guilt has thrown off his torturing sandals, and exclaimed, ".This is what I need," and has become "a living exposition of the truth." "'How beautiful, how tender, how kind,'—Anundo, a pupil in the General Assembly's school, Calcutta, was often heard to exclaim, while reading the Sermon on the Mount—'How full of love and goodness! O, how unlike the spirit and maxims of Hindooism! Surely this is the truth!' Never was there a more striking exemplification of what Owen calls 'the self-evidencing power of the Bible.'"* And so strong and sufficient does this self-commending internal evidence prove, that missionary converts are almost uniformly found to embrace the gospel independently of its external proofs. But this circumstance itself is additional evidence in its behalf. Hindooism, without leaving its native land to challenge examination, has been falsified and disproved. The microscope alone has laid its pretensions in the dust, by proving that the Maker of infusoria and animalculæ could not have been the author of its Shastres. Ge-

---

* Holt, p. 129; furnished by Rev. Dr. Duff, in the Scots Presbyterian Review.

ography has done the same for Mohammedanism, by showing that the "God of the whole earth" could not have been the author of the Koran; for to require its disciples, during the Ramadan, to fast from the rising to the setting of the sun, is to proclaim its ignorance of the arctic and antarctic circles. But wherever Christianity has gone, it has derived additional evidence of its self-commending excellence and universal adaptation; thus strengthening our conviction that the Maker of man and the Author of the gospel is one—" the only living and true God."

Still further is this conviction deepened by the illustration which the missionary enterprise affords *of the saving power of the gospel.* Had the primitive Christians been perplexed with doubts concerning the sufficiency of the gospel to meet cases of extreme depravity, how eminently fitted was the conversion of Saul of Tarsus to remove them! After him, of whom need they despair? Now, that the Christians of modern times did very generally entertain doubts of this description, is matter of authentic record. Whatever they might hope from its introduction among the civilized and inquiring, they were more than distrustful of its reception among the barbarous. How solemn but gracious a rebuke, then, have missionary successes been the means of administering to our unbelief, and what illustrious evidence have they supplied that the gospel is still "the power of God unto salvation to every one that believeth!" If Christianity has conquered Tahiti and Labrador, New Zealand and Caffraria, what country can stand before it when accompanied by the grace of its Author?

In the history of its progress we recognize almost every display of gracious power of which the mind can conceive. It has melted the inflexible Iroquois into penitence and tears; and has enabled the shrinking Hindoo to brave the loss of caste and the martyr's pangs. By a mightier exorcism than the negro or the Esquimaux had ever imagined, it has delivered the one from the enslaving fears of the Obeah, and cast out the terrible Torngak from the creed of the other. What other evidence of its power can be necessary? Under its subduing and humanizing influence, the convert from the frozen zone has been hailed as a brother in Christ by the Christian Indian in his native wilderness, and the once savage warrior of America has sent letters of peace and love to the fisher of Greenland. At its sound the barbarian veteran of a hundred battles, and of a hundred years, has become a little child; and a host of warriors, each of whom would once have preferred death to a tear, have wept, "so that there was a very great mourning, like the mourning of Hadadrimmon."* What other evidence can be necessary? Instruments which had never been used but for war and murder, it has converted to useful and even sacred purposes;† and tribes which had never met but in deadly conflict, it assembles together around the table of the Lord. It has declined no contest through fear of defeat; and wherever it has gone, it has erected monuments of its saving power.

What other evidence can be necessary? To my mind, says the eloquent Richard Watson, there is nothing in the history of the Church which so strikingly exhibits the power of our religion, as its triumphs over the moral evils so uniformly and necessarily inherent in a system of slavery. Glorious were the effects of Christianity among the slaves of the ancient world. It gave cheerfulness to submission, and patience to wrong; it created charity where gratitude could have no place; shut the lip of reproach, and silenced murmuring. But owing to the greater evils of modern slavery, religion, in our colonies, has triumphed more gloriously still. Its light has penetrated, so to speak, the solid darkness of mind left without instruction; it has struck the chords of feeling in hearts unaccustomed to salutary emotion; it has reconciled man to the degradation of color and feature; it has produced charity towards those who have dealt out to them the most humbling kinds of insult; breathed over passions which, when once awakened, are terrible, the calm of resignation; and taught the spirit, spurned from every other resting-place, to rest in God, and to wait for his salvation.‡

What other evidence of its power can be necessary? Among its converts are men whose depravity would have compared with that of a Jeroboam, a Manasseh, or a Saul of Tarsus: Ananke, the Esquimaux murderer; and the Mohican, Tschoop,

---

* Brainerd's Journal.
† Ellis's Polynesian Researches, vol. ii., p. 519.
[‡ See Introduction.—T. O. S.]

a monster of debauchery and vice; Africaner, the plunderer of neighboring tribes, and the destroyer of missionary settlements; Tamatoa, once blasphemously worshipped as a god; Vaza, the procurer of human sacrifices; and Romatane, the devastator of islands. By the ministry of the gospel, the Saviour speaks to them as from heaven, and "behold, they pray!" The epitome of vice becomes an epistle of Christ. The demon is transformed into "a pattern of the believers." The sanguinary chief is the first to beseech and adjure, with tears of entreaty, those to whom his name had been a terror, and whose race he had almost exterminated, to embrace salvation. What other evidence of its power can be necessary? If the success of the gospel on its first promulgation forms an evidence of its divinity, the success of the modern missionary enterprise must be received as an additional evidence to the same effect. It has been attended with spiritual triumphs of the same kind, and which can only be resolved into the same supernatural cause. Then surely our confidence in its sufficiency, as the instrument of human salvation, should be proportionally increased. Thus it was with the apostles.' And if doubts of the Divine sufficiency of the gospel ever haunted our minds, imparting feebleness to its ministry, and creating indifference as to its diffusion, what should, what must be the effect of its subsequent triumphs, but to impart ardor to our activity, and earnestness to our prayers, and a moral dignity to our onward step, eminently conducive, through God, to still greater success?

14. And not only has the missionary enterprise increased our confidence in the final conversion of the heathen—it has been attended by *the salvation of many of our own countrymen, both at home and abroad.* In commencing our remarks on the reflex spiritual influence of Christian missions, we adverted to the service they had incidentally rendered the Church in helping to break up the prevailing monotony of its religious occupations. Who can doubt but that, humanly speaking, many a youth whom that monotony would have repelled, has been held, by the new attraction of Christian activity, in allegiance to the outward service of God, till renewing grace has changed his heart? And who can question but that the missionary spirit, thus excited and bound up with early associations, has given its character to the man,

and is animating and determining the useful course of many, who, but for this, would have been lost to the Church, and devoted to the world? Indeed, the conversion of some has actually taken place, not in the sanctuary, and by the ordinary means of grace, but at the public meetings of our religious societies.

Still more marked have been the saving effects of the missionary cause upon our countrymen abroad. Between thirty and forty years ago, Buchanan wrote, "There are not ten righteous men to be found in Calcutta." "At that time," says another missionary, "you might have travelled from one extremity of India to the other, and have found no premonition of the Sabbath-day except the waving of flags at the military stations. As to the mercantile classes, to have closed a single house of agency on the Sabbath, would have been looked on as a strange deviation from the customs of commercial life. Now, it would be deemed as strange a departure from decorum in India, were a single commercial house to keep open its doors on that sacred day." Then, many of our countrymen went .there, not only almost as much strangers to the gospel of peace as were the Hindoos and Mohammedans themselves, but, amidst the polluting influence of heathenism, they became ten times more the children of hell than they were before they left their native shores. Now, among all classes, but especially the various armies in Her Majesty's and in the Honorable Company's service, a redeeming change is exhibited to a most remarkable extent. Many an officer emulates "the centurion of the Italian band," in devout and active piety. Many a regiment has its "praying company," and its active agents of Christian benevolence. Many a prodigal has there been met by missionary instrumentality; has himself become a missionary, and preached the faith which he once destroyed; and many others, after an absence in India of ten, fifteen, or twenty years, have returned to be the means of the conversion of their own parents, and to prove distinguished blessings where once they had been a curse.

15. And *innumerable are the occasions with which Christian missions have furnished the Church for glorifying God.* Not only did the design itself originate with God, in the sense of its being a duty to be found in his gospel, but, on looking

back and remembering the stony indifference to that design evinced by the Church in general; and the actual opposition to the first steps of the missionary enterprise, offered by many a professed Christian; and the truly insignificant measures in which the work began—measures in which the actors often owed their toleration to contempt—who can doubt that the primary human movers were themselves moved by God? If the apostle could say of the primitive Churches, "They glorified God in me," how often have we been constrained to recognize the hand of God in raising up and baptizing with a measure of the apostolic spirit many a modern missionary! If they acknowledge the Divine superintendence in selecting their spheres of labor, and preparing the way for their successful occupation, how often have we been called to adore the presence of the same agency in the missionary field, manifested in unexpected interpositions, in the universal concurrence of multiplied and repellent circumstances, and in the issue of the whole in some most unforeseen success! How many a burst of sacred joy has been occasioned by the intelligence of new conquests achieved over heathenism, and new honors accumulated around the name we love—joy, the most pure, ennobling, and rich, which grace can awaken in the faithful on earth, and which, more than any other sentiment, connects the Church below with the Church above in one spontaneous ascription of praise!

As to the manner in which some of the most distinguished of these triumphs were won: who can mark the sudden abandonment of idolatry in the Polynesian islands north and south—in the latter, when the mission was on the point of being relinquished in despair; and in the former, by the spontaneous will of the natives before any missionary had reached them—without perceiving how evidently God designed to secure the glory of the work to himself? How often and how emphatically have we been taught the same lesson by the superior success which has crowned the artless efforts of the native teachers—success which has frequently left the British missionary nothing to do, but, like Barnabas, to go and see the grace of God, and be glad. On comparing the missionary contributions and activity of the Churches at present—small as they still are—with the apathy of the past, and remembering the grandeur of the results to which they tend, how many a Christian has been led to say, with the mingled abasement and gratitude of David, "Who am I, and what is my people, that we should be able to offer so willingly after this sort, . . . to build thee a house for thine holy name?" What deep humiliation has been felt by thousands—and never perhaps was more deeply felt than at this moment—at the fact that the heathen world is crying to us for spiritual help, and perishing in its cries; that God is saying to us by his word and providence, "Hasten to their relief with the gospel," and yet that we should be so deplorably unprepared to obey! What grateful admiration, that God should have afforded us so many distinguished proofs that he is still in the midst of us; and what earnest entreaties that he would arouse the entire Church to a sense of its new and vast obligations, and would graciously pour out upon us his Spirit from on high! The direct tendency of all our missionary operations hitherto is to bring the Church on its knees before God in unfeigned gratitude for the past, and entire dependence for the future; prepared to inscribe on the sublime result of the whole, "To the praise of the glory of his grace."

From this review of the spiritual benefits of Christian missions on the Churches at home, we repeat the question with which the section commenced, in the full expectation that it admits but of one reply: Had the same amount of effort which the missionary object has received been devoted to the diffusion of piety at home, is there any reason to conclude that our country would have reaped greater advantage than it is now enjoying from the reflex influence of that object? Is it likely that more would have been done to impress a deep, salutary, and general conviction of the infinite importance of the gospel; more to call forth the resources and multiply the agencies of Christian usefulness; more to counteract the worldliness of the Church, and to give enlargement and elevation to its views and affections; more to illustrate the excellence, and to raise the standard, of Christian charity; more to silence the irreligious objector, to engage the intercessions of the faithful in the behalf of the world, to fill us with devout dependence and holy anticipation for the future, and to prepare the Church to arise and shine as the light of the world, and to prove, through God, a universal blessing? So far from this, we venture to affirm that not only would less have been done in all these respects, but that, humanly speaking, had it not been for the influence of the missionary cause, many a society now in active operation expressly for home would never have come into existence; many a heart, which now beats high with a hallowed patriotism, would have been cold to the claims of home; and many a Christian Church, now known as the centre of a large circumference of local benevolence, would have been comparatively living to itself. And, indeed, what is all this but saying, in effect, that the history of Christian missions will eventually be found to furnish a grand illustration of that sublime principle of a kingdom founded in love, that " it is more blessed to give than to receive ?"

CHAPTER IV.

ARGUMENT DERIVED FROM THE BENEFITS OF CHRISTIAN MISSIONS FOR THE INCREASED ACTIVITY OF THE CHRISTIAN CHURCH.

IF the Christian Church is expressly designed to embody and diffuse the influence of the cross, and if its full efficiency for this end depends, under God, on the entireness of its consecration to this office, we may expect to find that every page of its history illustrates and corroborates the fact. Such is the remark with which we opened this Second Part. But as the nature and limits of our subject forbade us to open the volume of ecclesiastical history, we contented ourselves with remarking generally, that the period of the first and greatest activity of the Church was the season of its greatest prosperity; that the subsequent decline of its devotedness was the decline of its prosperity; and that, as every departure of the Church from its missionary design has been invariably avenged, so every return to that character may be expected to be Divinely acknowledged and blessed. Such a return, in part, we professed to recognize in the operations and aims of our Protestant missions. And the subsequent chapters have been intended to enable us to show that, as far as their history is concerned, it may be made most clearly and impressively evident that every step in return to the aggressive design of the Christian Church is a proportionate return to its first prosperity. It remains, therefore, that we make such use of those chapters as shall tend to render this fact apparent; thus connecting them with the former part, and strengthening the whole by enforcing the additional motive supplied to entire Christian consecration.

I. Now, this may be done by showing, first, that *our missionary success has been fully proportioned to our efforts.* Perhaps the only persons disposed to question this proportion of success will be found among those who would have been the last to commence those efforts. For it is characteristic of a certain class, that, though they would never have originated an enterprise, they are among the earliest and the loudest in their complaints if it is not speedily crowned with complete success. No sooner do they awake from the slumber of doing nothing, than they seem to expect that every thing will rush to their aid, and are mortified at finding that they are doomed, like all their predecessors, to work by means and not by charms. But we would ask such persons what is the standard by which, in the present instance, they regulate their expectations of success. Is it by the rapidity with which the gospel was diffused in apostolic times? But surely they do not expect this, independently of the zeal, self-denial, and earnest supplications which distinguished those times. Or would they say that the proportion of success now is much less, as compared with the means employed, than it was at that time, even allowing for the present diminution of zeal? But how is the rate of this diminution to be ascertained? and yet, until it is, an essential element of the question remains undetermined. The truth is, that although the Church of late has begun to exhibit a spirit of missionary activity, of zeal it knows comparatively little. We might ask the persons supposed, for instance, How many years, or rather how many hours, have *you* given to this object of your professed solicitude? To how many seasons of wrestling in prayer with God; and to how many acts of practical self-denial; and to how many efforts to enkindle the zeal of others, has it led? Do you not think that it will be high time for you to complain of slender success, when you can return a less self-condemnatory answer to inquiries such as these?

Or would they regulate their expectations of success abroad by the standard of home? But we have shown, in a preceding chapter, that much of our domestic prosperity itself is ascribable, under God, to the reflex influence of our evangelical operations abroad. Independently of this, however, could we only bring together the happy results of those operations from the various parts of the wide field over which they are scattered, and place them beside the fruits which religion has reaped within the same period at home—making, of course, the necessary allowance for the vast disproportion of means—we should see that, if these fruits at home call for ordinary thankfulness, the results abroad demand the loftiest ascriptions of praise.

Are we asked, then, to sum up the benefits resulting from Christian missions? Enumerate them we can, and have; but estimate their value we cannot. We have no standard by which to rate the worth of even their temporal, much less of their spiritual advantages. We can refer the inquirer to the temporal good they confer on the land which sends them forth; and if he be a patriot, he will rejoice to hear of it. But unless he can furnish us with an instrument for determining the value of literature and science; of correct and enlarged views of the actual condition of man; of our own national character; of human life; of commerce; and of safety and supplies for our shipping; we must leave the precise worth of that good to his own imagination; for in all these respects have they been eminently useful. Does he ask for vouchers? Let him consult the records of learned societies; the voluntary testimony of disinterested travellers; the "Evidence on the Aborigines;" the incidental as well as direct testimony in official reports and government returns, to all of which we have distinctly referred. Let him ask the crew just liberated from cannibal hands, at what price they rate the value of the missionary influence which has saved them, and let him ascertain how many crews would by this time have been sacrificed but for that influence; or what would have been the amount of the waste of European life before commerce could have obtained even a footing in those barbarous regions where, owing to that same influence, it now finds a welcome and a home? Let him do this, and we will leave him to his own conclusions respecting its value.

Is he a philanthropist? We can take him into the distant missionary field, and point him to happy homes and peaceful villages rising amidst wastes where lately man roamed restless and ferocious as the beasts with which he contested for supremacy: to multitudes, now diligently busied in the arts of civilized life, whose hands were but yesterday red with the blood of their fellows: to thousands of children and adults trooping to their respective schools, where, a short time ago, all the visible signs of a language were utterly unknown : to organized societies and the ascendency of law, where, but recently, to be lawless was reckoned essential to enjoyment, and to kill at pleasure the highest prerogative : to sober, honest, highly moralized countries, where, lately, rage and intemperance revelled at will : to tribes which till lately never met but for mutual destruction, but whose intercourse now consists entirely in the reciprocation of benefits and tokens of love : to the animalized savage, acting the man : to the debased slave, now walking at large as an heir of freedom : to degraded woman, raised from the dust and restored to be the partner of man : to hundreds of thousands rescued from the curse of the darkest idolatry, and brought into the light of truth, and surrounded with the means of social improvement and unending happiness. But this is not enough. Having surveyed the happy change, let him place in strong imaginary contrast with it what would probably have been at this moment the actual state of all those human beings had it not been for missionary intervention. Let him imagine how many of those women and slaves would have pined and perished under brutal oppression : how certainly those implements of peace would all have been in request as weapons of murder and war; how many of those children would have been immolated ; how many of those islands would have been depopulated, and of those tribes exterminated; and then in what way the wretched survivors would most likely have been now employed. Let him then say, if he can, what is the value of the change which has been produced ; of the knowledge by which all that ignorance which was in actual possession has been displaced; of the morality and freedom by which all that vice, bondage, and idolatry have been swept away ; of the humanity by which that effusion of human blood has been prevented, and all those lives been saved; and of those moral principles, and social habits, by which all that has yet taken place will only be employed as means of improvement for all the future. Let him do this, and we will tell him the worth of the missionary enterprise to the cause of philanthropy.

Or is he who urges the inquiry a Christian ? To you, we might reply, to you we can speak of spiritual results. Not that you value the temporal benefits less than the patriot or the philanthropist, for you are both; but that you value the spiritual blessings more. Tell us, if you can, how all the property by which the missionary object has been sustained would have been employed; how all the time would have been spent which has been occupied in collecting, pleading, and laboring for the object, or in reading and hearing of it; and what would have been the character of all the myriads of thoughts and feelings which would, during that time, have left their eternal signature on the mind, had that object never existed to engage and engross it; for, in order to compute its value, it is necessary to know the evil which it has been the means of preventing, as well as the positive good which it has been instrumental in producing. Tell us, if you can, the value of that knowledge which maketh wise unto salvation; of that love which passeth knowledge; and of that peace which passeth all understanding, and we will tell you the worth of missionary instrumentality, for it has been the means of imparting all these to thousands. Tell us, in answer to the question of our common Lord, "What shall it profit a man if he gain the whole world, and yet lose his own soul?" and from the amount of that fearful loss we will compute the gain of missionary instrumentality, for it has been the means of saving the souls of thousands. Tell us, or ask the redeemed in glory to tell, by what line we can sound the depths of that pit from which they have escaped; by what scale we can take the height of the bliss to which they have attained; or where are the balances in which we can lay an eternal weight of glory, and we will tell you the value of missionary labor; for it has instrumentally saved thousands from hell, and prepared them for heaven. Think of the state in which the Christian missionary found "the nations of them that are saved;" of that horrid system composed of lies, and crimes, and curses, and woes, which he found in tyrannical possession; of the dreadful aspect with which it confronted heaven; of its mad devotedness to the spirit and purposes of hell. But now, see, the whole has vanished. The first house they build is the house of God. Almost their only book is the Bible. Among their days they now number and keep holy the Christian Sabbath. And almost the only form of society they know is that of the Christian Church. "Behold, the tabernacle of God is with men," and he graciously dwells among them. If you could not have looked down, with Balaam, upon the vast encampments of Israel on the plains of Moab, without emotions of delight: if you could not have witnessed the scenes of Pentecost, or have "seen the grace of God at Antioch," without being "glad," how can you adequately express your gratitude and joy at beholding these fruits of Christian missions? If you are truly conscious of Christian compassion, think of all the bodily sufferings, the moral evils, the mental anguish, which they have been the means of preventing or removing; of the hope, and peace, and joy, they have imparted on earth; of that "wrath to come," from which they have instrumentally snatched immortal souls; and of that "joy of your Lord," to which they have introduced them; and you will fall down afresh and bless God for the honor which he has put on the missionary enterprise. If you are sincerely "jealous for the Lord of hosts," think of all the instances in which they have been the means of converting idol temples into places of Christian worship; of disparaging idolatry in the very spot where for ages it had reigned; and of calling the idolater himself to join in the worship of the only living and true God. And think what honor has, in every such instance, been put on the love of the Father, on the mediation of Christ, and on the agency of the Holy Spirit; with what infinite complacency they have contemplated the glorious change; and what strains of seraphic joy it has called forth among the angels of God; and you will gratefully acknowledge, with a depth of conviction which, perhaps, you never felt before, that our missionary success has immeasurably exceeded the proportion of our efforts.

Yes, exceeded! for think how recently those efforts were commenced. The generation that began them has not yet entirely passed away. How much of the short time which has since elapsed has been necessarily consumed in preparatory work: in learning the languages of the people visited; translating the Scriptures into these languages; preparing elementary books; instructing the natives to read; in erecting the requisite machinery, and bringing it into working order! How many alterations and improvements have been suggested; and how much we had to learn, as to the best method of conducting missionary labors! And how small a proportion of the Church even yet is zealously engaged in promoting them! Many of these disheartening considerations were graciously allowed to remain hidden from the eyes of those who originated the missionary enterprise. But could we ask the most sanguine among them whether, notwithstanding, the event had equalled their first expectations of success, and could we show them at the same time all the salutary influence which that enterprise has reflected on the cause of religion at home, we should hear from them all a repetition of the grateful language, so often on their lips, "What hath God wrought! He hath done exceeding abundantly above all we asked or thought!"

Nor have our missionary successes exceeded our expectations in a single respect only. They have been the means of accomplishing good of a kind which we did not contemplate. Who thought, for instance, of their benefiting the slave in any but a religious respect? And had any one been heard to pray that they might lead to his emancipation, he would certainly have been silenced for his indiscretion or his presumption. So remote was such an issue from our views, that for years our missionaries rather concealed the miseries of the slave, lest, by displeasing the planter, they should be denied access to the objects of their solicitude. And yet to missionary influence, under God, the abolition of slavery is unquestionably to be ascribed.*

Nor has the *sphere* of this influence less exceeded our expectations than the kind of good which it has effected. We thought only of sending the gospel to heathen lands; but *our own country*, as we have seen, has been a gainer, by the enterprise, of the richest blessings.

And as in the sphere, so in the *time* when this reflex influence began to operate. While we were calculating on the good to result to others in a coming period, we found ourselves in actual possession. In merely designing to bless, we ourselves were blessed. The benefit flowing from Christian missions dates, not from the first year of their existence, nor from their first hour, but from their earliest moment. From that auspicious moment to the present, they have been discharging on the Churches, generally, showers of the richest influence. And have they been the means of doing so much

[* See Introduction.—T. O. S.]

good? Why did we not begin them sooner? and why are we not now prosecuting them with greater zeal?

II. We may expect to find also that advantages have flowed from our returning activity which nothing else could have conferred. And the reason of this is sufficiently obvious:—the planet is now moving in its appointed orbit: the Church is advancing in a line with the purposes of Omnipotence, and in harmony with its own principles. If, before, it had been hampered with forms, customs and corruptions, at every effort which it now makes to move, some portion of these old incrustations of evil fall off: a desire to advance aright sends it to consult the word of God; a concern to retrieve its past indolence fills it with a zeal that calls on "all men everywhere to repent;" the conversions which ensue furnish it with a means of enlarging its sphere of activity. The existence of all this both proves the presence of the Divine Spirit in the midst of it, and leads it to earnest cries for still larger effusions of his influence; and thus, by an action and reaction, an increase of its prosperity leads to importunate prayer for larger impartations of the Spirit, and larger impartations of the Spirit necessarily produce an increase of divine prosperity.

Let us look at the Christians and Christian denominations of Britain at present; and say, what but their activity for God, and the salutary effects of that activity on themselves, constitute the sign and means of their visible prosperity? Take away this, and what single feature would remain on which the spiritual eye could rest with pleasure? Their orthodoxy? That would be their condemnation; for, if their creed be scriptural, activity and zeal for God are necessary, if only to make them consistent with themselves. The numbers they include? The world outnumbers them; and it is only by their aggressive activity, blessed by God, that they can hope to keep their disproportion from increasing. Their liberality? Apart from this Christian activity, where would be the calls on that liberality? It is this which brings it into exercise, and by exercise augments it. Their union with each other? This activity for enlarging the kingdom of Christ is almost the only bond which, at present, does unite them; take away this, and nearly the last ligament of their visible union would be snapped. Their spirit of prayer?

That has been called into exercise almost entirely by means of their Christian activity; for, feeling the utter insufficiency of their own endeavors, they have earnestly entreated God to make bare his arm in their behalf.

From our returning activity, then, in the cause of human salvation, advantages have resulted which nothing else could have conferred. Amidst scenes of political strife, it has brought to us visions of a kingdom which is not of this world. Amidst scenes of ecclesiastical discord, it has provided one standard around which all can rally against the common foe. Amidst the icy selfishness of the world around, it has called forth warm streams of Christian liberality. It has given employment to energies which would otherwise have been wasted in the arena of angry controversy. It has been the means of originating various institutions, which are destined to hasten the great consummation; and of calling into existence specimens of Christian excellence and heroism of which the world is not worthy. To the visible Church it has given a heart, stirred its deepest sympathies for the world, brought considerable accessions to its numbers, imparted additional interest to its services, enlivened its piety, enlarged its views, and brightened its visions of the reign of Christ. It has been the means of disarming infidelity of some of its most specious objections, illustrated afresh the divinity of the gospel, increased the confidence of Christians in its ultimate triumphs, and furnished them with some of the most remarkable occasions for ascribing glory to God. Many of them it has filled with a sense of self-dissatisfaction, of utter dependence on God, of aching want and craving desire for something more and something better for the Church than it yet possesses; so that their loudest prayers are prayers for the promised outpouring of the Holy Spirit. From all of which we infer, that a full return in faith and prayer to the aggressive design of the Christian Church, would be a full return to its original prosperity.

III. But this is further apparent, and the whole of this Second Part connects itself with the former by the important fact that the history which it details of the missionary enterprise remarkably illustrates every particular there advanced on the theory of Christian influence. This, indeed, might have been expected; for it is only saying that the same principles, when put into operation under the same circumstances, produce the same effects. Accordingly, the records of modern missions might easily be made to furnish the most striking comment on the "Acts of the Apostles," and to illustrate every principle of the missionary constitution of the Church.

How strikingly do they exemplify at once the attractive and the expansive power of the cross of Christ! Here is an humble individual, a Carey or a Mills, a Hall or an Egede, meditating in solitude an attempt to convert the heathen. Never, surely, was a project more remote from the sphere of worldly calculation. It is almost beyond the range even of ordinary Christian sympathy. What is to account for it? Has some personal command, or supernatural visitation, called him by name to undertake the work? No, the love of Christ alone constrains him; and the known requirements of Christianity are his authority. The ignorant may pity him as foolish, the irreligious may pronounce him mad, and even his professed fellow-Christians may deem him rash and zealous overmuch. But he is simply "thus judging," that if the world is perishing, and if Christ died for its redemption, he, knowing the fact, is bound to proclaim it. He "cannot but speak the things which he has seen and heard."

Months, perhaps years, elapse, but still the fire of his purpose burns on with unabated strength. Reflection and prayer only increase its ardor; at length, he finds, with untold delight, that, like the caloric diffused through physical substances, the principle of benevolence lying dormant in the heart of some with whom he holds communion, is beginning to disengage by collision, and to ignite into a flame of sympathetic Christian zeal. They join him in prayer, aid his resources, and urge him to depart "far hence among the Gentiles."

If we follow him, after a while, to the scene of his missionary labors, what is the spectacle we behold? To an uninstructed observer we might say, See you those savages sitting, mourning, and melting around him? He is telling them the tale of the cross. Do you remark how the stolid countenances of others are awakening into intelligence, and their very attitudes indicating an anxiety to understand? "Jesus Christ has been evidently set forth crucified among them." Do you observe how others are busily occupied in building around? Blessed Saviour, thou hast triumphed; thou art drawing all men unto thee! for, in effect, they are building around the cross! Abandoning their idols and their wandering habits, they have found the true centre of attraction, and rejoice to be near it. "It was when I discoursed to the multitude," says Brainerd, "on that sacred passage, 'Yet it pleased the Lord to bruise him,' that the word was attended with a resistless power: many hundreds in that great assembly, consisting of three or four thousand, were much affected, so that there was a very great mourning, like to the mourning of Hadadrimmon." "How was that?" said the affected Kaiarnac—when, after the "rationalizing process" had long been tried on the Greenlanders in vain, the history of our Lord's sufferings was at length read to them—"How was that? tell me that once more, for I would fain be saved too."

But if the gospel of Christ possesses this power of subduing the heart to its own expansive purposes, *we may expect to see even the converted savage attempting the conversion of those around him.* Nor do we expect this in vain. Kaiarnac himself is an illustration in point. "His family, consisting of nine persons, were the first that were brought under conviction by his words and conduct; and before the month was over, three large families of natives came, with all their effects, and pitched their tents beside the dwellings of the Moravians."* Thus the gospel extends its influence from the individual to the family, and from the family to the neighborhood.

"The natives," writes a missionary in New Zealand, "are beginning to itinerate among their countrymen to preach the gospel. Surely good times are near at hand for this country. The desire which some of the young men manifest for the salvation of the souls of their countrymen evidently points out the nature of the religion which they profess."† In one station we behold a vast assembly of native converts addressed by Christian chiefs and others, and urged by compassion for "lost souls," and by gratitude for their own salvation, to embark in a missionary enterprise among the idolaters

---

* Carne, vol. i., p. 237.
† Evidence on the Aborigines, pp. 121, 122.

beyond. In another we hear a venerable chief lamenting in the midst of his people that he is not young enough to go on such an errand of mercy, and praying that the churches of the station might be honored to "supply brethren to bear the gospel to more populous lands." Elsewhere, we hear the chief of one island, who has sailed far to address the chiefs of another, exclaiming, at the close of his earnest appeal, "Grasp with a firm hold the word of Jehovah; for this alone can make you a peaceable and happy people. I should have died a savage, had it not been for the gospel." And there, another, under similar circumstances, exclaiming, as he steps forward and seizes the heathen chief by the hand, "Rise, brother, tear off the garb of Satan, and become a man of God."

"The inhabitants of eight islands," says one of the witnesses in the "Evidence on the Aborigines," "were entirely converted to Christianity by the agency of native missionaries. . . . . We have about sixty or seventy, and that number is increasing; *because wherever the gospel is attended with beneficial effects, a new agency is created there for its still further propagation.* . . . . The original station was only one island, that of Tahiti; and the knowledge of Christianity was conveyed to the islands where the American missionaries are, and to the Friendly Islands, by native agency. We have forty or fifty islands under instruction at the present time by native agency."

What a strong scriptural illustration of the expansive power of the gospel is here! "The Spirit and the bride say, Come." Every Church regards itself as a missionary society. Some of their first property was sent home to aid the cause of missions. Their best men are called forth and devoted to the missionary office. With a simplicity and singleness of purpose worthy of apostolic times, they go forth, often at the imminent hazard of their lives, to proclaim salvation to remoter islands. And wherever they have proceeded hitherto, unexampled success has attended their labors, "the Lord working with them." And thus the distant field of missionary labor presents at this moment the noble spectacle of a vast sphere in Christian activity; not for itself merely, but for an ever-enlarging circumference beyond.

IV. Now, what a powerful motive should all this supply to

the increase of our missionary zeal! If every event of Providence has a voice and a lesson, the only interpretation we can give to the language uttered by our missionary success is that of one unbroken call to greater diligence. After making the preceding circuit of the missionary field, and taking a survey of the results of our past attempts, can we return into the presence of the Lord of the harvest without feeling how justly he might say to us, as he did to his disciples at the close of their first itinerancy, "Lacked ye any thing?" and how confidently he might await the same reply, "Nothing, Lord." You were ignorant, he might continue to say, and one of the direct tendencies of my dispensations toward you has been to instruct you in the heavenly art of doing good. You were fearful and unbelieving; and I rebuked your doubts, not in judgment, but by affording you unexpected disclosures of my resources and my grace. You had enemies: many of them exist no longer; others I have changed into friends; and of those that remain I have taught you to believe that "their end draweth nigh." From many a scene of apparently fruitless labor you were inclined to withdraw dejected; but I gave you grace to persevere, and Heaven heard the result in your grateful shouts of rejoicing triumph.

Where have you labored in vain? Your own recorded testimony is, that "success, to a certain extent, has invariably attended your missionary exertions among the heathen."* Name an instance, if you can, in which an attempt to introduce the gospel among a barbarous people, and perseverance in the use of suitable means, have not been attended with a measure of success. Even where that success has been apparently delayed, was it not as much, if not more, eventually, than as if it had been early and gradually sent? Has not the scene of your greatest dejection repeatedly proved the occasion of your greatest triumph? And as to the tendency of your missionary activity to benefit yourselves, say by what other process you can suppose your advantage would have been greater. By what other means could you have equally learned the secret of mutual Christian influence; of the stimulating effect of individual devotedness upon a Church, and of one Church upon another, and of one denomination upon

---

* Evidence on the Aborigines, p. 132.

every other part of the Christian community; the great fact that for a single Christian to move in my service is sure eventually to move the entire Church, and to hasten the conversion of the world? Or by what other means could I have equally illustrated the fact that my Church is constituted expressly for this end, and that its welfare depends on its becoming the channel of my Spirit to the world, and of thus answering the great relative object of its existence?

But if so many ends have been answered, and so much good has been accomplished by the comparatively slender amount of instrumentality which you have already put into motion, what might you not have been the means of effecting, had your activity but equalled your resources? For though my sovereignty is at liberty to act as independently as I please, both of your instrumentality and of my own promises, in *exceeding* your just expectations; and though, in this sense, I will still be " found of them that sought me not," yet, as you have never asked but I have answered, never labored but I have blessed, think how many a region still sitting in darkness might have been added to those which you have been the means of bringing into marvellous light!

And now, when will you be satisfied with success? You say that you are grateful for the past; but remember that whatever you may profess, the amount of your present activity describes the exact degree of your gratitude. You profess to recognize a connection and a proportion between the measure of your instrumentality and your success: are you then already satisfied with the good effected, that you do not increase your Christian activity? This you profess to be quite impossible: nothing, you avow, can ever arrest your activity, or satisfy your desires, till my gospel has leavened the heart of humanity, and its laws have become interwoven with every human government; till wars have ceased to the ends of the earth; a sorrowing world has dried up its tears; till the reign of sin be ended, and one universal transporting song ascend from every land in honor of Him by whom the victory is achieved. Why then do you not aim at greater proportion between the splendor of your expectations and the measure of your endeavors? I am not exhausted with imparting: are you weary with receiving? As yet you have only received the first-fruits: when will you be prepared for the harvest? I have only at present begun to bless; but "prove me now herewith, saith the Lord of hosts, if I will not open you the windows of heaven, and pour you out a blessing, that there shall not be room enough to receive it. And I will rebuke the devourer for your sakes, and he shall not destroy the fruits of your ground; neither shall your vine cast her fruit before the time in the field, saith the Lord of hosts. And all nations shall call you blessed; for ye shall be a delightsome land, saith the Lord of hosts."

PART III.

*ENCOURAGEMENTS OF CHRISTIANS TO PROSECUTE THE MISSIONARY ENTERPRISE.

As far as human agency is concerned in the eventual triumph of the gospel, he who despairs of that triumph is doing all he can to prevent it; and he who confidently and consistently expects it is materially contributing to promote it. While it is admitted, therefore, as an axiom in Christian morals, that encouragements to duty do not form the ground of our obedience, yet when such encouragements are graciously afforded, not to regard them would be sullen ingratitude against God, and not to feel them is to remain insensible to some of the most cheering and powerful inducements to increased activity. Encouragements to missionary labor, and to anticipate the final success of that labor, lie around us on every side. In collecting and presenting some of the more obvious among them to Christian attention, it may contribute to clearness, and sufficiently answer our present object, if we consider them in succession, as historical, political, moral, ecclesiastical, and evangelical; after which we shall mark their relation to the preceding parts, and their practical application.

SECTION I.

ENCOURAGEMENT FROM HISTORY.

THE first encouragement to missionary labor to which we invite attention, is that which is derivable from the history of the propagation of Christianity. In attempting the diffusion of the gospel, we are not engaged in a novel experiment; nor is the gospel itself a system of truth hitherto untried. It has a long and an eventful history. In order to estimate its prospects for the future, then, let us question that history concerning the past; for if it shall appear that Christianity, regarded merely as one form of religion among many, has vanquished every foe which it has encountered, passed through every ordeal to which it is ever likely to be subjected, and is still vigorous and aggressive, even the skeptic must admit that, whether its success be owing to supernatural aid, to intrinsic excellence, or to both, its friends have strong encouragement to hope for its continued progress.

Now, the first question naturally arising in the mind of an inquirer on this subject would be—" Has the religion of the Bible triumphed already?" Open the first pages of its history, we reply, and you will find that its early history is a history of its triumphs. It matters not whether that history be written by an Origen or a Pliny, a Eusebius or a Tacitus, a Tertullian or a Gibbon—friends and foes alike bear testimony to the fact that during its early ages the gospel not merely maintained its ground, but extended its conquests on every hand with a rapidity and vigor which left numbers of its enemies no alternative but to ascribe it to the finger of God.

" Perhaps, however, the advent of Christianity took place at a time when the prevailing systems of religion were of a kind less hostile to innovation than those which exist at present; or, perhaps, the character of the gospel had a tendency to coalesce with them, and accept of their support." So far from this, the gospel was utterly unlike every system which the mind of man had imagined; nor would it accept the remotest alliance with any, but proclaimed a war of extermination against them all; and yet it triumphed. It found every human heart a temple filled with the worship of some idol god, and the world a Pantheon, crowded with the long-accumulated images and services of an ancient idolatry; and yet it triumphed. Never, perhaps, had the prevailing systems presented a more threatening front to the pretensions of any new and rival religion than at that period: this the ages of persecution which followed sufficiently testified; but not only did the gospel denounce *them*,—it went even deeper, and proclaimed eternal war against the very propensities and principles of human nature which had given them birth; and yet it triumphed. " But the gospel may have owed its early successes to an instrumentality of a kind so efficient as it may never possess again." As far as that agency was miraculous, it was doubtless demonstrative of the truth of the gospel; but the means employed for its diffusion were simply "the foolishness of preaching." No purple clothed it, no orators pleaded its cause, no secret bribes procured it access to the ear of the great, no army hewed for it a path; and yet it triumphed. The apparent impotence and meanness of its agents formed one of the great objections of the day against the divinity of its origin, and the possibility of its success; and yet it triumphed. And one of the reasons why such an instrumentality was employed, doubtless, was, that the Church might never, on this ground, have cause to despond: that it might feel that as long as it can furnish but "twelve fishermen," it possesses an instrumentality equal, under God, to repeat the triumphs of its primitive days.

"But it may be that Christianity triumphed only in one direction, and vanquished only a single kind of opposition." It evaded no difficulty—turned aside from no foe. It went in search of "Satan's seat." Not a people here and there merely, but many nations, and these in every stage of civilization, and exhibiting almost every variety of political and moral condition, abandoned their idolatries, and embraced the Christian name.

"But many a system which has prospered in its early days, and which has even gained energy by conflict, has no sooner been seated in the place of ease and power, than it has fallen before the first vigorous assault which it was called to sustain. One would like to see, therefore, whether or not Christendom could survive such an encounter." The irruption of the Gothic and Slavic nations into the Roman empire furnished the means of the experiment; and what was the effect? The conversion of these northern barbarians had been before but imperfectly attempted; yet now, when they came to vanquish the civilized world, the second increase of Christianity took place by their nominal adoption of the faith. And thus the very event which had threatened Christendom with irreparable ruin proved the second era of its enlargement.

"In this instance, however, the encounter of Christianity was only with barbarian force. What if the antagonist had been armed with knowledge, with elastic mind, and intellectual might?" The supposition has been realized—realized under circumstances the most unfavorable for Christianity; and yet it triumphed. At the time when ancient literature arose from the sleep of ages like a giant refreshed; when the newly-created press gave wings to thought; when philosophy rose like a sun on the old world, and science discovered a new world; and when mind, in consequence, received an impulse which threatened with extinction whatever was not true and good, Christianity was found overlaid and oppressed with centuries of corruption. But with an energy of self-renovating power which could have only come from God, it arose with the occasion, and, so far from avoiding, actually called to its side, and employed in its service, all those elements of greatness which had just come into existence. Ancient literature held its rekindled torch to the translation of the Bible: the press propagated it in all directions: an inductive philosophy has ever since been illustrating its truths, and augmenting its evidence; and from parts of that new world which Christianity was the first to colonize, it is now meditating the conversion of mankind.

"Still the test might have been more severe. Christianity might have remained unreformed, or the slumber of security might have come over it after the Reformation, while its enemies were secretly forging their weapons, and gradually preparing for its sudden destruction: what would have been the issue of such an onset?" The question is answered: the onset was made, and yet the cause of the gospel triumphed. The Neological Pantheism of Spinoza; the Casuistic Doubts of Bayle; the Phenomenonism of Hume; Kant and Transcendental Skepticism; the Ridicule of Voltaire; the Sentimental Deism of Rousseau; the Historical Infidelity of Gibbon; all the agents and hosts of evil fell on the cause of Truth in quick succession, and in the hour of its faintness, and felt secure of its utter extinction. Political convulsions, too, at the same time, seemed to conspire and make way for the most fearful changes. The revolutionized aspect of the social system, at this moment, testifies to the violence of that moral deluge by which mountains were brought down, and valleys raised, and the organic structure of Christendom changed. Yet not only did Christianity survive the conflict— the hour of its crisis was the season of its greatest triumph. While maintaining its ground with apparent difficulty at home, it was actually acquiring new territories abroad. At the moment when its enemies supposed that its doom was sealed, it was seen as a mighty angel flying through the midst of heaven, and preaching the everlasting gospel to all nations. The day of its fiercest trial is the day from which it dates its modern missionary enterprise.

Now, are we not encouraged from this review of the past to augur hopefully of the future? Shall not the weapon which has never failed be regarded by us with greater confidence than one which has never been tried? Is it too much to expect that the gospel which has triumphed so long and so gloriously will continue to triumph still? We pass to the field of missionary effort over the wrecks of former systems of idolatry, and through scenes of early gospel triumph, and shall we not feel the inspiration of the scene? Where now is Diana of the Ephesians? Where now are Jupiter and the gods of Greece? and where the whole Pantheon of Rome? The first Christians testified against them, and they vanished. Missionaries of Christ came to Britain; and where now are Woden and all the Saxon gods? Hessus, and all the more ancient and sanguinary rites of the Druids? The idols which we now assail in other lands have been long since routed, and the sword we wield routed them. The gods of India are the same, under different names, which Italy and Greece adored: the sword of the Lord chased them from the west, and shall it do less in the east? Remembering "the years of the right hand of the Most High," let us "thank God and take courage."

SECTION II.

MISSIONARY ENCOURAGEMENT ARISING FROM THE POLITICAL ASPECT OF THE WORLD.

A SECOND ground of missionary encouragement, and one deserving peculiar attention, may be denominated political, for it respects the external relations of Christendom, and especially of reformed Christendom, to the rest of the world. If the social condition of states, and their aspects toward each other, are to possess any weight in our estimate of the missionary cause, we may venture to affirm that it would be difficult to conceive of their occupying any position relative to that cause more encouraging than that which they now present.

1. For, first, all the rest of the globe appears to be placed by Providence at the disposal of Christendom. This will appear from a slight degree of attention to the following considerations: That which classifies and distributes the population of the earth is, not geographical lines, but religion. This is the centre around which humanity collects, and by which it is civilized and formed into masses; and hence the savage tribes, having nothing deserving the name of religion, know nothing of civilization, or of union among themselves. Now, if we look down upon the human race from a point of view sufficiently high, we shall find them divisible into three great families—the Mohammedan, the Brahminical, and the Christian, including the Jewish. Within the bosom of these families there are numerous points of difference. The nations which compose them are in various stages of progress; but still they are all marshalled and moving under one or other of these three banners.*

The Mohammedan division occupies South-western Asia, and the north and east of Africa. The Brahminic section, the most populous of the three, possesses Eastern Asia, and the neighboring islands on the east and south, including Japan, Chinese Tartary, China, and the Indies. The Christian portion comprehends Europe and America, penetrates Asia by the north and the south, Africa south of the tropics, and has colonies everywhere.

The Moslem division embraces a population of about a hundred and twenty millions; Brahminism, in its different sects, about four hundred millions; and Christendom about

---

* For many of the facts stated in this part of the present section, the author is indebted to a sketch of the "Present State of Humanity," by Mr. Jouffroy, Professor in the Faculty of Literature, Paris; in which, with much that is unsound in theory, there is blended much **that is useful in information.**

two hundred millions. The remainder of the human race, amounting to nearly a hundred millions, are savage. These are so scattered and surrounded, that, as a portion of humanity, they exert no influence on the three great divisions, but are probably destined to be assimilated and absorbed by them.

The great powers, then, which divide the civilized world between them, are Mohammedanism, Brahminism, and Christianity. Now, of these, it is evident from facts that the Christian division is the only one which possesses an expansive power.

Christianity alone entertains the idea of gaining savage tribes to civilization. Brahminism has few or no savages to civilize; for while, on one side, its dominion extends to the eastern borders of Asia, on the other it approaches Mohammedanism and Christianity, and consequently touches the other systems of civilization. Mohammedanism, also, on the east toward Asia, and on the north and west toward Europe, is arrested by Christian and Brahminic civilization. It comes in contact with savages only at the south, toward the centre of Africa; and these there is reason to conclude that it entirely disregards. But while Mohammedanism and Brahminism take no measures by which they may share in the mass of men who are yet to be civilized, if we turn our eyes to Christianity, we perceive that, with the exception of the barbarians of Africa—and even these it is on the point of disputing with Mohammedanism—it holds in its hands all the savages of the rest of the world.

For, in the next place, Christendom is the only one of the three divisions which colonizes. Mohammedanism, like Brahminism, keeps at home. The time when it subdued nations with the sword is past; while there is hardly an island of any considerable magnitude where one part or other of Christendom has not taken a station.

It is the only one of the three divisions capable of increase from population. The countries possessed by the other two have as many inhabitants already as comport with their respective systems of civilization. But this is so far from being the case with Christendom, that the population of modern Russia, for instance, doubles itself in about fifty years, and that of America in about half that period. It has before it, therefore, a vast prospect of increase, both at the expense of the savage portion of the human race, and by virtue of its own productive power—a prospect denied to the other two.

Christendom alone evinces a zeal for improvement. Among the Brahminic nations science is stationary; by the Mohammedan it is despised; while, among us, it is honored and cultivated, and is rapidly arming us with an ever-increasing power over them both.

Besides which, it is the only power which advances at the expense of the others. Not only does its superiority secure it from the attacks of the other two—it places them both, in a sense, at our disposal. Accordingly, neither Brahminism nor Mohammedanism penetrates, or attempts to penetrate, into Christendom. They appear smitten with death. They make no conquests even on each other, or among barbarians. They seem to exist merely because time is requisite for a dead system, as for a dead tree, to fall to pieces. Christendom, on the contrary, exhibits all the signs of a fresh and vigorous life. Everywhere it advances with ardor and deliberate purpose into the domains of Brahma and Mohammed; and almost the only resistance which it meets with is that of inertness and decay. Thus, while the aspect which the former two present is that of the Dead Sea, the latter, like the Jordan, is seen rushing into it, and we cannot forget that the promise is, " The waters shall be healed."

2. But if, on taking a survey of the civilized world, we are struck with the fact that, of the three systems into which it is divided, Christendom alone is aggressive, still more are we impressed at finding that, of all the nations of Christendom, those which are especially distinguished by Providence with political influence over the lands of Brahma and Mohammed are the Reformed and anti-Papal powers. Italy, with its enfeebling despotism, Spain, with its internal factions and suicidal passions, and even France, with its redundant peasantry, exhibit no symptoms of diffusing themselves over the world. England, English America, and Russia, are the only countries now standing in an interesting relation to the future. The former two may be regarded as one. Concerning its probable destiny, let us hear an opinion, which, considering the quarter whence it comes, is entitled to deep attention. It cannot be

denied that "the British race," says M. Tocqueville,* "has acquired an amazing preponderance over all the other European races in the New World; and that it is very superior to them in civilization, in industry, and in power. . . . The geographical position of the British race in the New World is peculiarly favorable to its rapid increase. . . . It has been calculated that the whites advance every year a mean distance of seventeen miles along the whole of this vast boundary, [about fifteen hundred miles.] Obstacles, such as an unproductive district, a lake, or an Indian nation, unexpectedly encountered, are sometimes met with. The advancing column then halts for a while : its two extremities fall back upon themselves; and, as soon as they are reünited, they proceed onwards. This gradual and continued progress of the European (British) race towards the Rocky Mountains, has the solemnity of a providential event : it is like a deluge of men rising unabatedly, and daily driven onwards by the hand of God. . . . Thus, in the midst of the uncertain future, one event, at least, is sure. At a period which may be said to be near, (for we are speaking of the life of a nation,) the Anglo-Americans will alone cover the immense space contained between the polar regions and the tropics, extending from the coast of the Atlantic to the shores of the Pacific Ocean—equal to three quarters of Europe in extent, with a population of a hundred and fifty millions of men. . . . This is a fact new to the world, a fact fraught with such portentous consequences as to baffle the efforts even of the imagination."

But it is not merely one quarter of the world of which the British race have taken possession. Southern Africa has received her language and her laws. In Australia—a new world, larger than Europe, and comparatively empty of men— colonization is spreading with a rapidity never before witnessed. And still about two hundred thousand emigrants annually leave the shores of Britain to take possession of the waste places of the earth, as if they were theirs by a Divine gift, or by the right of inheritance.

Our empire and political influence in the East, too, are of vast and still increasing extent. We speak not now of the unexpected manner in which England has been allowed to be-

---

* Democracy in America. *Paris and London*, 1835.

come the mistress of India, or of the solemn responsibility which the mighty transfer has imposed on us. These are subjects for consideration in a subsequent chapter. We advert to the striking fact, that Providence has permitted us to acquire political influence over about a hundred millions of immortal beings in India, as a very cheering view for those who meditate their conversion to God. And this fact becomes still more encouraging and significant of the Divine designs, when we remember that the country has already been in the hands of the Portuguese, who, by their cruelty, opposed its religious improvement, and of the Dutch, who neglected it, and is now intrusted to the only people who possess the means, humanly speaking, of benefiting it.

Now, what reflecting Christian but must perceive, in this view of the state of the world, strong encouragement to missionary enterprise? Let him not fear that we shall overrate its importance; or be tempted by it to withdraw our supreme confidence from Him "who is our hope." We are free to admit that our extensive influence has been acquired by no design or forethought on our part, but, in the providential course of events, from the expansiveness of our energies, and the inherent advantages of that civilization for which we are indebted to our religion. Nor can we forget that the occasion which led to the colonization of America by the Puritans, the bribery and bloodshed by which we have obtained large portions of India, and the countenance still afforded to its hateful idolatry, are all calculated to cast a stain upon our glory, and may well induce us to rejoice with trembling. Still, it is not the less our duty, rather it is calculated to augment our gratitude, to remark that, in defiance of all our own deserts, and of all human calculation, our political position abounds with encouragement to missionary exertion.

Suppose, for instance, that Christendom and Mohammedanism were to exchange their relative positions: that the former were declining and superannuated, existing on the mere sufferance of the latter, and expecting to be finally driven from Europe; while the standard of the prophet was planted in the heart of the continent, the scymitar flashing around the shores of the Mediterranean, and one province and island after another resounding for the first time with the cry of the muezzin: would the change cast no shade over our missionary prospects? Whatever our duty might be, would our hopes remain undiminished? Would not a revolution, which should cast Mohammedanism to the earth, and place Christendom in its present attitude of security and superiority above it, bring back a great accession of encouragement to the missionary cause, and be regarded by us as a loud call to increased activity?

Suppose, again, that those on whom the modern missionary spirit has descended, inhabited a country situated in the centre of the European continent, destitute of a navy, and strangers to commerce: would the want of all our present maritime facilities be unfelt and undeplored? Is it nothing that this spirit has been excited among those whose subject territory is thrice as large as that of ancient Rome, whose colonies people every quarter of the globe, and whose ships crowd every port of every shore? This is not accident. It is the finger of God pointing out our duty to the world, and the voice of God cheering us on to perform it.

Is it nothing, again, that India "is open?" Only a little more than a century ago, it was as likely, to all appearance, that the Mogul empire would have passed into the hands of France, of Portugal, of Denmark, of Holland, or even of Russia, as of England. But under the jealous despotism of Russia, or the ascendency of the Romish power, India would have been closed against the missionary. And is it nothing, then, that it has been given to the only Protestant power capable of efficiently discharging the high mission of genuine Christianity throughout the East? Let the Christian reader, who beholds in it a special providence, derive from it also special encouragement to increased missionary effort.

SECTION III.

MISSIONARY ENCOURAGEMENT ARISING FROM THE MORAL ASPECT OF THE WORLD.

1. ANOTHER source of encouragement to missionary exertion arises from the moral aspect of the various parts of the world. And here, if we begin our examination with the least hopeful

of those parts, the Mohammedan, and select the least auspicious sections even of these, Persia and Turkey, we shall find that never did the Moslem ranks present so broken a front, and invite aggression with so great a prospect of success, as at present. The political state of these countries is a correct representation of their moral condition. Persia, by its heretical adherence to Ali, divides the Mussulman power, and becomes a source of solicitude and weakness to Turkey. As Mohammed appealed to the sword in proof of the divinity of his mission, "every battle lost is an argument lost;" so that the evidence of his creed is nearly at its minimum. Science and philosophy are against it; for of all the systems of false religion, that of the imposter is the least true to nature; so that almost every fresh scientific discovery is the preparation of a new weapon with which to assail it, and every Mohammedan that begins to reason is a votary lost. The Ottomans themselves are possessed with a melancholy foreboding of their doom; and the events of every year only serve to deepen the gloom of their prospects. Their moral aspect now, therefore, is that of a foe comparatively disarmed and disheartened; and though he who should denounce the Caaba, or preach the Cross, in the streets of Constantinople, would probably find the cadi and bigotry as active as ever, yet the history of Henry Martyn shows us how patiently the Islamite will attend to the claims of Christianity, when judiciously presented, and how beneficial an influence may be exercised by religious conversation alone.

2. There was a time when the Polytheism of India was deemed unchangeable. It is evident, however, not only that multitudes of Hindoos adopted, from whatever motives, the religion of their Mohammedan conquerors, but that, without any foreign inducement, they have voluntarily passed through the usual gradations of error, and exhibited the ordinary love of change. From the worship of the elements they have advanced to Brahminical Polytheism; from Polytheism to the Pantheism of the Budhists; and from Budhism have returned to Brahminism again. So that all our fears of the immobility of the Hindoo character have been long since proved to be unfounded. It should be remembered also, that the religion prevalent through all the regions of the East is substantially the same. For the Brahminism of Hindostan

is only a more popular form of the strict Pantheism which prevails to the north and the east, and which is satisfied with the one incarnation of Budh. So that in dissolving the fatal charm of Hindooism, we should not be benefiting a single nation merely, but breaking the spell by which nearly half the race are morally enslaved.

Remarkable it is, too, that there should be one country of the East which has given religion, science, and civilization to all the rest; for from India have proceeded the missionaries of the Lamas, the Bonzes, and of Budh, the last of the Indian incarnations—a fact which awakens the hope that when the same land embraces Christianity, it will be equally ready to furnish missionaries of the cross for the very extremities of Asia. Still more remarkable is it that this one country, to which all the surrounding regions look as the fountain of holiness and wisdom, should be placed by Providence at our disposal. To heighten our encouragement, the ancient and antiquated religion of this one country has fallen into discredit, and is rapidly on the decline. Where one new temple is built, sixty are allowed to go to ruin. Many of the seminaries where the shastres are studied, are closed for want of pupils. Nodea and Santapore, the two most celebrated of these colleges, and which formerly had from three to four thousand students, have not at present more than three or four hundred. The Brahmins themselves have lost so much of their influence with the people, that their curses are but little dreaded, or their blessings desired. Hundreds of them have renounced the priesthood, as no longer able to afford them the means of living. The links of caste are fractured, and the very weight of the chain is threatening a powerful reaction against it.

Who does not behold in all this a grand work of Providential preparation for the missionary enterprise in India? And, as if nothing should be wanting to complete our encouragement, a large proportion of the population are already able to read and write: a very general desire is felt to acquire the arts and sciences of Europe; and the knowledge of these would necessitate and hasten the fall of Hindooism. A strong presentiment that its doom is sealed is daily extending; and such is the comparative indifference for its fate, that, in numerous instances, the Christian missionary denounces idolatry in the very temple of the god.

3. China—that world within itself—is doubtless surrounded with obstacles to conversion. But the existence of these constitute the very reason, and the only ground of necessity, why we should attempt it. She is guarded against the truth by more than one wall. Her material wall, as it has been justly remarked, is crumbling dust compared with her political: her political wall is a mere illusion compared with her moral barriers—for civilization in China can hardly be called religious: her moral wall of prejudice and pride is only that by which sin intrenches itself in every country and every heart. The wall which overtops the whole, and which we shall find it most difficult to surmount, is that which our own unbelief and ignorance have erected. Every other has been breached and entered. So far is China to be from being regarded as impregnable, that Judaism entered it probably prior to the Christian era, Budhism in the first century, Nestorianism in the seventh century, Mohammedanism in the eighth century, and Romanism in the thirteenth century. Such was the success of Popery in China, especially in the hands of M. Ricci and Father Schaal, that many of the mandarins embraced its doctrines: one province alone contained ninety churches and forty-five oratories: a splendid church was built within the palace: the mother, wife, and son of the emperor, Yung-leih, professed Christianity; and nothing apparently prevented China from being added to the Papal see but the disputes which broke out between the Jesuits and the Dominicans.

But besides the encouragement derivable from the fact that China has already been open to missionary aggression, it should be gratefully remembered also that obstacles existing elsewhere are absent here; and that many of those considerations which once operated as fears, have gradually vanished, or changed into hopes. The climate, for instance, so far from being relaxing or pestilential, is fully as salubrious as that of England, and much less changeable. The language, once deemed unattainable, has been mastered, and "made easy;" and what an inducement should it furnish to the Christian student, that when he has mastered the Chinese symbols, he will be able to make himself intelligible from the mouth of the Ganges to the Amoor, and to indite a book—for nearly all can read—for more than one-third of the human race! The despotic unity of its government, by which the will of one man moves and rules the entire mass, may itself be made the means, under God, of its more easy and effectual reconstruction on Christian principles. At all events, the unity of character resulting from this unvarying uniformity of literature and government, is attended with this advantage to the missionary—that to comprehend the sentiments and reply to the objections of a single mind, is to master the views and objections of three hundred and sixty millions of human beings. In this respect, too, the magnitude of the population, once regarded as appalling, presents the missionary with an advantage not to be met with elsewhere. But that which calls for special observation is, both that the Chinese mode of writing is current and legible far beyond the limits of China, throughout Cochin-China, Corea, and Japan, and that the population of China itself is bursting forth on every side, placing itself in voluntary contact with Christians, and seeking the shelter of European governments. Millions are already to be found in Burmah and Siam, in Pegu, Assam, and the Malayan Archipelago. All these are accessible to missionary efforts. What has been accomplished of late among these by the ardent and persevering zeal of two or three individuals, encourages the hope and points out the way of benefiting China at large. For only let suitable measures be taken to evangelize the emigrant Chinese, and a race of missionaries will be thus provided, which, in spite of imperial edicts, will find their way into all parts of the empire, and become, in the hands of God, the instruments of its renovation.

4. The most considerable body of barbarians on the face of the earth at present, living contiguously in the same region, is the forty millions of Central Africa. To the evangelization, or even the civilization, of this dense mass of barbarism, five obstacles formerly presented themselves, each of which was deemed insuperable — the judicial sentence of God against them, their mental imbecility, the demoralizing influence of slavery, the deadly nature of the climate, and the ferocious character of the native superstitions. To the first of these it is now considered a sufficient reply, that the gospel

repeals every national malediction, and addresses itself to every creature. Missionary culture has proved that, as to the second, the charge of mental inferiority must in future lie rather against those who bring it than against the African. The third will be gradually obviated in the universal abolition of slavery—for the sentence of indignant humanity has gone forth against it. While the emancipation of our slaves might go far to obviate the fourth; for what agency so fitted, physically and morally, to evangelize the inhabitants of the torrid zone, as their converted brethren of the West Indies?* And, as to the last,—the ferocious character of African superstition,—it is now well ascertained that while their religious creed is too meagre and undefined to possess a powerful hold on their minds, their religious practices, consisting of Obeah and Fetishism, form a "reign of terror" against which a very slight inducement would raise them in revolt. And hence, wherever the gospel has been preached to them, "Ethiopia has stretched out her hands unto God."

5. The other savage portions of the earth wear a more encouraging aspect still. As there is no peculiar obstacle to the religious instruction of the aborigines of the Americas which European injustice has not created, it may be hoped that the Christian sympathy awakened in their behalf will be successful in removing it; while their comparative vicinity to the American Churches encourages the hope of their more speedy recovery. Experiment has proved that the New Hollander may be reclaimed and elevated to Christian humanity; and that New Zealand may become a province of the Prince of peace. Nearly the whole of Eastern Polynesia is converted to the Christian faith. And still, as the missionary stretches away towards the Fijis, and approaches New Caledonia, New Britain, New Ireland, and New Guinea, he finds the islands waiting for the law of the Lord.

6. Christendom naturally divides itself into the Greek, Romish, and Reformed Churches: reserving the last for consideration in the next section, we may remark of the first, that, with all its unvarying childishness and love of toys, it is not without the prospect of improvement. Education is encouraged and promoted by the Emperor of Russia. The career of civilization on which that vast country has entered

---

[* See Introduction.—T. O. S.]

will necessarily bring her into contact with superior moral influences, and there is nothing in the constitution of the Greek Church to prevent her deriving advantage from them. According to a recent edict of the emperor, Russian Georgia is to be "evangelized:" signs of missionary activity, even of *the lowest kind*, are signs of hope.

7. There is reason to believe that the palmy days of the Romish Church have passed, never to return. In the activity which she here and there exhibits, we see only the restlessness of petulance, and the hurried and uncertain expedients of fear. The Reformation has left no part of Popery what it was before. The press has imparted a power to public opinion by which the Inquisition—the extinguisher of opinion—has itself been extinguished. The circulation of the Bible has kindled a light from whose beams that system of darkness will never be able effectually to retire. The light of truth and the force of opinion are both against it. Even in Spain and Portugal, two of its strongholds, principles obtain with which, in its present form, it cannot long coëxist.

But let us glance at European Christendom in its two great divisions of north and south—Germany and France. The *Rationalism* of Germany has been long on the decline. Almost of a sudden, and without any cause which could be historically traced, a general dissatisfaction and disgust with it seized the community. The teachers who favored infidelity saw themselves in the minority. Philosophy, previously hostile to religion, declared itself the servant of the Christian faith. Supernaturalism obtained ascendency; and the still growing popularity of the "Pietists" augurs well for the diffusion of evangelical religion.

The *Naturalism* of France, like the Rationalism of Germany, is on the wane. Voltaire, Diderot, and Cabanis are no longer authorities with cultivated minds. And, though the great bulk of the people are still plunged in materialism, the philosophy of spiritualism alone (such as it is) is popular with the educated; while, among the most enlightened part of the nation, a strong presentiment is said to prevail, of some approaching religious change. A spirit of religious inquiry is certainly abroad in France, such as has not been known since the time of the Reformation. And the multiplication of Protestant Religious Societies, the gradual increase of faithful pastors in the Reformed National Church, and the eminent names of Neff, the Baron de Stael, Gonthier, with those who are at present living, exert an influence which naturally awakens the hope that that spirit of inquiry may lead, under God, to the happiest results.

8. Nor can we conclude these remarks on the moral condition of the various divisions of mankind, without adverting to the fact that even the mind of the Jews is beginning to awake. And though the philosophy of Mendelsohn is transferring them from the silly reveries of their rabbins to the anti-supernaturalism of Spinoza, the very circumstance of their change shows that much of their obstinacy is to be ascribed to their ignorance, and that Christian kindness and instruction could never meet them more seasonably than now, in their passage from credulity to infidelity. Reformed synagogues have been opened at Berlin, Leipsic, Vienna, Carlsruhe, Breslau, London, and other places. The Karaite Jews, or Scripturists, have an especial claim upon the attention of Christians. And let us remember that "the partial blindness that has fallen upon Israel shall continue (only) till the full complement of the nations shall have been brought in, and then shall universal Israel be restored." So that, as nation after nation opens its gates to welcome the entrance of the Christian faith, the Jews cannot look on without being in some degree " provoked to jealousy," nor can we fail to recognize signs of their approaching recovery.

Such are the moral signs of the times. We do not for a moment mistake them for signs of incipient conversion. We do not even interpret the most hopeful indication among them into a token of direct readiness to embrace the truth. The mind may leave one class of errors only to embrace a worse. All that we infer from the moral aspect of the world is, that if it be a more promising undertaking to assail a system of error in the season of its age and weakness than in the hour of its strength, that encouragement is now held out, for that season has arrived. If the time for recasting the metal is when it has reached a state of fusion, now is the period for employing the mould of the gospel, when the human mind is so generally indicative of being in the crucible, and of possessing unusual susceptibility for new impressions. Look in what direction we will, the horizon of hope enlarges and brightens. The fanatical zeal of the Mohammedan has burnt out. The priestly power of the Brahmin is broken, and his demons wait in vain for their prescribed libations of blood. The altar of the Chinese, empty, but standing, is waiting to welcome the advent of an unknown God. The South African chief comes from the remote interior, and offers his herds for a Christian teacher; the vast kingdoms and islands beyond the Ganges are ready for the reception of a number of missionaries. In one quarter, Idolatry is losing its hold on millions; in another, the savage is awakened from the sleep of centuries; here, Popery is falling off from a nation, as a snake casts its gaudy but shrivelled skin; there, philosophy is wearied out with its ever promising but unsatisfactory illusions; and, elsewhere, childish credulity is becoming a man and putting away childish things. Everywhere are to be seen an impatience of the present, a deep presentiment that it is hastening to decay, and a spirit of inquiry, anticipation, and change, looking out on the future. As it was with Judea and the East generally about the era of the advent of the Son of God, the world is waiting for the advent of some principle or means which shall change its destinies. Now, then, is the time for the Church to proclaim to it, "Behold your God!"

SECTION IV

ECCLESIASTICAL ENCOURAGEMENT TO PROMOTE THE MISSIONARY ENTERPRISE.

OF Protestant Christendom we propose to speak separately. And as our subject here will be to point out the ecclesiastical auspices of the missionary enterprise, we shall direct our attention chiefly to England and English American. For, although some of the Protestant Churches of Switzerland and Holland, France and Germany, are prepared to send their contingents into the field of missionary labor, it may be expected that their resources will be almost entirely needed for years to come to meet the demands of home; while the similar resources of England, meantime, and of her religious ally, are of a degree which devolve on them preëminently the office of the religious instructors of the world.

That peculiar encouragements for the execution of the office exist, we have already seen. In vain would it be, however, to show that considerations, historical, political, and moral, conspired to animate the missionary enterprise, if, at the same time, every thing in the Church itself seemed to forbid the attempt—if the missionary spirit, for instance, had yet to be enkindled; or if, having been excited, it was evidently on the decline; or if, having existed for years, it yet exhibited no signs of improvement at home, nor was attended with any success abroad. But in reality, the direct reverse of each of these suppositions is found to be the truth; and hence our ecclesiastical encouragement to advance.

1. For, first, a missionary spirit does exist in our Churches. There was a time, and that not many years ago, when it did not exist. Here and there a Christian divine might occasionally advert to the desirableness of such a spirit; a Christian poet might tune his lyre to celebrate its glorious results; and a Christian philanthropist wish to behold the sublime reality. But so far from entertaining any definite views or manifesting any active zeal on the subject, the Christian community, in general, resembled rather the altar and offering of Elijah when immersed in water. And as, in great undertakings, the first step is commonly the most difficult and important, so here, now that fire has descended from heaven to ignite the mass, we are prepared to see the whole gradually become a flaming sacrifice for the glory of God. That such a sacred kindling has commenced, we have already demonstrated at large. Holy men of God have devoted themselves to the missionary enterprise; Christians have associated for the purpose of sending them forth; and the result has been, that voices have been heard in various parts of the moral wilderness of the world, crying, "Prepare ye the way of the Lord."

2. But let us rather proceed to show that not only does the missionary spirit exist, but that it is also progressive. It has, we presume, passed that critical period in the history of a society or institution when, losing those sympathies which kindle so easily on contact with new objects, it must rely on principles, or perish. At first, the warm impulses of pious

feeling alone might serve to prompt to the effort, and to supply the place of sober and substantial principles.

But "that spring-time of novelty has passed. The ardent feeling and the excited imagination which threw so much interest over the prospect of the work, have given way to the grave reality of the work itself." Every year has increasingly based its support on its own intrinsic claims. The great truth that every Christian is bound to do something for the diffusion of the gospel, long hid from view, like a sand-covered pyramid of the east, has been gradually disinterred and brought to light; till now it stands before the Church in its majestic proportions, and is universally recognized as the fundamental principle of the missionary enterprise. No longer is it deemed necessary to support it by arguments. Being admitted as an axiom in Christian ethics, all that remains is to point out its application, and to enforce its importance. And, further, to show that the Church has been brought to act from a calm and simple sense of obligation, we might advert to the fact that, since its modern missionary activity commenced, it has, in some instances, endured protracted trials and severe discomfitures, which would have put to flight all mere impulse, and which only a grave and deep-seated conviction of duty could have sustained. Notwithstanding the conviction that in this, as in every grand and lasting enterprise, the great law will obtain, that "one soweth and another reapeth," the friends of missions have continued to go forth to sow.

It is an auspicious sign of the progress of a cause, when it can not only dispense with the impulse of mere excitement, and fall back on its principles, but when, at the very same time, it is found to extend and deepen its influence on the public mind. Now, the missionary cause has done this. "Not to pray for the coming of the Messiah," said the ancient Jewish proverb, "is not to pray at all." And not to pray for the diffusion of his gospel, it may now be said, is not to pray at all. Every prayer is expected to include it. In every religious family, the infant lisps of it in his earliest hymn. The "missionary box" is an object of notice alike in the nursery and the school-room, in the private residence and the public shop. The missionary tract is in universal request in every Sunday-school. The missionary "branch," or "auxiliary," is to be found in activity in every district and every congregation. The missionary anniversary is hailed as the return of a most welcome festival. The subject is to be met with in newspapers, and journals, and libraries, of almost every description. Far and wide through the land does it enter into our literature, and form a part of the public reading.

Nor is it confined to any one class of society. Beginning principally in the middle ranks, the missionary spirit has descended and pervaded the mass of the Christian poor, and at the same time has gradually drawn within its influence many in the highest circles of the nobility. Nor is it limited to any one denomination of the Christian community, or even to any particular portion of Christendom. Though some Churches have attached themselves to the great missionary organization more tardily, and are less powerfully influenced by the object than others, yet every orthodox Protestant body in Christendom has at length joined it, and gives signs of being affected by it in a similar manner. Among all Christians holding the doctrines of the Reformation, there is now a common mind in favor of the missionary enterprise.

The prosperity of a cause is indicated also when the numerical increase of its supporters is not made an excuse for the reduction of individual effort, but both are seen advancing together. Now, the missionary cause exhibits this sign. Each successive year has witnessed an increase on the income and activity of the year preceding. Christians, trained to liberality by its beneficent spirit, have, in many instances, doubled and quadrupled their subscriptions. A salutary reaction has been constantly going on between the increase of our labors abroad and the enlarged demand on our resources at home. The more we have given, the more we have been enabled to do; and the more we have done, the more we have been constrained to give. The spiritual wants of the world have been brought to light so much faster than we have been prepared to supply them, that we have happily been able to think little of what we have done, in the prospect of the prodigious field of labor yet to be occupied; while every attempt to raise the standard of Christian liberality and activity has been, upon the whole, so promptly responded to by the great body of the faithful, that we are impelled to the conclusion that considerable resources are yet to be explored, and to the holy resolution that every succeeding year shall continue to develop and employ them. And may we not on these grounds warrantably hope that, though partial relapses may occasionally mark the missionary spirit, and even particular societies fail, the next generation will prosecute the work with greater ardor than the present, and the generation following with still increased zeal; and that thus the devotedness of the followers of Christ will approximate nearer and nearer to the elevated standard of his blessed gospel?

And it augurs well for the prosperity of a cause when it allows of receiving, and actually adopts, from time to time, the improvements which, being human, it indispensably requires. Many an institution, full of promise at first, has perished through want of compliance with this easy but important condition. Now, the history of Christian missions is a record of successive corrections and improvements. We may instance the gradual improvement in the kind of instrumentality which they have employed. To say nothing of the sword alone; and then of the sword and the symbol of the cross, conjoined—for these belonged to a too distant period and a too questionable object—we behold in the early history of modern missions the strange conjunction of the missionary and a royal edict, as in the mission sent to Lapland by Gustavus Vasa; the missionary and commerce, as in the first Danish mission to Greenland;* the missionary and the promise of civil distinctions, as in the attempts of the Dutch to evangelize Ceylon. And even in the early history of our present institutions, it was considered in some instances essential to success that the missionary should be *preceded* by civilization rather than be the means of introducing it; while in others, perhaps, there was too great a tendency to neglect the means of civilization, even after Christianity had obtained a footing. The missionary without the Bible has been, and ever must be, while Popery remains what it is, the great defect of Catholic missions; and yet some of our early efforts to convert the heathen were in danger of suffering from the same deficiency. Then came the full conviction that education,

---

* The King of Denmark ordered a lottery in favor of the Greenland mission and commerce.

never, perhaps, entirely neglected, should uniformly accompany the preaching of the missionary, and form an essential part of his regular labors. On this followed the clear perception, that if the Bible was to be translated, the barbarian to be civilized and instructed, and a Christian community built up, the missionary *corps* should be "picked men;" that, instead of rating their requirements lower than those of the ministry at home, the holiest and ablest men the Church could send forth were the fittest. And then came the conviction of the importance of training and employing native Christian agency—a step, perhaps, more pregnant with good to the missionary enterprise than even the increase of our own missionaries.

During all this time, too, the friends of missions have been learning the importance of system in their proceedings; while the wisdom which they have been acquiring by experience has enabled them to systematize in the manner best adapted to their ultimate object. On the happy reciprocal influence of home and foreign activity; on the kind of preparation necessary for the missionary work; on the right selection of missionary stations; and on the mutual adaptation of agents and stations—on these, and a variety of correlative particulars, their views have been receiving perpetual correction and expansion. And it may not be out of place to remark here, that if their object be to publish the gospel everywhere in the shortest time, a more judicious selection of missionary posts could hardly have been made than that which, by a wisdom higher than their own, they now occupy. Few as those stations are, compared with the vast field of heathenism, they are so distributed that the efforts of the Church must soon be heard of by the great proportion of mankind; and the entire world, meantime, may be said to be calling for relief within view and hearing of the Church.

3. Another auspicious fact is, that at such a conjuncture the providence of God should furnish so many facilities and auxiliaries for the prosecution of the work. The intercommunity between all the provinces of the Roman empire which aided the early propagation of the gospel, and the newly-formed power of the press which came in aid of the Reformation, though parallel facts, are not to be compared with the subsidiary aids in the service of the gospel at present. What,

for instance, was the intercommunity to which we have alluded, compared with the facilities afforded now, by improved navigation alone, for visiting the remotest parts of the earth? Was the central position of Judea a favorable circumstance for the first diffusion of the gospel? Britain is the Phœnicia of the modern world, with every part of which we are in constant communication. Was the early propagation of Christianity materially promoted by the dispersion of the Jews among the surrounding nations? Still more widely are British Christians distributed among the nations now, and still more effectually, therefore, have they the means of contributing to the same glorious end. Did the greatness of the Roman empire present an ample field for missionary exertion? It is only an angle of the field which now awaits our labor. The transmarine possessions of Britain have an area of 2,200,000 square miles, a sea-coast of 20,000 nautical miles, and a population of 120,000,000. But our labors are not limited to these: our "field is the world." Did "the gift of tongues" conduce to the primitive diffusion of the gospel? The power of the press has come to us in its stead, enabling us to speak to the nations in a manner not dependent on the utterance of the speaker, but which often anticipates his arrival, prepares the minds of a people for his message, and continues to echo it, after his departure, from generation to generation. So mighty a power and so rich a gift is this, that had we to choose between it and the gift of tongues, we should all probably give it our decided preference. In a single year it multiplies copies of the Holy Scriptures by thousands and hundreds of thousands; and, if need be, it could multiply them in the same time by as many millions. So that as far as the means for the propagation of the gospel are concerned, the Bible Society alone gives us a decided advantage over the primitive Church. Having "rolled a noble stream of truth through the earth, it requires that the missionary should stand upon the banks and cry, ' Ho, every one that thirsteth, come ye to the waters !' "

Success is seldom or never the result of a single influence; and in addition to the complex aid to the missionary enterprise we have already named, we may notice the favorable influence of the British character. The fact of our success in arms, our love of regulated liberty, and our priority in the race of scientific and civil improvement: our national enterprise, and the unparalleled extent of our colonial possessions: our reputation for commercial integrity, for all that is humane, generous, and noble in designs of benevolence; and the multiplicity of our moral means for accomplishing them: these, and many other elements of individual worth and national greatness, tend to invest our missionary character with additional weight in every part of the earth. How far the general diffusion of the English language and literature may have already subserved the missionary object we know not, nor how much that object would be likely to be promoted by their ultimate universality; but it is clear that if any language is likely to become universal, that language is the English; and that, considering how deeply most of our early standard works are imbued with a religious spirit, none could have fallen in with our evangelical design more directly than this.

We might invite special observation to the fact that certain influences which a few years ago were arrayed, not against the missionary enterprise merely, but against evangelical religion itself, are now ranged on their side. Science—chemistry alone—destroys polytheism, root and branch. All the superstitions of the world involve more or less the worship of the elements; but chemistry can decompose those very elements themselves, and thus leave the Hindoo without his gods; so that a child armed with a microscope is mightier, and more to be dreaded by Brahminism, than Samson by the Philistines when he slew them "heaps upon heaps."

The aspect which the national government, and that mighty power called public opinion, now presents to the cause of missions, exhibits an auspicious contrast with the past. There was a time when the English missionary in India was indebted for protection to the Danish crown. There was a time when the cry was raised, for anti-missionary purposes, *that our empire in India was an empire of opinion*, and when all the force of that empire was against us. There was a time when the press was kept in spasms of activity by the Christian advocates of heathenism for India: when pamphlet after pamphlet proclaimed their veneration for the ancient Hindoo pantheon, and their rage at any mark of contempt shown **to** it, as if an affront had been offered to a valued friend, which they were bound most indignantly to resent. But let us mark, in a single instance, the indication of a change. " It is a happy circumstance," says the " Friend of India," " that Providence has placed so great a number of the Burmese provinces under the sway of Britain, in which the missionaries" (driven from Ava and Rangoon, where a cruel persecution has been raised against the native converts) "are at liberty to carry on their benevolent labors without hindrance. It is not a little singular that whereas the Burmese mission grew out of the persecution of the British government thirty years ago, which constrained the missionaries to seek for spheres of labor beyond the reach of British interference; at present, the salvation of the Burmese mission is owing, under God, to the protection which that same government, more alive to its Christian obligations, is enabled to afford in its conquered provinces."

In addition to all these auxiliaries to the cause of missions, we might point attention to two to which we have already incidentally adverted,—to education and native agency. By the former of these we are comparatively foregoing partial and immediate success, for the sake of preparing with much greater certainty, and to an incomparably wider extent, the future overthrow of idolatry, and a consequent way for the march of the truth over its ruins. And, by the latter, we are not only taking to the converted heathen the fruits of the tree of life, but, in a sense, are planting the tree in their soil, and leaving it to grow and flourish among them.

Now, if our remarks on missionary progress proved that there is more of a missionary spirit in the Church at present than has ever existed since primitive times, our observations on missionary facilities tend to show that our amount of means for the conversion of the world is considerably greater than existed even during those times. All the weapons of victory which they possessed, with the exception of miracles, are at our disposal; and others of equal and even superior power are added to them. Some of these, indeed, are chiefly in the service of the world, but they exist for the Church. Others were obstacles, but have become auxiliaries. Indeed, whatever designates Britain as the country destined by Providence to take the lead in works of beneficence, must be regarded as an encouragement to the missionary enterprise; and to a Church alive to this object, all things around are ready and offer themselves as an apparatus for its successful prosecution.

4. But not only is the missionary spirit in existence, in progress, and surrounded by numerous and powerful auxiliaries—it has been crowned with signal success. Had only a single instance of usefulness attended its endeavors, even that would have been sufficient to redeem the enterprise from mere hopelessness. But the preceding Part contains abundant evidence to show that our success has been fully proportioned to our efforts: that advantages have flowed from our activity which nothing else could have conferred; and that the glorious result has abundantly exceeded the most sanguine expectations of those with whom the enterprise began.

We will here add only two remarks, that, great as our missionary success has been already, the Christian Church is filled with the expectation of seeing greater things than these. While a sentiment of despondency and vague apprehension hangs over the regions of false religion, in the Christian Church the present is an era of expectation and hope; and the influence of hope contributes not a little to the accomplishment of its own predictions. Besides which, the friends of Christian missions are entertaining a confident persuasion of the approach of a period when the influence of the Spirit will descend with much greater efficacy, and their success will be far greater than at present, in proportion to the measure of their exertion. They deem it "reasonable to believe," says Foster, in the admirable Discourse already adverted to, "that when once a certain point of success has been attained, the mere accumulation of power and influence on the side of truth will impart an irresistible momentum and a greatly accelerated velocity to religious principles, so that the last conquest of Christianity shall be accomplished in an incomparably shorter period than has been occupied in achieving its first successes." Judging from the past, they think it likely that when the native mind of a populous heathen land begins to awake and act, it will act in masses; that the law of sympathy becoming subservient to a higher influence, the "wind will blow where it listeth," so that no one will be able to say whence the impulse came, or what is the direction it will take. Thus may "a nation be born in a day." "Behold, the days come, saith the Lord, that the ploughman shall overtake the reaper, and the treader of grapes him that soweth seed."

The conversion of many parts of the earth, like that of Polynesia, will probably be effected with a rapidity which will take even the Church by surprise. And thus it will be seen that "God had prepared the people, for the thing was done suddenly;" and "he shall bear the glory."

SECTION V.

EVANGELICAL ENCOURAGEMENT TO PROMOTE THE MISSIONARY ENTERPRISE.

BUT our great fund of missionary encouragement is evangelical, being derived exclusively from the word of God. And so animating and ample is this, that were all the others not only wanting, but converted into so many sources of apprehension, we should yet rely on the ultimate success of our endeavors.

1. In order, however, that we may not retread the ground we have already passed over, nor open too wide a field for fresh observation, we shall here confine ourselves to three specific grounds of encouragement. The first of these consists of the fact that the missionary enterprise has to receive the benefit of a vast amount of prayer, as yet unanswered, in its behalf. It was predicted of Solomon, as typical of Christ, "prayer also shall be made for him continually." And it is cheering to reflect, that in the present day there is a sense in which the prophecy has received, literally, its evangelical accomplishment. "Last evening," wrote a missionary from China, a few years ago, "a small party of the disciples of Jesus held a meeting for prayer in my rooms, in behalf of the heathen around, and for the kingdom of Christ throughout the world. In this land of the rising sun, we may probably be considered as beginning that series of prayer-meetings which are kept up all around the world on the first

Monday of the month; a chain of prayer, beginning at the farthest east, and carried round successively as the sun advances to the farthest west in the islands of the Pacific Ocean, and thus continued for twenty-four hours, monthly."

Now, it is only to pursue this calculation, and to suppose that wherever there are Christians to pray monthly in public for the kingdom of Christ, there are some to pray daily in private for the same object, and then we are brought to the delightful conclusion, that prayer is made for him continually; that as the aged believer, like David, breathes out his last prayer for the glory of his reign, another generation is just beginning to lisp, "Thy kingdom come;" and as the Christians of one province are rising from their knees before the throne of grace, the Christians of another province are just beginning to take up the language of supplication for Christ; and thus a chain of prayer, beginning in the farthest east, is carried round with the sun to the farthest west, in the islands of the Pacific, through all the hours of time.

And how much more pleasing does this reflection become, when we add to it the thought, that of all the prayers which are thus offered for the reign of Christ, making one unbroken strain of supplication, not one ever has been or can be lost Is it true that every sin committed by his enemies is noticed by a God of unspotted holiness? that every transgression adds something to the treasures of his wrath; and that when the cup of vengeance is full, he pours it forth on the heads of the guilty? As certainly true is it that every prayer of faith offered by his people in behalf of his Son, is noticed by a God of infinite love; that every such prayer adds something to the treasures of his grace; and that when these treasures have accumulated to a certain amount, he pours them forth upon the Church and the world. It is as certainly true that at the very moment when such a prayer is offered, in that very moment he answers it in his Divine intention, though he may wisely delay for a time to answer it really. The suppliant himself may forget his own supplication, or may despair of obtaining an answer; but He is still mindful of it. And, however obscure the suppliant, he prizes it. It is a prayer for his Son, and, as such, it is music in his ear, of which he loses not a single note. It is a prayer for the coming of his kingdom, and, as such, he places it among the perfumed supplications already offered by the saints of past generations; he places it among the last aspirations breathed by "David, the son of Jesse," and of every ancient worthy; among the mighty prayers which ascended from the fires of the early martyrs; among the loud cries of those whose souls are heard from under the altar; among the earnest entreaties of the wide creation, which sighs to be delivered from the bondage of corruption into the glorious liberty of the sons of God. It is a prayer for the salvation of a world which he loves; and, with delight, he beholds it flow into a channel in which a stream of prayer has been for ages flowing and accumulating without a moment's pause, and which shall finally overflow and pour forth a healing flood of heavenly grace over the whole earth. If the success which has hitherto attended our missionary efforts is to be regarded as sent partly in answer to prayer, an indefinite amount of success is yet to come, if only to complete that answer; for that prayer has aimed at nothing less than the salvation of the world. And our partial success proves that it will come; proves that, like the vapor which the earth sends up to heaven to be returned again in fruitful showers, the supplications of the Church form a cloud which is at this moment suspended over the whole field of moral cultivation, ready, at the word of God, to discharge its fertilizing contents. "Ye that love the Lord, keep not silence."

2. But the efforts of Christians to evangelize the world have also to receive the benefit of many a yet unfulfilled promise and prediction of Divine influence. This is a source of encouragement additional to the former; for it both anticipates our prayers, and directs us to the object at which they should aim.

We are taught to believe, in the word of God, that for every degree of spiritual success we are entirely dependent on the agency of the Holy Spirit. But, in order that this doctrine might tend to animate our efforts, as well as to render us humble, we are also assured that a measure of his influence shall accompany every scriptural effort we make, and be imparted in answer to every prayer of faith we present. The whole system of religious means, indeed, is Divinely appointed, and expressly intended, as that in immediate connection with which He is to act; and all the spiritual good already accomplished has been effected, so far as we can ascertain, by the Holy Spirit in this connection. But we are taught, also, that this gracious arrangement still leaves him at liberty to exceed that assurance as he pleases. Indeed, we are taught this by the manner in which he often fulfils that very assurance; for while he never disappoints the just expectations which it has excited in his people, the circumstances attending their fulfilment exhibit the endless diversity of unconfined and unconfinable power. Hence the reason of the language, "In the morning sow thy seed, and in the evening withhold not thy hand; for thou knowest not whether shall prosper, this or that."

But while we are to regulate our expectations as to the success of particular efforts, we are animated with confidence as to the final success of the entire work. If it is not given us to assign the manner or the degree in which particular instances of success will take place, it is only, perhaps, that our confidence may be more undivided and fixed on the success destined to crown the great system of means taken as a whole. For the substantial import of numerous Divine predictions is, that the Spirit shall be poured out from on high; that he shall be poured out upon all flesh; and that then the wilderness will be a fruitful field, and the fruitful field be counted for a forest. Now, as he uniformly operates for the truth, or in connection with it; and as the object of the missionary enterprise is the universal diffusion of the truth, we are encouraged to look for the fulfilment of these predictions in the success of this enterprise. And since the only way in which he has ever acted as if he had forgotten his promise, is by doing exceeding abundantly above all which it had led us to ask or think, we are encouraged to hope for a period when the amount of his influence will be much greater than at present, as compared with the amount of our activity. But if such a period be in reserve, it must be nearer now than at any preceding moment; and if any signs are to indicate its approach, we may surely recognize some in the returning anxiety and activity of the Church for the salvation of the world, and in the preparation which the world exhibits for some great moral change. And what else will be necessary but the arrival of such a period for the consummation of all our missionary designs? Only let the Church behold the fulfilment of the promises and predictions which relate to the impending influences of the Holy Spirit, and the work will be as good as accomplished. The three thousand souls added to the Church in one day by the preaching of St. Peter, would then prove to have been intended as a mere earnest of the rapid progress which the faith should make universally. Like the first rumor of victory, the news of salvation should seem to fly swifter than the speed of the messengers sent to proclaim it; and wherever proclaimed, the people should bow before it.

3. And then, finally, all our scriptural activity for the diffusion of the gospel is in obedience to the will of Christ, and its final success is secured by the fact of his mediatorial reign. The essential connection of these two propositions was established by Christ himself, when he said, "All power is given unto me, in heaven and in earth. Go ye, therefore, and teach all nations;" intimating, that not only is the great system of universal providence committed to his hands, but that it is committed to him expressly that it may be made subservient to the successful diffusion and eventual triumph of his gospel. As if, having entered the spacious treasury of God, and taken account of all its infinite stores : having reckoned up all the orders of heavenly intelligences, and marked their respective capacities for his service; having looked down through all the ages of time, counted its generations, and numbered its events, he had said, All these shall be harmonized, combined into a system, and made contributory to the one object of human salvation. Vast as is the space they occupy, there is not a point in it which shall not in some way be impressed with the signs of their activity : a theatre less ample would not be adequate to the development of my plan. Diversified as are the kinds and degrees of influence they are calculated to exert, and even hostile as many of them are to my purpose and to each other, there is not one of them all which cannot, and which shall not, yield its proportion of willing or unwilling service. And distant as is the period when the last soul shall be saved, there shall not be a moment through the whole of the mighty interval in which all these countless and far-reaching agencies shall not be gradually concentrating their forces, and pointing, more and more directly, to that grand consummation. "All power is given

unto me in heaven and in earth; go ye, therefore, and preach the gospel."

The connection of these encouraging views with the preceding Parts, as well as their practical application, are direct and important. The facts and sentiments of which these Parts consist, are themselves encouragements to missionary exertion; and as such, they naturally fall in with our present train of remark, and multiply our incentives to increased activity.

For instance, is it a slender encouragement to those who are embarked in the missionary enterprise to find that the Christian Church is constructed expressly with a view to that great object? Should it afford us only slight encouragement to find that the aggressive principles of such a Church were shown to be practicable as soon as they were made known, and were attended with unexampled success as soon as they were put into activity? Ought it to yield us only small encouragement to find that the tenor of prophecy, even to its last words, tells of missionary labors and of a triumphant gospel? Or ought it to be regarded as auspicious only in a very slight degree, that, as far as we have acted under the influence of these encouragements in modern times, they have proved authentic? that our missionary usefulness has been fully proportioned to our endeavors? and that advantages have flown from it both of a kind and a degree on which the most sanguine of those with whom it commenced had never calculated? And, considering the obstacles which stood in the way of this success, and the remarkable manner in which many of them have been removed, how considerately and kindly our impatience has been rebuked, our errors corrected, and our ignorance instructed; how opportunely suitable agents have been raised up for occupying peculiar spheres of usefulness; and how unexpectedly aid has come in from the most unlikely quarters, and enemies and apparent evils been converted into valuable auxiliaries and friends—are we not constrained to trace it to the glorious fact that "The God of our Lord Jesus Christ . . . . . hath put all things under his feet, and gave him to be the head over all things to the Church, which is his body, the fulness of him that filleth all in all?"

We commenced the present Part by showing that the history of Christianity, from the earliest times to the present, is replete with encouragement to attempt its further propagation; that even in the first age of its existence, when it was the mark at which every weapon, human and infernal, was levelled, each of its conflicts was a splendid victory; that even its moral weakness has been too strong for barbarian might; that its false friends have never been able to corrupt it beyond its power of self-renovation, nor its avowed enemies to assail it, even at its greatest disadvantage, without finding to their cost that it is still as vigorous and aggressive as ever? Now, after all this accumulated evidence that Christ is invested with supreme power, and that he wields it for the protection and progress of his gospel, can we believe that he is the same yesterday, to-day, and for ever, without feeling that our cause is invulnerable, and its triumphant issue secure?

On taking a survey of the political world in its relation to the Church, we have seen that all the rest of the globe seems placed by Providence at the disposal of Christendom; that of all the nations of Christendom, those which are especially distinguished with political influence over the pagan and Mohammedan regions are the Reformed and anti-Papal powers; and that of these powers, Britain and America, the only Protestant nations capable, at present, of becoming the religious teachers of the world, are the nations to which has been given the political command of those regions. Now, can we mark these "wheels within a wheel," can we account for these *imperia in imperio*, without resolving them into the sublime truth that the Lord reigneth? Or can we believe that this threefold collocation of the various parts of the world around the missionary portion of the Church, results from his mediatorial arrangements, without hearing the loud and encouraging call which arises from it to "go forwards?"

Besides which, the moral aspect of the mass of mankind, as we have seen, presents encouragement to the same effect. Not only is the heathen world arranged, in a sense, around the Church, but its state is that of feebleness, exhaustion, and desire of relief. Without knowing what is the nature of its malady, it is sick at heart, and panting for a change. Now, if its political position in relation to the Church evinces the provident activity of the reign of Christ, is not that evidence materially increased when viewed in connection with its moral condition? It is not only brought to our door, but brought at a moment when it is famishing. It is not merely placed within our reach, but is actually fallen at our threshold. Could any conjunction of circumstances afford us a better opportunity of presenting the gospel, or a more encouraging prospect of its favorable reception?

And should it not add something to our hopes that this happy juncture has arrived at the very moment when the Church, after neglecting the world for centuries, is awakening to its missionary obligations? Is not such a coincidence indicative of providential arrangement, and worthy of it? Is it nothing that the commencement of the missionary enterprise should have proved like the bursting forth of a fountain of internal prosperity in the Church itself? Is it nothing that Missionary, Bible, and Educational Societies should have arisen precisely in that order of succession which the nature of the case required? Should it pass unnoticed that all the great discoveries and improvements of science are more or less auxiliary to missionary purposes? and even if no other encouraging consideration could be adduced, ought not the single fact that God has smiled on our efforts to be sufficient of itself to induce us to proceed? Ought not the firm persuasion that there are many who, by the blessing of God on our instrumentality, have been rescued from the depths of heathenism, and who are at this moment swelling the chorus of the blessed above, to animate our zeal, and redouble our endeavors?

But the great evangelical fund of encouragement remains to be considered. Does the effectual fervent prayer of a righteous man avail much? The missionary enterprise inherits the prayers of the entire Church. All the redeemed in heaven have prayed for it; and it engages their sympathies still. And, what is infinitely more, it enjoys the intercession of the Great Advocate himself. Is the influence of the Holy Spirit essential to missionary success? Drops of the coming shower have already fallen; and still the cloud enlarges and descends, and gives signs of the impending blessing. Is it necessary that infinite faithfulness and power should show themselves interested in it in order to assure us of its success? All power in heaven and in earth is given to Christ to render the success of his gospel certain. The present evangelical economy exists for it. All the machinery of Providence is constructed to advance it. The world itself is maintained only as the theatre for its progress. Nature, providence, and grace, are not three independent departments of the Divine government; they are only concentric circles revolving around one centre—the cross of Christ. For the diffusion of its influence Christ himself reigns, and harmonizes and administers all their revolutions. To this object, nothing within the vast circumference of his government is indifferent. Nothing is too great to serve it, or too minute to promote it. Nothing opposed to it is allowed to triumph; nothing friendly to it can fail to yield its mite of auxiliary influence. Nothing, absolutely nothing, is allowed to quit the stage of activity, without leaving behind some tribute to its claims.

And are these our encouragements to prosecute the missionary enterprise? What else means the mediatorial Sovereign by associating the command to proclaim his gospel with the announcement that all power is his? What else means the sublime declaration that all things are *by* him and *for* him? What else mean the conspicuous and undeniable facts that only two or three thrones of paganism are left; that a hand mightier than Samson's should be laid upon these; that the gospel, after surviving a thousand conflicts, should be seen exhibiting the vigor and activity of its youth? and that the Church, in awaking to its diffusion, should have opened a new source of internal happiness and prosperity for itself?

Are these our encouragements to expect success? Then "be silent, O all flesh, before the Lord; for he is raised up out of his holy habitation." Be hushed the language of complaint and unbelief: be silenced the taunts of infidelity, inquiring, Where is the promise of his coming? be stilled the din of opposition to the progress of his cause, and the shouts of frantic superstition in every idolatrous temple. Then "the idols he will utterly abolish." Kalee, Vishnu, Juggernaut, your shrines are doomed, your days are numbered, your end draweth nigh. Then *it is* the voice of him that crieth in the wilderness which we hear—" Prepare ye the way of the Lord: make straight in the desert a highway for our God. Every valley shall be exalted, and every mountain and hill shall be made low; and the crooked shall be made straight, and the rough places plain, and the glory of the Lord shall be revealed, and all flesh shall see it together." Islands of the sea, ye shall not wait in vain for his law. Africa, there is hope in thine end : the hands of all thy children shall soon be stretched out to God. All thy myriads, India, shall rejoice in a true incarnation, " God manifest in the flesh." And, China, thy only walls shall be salvation, and all thy gates praise. All for which the Saviour endured the cross, despising the shame; all for which the past has been preparing, and which the present is needing and desiring—all shall be accomplished. "The great trumpet" has been blown : its reverberations of mercy roll round the earth, and the world shall hear it and live.

And are these our encouragements to proceed? Then our course is obvious, our duty clear. At the most dim and distant prospect of such scenes, the ancient prophets were rapt into an ecstasy of delight. With encouragements incomparably less than we possess, an apostle was inspired with a confidence of success which nothing could dismay, and with an ardor of activity which nothing could quench. For us, then, to decline the missionary cause, or to look coldly on its progress, is to merit the execration of the world we are neglecting, and of the Church we are refusing to assist. But scripturally to aid it, is to place ourselves in harmony with all the purposes of God, and to hasten the recovery of the world to Christ.

PART IV.

OBJECTIONS TO THE MISSIONARY ENTERPRISE, OR PLEAS AND EXCUSES FOR NEGLECTING IT.

So obvious are the obligations of the missionary enterprise, and the encouragements to discharge them so numerous and strong, that, if facts did not loudly proclaim the contrary, we might well believe it impossible for a single objection to be raised against it. We know, however, that no degree of excellence, even when accredited from Heaven, has ever proved sufficient to exempt a cause entirely from opposition; and that its success, whether great or little, has never been owing to any lack of difficulties feared by its professed friends, or created by its avowed foes. Indeed, the loftier its aims, and the greater the spirituality of its character and claims, the more numerous the obstacles likely to be cast in the way of its progress. The missionary cause, then, by aiming at the most unworldly ends, and by taking the whole earth for the sphere of its activity, may be expected to exasperate every form of irreligious hostility, and to be encountered by every kind of objection. And when it is remembered that the ignorant are always ready to accept such objections, however futile, as so many unanswerable arguments against it; that the indolent are glad to construe them into a full discharge from all activity in its behalf; that the timid are for waiting until they are all silenced, and the ground completely cleared of difficulties; and that, however often they have been met already, error is likely to revive and repeat them again with the lips of each succeeding generation—it is by no means supererogatory or unimportant that such objections should be obviated again;

especially, too, when nearly all of them may be so easily converted into arguments for serving the very object they were intended to weaken or destroy.

I. Now, if we propose to notice these objections* in order, the first, perhaps, which demands our attention, is that which would represent the missionary enterprise as unnecessary. According to the objector, the heathen are comparatively safe already: their ignorance of the gospel is involuntary: they are a law unto themselves: they will not be judged by the high requirements of the Bible, but by the light of nature: their eternal destiny, therefore, is far from hopeless; and to pronounce it otherwise is uncharitable and cruel.

To this representation we should object, 1. That it overlooks the true condition of mankind in relation to the moral government of God. It forgets the momentous truth that "all have sinned," and are condemned already. 2. It makes the salvation of the heathen a question of right and justice. It supposes that, by saving those who believe the gospel, the Almighty has brought himself under a kind of obligation to throw open the gates of heaven to the whole mass of the heathen world. 3. And it virtually constitutes idolatrous ignorance a better security for the future happiness of mankind than is afforded by the means of grace enjoyed under the gospel.

The question is not, be it remarked, whether or not, in consequence of the mediation of Christ, the heathen are in a salvable state. This we not only joyfully admit, but are prepared, if necessary, earnestly to contend for. But this fact only proves their present condition to be more fearful than if no such salvability existed; for it shows they are the subjects of moral government, and as such exposed to punishment for disobedience. Nor is the question whether many, but whether any, of the heathen are saved; for we presume that the objector himself does not suppose that any large proportion among them are rescued from destruction; that he is not even prepared to prove that any of them will certainly be

---

* Some of these objections are very ably met in a work entitled "The Missionary Convention at Jerusalem; or, An Exhibition of the Claims of the World to the Gospel. By the Rev. David Abeel, Missionary to China."

saved. And where, we ask, is the charity of abandoning them all to a vague hope of deliverance? or what is gained by the admission that one here and there is possibly saved? This single ray leaves the nations sitting in the darkness of destruction still. The true question is, Are the heathen, as a whole, idolatrous and immoral as they are, spiritually safe? Every part of the word of God—the only authority competent to reply—affirms that they are not.

For, *first*, they are condemned by the light of nature. They will not be condemned for the infraction of a law of which they never heard, nor for the rejection of a Saviour who was never proclaimed to them. The ground of their condemnation will be, that they loved darkness rather than the dim light of reason, conscience, and tradition, which they enjoyed: that bad as their creed was, their character was worse: that single as their talent was, and on that account all the more precious, they hid even that in the earth, "so that they are without excuse."

Secondly, the word of God confirms the sentence of their condemnation. Although the heathen of the present day are involuntarily ignorant of the Sacred Scriptures, never having heard of their existence, yet as the first act of idolatrous worship in every nation must have been perpetrated in defiance of every thing sacred; and as the descendants of these idolaters evince as strong a dislike to recover the knowledge of God as they themselves did to retain it, not only neglecting to avail themselves of "that which may be known of God," but entailing their idolatry from generation to generation with accumulated abominations, they are Divinely pronounced to be inexcusable. The opening of the Epistle to the Romans is devoted directly to the establishment of this solemn fact. Having affirmed that "the Gentiles who have not the [revealed] law are a law unto themselves," the apostle convicts them of the grossest violations of that unwritten law; and draws the solemn conclusion that they who have thus "sinned without [the revealed] law, shall also perish without law."

Nor, *thirdly*, does the gospel afford us any ground to hope that the sentence of their condemnation will be reversed through the mediation of Christ. That faith in the mediation of Christ is indispensable to the personal salvation of those to whom the gospel has been proclaimed, will be generally admitted. But when the apostle inquires concerning the heathen, "How shall they believe in him of whom they have not heard? and how shall they hear without a preacher?" if there be meaning in language, he obviously intends that it is as impossible for a heathen to be saved by Christ without believing in him, as it is for him to hear of Christ without a preacher.

But salvation includes the renewal of the heart by the agency of the Holy Spirit, as well as the remission of sins through faith in Christ. Now, that this spiritual change is indispensable to the salvation of all to whom the gospel comes, and that the truth is the instrument by which it is effected, will also be generally admitted. But when we hear it Divinely declared to the great apostle of the Gentiles, that the object of his mission was "to open their eyes, and to turn them from darkness to light, and from the power of Satan unto God," what can we infer, but that a spiritual renovation is essential to their recovery, and that the instrumentality of the gospel is essential to that renovation? To such as would argue against these conclusions, from the probable salvation of the offspring of heathen dying in infancy, we need only say, You are arguing from the case of those who have no actual sin, to those who are covered with the guilt of personal transgressions: from those who *can* neither sin nor believe, to those who have the capability of both: by a very slight extension of your argument, therefore, you may proceed to infer that as those dying in infancy are probably saved through Christ without exercising faith in him, all are probably saved by him, though in the same destitution of faith.

But, *fourthly*, we cannot be adequately impressed with the danger of the heathen, unless we remember that their idolatrous condition is never represented in Scripture as a palliation of their guilt, but as constituting its vilest element. In speaking of its origin, it is there traced to two sources: "because they did not like to retain God in their knowledge, God gave them up to vile affections." Here, a hatred for the truth combines with an act of judicial dereliction to seal their doom; for if the former adds the last shade to their guilt, the latter entirely extinguishes the hope of their deliverance.

And hence, *fifthly*, the Divine punishment of idolatry has frequently commenced in the present life. The Jewish dispensation was one perpetual protest against it. Whole nations of idolaters were exterminated to make way for the worshippers of the one living and true God. Almost the only thing against which "the wrath of God was revealed from heaven" for ages, was idolatry and its immediate fruits. In the punishment of these, the great cities, thrones, and nations of antiquity were involved in a common ruin.

But, *sixthly*, if we have recourse to the word of God for direct statements on the subject, the answer of the living oracle is strictly corroborative of our worst fears: "The whole world," saith St. John, "lieth in wickedness." A people destitute of Divine revelation are spoken of as "having no hope, and without God in the world." If we ask of their future state, we are told that "idolaters" are adjudged to "the second death," and that the "nations who forget God are turned into hell." And how truly affecting to find that this fearful view receives an appalling confirmation in the fears and distressing convictions of the converted heathen themselves, concerning those of their relatives who have died in heathenism! Strongly predisposed, as we may well imagine them to be, to hope the best of their eternal state, they are free to confess that, taking the Bible for their guide, they can see no escape from the dreadful conclusion that every impenitent idolater is lost. And from this harrowing consideration they derive a strong ground for upbraiding us that we did not earlier send them the gospel, and for an earnest appeal that we would now redeem the time by redoubling our efforts for its universal diffusion. Away, then, with the false philanthropy which indolently and charitably abandons the everlasting happiness of millions to a mere peradventure. Let ours be the only scriptural and consistent charity, which, while it fears the worst, aims at the best; and while it dreads their destruction, labors to the utmost for their salvation. By this method, at least, we cannot injure them: by any other, we may be probably leaving them to hopeless destruction.

II. Another class of objectors are inclined to regard the missionary enterprise as impracticable. They entertain a vague opinion, the grounds and merits of which they have never examined, that heathenism is a system too old to be altered, too deep-seated to be subverted, and too vast to be materially reduced. And hence they are apt to fortify this objection by the addition of another—that little or no good has been hitherto accomplished by missionary efforts, and that some stations have been actually deserted by the missionaries, through want of success, or the fierceness of heathen opposition.

Now, we might justifiably satisfy ourselves by bringing this objection under the neutralizing influence of the preceding, and asking, how the view that the heathen are so good as to be in little danger of destruction, is to be reconciled with the opposite assumption that they are so bad as to defy all means, human and Divine, for their moral improvement. But we do think it enough to refer the objector to the Second Part of this Essay, on missionary successes, as containing a full reply to his opinion that but little benefit has hitherto resulted from Christian missions; and to the Third Part, on missionary encouragements, in answer to his objection on the impracticability of the work.

As to any difficulty which he might feel arising from the occasional reverses and partial failures of the missionary enterprise, we would remind him, *first*, that temporary reverses are not peculiar to the diffusion of the gospel; that science has sustained them, and yet ultimately triumphed; that an Alexander encountered them, and yet became the conqueror of the world; that from many of our present colonies the British arms have more than once been beaten off, and compelled for a time to retire, but have finally gained their object; that even where our hopes have been most disappointed, and are at this moment at the lowest point, our prospects are such that, were our object military conquest or national aggrandizement, instead of Christian usefulness, we could not entirely relinquish our attempts without incurring the charge of cowardice or treason; and on what principle are *we* to expect immunity from similar trials, or to construe them into a sign of certain and universal defeat?

We would remind him, *secondly*, that such reverses are not attending the diffusion of the gospel now for the first time; that its plantation in our own country was not the work of a day, nor effected without the endurance of persecution and death; that the apostles themselves were often driven from city to city; and that we have no right to expect exemption from similar vicissitudes.

But, *thirdly,* we have reason to believe that, owing to a change of circumstances, the instances of missionary stations once occupied, but now deserted, are incomparably fewer than similar reverses were in primitive times; that, if these few instances were examined, it would be found that the majority of desertions had arisen from the opposition, not of heathen, but of nominally Christian governments; and that such opposition from this quarter is gradually ceasing to exist.

Fourthly, we have to remind him that such failures, so far from being final, have commonly been followed by the most signal successes; that as, in primitive times, the "bonds" of the apostle "turned out rather for the furtherance of the gospel," so, in the history of modern missions, the scene of our greatest discouragement and disaster has often become the scene of our most grateful triumph. The Caffre tribes, which formerly came down on the missionary community in marauding bands, approach it now only to invoke the instructions of a Christian teacher. Where once the missionary was prevented from landing, the New Zealand chief has since been seen heading hundreds of natives to honor and welcome his arrival. And in the Sandwich, Tahiti, and Society Islands; in the Hervey, Navigators', Friendly, Austral, Paumatu, Gambier, Marquesan, and other groups, where once the Christian preacher dared not approach, or fled with unconcealed terror, are now to be found exemplary Christian churches, and societies for sending native missionaries into the regions beyond.

Let the objector remember, *next,* that even if the missionary enterprise had been attended with no direct benefits whatever abroad, its reflex influence on the state of piety at home has been most amply remunerative; so that even if the salvation of our own countrymen were our exclusive duty, we could not think of limiting the gospel to our native land: if we were at full liberty to seek the welfare only of our own people, in order to attain that end in the shortest time, and in the highest degree, we should feel bound to obtain the reacting influence of Christian missions.

But, *finally,* we have to remind him, that eminently useful as their legitimate reaction has been on the state of religion at home, there is reason to believe that a greater number of conversions has taken place in heathen lands, in proportion to the amount of means employed, than has been effected in the same time in Christendom. So that, unless the objector is prepared to arrest and destroy all the Christian instrumentality now in operation at home, on the plea of inutility, consistency requires that he should advocate the continuance and encouragement of the same instrumentality, on the ground of its usefulness abroad.

III. Having yielded to the preceding reasons, the objector may allege, further, that "If the conversion of the heathen must needs be attempted, philosophy and learning must, in the nature of things, take the precedence. Indeed, it should seem hardly less absurd to make revelation precede civilization in the order of time, than to pretend to unfold to a child the Principia of Newton, before he is made acquainted with the letters of the alphabet." This, be it remarked, is not an objection imagined for the occasion, but the veritable language of one who was literally applauded by thousands for uttering it, and whose words doubtless echoed the thoughts of thousands more. Indeed, at the commencement of modern missions, the opinion very generally prevailed among the friends of missions themselves, that, in barbarous lands, civilization must pioneer the way for Christianity, but on this important condition—that the Christian missionary himself should be the pioneer; while the class of objectors in question would have him to remain at home till his way is prepared by philosophy and science.

1. Now, conceding to the objector the credit of being himself a philosopher, we might begin our remarks by inquiring, Do you not know that philosophy has not yet decided whether the most perfect state of man be not the least civilized? And lest you should suppose that such a question was peculiar only to the dreaming school of Rousseau, we have further to remind you that travellers and historians are still found describing the life of the savage with so much rapture, as to compel the belief that they would fain propose it as a model to the rest of the species; and so copiously applying to that state the epithets "simple," "virtuous," and "happy," as to awaken the inquiry whether it would

not be wiser to employ missionaries for restoring the civilized to barbarism, rather than for raising the barbarous to civilization.

2. We will suppose, however, that all men pretending to philosophy have arrived at the philanthropic conclusion that the savage tribes of the earth should, if practicable, be civilized. But here we have next to ask the objector, Are you not aware that the almost unanimous conclusion to which your order has arrived is, that those tribes are utterly irreclaimable? Nearly two centuries elapsed, for instance, after the discovery of America, before its inhabitants attracted the attention of philosophers. And when they did, it was only to be described by one as "a race just called into existence, and still at the beginning of their career;" * and, by another, as "animals of inferior order, incapable of acquiring religious knowledge, or of being trained to the functions of social life." † And do you not know that this representation of the natural inferiority of uncivilized man became so prevalent in the class of philosophic writings referred to, that had the writers been constituted a committee on the subject, they could not have "brought up" a more consistent report? Do you not know that the consequent belief of this inferiority became so popular, that the public mind is yet far from being disabused of it? but that, as far as it has been disabused, Christian missionaries have been mainly instrumental in dislodging the error by developing the intellectual and moral capacities of the traduced aborigines, through the medium of religion?

3. Now, it must be allowed that to report a people irrecoverably brutish, is a strange and ominous commencement of their civilization. For, "having classed their fellow-creatures among the wild beasts of the forest, these claimants to the exclusive title of human beings are likely to find little difficulty in defending, at least to their own satisfaction, whatever measures may be necessary for the subjugation or destruction of the common enemy." ‡ Accordingly, we have next to remind the objector that, with singular unanimity,

---

* M. de Buffon, Hist. Nat. iii. 484, etc.; ix. 114.
† M. de P. Recherches Philos. sur les Americ. passim.
‡ Lord Glenelg's Dispatch to Governor Sir B. D'Urban.

they have decreed that untutored man must be destroyed. Yes, the very men who would scout the idea of the Christian missionary attempting to benefit the savage before they have visited him with their grand specific of civilization, have yet banded together, in effect, for his destruction. "Nothing but powder and ball," said a European officer, "can civilize these savages." The tribes to which he referred have since been both civilized and evangelized, by the Divine blessing on missionary endeavors. "Do you think it possible," said Sir Rufane Shaw Donkin to Doctor Philip, in the Committee of the House of Commons, "to prevent *enlightened* Europeans, who settle in a country, from ultimately exterminating the unenlightened inhabitants?" from which we must infer that the certainty of the destruction of a barbarous tribe is in exact proportion to the advanced enlightenment of the colonists.

In a proclamation issued by Sir B. D'Urban, the Caffres are denounced as "irreclaimable savages;" and this in the very face of the fact, as stated in the dispatch of Lord Glenelg, that "under the guidance of their Christian ministers they have built places of public worship: have erected school-houses, and sent their children thither for instruction: have made no inconsiderable advance in agriculture and in commerce: have established a trade amounting to not less than £30,000 per annum in the purchase of European commodities; and when as many as two hundred British traders were living far beyond the boundaries of the colony, protected only by the integrity and humanity of the uncivilized natives." And yet it is of this same people that we read in a volume just issued from the press, that "it furnishes matter of amazement to every thinking person, how those who have legislated for the affairs of the colony should not long ago have seen the imperious necessity, dictated alike by *reason*, *justice*, and *humanity*, of exterminating from off the face of the earth such a race of monsters."* "The uncivilized must give way to the civilized," says the editor of the journal of the Royal Geographical Society, "and better sooner than late."† But,

---

* Narrative of an Expedition into Southern Africa, etc., by Captain W. C. Harris.
† Vol. v., part ii., 1835, p 315.

for the full exposition of this exterminating philosophy, we must refer to the following passage in Sir John Ross's Second Voyage to the Arctic Regions: "Our brandy was as odious as our pudding to our Esquimaux visitors, and they have yet therefore to acquire the taste which has, in ruining the morals, hastened the extermination, of their American neighbors to the southward. If, however, these tribes must finally disappear, as seems their fate, it is at least better that they should die gradually by the force of rum, than that they should be exterminated in masses by the fire and sword of the Spanish conquest, since there is some pleasure, such as it is, in the mean time; while there is also a voluntary but slow suicide in exchange for murder and robbery. Is it not the fate of the savage and the uncivilized on this earth to give way to the more cunning and the better informed, to knowledge and civilization? It is the order of the world, and the right one; nor will all the lamentations of a mawkish philanthropy, with its more absurd or censurable efforts, avail one jot against an order of things as wise as it is assuredly established."*

4. But next, we have to remind the objector that those who should have been the advocates and agents of civilization, having concluded, to their own satisfaction, that the uncivilized must be destroyed, have destroyed them accordingly. "An uncivilized people," says Niebuhr, "has never derived benefit from contact with a civilized race." So uniformly has the extirpation of the former followed the arrival of the latter, that, as we have seen in the preceding paragraph, a theory has been formed to account for and justify the wide-spreading calamity. Man has impiously appealed to the purposes of God in vindication of his own atrocities. The ordination of Divine Providence—a Providence ever just and kind—has been represented as obtaining its fulfilment in the erection of an altar to Molech, at which millions of human victims have bled. And here, let it be observed, we are not speaking of days long gone by—of the Red Cross Knights of Mexican and Peruvian butcheries— but of the deeds of to-day; of the last new creed of philoso-

* Narrative, etc., vol. i., p. 257.

phy on the subject of civilization; of the principle just evolved by the spirit of the times from an induction of multiplied facts, as the only principle to be relied on and embodied in practice; and this is it—*the uncivilized world must be blotted out.*

5. Next, we have to show the objector that where the civilization which has hitherto attended the progress of our arms, commerce, and colonization, has not exterminated a people, so far from preparing them for the reception of Christianity, *it has proved the greatest obstacle to its introduction.* And how could it be otherwise? For what have the means of such civilization been, but the overflowing of our national depravity, and the exercise of injustice and oppression? Philosophy has prepared the way for the demons of avarice, cruelty, and licentiousness, by proclaiming the hopeless brutalization of savage tribes. A civilized legislation has transferred whole regions to colonists—transferred those regions from under the feet of the aboriginal inhabitants, without rendering them an atom of compensation. A legalized commerce has for ages devoted one quarter of the globe to a market for human flesh. And, in its considerate regard for the welfare of the native tribes, one of the first buildings which a Christian government has erected in some of its colonies has been a jail for the reception of the superabundant depravity of home; and one of the first colonies which it has planted has been a colony of convicts. About two thousand runaway sailors and convicts are at large in New Zealand and the adjacent islands alone, carrying demoralization and ruin wherever they come. And again philosophy steps in with her timely aid; and, lest the work of destruction should proceed too slowly, announces the crowning and seasonable discovery, that such destruction is perfectly in harmony with the plans of Heaven.

Are we to wonder that, influenced by such examples, and in obedience to such doctrines, the civilized savage should have degraded the uncivilized savage from a brute into a demon, making him twofold more the child of hell than before; that he should have introduced among the natives European vices, violently seized their women, taught the horrid traffic of licentiousness, and introduced a train of new diseases and frightful evils too revolting to meet the public eye?* that he should have forcibly seized their lands, plentifully supplied them with ardent spirits, excited quarrels among the different tribes, and then furnished them with arms for the purpose of mutual destruction? and that the direct effect of all this should be to prevent the progress of education and religion?† Are we to wonder that the only question of colonial policy with many of the colonists themselves has come to be simply this, whether the natives should be destroyed slowly or speedily—by the gun, or by drunkenness and disease? Are we to be surprised at finding that they themselves have come to stand in much greater need of the restraints of law than even the natives; that while these only need the Christian missionary, those require both the missionary and "the supervision of an efficient police?"‡ or that a society should have at length arisen for the protection of those aboriginal victims of civilization? Are we to wonder that one missionary should be heard deprecating the influence of such civilization on the natives? that another should declare, "I had ten times rather meet them in their savage state than after they have had intercourse with Europeans?" and that all should unite in deploring the effect of such intercourse, as amongst the greatest obstacles to success which they are called to encounter?§ And can we be astonished to find the prejudiced, injured, and demoralized native turning away, and spurning the cup of salvation, because it is proffered to him by a Christian hand?

6. Advancing a step farther, we would show the objector, next, that instead of civilization being necessary to prepare the way for Christianity, Christianity is indispensable to a true civilization. When we speak of a *true* civilization, we mean to imply that a spurious and superficial state of social advancement—in which houses are built instead of wigwams, the clothing of the loins extended over the body, and the work of conquest and human butchery is conducted scientifically—may obtain independently of religion. But if by

---

* So revolting, that, in the "Evidence on the Aborigines," it is necessarily omitted. See pp. 20, 23.
† Evidence on the Aborigines, passim.
‡ Idem, p. 68.   § Idem, pp. 27, 173, 277.

civilization we understand a state in which the rights of men are respected, and the proprieties and charities of life are cultivated, we are prepared to show that it has never been found but as the inseparable companion and effect of Divine Christianity. For, first, admitting that barbarous tribes could be reclaimed without the intervention of Christian missionaries, "the mere civilizing plan does not furnish motives strong enough to induce men to give up the comforts of home merely to teach them civilization." Hence, when Dr. Coke, about forty years ago, was induced to form a plan for civilizing the Foulahs of Western Africa, preparatory to the introduction of the gospel, a plan patronized by Mr. Wilberforce and other leading men of the day, it failed entirely, "and failed for this very reason, that the agents [mechanics] engaged to carry the scheme into effect did not find sufficient motives to induce them to persevere. On reaching Sierra Leone, their courage failed them." But Christianity could find agents for that very sphere—has found them; and the result is, that religion and civilization are advancing among the Foulahs hand in hand.*

Nor, secondly, does civilization furnish motives sufficiently powerful to induce the heathen to be taught. "The fruit ripens," they say, "and the pigs get fat, while we are asleep, and that is all we want; why, therefore, should we work?" In vain did the Governor of Upper Canada repeat his attempts to induce the Chippeways to renounce their wandering life, and to attend to civilized pursuits. "Who knows," said they, "but the Munedoos [gods] would be angry with us for abandoning our own ways?" and the homes which he had kindly built for them remained unoccupied—monuments of the impotence of civilization without religion. The apparent tameness of civilized life possesses no attractions sufficiently strong to induce the barbarian to abandon his roving habits, and to encounter the anger of his gods for its sake. Such is the explanation of the fact furnished by the barbarian himself, when reclaimed by the influence of the gospel. And, consequently, so uniform and complete has been the failure of the mere civilizing plan, that many intelligent Americans have been led to adopt the conclusion that the aborigines are utterly

---

* Evidence on the Aborigines, pp. 124, 125, 129, 388.

incapable of being reclaimed, and must be banished from the neighborhood of the white population.*

But thirdly, if these difficulties were surmounted, the civilization of the heathen would not predispose them to the reception of the gospel. That part of our nature which religion especially addresses would still be left unimproved. And hence India and China are not found to receive the gospel the more readily for the fact that they have been for ages in a state of semi-civilization. The plan which the Society of Friends adopted in their early intercourse with the Indians was, to attempt civilization first. This plan they have steadily pursued for years, for ages, at a considerable annual expense. And what is the result of this long and costly experiment? "Within the last few years," says one of the members of the committee for conducting it, "we have had occasion to review the whole course of proceedings, and we have come to the conclusion, from a deliberate view of the past, that we erred, sorrowfully erred, in the plan which was originally adopted in making civilization the first object; for we cannot count on a single individual that we have brought to the full adoption of Christianity."†

And then, fourthly, while we are not aware of a single instance in which civilization has prepared the way for Christianity, facts innumerable might be added to those already adduced, to show that it has had a contrary effect. Why is it that the most savage tribes are more easily brought under the influence of the gospel, than the partially-civilized nations of China and India? Which of the Indian nations offered the most obdurate resistance to the gospel, but the Mohawks of Upper Canada, who, through the kindness of his Majesty, had enjoyed the educational and civilizing process for forty years? Their proverbial abandonment to vice was often urged by their ignorant heathen neighbors as an objection against the Christian religion itself.‡ And the reason why the influence of civilization is thus unfriendly to religion is obvious. "Man," says an eloquent writer, "may master nature, to become in turn its slave. Civilization, so far from being able of itself

---

* Evidence on the Aborigines, pp. 126, 127, 142, 143, 154, 178, 294, 387.
† Idem, pp. 187-197. ‡ Idem, pp. 133, 134.

to give moral strength and elevation, includes causes of degradation, which nothing but the religious principle can withstand." It multiplies the desires and passions of the heart, without any increase of power to the regulating principles; and thus only adds to the length of the lever by which vice subverts both our moral constitution and the fabric of society. "Reason and experience forbid us to expect," said Washington, on resigning the presidency in 1796, "that morality or political prosperity can prevail in exclusion of religious principles." And in 1802, the French republic were constrained to confess, "For want of a religious education for the last ten years, our children are without any idea of a Divinity, without any notion of what is just or unjust: hence arise barbarous manners, hence a people become ferocious."

7. We have to show the objector, further, that wherever Christianity and civilization have presented themselves before a heathen tribe in company, the former has been invariably embraced before the latter. Now, this fact, we should suppose, ought to be conclusive. The plan of missionary proceeding which wisdom and experience sanction is, not to act as if a savage tribe would be civilized by merely preaching to them the doctrines of the gospel,—this would be only the opposite error of those who imagine that rude people may be civilized without the influence of religion,—but to act on the principle that, while Christianity alone can excite in them a desire for improvement, nothing should be omitted of a civilizing nature likely to subserve that desire. For from the moment that the Christian principle begins to operate upon the mind of man, from that moment the wants and cravings of civilization begin and advance. And we repeat, that wherever, in harmony with these views, Christianity and civilization have thus labored among a barbarous people conjointly, the former has been invariably embraced first. Fifteen years of effort were made by the missionaries in the South Sea Islands to introduce the arts of civilized life with instruction in the truths of the Christian religion—but apparently in vain. At the end of that time, Christianity was adopted by the people, and from that moment their civilization commenced.* Another fifteen years of missionary effort were

---

* Evidence on the Aborigines, pp. 176, 177.

occupied in New Zealand in a similar manner, and apparently without effect; but the "very moment that Christianity established itself in only one instance in the island, from that moment civilization commenced, and has been going on hand in hand with Christianity, but never preceded it."*

8. And, finally, let the objector know, that wherever Christianity has gained a footing, civilization has invariably followed. The first house which the barbarian builds is commonly a house of God. In vain did government erect habitations for the Chippeways in order to lure them to the habits of civilized life; but no sooner did the gospel affect them than they applied to the governor for that very aid which they had before rejected: this was afforded, and they settled on the river Credit. In vain were the influences of civilization showered on the Mohawks: the only effect was increased demoralization. But no sooner did they begin to embrace the Christian faith, than "each appeared to vie with the rest which should give the strongest proofs of industrious habits."† The same mere civilizing process has been tried on the Wyandot Indians and the Cherokees, and with the same comparative failure; but "the missionary has marched up to the savage heart, adapted his mode of instruction to the condition of the Indian, and his conversion to Christianity has followed. This accomplished, he has been easily brought by gentle steps to walk in the path of civilization."‡ Evidence to the same effect might easily be adduced from the history of Christian missions among the West Indian negroes, the remains of the Carib race, the various tribes of West and Southern Africa, the Hindoos of India, the Budhists of Ceylon, the cannibals of New Zealand, and the other islanders of the South Sea.§ The missions of every denomination of Protestants, says Bannister, in his "British Colonization"—those of the Church of England, the Moravians, the Independents, the Baptists, the Wesleyans, the Scottish—all present animated spectacles of workshops, farms and school-houses thickening around their churches and chapels; and the occupations of merely civilized men carried on with vigor and success, hand in hand with Christian duties, by

---

* Evidence on the Aborigines, p. 250. † Idem, p. 142.
‡ Idem, pp. 146-153. § Idem, pp. 132, 166, 174, 250

tens of thousands whose fathers, and often themselves, were lately naked, and houseless, and possessionless barbarians.* While they are under the influence of their superstitions, they evince an inanity and torpor from which no stimulus has proved powerful enough to arouse them, but the new ideas and principles imparted by Christianity. And if facts can convince—if the question is to be decided by evidence—the objector is bound to receive it as an adjudged case, that the missionary enterprise is incomparably the most effective machinery that has ever been brought to operate on the social and civil, as well as on the moral and spiritual interests of mankind.†

IV. Convinced that Christianity is the great agent of civilization, an objector may yet allege in excuse for not assisting to send it abroad, that we have heathen enough at home: that charity begins at home, and that we must evangelize home first. These are pleas which, by wearing the appearance of a pious patriotism, often beguile the sympathies of the unreflecting, and tend to foster a spirit of indolence in the cause of God, whose exposure should be its utter condemnation. Let us first endeavor to exhibit their hollowness, and then specify certain principles by which they are to be met, and the truth defended.

"We have heathen of our own at home," you say, by which we are to suppose that you intend persons who are very ignorant and very vicious. But if such persons are existing around you in any considerable number, does not the fact implicate you in the tremendous guilt of having neglected them? And will you plead that which results from your own sinful omission of duty towards those thousands, as an excuse for neglecting a similar duty towards as many millions? But in extenuation of your conduct towards your irreligious neighbors, you probably plead that they have been far from entirely neglected: that the knowledge and means of religion have been within their reach from infancy. From which we learn, on your own admission, that they are ignorant, not by necessity, but choice—self-constituted heathen men, who deliberately prefer practical atheism to Christianity. And we ask, Is the world to be kept in ignorance—are the millions abroad

---

* Evidence on the Aborigines, p. 174.　　† Williams, M. E

to be left to perish—because there are those at home who "hate instruction," and "love darkness rather than light?" Such a sentiment you profess to repudiate; but while you theoretically admit the heathen to a share in your sympathies, you still contend that—

"Charity begins at home." To which it should be sufficient to reply, that this is a saying which, so far from subserving an objector to the missionary enterprise, tells directly against him; for it obviously implies that charity is diffusive, and, instead of remaining at home, only begins at home. There is but one way, then, in which this proverb can avail you, and that is by implying that there has not yet been sufficient time for charity to begin her domestic duties; in answer to which we will only suggest the inquiry, If upwards of a thousand years form too short a period for the mere work of preparatory benevolence at home, how many thousands are likely to elapse before the ends of the earth will be blessed with the gospel?

For your third proposition, that "we must evangelize home first," implies not only the order of benevolent operation, but also the high degree of success which must attend it before you could think of aiding Christian missions. But for such a requisition we are surely justified in expecting that you can plead the most substantial warrant both from Scripture and experience. You should be able to show, for instance, that the apostles made the evangelization of Judea the condition of their attempting the conversion of the Gentiles, and that, as they failed of entire success at home, they never proceeded abroad. And you should be prepared to prove, in addition, that this course has been uniformly sanctioned by the Divine blessing wherever it has been followed; so that to confine our Christian activity to the limits of home, is the true secret of real prosperity. Now surely you need not be reminded that almost the only particular in which the apostles incurred the public rebuke of Providence, was for indulging the very disposition which you exhibit—for confining to their own country labors which were meant for the world: that you owe it to the violation of that rule which you hold so sacred, that you yourself, and all your countrymen, are not living in heathenism; and that when the apostles came to understand their duty, they no sooner encountered rejection from the

Jews in any of the cities and regions they visited, than they forthwith "turned to the Gentiles." And as to the conclusion derivable from experience on the subject, we would merely suggest the inquiry, whether it is not high time to suspect the wisdom of a plan whose practical operation and proposed result never promise to approach each other.

The following principles, we think, require but a very slight effort of attention, and of application to the subject, in order to show you that your objection is utterly untenable. The *first* of these principles is, that as the gospel is designed for every creature, we are bound to attempt its universal diffusion. This obligation arises partly out of our community of nature and interest—a relationship by which the entire race, instead of consisting of a multitude of detached and isolated individuals, is formed into a family so closely united by reciprocal ties, that the well-being of each is connected with the good of all. To complete the obligation, however, the will of Christ has made it authoritative and divine. Do you ask where and how he has expressed that will? Not merely by commands to be found on almost every page of his gospel, and which require us to "do good unto all men." Not merely by the authority of his own example in "taking away the sin of the world." But also by the diffusive nature of the gospel itself, by which it no sooner takes effect on an individual than he feels himself impelled to proclaim its virtues to others, and to urge its acceptance. And still more, if possible, by the divine constitution of the Christian Church; by which, as we have shown at large in the First Part, having composed it of such as have themselves found mercy, he requires them to act as a body organized and appointed for the recovery of others.

But while every Christian is thus bound to aim at the welfare of the entire race, a *second* principle is, that there is an order in which his benevolent efforts are to be made. This law of succession is the order of nature, by which those who are most nearly related to us have the first and strongest claims on us; the order of Providence, by which we are enabled to administer the means of salvation to those who are placed near to us earlier, and at less expense, and in greater variety and abundance, than we can to those who are more remote from us; the order of Scripture example, in which we see the apostles uniformly preaching first, wherever they went, to those of their own nation; and also the order of the future judgment, according to which no plea of attempting good at a distance will be admitted as an answer to the charge, "I was a stranger, and ye took me not in." But in saying all this, we may appear to be only repeating the sentiments of the objector. So far from this, however, we are insisting on a very different subject, and one which, by implication, refutes his objection. For while we are only showing the *order* in which we are to work from the centre of our own circle outwards, he is contending for the time we are to remain in that circle, and the amount of good we are to accomplish there, before we attempt any thing beyond it, and is thus practically denying any order of usefulness at all. Whether the command of Christ to his apostles, that they should "begin at Jerusalem," is applicable here, admits of a question; for it is quite possible that the reason of that injunction arose out of *his* relationship to the Jews, and not from that of the apostles: a relation which, as it was perfectly unique, cannot be a ground of obligation to his followers. But allowing that it is applicable, and that it thus harmonizes with our present position; you, we say to the objector, you, by pleading exclusively for home, are acting directly at variance with it; for while it allows you to begin at home, it does not permit you to rest till you have aimed to diffuse the gospel "among all nations." And this shows that the order in which our benevolent efforts are to be made is not only the order of nature, of Providence, of scriptural example, and of the final judgment, but also the order of self-increasing Christian usefulness; the order, that is, by which, in seeking the salvation of those immediately around us first, we multiply our means, through the grace of God, for usefulness to the world at large.

Hence, a *third* principle is, that by observing the scriptural order of Christian activity, success at home becomes the means of increased usefulness abroad. Home duties, then, are to be discharged partly with the view of ultimately augmenting our resources for every sphere of usefulness beyond; so that we may say to the objector, The Christian philanthropist has all your motives for seeking the welfare of those around him, and one in addition of which you know nothing, —the powerful motive of thus multiplying his means of bene fiting the world at large. How many a Christian mother has found a strong additional inducement to the discharge of maternal duties, from having devoted her Samuel in heart to the public service of God! How many a Sunday-school teacher has labored in his high vocation with increased devotedness, when the thought arose that perhaps his class contained some youthful Eliot or Brainerd for the missionary field! And what a strong incentive to persevering diligence has the faithful pastor found in the recollection that the prosperity of his flock was an element in the prosperity of the Church at large, and consequently in the welfare of the entire world!

But from this arises, *fourthly*, the important principle that, in proportion as we scripturally seek the good of others, we ourselves are benefited. For, in the instances referred to, the mother, the teacher, and the minister, would be the first gainers by their increased attention to their respective classes of duties; and the son, the pupil, and the flock, would be the next, though the ultimate object aimed at was the good of parties still more remote. And do you not know, we might say to the objector, that this is only in harmony with the law of the Divine government, which ordains that "he that watereth others shall himself be watered?" You surely do not suppose that the fulfilment of this gracious declaration depends on geographical limits. If it guarantees to the individual Christian the reflex benefit of all the good he aims to impart to his friend, and if it secures to a particular church the advantageous reaction of all its efforts for the welfare of home, it equally engages that Christians at home cannot unite to benefit the world, without finding the benefit return in showers of blessings upon themselves. The history of modern missions is, as we have already shown, a continuous illustration of this great truth. So great has been the beneficial influence which they have been the means of exerting upon the Church at home, that, if the missionaries had effected little or no good among the heathen, they have accomplished more for their own countries by going abroad than if they had remained to occupy the most distinguished station at home. But of all this reflex influence you would deprive your country. By limiting benevolent exertion to your own circle, you would arrest the operation of a law by which all you do beyond that circle is repaid a hundred-fold, and without which, probably, there would be no benevolent activity at this moment within that circle itself.

And then, *fifthly,* this reciprocity of religious advantage reminds us of the great principle that the cause of human welfare is indivisible and one. Whereas your objection proceeds on the assumption that the interests of religion at home and abroad are opposed to each other; so that whatever is done to promote the one is so much lost to the other. But is this a supposition worthy of the professed follower of Him who embraced all the interests of humanity in his own person, and who left his gospel in trust for "every creature?" It is true that the claims of a religious society are sometimes magnified beyond their due proportion of importance, and enforced in a manner which threatens with neglect or collision certain kindred institutions. And in some instances, a prior duty of inferior importance is underrated and neglected for a more remote but magnificent enterprise. But these are errors and evils incident alike to the cause of religion at home and abroad. The advocates of each, however, should remember that all our duties, temporal and spiritual, are so related, that he who neglects the least will find no excuse in pleading that he was attending to the greatest; and that all our Christian societies are so connected, that he who promotes one at the expense of another, inflicts injury upon them all. The example of our blessed Lord in looking down from the cross, and tenderly providing for a mother's comfort in the very crisis of the world's redemption, shows that all the true interests of humanity are indivisible, and that all duty is sacred and one.

V. Supposing the objector dislodged from the preceding position, he may yet allege that, even if it be our duty to attempt the evangelization of the heathen, we have not the necessary funds. This objection, we might reply, is untenable on various grounds: it proceeds on the assumption that we have already reached the maximum of our contributions for missionary objects; whereas the steadiness with which, for so many years, they have gone on annually increasing, warrants the expectation rather that they will still continue to increase. The objection assumes, too, that the Christian Church is either so good or so bad as to admit of no improvement; whereas we confidently anticipate that, in answer to prayer, the Spirit will exalt the character of its piety, and that, as one of the necessary consequences, the pecuniary resources of Christians will be consecrated in a larger proportion than ever to the service of God. Another of the false assumptions on which the objection proceeds is, that the expense of evangelizing the nations is always to devolve entirely on the Church at home. But let Christianity begin to consecrate to Christian purposes those immense sums which paganism lavishes on its vain superstitions, and the Church at home might be reimbursed, if necessary, of the expenses already incurred. Christianity would need little for its support, compared with what idolatry requires. The celebration of the feast of the Hindoo goddess Doorga costs, at Calcutta alone, not less than the annual sum of five hundred thousand pounds sterling. "In the kingdom of Siam alone, with a population of four or five millions, there are at least twenty thousand priests, besides a great number of splendid and costly pagodas, supported by the voluntary contributions of the people. In Burmah, India, and many Mohammedan countries, we find the same lavish expenditure of talents and money in honor of their objects of adoration."* Let these resources be turned into the channels of Christian benevolence, and not only will they be sufficient, by the Divine blessing, to irrigate their own desert, but even to help in fertilizing whatever waste places might still exist in our own borders.

But most of all do we demur at the grave assumption, that the ultimate success of the missionary enterprise depends on the amount of our funds. That money is necessary for the prosecution of our object, we admit; but, remembering that an almighty Agent is graciously working with us and by us, the question of "how much?" admits not of human calculation. And remembering also that in the promises of Divine approbation and success, the stress is laid, not so much on the intrinsic value of the offering or service, as on the manner in which it is rendered, we are warranted in affirming that the consummation at which we aim depends not on the amount of our resources, but on the entireness with which we consecrate that amount, whether great or small, to the

---

* Abeel on Missions, p. 142.

service: that were we, on the one hand, to devote a thousand-fold more to it, we should not be warranted to expect success, if still we sacrilegiously kept back a portion unemployed; but that if, on the other hand, our funds, and agents, and resources, were to be ever so much reduced from what they now are, still, if they were all we *could* furnish, we should be justified in expecting complete success. Let the multitude to be fed be ever so large, and the means of feeding them ever so small, still, if the whole of that scanty provision be cheerfully placed in the hand of Christ, in that hand it will be so greatly multiplied, that they shall "all eat and be filled." To suppose, in such a case, that we should fail in diffusing the gospel over the earth, is to suppose, either that we are not responsible for that diffusion, or it is to make that responsibility return, and rest on him who had imposed it.

VI. Still the objector may plead, that, since our Lord prayed for the visible union of all his followers in order to the conversion of the world, we ought not to embark in the missionary enterprise until that union has been effected. Not only do we admit that this representation of the prayer of Christ is correct—we believe that the spirit of disunion among Christians is doing more at this moment to prevent the diffusion and success of Christianity in the world than all other causes together. But the propriety of deducing and adopting the objector's inference from this admission we unhesitatingly deny. We have to remind him first, and chiefly, that the duty of diffusing the gospel is not made to depend on our union, but on the explicit command of Christ. And, next, we have to suggest, that our Lord may have evinced his wisdom in this respect, by making our efforts for that diffusion conducive to the restoration of that union. Now this, we submit, is actually the fact. The common ground of benevolent activity is almost the only bond of the visible union of Christians which remains unbroken. And it is the growing conviction of the writer, that, as this is almost the last ligament which visibly holds them together, so it is likely to be the first and the principal means which God will employ in again restoring them to each other's love. Whether he will compel them thus to unite, in mere self-defence against the counter-activity of a world whose interests they are betraying and neglecting by their divisions, or whether, by an effusion of the Spirit of love and zeal, he may lead them to think more of the will of Christ than of the claim of party, we stay not now to inquire. But judging of the superior facilities for union which plans of benevolent activity present, and from the deepening conviction of Christians that such combination is made essential to the conversion of the world, we repeat our belief that benevolent coöperation is likely to be the principal means of restoring Christian union.

Thus the objection against Christian missions is turned into an argument in their behalf. They make us feel that we have a common object and a common interest; and what can the effect of that be but to inspire us with sentiments of reciprocal affection? Let us only meet on common ground, hail each other as auxiliaries to the same grand cause, and coöperate for the common interests of the world, and how necessarily would our groundless dislikes give place to a feeling which would deprecate every project to disjoin, and welcome such measures only as tended more closely to unite! If it be true of the blessed God, that "they who know his name will put their trust in him," it must be true, in a subordinate but corresponding sense, that the more his people, as such, know of each other—of their mutual resemblance to him, their common concern for the salvation of the world, and their zeal for his glory—the more sincerely will they admire each other's piety, and the more will they unite for the achievement of their common object; while the only contention between them will be that of the vine with the olive, which will bear the best and most abundant fruit.

VII. The objection of the millenarian—that the conversion of the heathen is reserved for the second coming of Christ, and, consequently, all attempts to effect the object by the diffusion of the gospel will prove useless—we have considered at length in the First Part of this treatise. The reader may remember that we have there endeavored to show that such an inference is at variance with some of the admitted principles and necessary deductions of Divine revelation; that it is not warranted by prophecy; but that the very reverse is the doctrine of the prophetic Scriptures, and is found to be in perfect harmony with every other part of the word of God by which its correctness can be properly tested.

The prosecution of the inquiry discloses, if we mistake not, the important facts, that whatever conflicts may hereafter ensue between the Church and the world, will arise from the success of the gospel; and that whatever judgments the earth may yet be called to witness, will only concur with the power of the gospel to enlarge the domains of the Christian faith. So that those very predictions which are too often made to depress the hopes and dishearten the zeal of the Church, will be found calculated, when rightly understood, to animate its activity as with the blast of a trumpet.

VIII. And another objection, not very remotely allied to the last, amounts to this: "The time is not come, the time that the Lord's house should be built." When that selected time arrives, the Almighty will easily find means to accomplish the conversion of the world; and till then, all our efforts are premature and presumptuous, and must prove abortive. In reply to this Islamite doctrine, we might say to the objector, Your conduct in urging this objection is inconsistent with your creed; for how do you know that it is the will of God that you should urge it? Why "use the means" for correcting our supposed errors? Are you not by this very act "taking God's work out of his hands?" Had you not better leave him to take care of his own cause? When "the time comes" for God to correct our errors, will he not find an abundance of means without disquieting *you?* and till then, is it not presumptuous for you to attempt to "take the work out of his hands?" If, however, on some inexplicable ground, you still consider yourself justified in "using means" to denounce the missionary enterprise, are you using means enough? Ought not your opposition to become more practical and laborious? If you really believe we are forestalling the appointments of Heaven in assailing the idolatries of the heathen world, and tormenting the demons before their time, ought you not to employ counter-missionaries, for instance, to protect those abominations, and to prolong their reign for a season longer? But perhaps your principle of interference only applies to those cases in which labors are unnecessary, and serious sacrifices not required.

You surely do not presume to plead that because God permits the existence of heathenism—does not arbitrarily destroy it—therefore it is not for you to attempt to reduce it.

This plea would not avail you unless you could assign the same reasons for *your* conduct which God can for *his*. And not only must your reasons be identical with his—your conduct in relation to heathenism must harmonize with his. But this it cannot, except by your cordially embarking in the missionary enterprise. For has he not maintained an unbroken contest with the evil? Have not cities, nations, a world, perished for it? Has your zeal ever flamed against it? He has appointed and put into operation a grand system of means divinely adapted to subvert the reign of evil: what are you doing to give that system impulse and activity? He has laid a command on every member of his Church to assist in sending the gospel to every creature; so that, if you are not rendering it obedience, and calling on others to join you, the sense in which you are content to permit the continuance of heathenism differs essentially from the only sense in which he can be said to suffer it. Every attribute of his nature is in hostility to it; every principle of his government—the whole course of his providence—is arrayed against it; the great wonder, the miracle of his mercy, is, that he should permit the continuance, age after age, of a Church which he has called into existence, partly for the purpose of extinguishing that evil, but many of whose members still plead, "The time is not come—the work is not ours, but God's."

Perhaps, however, you profess to be only waiting for the necessary indications, in order to evince your perfect readiness to act. But yours must be a very controllable zeal, if it does not sometimes quicken into impatience for the arrival of the sufficient signs. Inspired men of old often expressed themselves in language which showed that they would fain have multiplied themselves and their means a thousand-fold against the prevalent idolatry. Now, that must be a state of mind of a very different order which leads you to regard exemption from such hostility as a favor, and to denounce the activity of others as presumption.

But what are the signs from heaven which you would deem sufficient to warrant you in joining the missionary enterprise? Would a direct and express command possess any weight with you? Never has the Lord of the Church ceased to say, not to you merely, but to every member of that Church, "Preach my gospel to every creature." Would you regard the concurrence of the providence of God with the command of his word as an additional call to action? Behold it in the disappearance of numerous obstacles to missionary exertion; in the rapid accumulation of important facilities; and in the fact that so many hundreds of agents are at this moment actually occupied in the missionary field. Would you regard their success as another indication that the time for action has arrived? How could you venture a different interpretation? Here, then, are thousands converted by their instrumentality: you surely will not think, for the sake of a theory, of ascribing their change to any other than a Divine agency. Remember, then, that each of these conversions is to be regarded as an argument from heaven against your non-interfering views; and as a Divine reward to the friends of missions for having acted on principles directly opposite. And would you interpret the readiness and anxiety of the heathen to receive Christian instruction as an additional sign that the missionary era had come? The Lord of missions appears to have regarded such readiness as a call to activity, when he directed his disciples to mark that the fields were white to the harvest. Far wider fields invite our attention. In every direction, the vision of the "man of Macedonia" is, in effect, repeated, and heathen voices are heard lifted up in earnest application for help.

Now, is it possible that you should still require other signs that the period for labor has come, before you will consent to move? The reformers, there is ground to believe, deemed less than these sufficient to justify them in attempting to shake the Church and the world. And, judging from the results, you would not say that they displeased God by the attempt. His most distinguished servants appear to have regarded his express command, and opportunity to perform it, as always sufficient to create obligation to obedience; and the success of their endeavors has convincingly shown that they were not mistaken. With such strong and numerous inducements to missionary devotedness as we possess, then, our only fear for ourselves is, lest we should incur the rebuke of "the unprofitable servant;" and for you, lest you should fall under the spirit of the fearful denunciation, "Curse ye Meroz, curse ye bitterly the inhabitants thereof, because they came not to the help of the Lord, to the help of the Lord against the mighty."

One of the remarks inevitably suggested by our survey of the preceding objections is, that each of them, relying on some *partial* view of the truth, overlooks the great principle of revelation to which it belongs, and by which it must be decided. Who, for instance, could ever have brought himself to look on heathenism as if it were in amicable coëxistence with the Divine government, or on the heathens themselves as being in any other state than that of the most fearful exposure to everlasting death, unless he had lost sight of the universal and unrepealable law, "Thou shalt have none other gods before me?" Or who could have deemed it a valid objection to say that heathenism is unalterable, until he had forgotten that the gospel was launched at first into an ocean of heathenism—for, with the exception of Judea, the whole world was an idolatrous temple; that if the case is altered now, the gospel has been the means of effecting the change; that he himself and those around him are, in their own persons, an answer to the objection; and that the gospel is still the power of God unto salvation to every one that believeth? Or who could think that he was acting scripturally in confining his evangelical desires and endeavors exclusively to one nation, even though that nation be his own, until he had forgotten the great principle of our Lord's command, that the gospel is designed equally for all nations?

Another reflection forced on us by these objections is, that many, if not all of them, have been defended with a pertinacity which zeal for the truth can seldom command. If those who entertain them set a high value on religious distinctness from the world, they are certainly unfortunate in having adopted objections to the missionary cause which, as far as they go, completely identify them with the world. And we will venture to suggest whether it ought not to awaken their suspicion as to the soundness of their views, on finding that, if indolence, self-indulgence, and unbelief could speak on the subject, it would be to repeat the very same objections, in the same language.

But chiefly we are reminded, that Christian missions have this mark, in common with the gospel, that they are not of men, but of God; that every objection brought against them can be so easily converted into an argument in their behalf. And this removal of the war from our own into the enemy's country, takes place, be it observed, in every instance, not merely by a triumphant appeal to undeniable and accumulating facts, but also on the authority of one or more of those great principles of the word of God which the objector had overlooked. Thus, does he plead that missionary effort is unnecessary, because the state of the heathen is not so desperate as we seem to imagine? We can show him that, if rampant rebellion against God be a state of guilt; if to be hopeless and godless be a condition of misery; and if the most fearful threatenings of the offended Majesty of heaven be a just ground of terror, then is the whole idolatrous world in a state of the most crying and appalling want; for such are their guilt, and wretchedness, and danger, that hell may be said to have come to them on this side death. Does he regard the missionary object as impracticable? We can show him that the difficulties are vanishing while he is speaking of them. We can call for the trophies of Divine success, and they come from the four quarters of the earth. Impracticable! What! when hundreds of missionaries are actually in the field; thousands, tens, hundreds of thousands of heathens converted and collected into Christian societies, and of their children receiving Christian instruction! No good done! Spirits of the blessed, who have ascended from the missionary churches to join the ranks of the redeemed out of all nations and kindreds, and who are now before the throne—is your salvation nothing? Nothing to yourselves, as you glance from the depths you have escaped to the heights you have attained! Nothing to the society you have joined! Nothing to Him, the light of whose countenance is at this moment falling on you, and making your heaven! The objection is turned into a rebuke that we should have been detained by it so long. In a word, whatever his pleas may be, unless he can show that the great command of Christ to preach the gospel to every creature—a command frequently repeated and variously enforced in Scripture as the law of the Christian Church—has been modified or repealed, we confidently bring down its annihilating weight on all his objections, and challenge him, as one included in the principle which it contains, that all who possess the gospel are bound to coöperate to the extent of their ability in giving it to the world.

PART V.

THE WANTS OF THE CHRISTIAN CHURCH IN RELATION TO THE MISSIONARY ENTERPRISE, OR THE NECESSITY OF EMINENT PIETY AND ENTIRE CONSECRATION IN ORDER TO ENLARGED SUCCESS.

THE WANTS OF THE CHRISTIAN CHURCH IN RELATION TO MISSIONS.

THE prosecution of our prescribed course has brought us to a very important part of our subject. If, as we have shown in the First Part, the Church is constructed expressly to embody and diffuse the influence of the cross throughout the world; if the Second Part proves that, as far as the Church has answered this end in the modern missionary enterprise, its success has been fully proportioned to its efforts; if the Third Part has shown that encouragements from every quarter urge and animate us to advance in our missionary career; and if the Fourth Part assures us that every objection to our course becomes, when rightly considered, an argument to redouble our efforts, an unreflecting reader might be ready to conclude that nothing remains for us but mutual congratulations and unalloyed satisfaction.

The enlightened Christian, however, need not be reminded that as, in his own experience, a sense of joy in God, and of dissatisfaction with himself, often meet together in the same moment, so the hour in which the Church may have the greatest reason to rejoice through God in its relative usefulness, may be the hour in which the dust of self-abasement may most become it on account of its own defective instrumentality. He will remember that, however "the manifold wisdom of God" may have been displayed in organizing his

Church for usefulness, but few of its members as yet may have perceived that adaptation, and fewer still have combined to exemplify it in practice. He will remember that, while the Church now, as compared with what it has been, may be doing much, yet, compared with what it should be, it may be doing nothing; that its fitness for one office by no means implies a fitness for every order of duty; and that its very improvement may be made in a manner which may justly incur rebuke. He is aware that much collective activity may exist where there is but very little individual zeal: that, owing to the blessing of God on that activity, opportunities of usefulness may increase more rapidly than our readiness to seize and improve them; and that, in this manner, success itself may become a snare and a burden. And remembering all this, the effect of the preceding survey will be that so far from hastily surrendering himself to the pleasing but hazardous conclusion that all is well, he will feel that now has arrived the time for humble, searching, anxious self-examination; that to detect an evil now, may be the means of saving us from undue elation at present, and from much mortification in the future; and that to point out the great want of the Church now, may be to bring to it present prosperity, and to hasten by ages the glory of God in the salvation of the world.

But how is this examination of the Church to be conducted; or where is to be found the test of its fitness for converting the world? This can only be found in its original constitution. Now, on looking back to our exposition of Christian instrumentality, it will be seen that, according to that constitution, the individual Christian, the particular church, the entire Christian community—the whole, penetrated and actuated by the Holy Spirit—is intended relatively to act in harmony with the cross for the good of the world. Every addition made to it is meant to be an additional agent for carrying out the purposes of the cross. Every element at work in it—whether it arises from numbers and combination, from eminent piety, self-denial, and zeal, or from prayer, and the influence of the Holy Spirit uniting with the whole—is an element for drawing men to Christ.

But if the full efficiency of the Church for this end depends, under God, on the entireness of its consecration to this office, it will follow that the slightest diversion of its influence from this object is so much given to the very power which it was called into existence expressly to counteract; and that this is, in effect, the secret of its long decline and fall.

But, then, it follows also that if, at length, in that depressed state, the Church should awake to a sense of its responsibility as a missionary agent for the world's recovery to Christ—if, then, it should withhold any proportion of its influence, in that very proportion it would stand disqualified for answering its great original design. In this position the Church now stands; and here, we repeat, is the test of its fitness, at present, for its missionary office. To bring it to this test, indeed, has been the duty of every age. But never so much so as now, when, after the slumber of centuries, it is meditating the renovation of the world.

Now, on calling upon the Christian Church to muster for this review, is it not ominous at the outset that we know not who will appear? In answer to the name of Christian, indeed, about two hundred millions present themselves. But the great majority of these Christianity disowns. She knows them not. Many of them are among the chosen of Satan. The heathen around them are the worse for their vicinity. They must be dismissed by millions to the ranks of the foe. And thus, like Gideon's army, the number is reduced by a single sweep to a comparative few. And here goes, at first, the influence of numbers.

But perhaps it may be said that large portions of Christendom make no pretensions to the missionary spirit, and ought not, therefore, to be subjected to the examination. Without stopping to contest the point, and in order to be definite, let us suppose that, after all such portions have been dismissed, those who remain before us consist of the various denominations professing evangelical Christianity. Let us indulge the hope that as they are so reduced in number, and as each equally professes to live for the salvation of the world, they have at least learned the unspeakable value of union. United! Union! What does it mean? When did it exist? Is it not a fiction of the fancy? If there be such a thing, the Church practically disowns it. Whatever sympathetic connection may here and there exist among individual Christians, the

Church, as a Church, disowns it. See how these Christians hate! In their visible and public capacity, they scorn to approach each other. They expend more strength in struggling with each other than in encountering the world. The world looks on amused Infidelity claps her hands. And thus is lost the influence of union.

But, though it be thus divided as a whole, let us hope to find that the members of each particular Church are alive and devoted as one man to its missionary design. Let us take one Church as a specimen of all. Here are a thousand souls, we will suppose, assembled for Christian worship. As the service proceeds, the time for commemorating the great doctrine of the cross arrives. The majority arise and quit the place; thus practically disavowing all belief in the doctrine, or all interest in it; and leaving it to be inferred that, for aught they care, the world may forget, if it will, that Christianity has a cross, or that Christ died on it for our redemption.

But still we will suppose a large minority remains. Do we, however, flatter ourselves that we shall find general co-operation and devotedness here? We only evince our ignorant simplicity. True, they have just pledged themselves anew at the table of the Lord to the cause of the world's salvation; but let us wait a while, and we shall soon see how little that means—nothing incompatible with the most unmoved worldly self-indulgence. We expected to see them all equally interested in the object; but let us wait a while, and we shall see that the task of keeping them thus partially awake devolves entirely on two or three. We might have expected to see these, at least, nobly devote to Christ a portion of the time which the world devotes entirely to the pursuits of gain; but no: religion must wait till the world has been fully satisfied; and then, if a few of the jaded moments of evening are of service, they are spared.

Agents of mercy are wanted for distant lands; and we might have expected to see them start forth from the ranks of the rich and the poor alike; or, rather, we might have looked to see those who would require the least delay for educational preparation and support, offer themselves first. Might we so? What, when the act would involve the danger of losing caste with the world? Surely we did not expect to see them incur such a risk merely for the sake of saving immortal souls. True, the act would have the noblest effect, both on the Church and on the world; but we cannot expect them to sacrifice gentility, and ease, and the prospect of worldly gain, for such an object!

Wealth is wanted to prepare and send forth those who do offer themselves—all the superfluous wealth of the Church. But what do we behold? Not only is every other claimant satisfied first; not only is self, the most clamorous of them all, appeased; but only a fraction of what is left is then placed on the altar of Christ.

Prayer is wanted; and from what we hear them say of its efficacy, we might expect that, however remiss in other means, they would not neglect this; that perhaps they were indifferent to the others, only to reserve the ardor of their souls for this. But when the monthly or periodical season comes round, when the Church is supposed to be all collected and intent on obtaining an audience of Heaven on the subject of the world's salvation, what do we behold? Crowds thronging and besieging Heaven with supplications? the strong cries of a Church travailing to bring forth? The reply is too obvious to be necessary. Here, then, is lost the influence of self-denial, consistency, and prayer.

That exceptions to this representation exist, we gladly admit—exceptions which stand out in bold and bright relief—and owing to which it is that the Church is not actually retrograde. But that this is the rule, we confidently appeal to observation and experience. Need we then ask if the Spirit is visibly and gloriously present with the Church? Present with individual ministers and members of the Church, to a certain extent, he is; present with certain societies composed of a number of such ministers and members, he is—societies which are the salt of the Churches, as Christians are said to be the salt of the earth—but present with the Church, as a Church, he is not. As a Church, Christians do not invoke him. As a Church, they are not awake to their responsibility. And how can he, the great Missionary Spirit, sent to convince the world of sin, honor a Church which is so generally content that the world should remain unconvinced? How can his activity combine with its comparative indolence? his love mingle with its internal hatred? his gushing benevolence with its supine self-indulgence?

In thus exposing the defects of the Christian Church, in relation to its missionary office, we have abridged the unwelcome task as much as is consistent with the object of showing that defects exist with a view of pointing out the remedy. And if this sketch be correct, can we wonder if the world is slow to receive the gospel at our hands? What reason has the Church, as a Church, yet given the world that she herself believes it? Here and there an individual member acts out his principles, and the world admits his sincerity; and, however it may dislike his holiness, is almost as ready to admire his consistency and exemplariness as the Church itself. But what reason has the Church generally given the world to believe it sincere? For fifteen hundred years the wealth of the world was passing through its hands: did it employ that mighty talent for the world's conversion? The world itself was at its feet: did it do much better than trample on it? Again, the world, in a nobler sense, is at *our* feet; asking us, if not in anguish of soul, at least with marks of visible concern, what it must do to be saved. Providence is urging us to answer the question: Christ is saying, "Go and proclaim the cross to every creature;" and we ourselves, professing to believe that we hold in our hands the means of success—professing to exult that the gospel is the power of God unto salvation—can yet hardly bring ourselves to tell more than one in a thousand that there is any salvation; and, professing to believe that Christ has an absolute claim on all we have, can hardly bring ourselves to surrender sufficient to tell that one in a thousand. O, if our Lord had forbade self-denial—if he were now to repeal the law of self-consecration, and to enact a law of self-indulgence—would not the great majority of his people be found in a state of perfect obedience? If living to themselves would convert the world, how long since would the world have been saved!

Do we—can we—wonder that no more good has been effected by us? What! when we are acting in almost entire oblivion of the Scripture theory of Christian usefulness? when, as members of the Christian Church, we are violating almost every part of that theory? What! when we have had to act in the face not merely of a sinful world, but of the still more hostile influences arising from our own selfish inconsistency? when the influence of the little we have done has been fearfully diminished by the neutralizing effect of the much we have left undone? We have had to act against ourselves. The world quotes us as authority against ourselves. Our habits neutralize our acts. Our deeds contradict and silence our professions. The powerful influence which should have arisen from our evident union, disinterestedness, and self-consecration, though lost to us, is not lost to the conflict in which we are engaged; it is arrayed against us; it is more effectual than all other influences combined, in rendering powerless the effect of our actual efforts. The wonder is, then, that efforts so slender, divided, and languid as ours are, should have been attended, not with so little, but with so much success. The glory is more evidently the Lord's.

Can we doubt, then, what it is which the missionary Church of Christ requires? *Simply to realize the Scripture requirement of entire consecration to its office.* Let us not say, in excuse, it has never been realized. Never by a Church, perhaps, but by more of its individual members than history records, or than we may imagine. Religion has ever had a few such on the earth; and to that two or three the Church has been more indebted, under God, than to all its other contemporaneous members together. If corrupt, they have saved it from sinking under the weight of its evils. If sunk, they have helped it to rise. And, hence, when an enlightened posterity records the annals of their age, their names are almost the only honored. When the Holy Spirit himself indites the "Acts of the Apostles," he comparatively passes by all the rest, to do honor to the man who went through the world exclaiming, "None of us liveth to himself." Let us not say again, "My domestic claims—my children—require my time, absorb my property, and thus curtail my usefulness." They were meant to increase our usefulness; to augment the moral treasures of the Church; to multiply its agencies of good to the world. Are they not training up for God? What! is the sum of our moral history to be, that we contributed a trifle in money to the cause of Christ, and left our children to carry on the cause of Satan? Better for the Christian cause had we never been born. As if they had been sent down to us from heaven with a charge from Christ to prepare them for his service, let us look on them as the instruments by which, while we live, we may extend our usefulness; and by which, when dead, we may still continue to say to posterity, "None of us liveth to himself."

Can we doubt, then, we repeat, what it is which the Church requires? A growing desire to be useful we have; and a growing disposition to be active. But that which we most require, and for the want of which no activity can ever compensate, is a fitness, that moral fitness which springs from disinterested devotedness to the one object of the world's salvation. If religion has not yet mastered us, how can we expect by it to master others? How can we speak effectively for religion to the world, when it is so necessary that some one should plead for religion with us? How can we expect to reclaim the world to Christ, when large tracts of our own character are unreclaimed; when the most fruitful and cherished tracts within us are pagan tracts, where the objects and idols of sense are worshipped?—Mohammedan tracts, where self-indulgence reigns—a moral waste? Unless all the rules of fitness between means and ends are to be dispensed with, how can we expect the world to believe that it is perishing until they behold us in anguish for their rescue? The world is selfish: how can we hope to reclaim it if we ourselves are not models of disinterestedness? "If you Christians have known all these things," says the pagan, "and really believed that we ignorant heathen must perish unless we believe in your Jesus Christ, how could you leave so great a part of the world, for so many generations, to go down to perdition, without coming sooner to tell us of this only way in which we can be saved?" What can the missionary say? This is not idle fancy; it is matter of distressing fact.*

When a great experiment is to be made in natural philosophy, the preparation of the apparatus to be employed will often occupy a longer time than the experiment itself. The uninitiated spectator is surprised at the patient and laborious anxiety evinced by the experimenter to bring his instruments into a state of working perfection. But well he knows, from

---

* The Claims of 600,000,000 of Heathen; by Hall and Newell, American missionaries at Bombay, p. 77.

many a previous failure, that the presence of a single particle of matter foreign to the experiment is often sufficient to vitiate the whole process. Christ proposes the great moral process of drawing the world to himself: the Christian Church is the apparatus to be employed, and worldly selfishness or sin the object to be operated on. Do we not see the vital importance that not a particle of the thing to be destroyed should adhere to the instrument employed to destroy it? Do we not see the nature of the fitness we need—perfect contrast to the world? And that this fitness is indispensable to success? O for such an instrumentality! We ask not that it should consist at first of many Christians—their success would not depend on their number—but of men penetrated, possessed, with the conviction that Christian consistency and entire devotedness to the world's recovery are one and the same thing; that without such intense devotedness to that one object nothing morally great has ever been achieved; men who feel that they are not their own as intensely as if their persons were marked and sprinkled with the blood of Christ; and who, in the spirit of that self-consecration, should resolve that, by God's help, the world should feel their influence before they die. O for such an instrumentality! The Church should be converted, and the world too!

1. Now, if eminent Christian devotedness constitute the great want of the Church in its missionary relation, *deep humility* must be regarded as our first requisite, both on account of that essential deficiency, as well as to prepare us for greater improvement and success in the future. Had we "done all those things which are commanded" us, it would still have been our place to come into our Master's presence, saying, "We are unprofitable servants: we have done that which was our duty to do." Where, then, is the depth of abasement equal to the necessities of the case, now that we have almost entirely neglected that duty? And yet where are the tears of the Church on account of that neglect? How much easier it is to find the signs of self-gratulation on account of the little which we have done, than of self-condemnation on account of the much we have left undone? Where are the broken-hearted confessions which should ensue on a thoughtful calculation of the souls which have probably perished, and the revenue of glory consequently lost to the name of God,

through our want of fidelity to our trust? Where is the disposition which might be looked for, to ascertain our guilty omissions and most crying wants, and to take them into the presence of God, and cast ourselves at his feet in order to our forgiveness and improvement?

And yet, until these questions can be answered satisfactorily, we have no ground to expect the growing success we profess to desire. The law of the Divine economy on this subject is, "He that humbleth himself shall be exalted, and he that exalteth himself shall be humbled." God will not trust those with success who are likely to appropriate the glory to themselves. One of the principles by which he regulates this part of his conduct is, to proportion the usefulness and prosperity of his people according as they are able to bear it. The measure of our present success, then, is to be regarded as the measure of our present humility; so that, if we would not stop at the point of usefulness to which we have attained, nor be prepared for a higher degree by a course of painful providential discipline, we must humble ourselves under the mighty hand of God. Eminent devotedness to God will recognize and rejoice in this as a primary duty, while the sincere performance of the duty cannot fail to promote eminent devotedness to God.

2. The next requisite for the Church in its missionary capacity which we venture to specify is, *the due appreciation of the spiritual nature of the work in which we are engaged.* Independently of the danger on this subject to which we are naturally and always liable, the present day has dangers peculiar to itself. Our claims, as the benefactors of mankind, are not, as formerly, passed by in contempt, or summarily dismissed by the world as mischievous or chimerical; but hence the danger of lowering our tone as the servants of the Most High God, and of aiming to make out a case for its commendation which will compromise our character for fidelity to him. Our claims are not only canvassed by the world generally, but partially patronized by the great; but let us remember that, if they have not the mind of Christ, that which constitutes the true distinction and glory of our object is "far above out of their sight," and that what they admire in it are merely its outward accidents and adjuncts. Nor do we now occupy the field of benevolent activity alone; a phi-

lanthropic philosophy professes to join us, to aim at the same end with ourselves, and to be emulous of excelling us in benefiting mankind; but let us remember that our proper work is unique, and that we cannot contest with a worldly philanthropy without coming down from our high vocation, and forgetting that our great aim is, not the temporal, civil, or social improvement of mankind, but their spiritual recovery to God.

But in order to this, we must sympathize with God. This is our only security. And yet how few comparatively do this! How much more frequently do we act from the lowest allowable, rather than from the highest possible, views of Christian duty! How content are we with mere occasional glimpses of the loftier order of Christian motives! as if it were quite sufficient to satisfy us if we can thus assure ourselves now and then of their existence. How seldom do we stand and gaze on our enterprise in the only light in which it is viewed from heaven; as having been revolved from eternity in the mind of God; as asking the universe for a theatre; involving the endless well-being of a race of immortals; requiring the Prince of life for a sacrifice; and all spiritual natures, even the Infinite Spirit himself, as its only adequate agency; and the coming eternity for the full development of its issues! How little do we sympathize with God on that particular point on which, if on no other, the strongest bond of union might be supposed to exist—compassion for depraved, guilty, suffering souls! Who is there that makes the burden of a dying world his own? that goes about with "great heaviness and continual sorrow of heart," oppressed and borne down by the weight of its woes? Jesus wept over the guilt and obduracy of Jerusalem: who are there prepared to mingle their tears with his over the guilt and impending destruction of a thousand cities wholly given to idolatry? Enoch and Noah, Abraham and Moses, David, and Jeremiah, and Paul, evinced the tenderness and depth of their compassion for men by tears, entreaties, and unappeasable anguish of soul: who is there now that can say, "Rivers of waters run down mine eyes, because they keep not thy law?" Who now is heard exclaiming, "O that my head were waters, and mine eyes a fountain of tears, that I might weep day and night for the slain of the daughter of my people?" Who now asseverates, "I could wish myself accursed from Christ for my brethren?"

And yet, until we approach this state of sympathy with God on the spiritual and lofty character of Christian missions, are we likely to be eminently devoted to their prosecution? Will not comparatively trifling acts of service too readily satisfy our feeble sense of duty? But what could appease the anxiety of him who was accustomed to stand in the counsels of God, and daily to look around on mankind from the moral elevation of the cross, or to view them in the light of the judgment fires—what but his total consecration to the work of their rescue? Were this state of mind to become general in the Church, one of its first effects would be that we should think much more highly and honorably than we now do of the missionary character and office. Let a ship be perishing within sight of an assembled multitude on the shore, and let some of these volunteer an attempt to save the sinking crew, with what strained and earnest looks are they followed by those who have sent and cheered them off, and how deep and panting the desires for their success! The missionaries of the cross, in the case supposed, would carry with them the sympathies of the Church. Their office would be regarded as the highest and holiest out of heaven. Selecting them, as we should, within the view and hearing of the perishing millions, how careful should we be, as far as it depended on us, that none but the most compassionate and devoted men went forth! The Saul and the Barnabas of each Christian society would be deemed the most eligible to the office. And having dispatched them, what holy anxieties would follow them! and what earnest intercessions would ascend for their success at the footstool of grace! Hitherto, the Christian missionary may be said to have raised instrumentally the character of the Church; but never till the Church, eminent in its devotedness, imparts its character to the missionary, will the sympathy between them be complete; and in order to this we must appreciate more highly the spiritual nature of the work in which we are engaged.

3. It must be obvious that whatever else may be necessary, a vivid and all-pervading apprehension of *the missionary constitution of the Christian Church, and of the corresponding obligations of each of its members*, is of the first import-

ance. "But do not the various aggressive efforts recorded in the preceding pages show that we have already recovered that apprehension?" To a very limited extent. Until recently, the Christian Church was well-nigh as local and stationary as the Jewish. And is not the clear apprehension of its missionary design still confined to a small minority? Or, if felt by the many, felt only as a passing impulse, the result of an annual appeal, rather than as a personal obligation and a universal principle? Or, if felt as a claim, felt as one which may be easily devolved, and discharged by proxy?

Now, the constitution of the Christian Church supposes that every individual member is prepared to take his post as an agent for Christ. It does not allow the indolent to fold his arms, and transfer his duty to another. It does not permit the fashionable professor to wait till Christian labor becomes genteel. It does not permit the wealthy to buy off his personal services by the bribe of large donations. It requires both—his activity and his donations too. Whether it contains a man for every post or not, it is certain that it contains a post for every man; and hence the first inquiry which some Christian communities make of a newly-admitted member is, "What shall your post be?"

Were the writer to be asked to what it was owing, chiefly, that the early triumphs of the gospel were arrested; how it was that Christian usefulness died out of the world, and piety out of the Church, he would suggest that it was to be ascribed principally to that master-device of Satan by which the Christian professor was led to suppose that he could do every thing by proxy: that there was an order of men on whom, for a certain consideration, he could devolve his duties both to God and to man. Now, this, we hardly need remind the reader, is substantial Popery. The very essence of that system consists in undertaking to exempt its votaries from their personal responsibility—in finding a price for every duty, and a discharge from every claim of personal accountableness. We pride ourselves, indeed, in our Protestantism; but if this representation of Popery be correct, it is high time to inquire from how much of that enormous system we have been rescued. For just as much of it as still cleaves to us, by just so much are we effectually disabled from doing the first works and emulating the first days of the Christian Church.

Now, judging from the past, we should say that the Reformation rescued us from only one half of the evil—from that part which blinded men to a sense of their personal concern in the affairs of their own salvation. But while the Protestant wonders at the infatuation of the Papist in imagining that any thing can exempt him from the necessity of *personal* diligence in seeking his *own* salvation, are not we the objects of equal wonder in acting so generally as if we thought any thing could exempt us from the duty of personal activity in seeking the salvation of others? If the one is essential Popery, equally so, in spirit, is the other also. Glorious, therefore, as the Reformation was *for the Church*, in rescuing its members from the grasp of a spiritual despotism, and making each one feel the necessity of personal faith and personal holiness, as glorious will that Reformation be *for the world* which shall complete the work of deliverance, by rescuing them also from the grasp of selfishness, and making each one feel his accountability to God for personal activity in the work of human salvation.

But, in order to this, the doctrine of individual Christian obligation must be clearly understood, and generally felt. Until the Christian sees that it is not rhetorically but most strictly true, that *he is not his own*, he will be often acting as if his own will were his only law. Even when he sees theoretically that he is the property of God, unless he remember, at the same time, the subduing nature of that price by which he has been bought, he will often act from a stern sense of duty, instead of feeling constrained by the power of love, and will be tempted to reduce the amount of his service as much as he can, without refusing it entirely, instead of presenting himself a living sacrifice unto God.

But even in addition to this, it is necessary that he should feel that he is redeemed for a specific end—an end which leaves no moment of his time unclaimed, and no property of his nature untaxed. Never, till every Christian feels himself as much ordained to *diffuse* the gospel as the minister is ordained to *preach* it; never, till every Church regards itself as a society organized expressly for that diffusion, will its members be aware of its vast capabilities, in the hand of God, for blessing the world! What but this feeling in the hearts of a few has originated all the Christian instrumentality which at this moment is at work? And if a sense of responsibility for personal activity in only a few instances has led to so much, what might we not hope, under God, from the individual and united activity of the universal Church?

4. In order to maintain and enlarge our sense of Christian obligation, *missionary information should be more widely circulated, and more seriously pondered.* What Christian could be insensible either to his own obligations, or to the crying wants of the heathen, at the mouth of the pit of perdition? Now, the direct tendency of all the missionary accounts of heathenism, when rightly considered, is to make us feel that around that gulf the idolatrous world is assembled, and that, but for the interposing grace of Christ, there should we have been mingled with them. We have admitted, indeed, in a previous page, that information from the missionary field is periodically and increasingly diffused, and that a missionary literature for the rising race is in the course of rapid formation; nor can we fail to regard this as tending to the end at which we now aim. Our great concern is, that Christians generally would lay the moral statistics of the heathen world to heart; that they would not merely read a page or an anecdote now and then, but would regularly peruse a portion of the accounts transmitted as if endorsed by the hand of Providence for them, to be taken into the closet and read at the throne of grace. Mere cursory reading can only produce evanescent impressions. And hence, let the members of any Christian congregation, even of one assembled on a missionary occasion, be taken and examined on the subject of Christian missions—how small the number of those who could render an account of even the more recent and familiar facts in its history; and how much smaller the number of those who have so far made it a study as to have a single question to ask concerning it, or a single suggestion to offer for its improvement!

And why is it thus? And how long shall it remain? Till we not merely listen to an occasional appeal on the subject, but take it in all its appalling magnitude into our stated and devout consideration before God. Till we read the history and geography of the heathen nations with a view to it, and study it in maps. Till we make it a standing topic of Christian conversation; and, like the primitive saints, repair to the missionary assembly with minds, not requiring additional excitement, but already filled with intense interest. Till we have laid the state of the heathen world upon our naked hearts, and vividly pictured its miseries to the eye of our mind, as an object at which habitually to gaze. Would the Almighty affect his prophet with the spiritual death of the Jewish nation? He called him *to look* on a valley full of dry bones. Was the spirit of the apostle, when at Athens, stirred within him? It was when he *saw* the city wholly given to idolatry. Did Jesus weep over Jerusalem? It was when he drew near and *beheld* the city. And if we would be duly impressed with the spiritual destitution of mankind, and with the consequent urgency of missionary claims, we must *look*, and *gaze*, and *dwell*, on the subject. By a well-known law of our nature, our eye will soon affect our heart; and, by a gracious law of the Divine economy, that compassionate emotion will be turned into practical effort and missionary success.

5. The preceding considerations suggest the existence of another want—*a greater depth of personal piety*. Fears are entertained by many Christians lest religion, in the present day, should be made to consist more in imparting than in receiving. While they would not have it less abroad for useful purposes, they question whether it is not too little at home. They are apprehensive lest our spiritual expenditure should be exceeding our spiritual receipts. The ground of these fears may be right or wrong. If they arise from the idea that Christian activity and the growth of personal piety are naturally incompatible, so that attention to the one necessarily involves the proportionate neglect of the other, they are utterly unwarranted. For not only were the most active servants of God, as described in Scripture, the most eminent for spirituality and devotion, but their very activity formed a part of the means by which their spirituality was sustained. If, however, those fears arise from the well-known tendency of our nature to substitute a morality however ascetic, a ritual however irksome, or a philanthropy however costly, in the stead of personal piety, and to mistake it for piety, they are not unfounded. But whatever the grounds of fear, it cannot be denied, and need not be concealed, that the danger apprehended exists—the danger of religion losing in depth what it gains in surface.

Nor do we fear lest, in saying this, we should damp the missionary zeal of the Church. On the contrary, our aim is to render that zeal more scriptural and effective; for as long as it remains a principle of Divine appointment that personal piety is the proper foundation of relative usefulness, he who assists in raising the Church nearer to God is enabling it to act more beneficially upon the world. Hence the wisdom of the inspired Psalmist in praying for the prosperity of the Church as preparatory to the conversion of the world: "God be merciful unto us, and bless us; and cause his face to shine upon us: that thy way may be known upon earth, thy saving health among all nations." It is observable that while the calling of the apostles is placed, by one evangelist, in immediate connection with the command that we pray the Lord of the harvest for an increase of laborers,* it is described by another as immediately following a whole night spent by our blessed Lord in prayer to God.† Thus the foundation of missionary activity was laid in the very element of prayer. It was when the apostles had been day after day "with one accord in one place" calling upon God, that they came forth to enjoy pentecostal successes, and to reap the field of the world. And as long as it is true that spiritual influences, like the water, which is their material emblem, cannot rise above their own level, the higher their source, the wider will be their diffusion through the various channels of Christian activity. While this activity, by the occasions with which it will be constantly furnishing us for renewed application to God, will be the means of keeping us in habitual communication with the Fountain of spiritual life; so that by action and reaction our piety will give activity to our benevolence, and our benevolence invigorate our piety.

6. Were the preceding requisites supplied, one of the first effects apparent would be an *increase of holy wisdom*—wisdom to mark the characteristic features of the age and the movements of the world, to appreciate the peculiar position of the Church in relation to them, and to apprehend and obey the indications of God concerning them. The Saviour may be regarded as saying to his people, but especially to

---

* Matt. ix. 38; x. 1. † Luke vi. 12, 13.

his ministers, in every age, "Can you not discern the signs of the times?" Each period is preceded and attended with its own peculiar signs, and it is a part of their duty to mark them,—that to the inquiry of the Church, "Watchman, what of the night?" they might be able to return the correct and seasonable reply. Never was there an age when the wide field of human misery was so fully explored, and so accurately measured, as at present; and consequently there never was a time when the obligation of the Christian Church to bring out all its divine resources and remedies was so pressing and so great; hence the importance that its ministers should be prepared to bring forth the strong reasons of the gospel for entire self-consecration. Never was there an age when science attempted so much and promised so largely—challenging the gospel, in effect, to run with it a race of philanthropy; and, consequently, never was there a time when it so much concerned the Church to vindicate her character as the true angel of mercy to the world; and to do this, not by decrying the human expedients which unenlightened man employs, but by surpassing them in the strenuous application of God's remedy. Never was there a time when the elements of universal society exhibited so much restlessness and change, and when the field of the world was so extensively broken up and ready for cultivation; and, consequently, never was there a time which so loudly called on the Christian sower to go forth and sow; but as long as the laborers are comparatively few, a wise selection of the spheres to be occupied is of the first importance. And if there never was a time since the days of the apostles when the various sections of the Church were so aggressive in their movements, the obligation is proportionate on each community to mark the operation of the others, not to envy, but to learn from their experience, and to emulate their excellence.

To a mind alive to the erection of the kingdom of God in the earth, numerous questions of surpassing interest are always present. Some of those which engaged the attention of the fathers of modern missions, the events of Providence have already answered and set at rest. Of those deserving consideration at present, we might specify such as these; whether or not the claims of the ancient people of God are engaging a sufficient measure of Christian attention; whether, considering the geographical position of Russia, stretching across the whole northern continent of Asia, from the banks of the Vistula to the shores of America, as the dominion of Britain stretches across the south, and thus having between it and us five-sixths of the heathen world—something should not be attempted toward purifying its Church, and rendering it a missionary co-worker with ourselves for their salvation; what the design of God may be in the remarkable distribution of Christian communities—old and corrupt though they be—all over the Mohammedan empire; whether, without diminishing our endeavors for heathendom, more ought not to be done for Christendom; what are the comparative claims of education and preaching in our missionary operations; whether sufficient importance is yet attached to the preparation of a native agency in the various parts of the missionary field; and whether the time has not come when the standard of education for our missionaries might be advantageously raised, especially in the department of science. These are only a few of a great number of topics of growing interest; most of which are likely, at no distant time, to force themselves on our attention in a manner for which present consideration, and devout inquiry of God, can alone prepare us.

But if there never was a time when the great missionary subject teemed with more interesting inquiries, it is equally true that never was there a land blessed with such peculiar facilities as Britain for answering those inquiries, and for obeying the calls of Providence to give the gospel to the world. Why is it that the gospel is at this time in trust with a people whose ships cover the seas—who are the merchants of the world? Has He who drew the boundaries of Judea with his own finger, who selected the precise spot for the Temple, who did every thing for the Jewish Church *with design*, abandoned the Christian Church to accident? And if not—if he has placed the gospel among us with design, what can the nature of that design be, but that it should be borne to the world on the wings of every wind that blows? Let us ask ourselves why it is that Britain and her religious ally, America, should divide the seas, and thus hold the keys of the world? Were we but awake to the designs of God, and to our own responsibility, we should hear him say, "I have put you in possession of the seas: put the world in possession of my gospel." And every ship we sent out would be a missionary church—like the ark of the deluge, a floating temple of God—bearing in its bosom the seeds of a new creation. Ours is indeed a post of responsibility and of honor! On us have accumulated all the advantages of the past, and on us lies the great stress of the present. The world is waiting breathless on our movements; and every sign of Providence finds a voice to urge us on.

And in saying that a missionary Church, to be effective, should be thus wise to mark, and quick to avail itself of, every providential indication, what are we saying, after all, but that God is conducting the affairs of the universe on a plan; that in every age that plan advances; that his people are to mark the signs of that advance, and to fall in with it; and that, in proportion as they adjust their movements to his, link themselves on to his plans, and keep pace with his progress, they move with the force of Omnipotence simply by moving in a line and in harmony with it? O for celestial wisdom, to place ourselves in harmony with Providence, and to seize the crisis which has come for blessing the world!

7. One of the first wants which that wisdom of which we have been speaking would discover, and one of the first steps to which it would lead, would be *a spirit of greater devotedness to the missionary work among ministers at home.* If a considerable number of those who are now preparing for the Christian ministry, and of those who have already entered the sacred office, were to devote themselves, as one man, to the spiritual rescue of the heathen, who can calculate the impulse which would be given to the general cause of religion? What exalted piety would it evince; and what an increase of energy and devotion would it tend to call forth! No fear need be entertained for the safety of the work at home: the spiritual efficiency of those who would find it obligatory to remain at their present post would be increased in a far greater ratio than the numerical reduction of their ranks: many a youth now devoted to secular pursuits would give himself up to the service of God; and, more than all, the act would discover so high a degree of devotedness to God, that he would be able, consistently with his character, to say, in acts of unusual

blessing, what he has already declared in words of promise, "Them that honor me I will honor."

There is reason to fear that, at present, the number of ministers adequately acquainted with the missionary aspect of the Church, and interested in it, is comparatively small; that the subject is introduced to the attention of the people too exclusively at stated times, on annual occasions, and in connection with pecuniary collections; and too seldom as forming a legitimate topic of ordinary ministerial discourse, and to every part of which the heart of the Church should be supposed to be ever ready to vibrate and respond. And yet to this advocacy, partial and feeble though it be, it is owing, under God, that the missionary enterprise has risen to its present position in the Church. What, then, might we not hope to see result, were deeds added to words, and personal devotements to arguments and professions! Let them be respectfully reminded that, besides their special relation to their respective churches, they and their churches sustain a universal relation; that the gospel they preach embraces all interests; that the pulpit they occupy stands, in a sense, in the centre of the universe; that there are lines of relationship connecting it with every object and event within that vast circumference; that they are placed in that central position to watch and report to their people the progress of events, to impress on them the dignity and responsibility of their character as the agents of "Him for whom are all things, and by whom are all things;" and thus to induce them, as their highest honor and happiness, to fall in with that vast procession, including all orders and all worlds, which even now is moving on to the one appointed spot, where all the diadems of the universe shall be laid at the feet of Him on whose head already are many crowns. "This is a true saying, If a man desire the office of a bishop, he desireth a good work;" but let them remember that he who said this regarded a participation in the work of missions as a higher distinction still: "Unto me, who am less than the least of all saints, is this grace given, that I should preach among the Gentiles the unsearchable riches of Christ." Let them estimate the missionary office as highly as he did, and remember how much may depend on their adoption of it: much in the Church;

for while the private Christian is to be an example to the world, they are to be "an ensample to the flock"—a model among models; and much in the world; for their central station and official character invest them with influence which renders their every movement an object of interest to superior beings, and which, in reference to the heathen world, may implicate the everlasting welfare of myriads. Only let these considerations be devoutly laid to heart, and many a minister who now supposes himself bound to remain at home, would be heard saying, "Here am I: send me:" others, who could not go abroad, would become missionaries at home; while the Church generally would find her highest interests benefited as much as by any event which has occurred since apostolic days.

8. Another requisite is *Christian union*. We have already intimated that it is very much owing to the fraternal influence shed on the various denominations of Christians by missionary and kindred operations, that even a vestige of visible union remains. And how is it that on particular occasions we are induced to quit our denominational camps, and to proclaim the truce of God? By paying greater deference to the will of Christ than to the claims of party; by looking out on a world perishing; by erecting the cross for its salvation, and rallying around it: in a word, by reverting practically to the primary design of the Church. Who has not been ready to say at such times, Would that the whole Church could be converted into a Christian missionary society, and meet in that capacity alone!

The union wanted is not the union of one day in a year, but the union of every day; not the hollow friendship which merely forbears to misrepresent or to injure those who "follow not with us," but the Christian sympathy which sincerely mingles alike in their sorrows and their joys: not merely a oneness of purpose, but, as far as practicable, a union of means for the attainment of that purpose. One Church abounds more, it may be, in the zeal which burns for active exertion; another, in the wisdom which is profitable to direct; and a third, in the funds which are necessary to support the holy war. Here, sympathy with each other's wants, by uniting their respective means, would happily supply them all; while a spirit of division makes that which is already little, still less. "One rule of action there is," says a distinguished American missionary—Abeel—"which, if observed by all sects, would result in the greatest benefit to the Church and the world. It involves no sacrifice of party interests, and it is the only plan which, while Christians remain in distinct communities, does not sacrifice the interests of the Redeemer's kingdom to mere sectarian aggrandizement. In selecting their spheres of action, let each denomination pass by the place already occupied, and fix upon those where their services are most needed. Let it be a mutual understanding that, if education or predilection dispose the inhabitants of any part of a country to a particular sect, all others will yield the ground. What endless collision and confusion this would prevent! What desirable consequences it would produce! If the attention of Christians could only be diverted from each other, and from the places already occupied, and fixed in deep compassion upon the destitute parts of the world, how soon their dying fellow-men in every land would feel the quickening influence!"

It is in vain to plead the beneficial rivalry of sects. This only shows that we are so much accustomed to our divisions, that we can see beauty in that which forms our deformity and disgrace. But let us see the natural fruits of past divisions in the fact that Mohammedanism, Popery, and irreligion, still divide the civilized world between them: that reformed Christianity finds, on numbering her followers, that she still stands in an insignificant minority. And are we to suppose that what has hitherto proved the curse of the Church is now converted into a blessing? A spirit of disunion is still dishonoring Christianity in the eyes of the world. By confirming the irreligious in their impiety, disheartening the sincere inquirer after the truth, and blinding numbers with the idea that the sectarian spirit is true piety, it is still ruinous to the souls of men: by dividing our limited instrumentality at home, and tending to counteract our Christian influence abroad, and, incomparably more than all, by grieving the Holy Spirit of God, it is still enfeebling and endangering our missionary operations, and delaying the conversion of the world. It is in vain to say that but little disagreement exists as yet among our Christian agents abroad: the seeds of discord only ask for time, and they will not fail to bear their proper fruit. It is in vain to urge that good is done notwithstanding our disunion: the partial good which is effected abroad is effected by merging the disputes at home—in fact, by uniting—or by pretending to a degree of fraternity which the relative state of parties at home will not justify. And would not a knowledge of our differences there be to a great extent fatal to our usefulness? Would it not shake the confidence of the religious novitiate there, and embroil the Churches, and cover the breast of the idolater with an additional coat of resistance to the arrows of the Lord, and arm the Brahmin, the skeptic, and every hostile hand with a new weapon of attack?

On the other hand, how greatly would the mutual regard and sympathetic coöperation of which we speak tend to increase our capacity for missionary influence!—by promoting our own piety and happiness; for, having ceased from the comparative trifles which now vex and engross us, we should feel more than ever the force of high and ennobling motives: breath, now wasted in controversy, would be turned into the incense of prayer; and the only spirit invoked in the Church would be the Spirit of grace—by the increase of sanctified agency which it would set at liberty from the present imprisonment of controversy, and send forth into the field of the world—by a wise combination of means, so that resources which, divided, are not equal to the religious cultivation of a district, would, when united, be equal to an attempt on a continent—by affecting the public mind, and preparing the world to yield to the claims of the Son of God; for Christian union is not merely a Scripture doctrine: its practical and visible exhibition is evidently intended, according to the prayer of Christ, to be the grand means for the conversion of the world, and a leading design of the Christian dispensation. Such a union, therefore, as that of which we speak, would humbly challenge his blessing, for it would be a substantial fulfilment of his prayer. And, then, how directly would it increase the capacity of Christians for usefulness, by increasing their capacity for the reception and coöperation of that Holy Spirit, who alone can crown their activity with success!

In order that the slain in the valley of vision might become an efficient body, it was necessary, not only that life should enter into each separately—they must fall into order with a view to the union and organization of the whole; and then, as an exceeding great army, a skilful commander alone was wanting to lead them forth to conquest. The leader of the hosts of God is already waiting. Let them be not only compact in their several sections, but let those sections be united with each other, and as one body he will lead them forth, "terrible as an army with banners." Nothing shall be too great for them to attempt; and every conflict shall be a victory.

9. And is not *greater pecuniary liberality wanted?* To assert, indeed, that it is not already on the increase, would only evince insensibility to the obvious facts we ourselves have adduced, and ingratitude to the great Head of the Church. But while the increase of funds which our great benevolent institutions have almost annually to announce, concurs, with other circumstances, to show that the Church is not only dissatisfied with its past parsimony, but is gradually awaking to the claims of Christian liberality, we can regard them as little more than *indications* of improvement.

Nearly all the great defects in the charity of the Christian Church remain, with very slight modifications. It still waits for impulses and appeals. It wants calculation, proportion, and self-denial. It does not keep pace with the growing demands of the kingdom of Christ. It wants principle and plan. The great current of Christian property is as yet undiverted from its worldly channel. Many of the scanty rills of charity which at present water the garden of the Lord, are brought and kept there only by great ingenuity and effort. Here and there an individual is to be found who economizes his resources that he may employ them for God; but the very admiration in which such a one is held in his circle implies that he stands there alone. In which of the sections of the Christian Church shall we find a spirit of worldly self-indulgence to be only the exception, and a spirit of self-denying benevolence the rule? How small, it is to be feared, is the number of those who really and practically believe that "it is more blessed to give than to receive;" or who truly act on the principle that they hold their property in trust for God! And hence, is it not the fact that our very success in the cause of God is, in an important sense, found inconvenient and burdensome? Do we not, consequently, stand disqualified for extensive usefulness? Is not the great Head of the Church himself placed under a moral restraint from employing and blessing us only in a very limited degree? A covetous, self-indulgent community! how can he consistently employ such to convert the world, especially, too, as that conversion includes a turning from selfishness? Not, indeed, that his cause is necessarily dependent for success on our liberality; and, perhaps, when his people shall be so far constrained by his love as to place their property at his disposal, he may most convincingly show them that he has never been dependent on it by completing his kingdom without it. But while he chooses to work by means, those means must be in harmony with his own character, and with the character of the Christian dispensation; and what is that character but self-denying, infinite benevolence?

It is recorded, to the high honor of certain ancient believers, that "God was not ashamed to be called their God." So plainly did they " declare that they sought a better country, that is, a heavenly," and so entirely did they live for his glory, that he could point the attention of the world to them with Divine complacency: he could intrust his character in their hands: he could leave the world to infer what he was from what they were: he was content to be judged of by the conduct of his people. Could he leave his character to be inferred from the conduct of his people now? Is there any thing, for instance, in the manner and extent of their liberality which would remind the world of his vast, unbounded benevolence? They know the grace of our Lord Jesus Christ, that though he was rich, for our sakes he became poor, that they through his poverty might be made rich; but from what part of their conduct would the world ever learn this melting truth? No: in this respect he is ashamed to be called their God. Their self-indulgence misrepresents his self-sacrifice. Their worldly spirit of appropriation is a shame to his boundless beneficence. His character is falsified by them in the eyes of the world. Nor could he honor them in any distinguished manner before the world, without endorsing and confirming that falsification of his charcter. He is yearning for the happiness of the perishing world; but such, at present, is the nature of his Divine arrangements, that he has only the instrumentality of his people to work by, and that is so steeped in selfishness, that his grace may be said to be held under restraint.

Now, the liberality wanted is that which originates in Christian principle. As long as it is subjected to any inferior motives, its defects will be numerous, unavoidable, fatal. It will think highly of its smallest gifts: will be unduly influenced by the conduct of others: will wait for public excitement; and will ever be in danger of diminution, and even of total cessation. Nothing but a deep and abiding conviction of our vast, solemn, subduing obligations to God in Christ, can ever insure that cordial and entire consecration of our property, which his Divine commands, and the necessities of his cause, imperatively require. By taking the Christian to the cross, and keeping him there in the presence of the great Sacrifice, he is made to feel that he is not his own—that his costliest offering, could he multiply its value a thousand-fold, would be utterly unworthy of Divine acceptance; and if called to pour forth his blood as a libation on the altar of Christian sacrifice, he would regard it as an ample explanation of his conduct to say, with an apostle, "The love of Christ constraineth us."

The liberality wanted is that which provides itself with regular resources by acting on a plan. Business plans and systematizes in order to gain; covetousness schemes for selfish purposes: why should the cause of Christian benevolence alone be left to the uncertainty of impulses, and to the mercy of what the world may chance to have left? "Upon the first day of the week, let every one of you," says the apostle, "lay by him in store as God hath prospered him, that there be no gatherings when I come." Acting in the spirit of this direction, we should statedly invite the Divine presence, so to speak, to audit the accounts of our worldly affairs: our offerings would be presented with cheerfulness, because coming from a fund designed expressly to no other end than charity; and the cause of benevolence, no longer dependent on precarious alms, would be welcomed and honored as an authorized claimant, a Divine creditor; while what we retained for our own use would be Divinely blessed by the dedication of the rest to God.

According to the apostolic language just quoted, the liberality of the Christian should be distinguished not only by plan, but also by proportion. In assisting him to determine the amount of that proportion, the only step which the gospel takes is to point him to the cross of Christ; and, while his eye is fixed there in admiring love, to say, "Ye know the grace of our Lord Jesus Christ;" "Freely ye have received, freely give." And can he, after that, experience any difficulty in deciding the proportion to be made sacred to God? Surely he would rather exceed than fall short of the exact amount. *With* whom is he stipulating? *For* whom is he preparing the offering? Well may the recollection put every selfish thought to flight; tinging his cheek with shame at the bare possibility of ingratitude, and impelling him to lay down his all at the feet of Christ. Only let him pass near the cross on his way to the altar of oblation, and he will not be long lost in the question of proportion; his only subject of anxiety will be that his richest offering should be so utterly unworthy. If poor, he will soon detect some small superfluity which can be retrenched, or some leisure time which can be profitably employed, "working with his hands the thing which is good, that he may have to give to him that needeth." If rich, he will not, cannot be satisfied with the gift of money merely, however large the amount: the cause of Christ will have his activity and his sacrifices also. Yes, the liberality wanted is that which gives, not a little from much, but much from a little; that which shall induce the wealthy Christian parent to offer up his pious son on the missionary altar, and to lay beside him, at the same time, whatever may be necessary to make the oblation complete; that which shall constrain the wealthy Christian to ascend that altar himself, taking with him all he has, and offering the whole as a missionary oblation to God.

In other words, the liberality wanted at the present crisis is the liberality of Christian self-denial. And here we would not be understood to mean that the gospel requires that every Christian should, at all times, be found in a state of voluntary and comfortless poverty. Were the thousand drains of selfishness cut off, the cause of Christ would find an abundance from his friends, and would leave an abundance to them all. When every Christian brings his all to Christ, every Christian will be able to take away with him again an ample supply for his most comfortable subsistence. But till then, is it not the duty of every one who would be deemed benevolent to institute the momentous inquiry which the Church is now more then ever called on to decide—whether, under existing circumstances, there can be any Christian benevolence without self-denial? Does not the Church itself require to be moved by examples of self-denial? Do not the very terms of Christian discipleship include a readiness to lay down life itself, if required, for the sake of the gospel? Is not the teeming population of many a heathen district perishing at this moment in ignorance of Christ, because Christians will not lay down —not life, but some of its superfluities? And yet, are these Christians living around the cross, in sight of the crucifixion, and ever ready to acknowledge that they are bound, by their obligations to it, to withhold nothing they possess, that has in it the least tendency to draw the world to the same centre!

Nor can we be supposed to imply, after what we have already said, that the Christian cause is originally and necessarily dependent for success on the property of the Church. God, however, has been pleased to employ the instrumentality of his people for the conversion of the world; the value of that instrumentality depends entirely on its moral character; and that character, to be acceptable to God, must be perfectly congenial with his own character. Now, it is worthy of attentive regard that, while he has thus made the duty of giving imperative, he has taken away all pretext for supposing that it is necessary on any other account than as an exhibition of Christian principle, by making its usefulness to depend, not on the amount given, but on the spirit and entireness of the gift, so that, were the amount of our contributions, on the one hand, to be multiplied from thousands to millions, that alone would not entitle us to look for an increase of usefulness. Success is not to be purchased. That *no* increase of good would arise from such multiplication we dare not affirm; for we know not the plentitude of sovereign grace. But that no promise in the Bible would entitle us to look for it, we do affirm. Success is there promised, not to acts, but to the Christian principles whence those acts should flow. And hence, on the other hand, were our contributions a thousand times less than they are, that alone would not warrant us to apprehend a decrease of usefulness. The question would still return, What is the *character* of our liberality? Does it partake of the unworldly and self-denying character of the cross? We ask not the amount of what the Church has given, but how much it has kept back for mere self-indulgence. We ask not how many agents of mercy have been sent forth, but also how many more might, and therefore ought to, have been sent forth, but which through our selfishness have been kept unemployed. What we have left undone, owing to our worldliness, has an influence as positive as that which we have done; and the only influence which it can have is to weaken the effect of our actual efforts. In the eyes of the world it convicts us of gross inconsistency, and thus directly tends to neutralize the influence which belongs to Christian character. And in relation to God, it suspends the shower of his blessing, and allows us only a few prelusive drops; for how could he distinguish with his copious blessing a liberality which puts off his cause with merely a few of the drops of its superfluity, without exposing his own glorious character to the suspicion of inconsistency?

The liberality wanted, then, is not that empty benevolence which makes no retrenchments, takes no pains, costs neither effort nor sacrifice; but that which, actuated by the love of Christ, plans, proportions, and adds to its superfluities the precious savings of self-denial. And the principal ground on which we urge it is, that it is the only liberality congenial with the character of Christ, and therefore the only liberality which he can consistently honor, to any great extent, with his blessing. Till this comes, the great shower of his blessing will not come. But when it does, what can stand before a spirit which evinces a readiness to give up all for Christ? for the Spirit without measure will come with it. The world will behold in such conduct an argument for the reality and power of the gospel which it could not misunderstand, could not gainsay. "God, even our own God, shall bless us," shall glory to own such a people before the eyes of the world—"God shall bless us," and, as a consequence, "all the ends of the earth shall fear him."

10. The Christian principle which originates the liberality wanted would not stop here, but would proceed to supply another important want—*the Christian agency of missionary laymen.* No reason, except our defective devotedness to

Christ, can be assigned, why the wealthy Christian should so generally confine his missionary instrumentality to the mere act of giving money; why he should not himself accompany the missionary preacher; why he should not select for his residence some unenlightened region, and take with him "a man of God" to be the ministerial instructor of his own family, and the missionary of the district around; why the Christian female whom God has prepared for missionary usefulness should not emulate "those women who labored in the gospel" in apostolic days; or why the colonization of heathen districts should not be attempted by the settlement of Christian societies.

It cannot be alleged, in excuse, that there are no persons eligible for such a duty. There is many a Christian at this moment who possesses an affluent proportion of independent property; who has no indissoluble ties which bind him to his native land; who can occasionally leave that land for a continental excursion; who is often at a loss for occupation; and who consequently spends much of his time in a way which absolutely endangers his piety. It cannot be said that there are no places eligible in heathen lands for such to reside in. There are many situations in the British colonies and dependencies, at least, where they would find salubrity, security, and as many of the comforts of life as those can consistently desire to possess who profess to be the followers of Him who had not where to lay his head, and whose treasure is in heaven. Nor can it be alleged that the preaching of the gospel is the only instrumentality required for the heathen; or that the effect of the addition of lay agency would be experimental and uncertain. "I have scarcely been in a foreign port," says the American missionary already quoted, the Rev. D. Abeel, "where I have not met with men from Christian lands engaged in business. These persons are found wherever they can reap advantage from their worldly professions. After remaining some time in a place, they not only feel themselves at home, but are regarded, by those around them, as naturalized citizens. They gain the confidence of the natives, and become influential. They are looked up to with respect, and their opinions are sought for with avidity. I have been in countries where these persons had become so popular as to receive from royalty itself marks of honorable distinction. Now, the missionaries have often inquired why Christian merchants and mechanics might not pursue the same course of life from the motive of glorifying their Redeemer and benefiting their fellow-men. They could certainly engage in the same employments; they might probably secure the same confidence; and, at the same time, they could make all their relations and honors subservient to the progress of Christianity. I have known a few persons in heathen countries who acted on high religious principles, and it is impossible to tell how much good they accomplished. It is not only their personal exertions which render them useful, but the countenance and assistance they lend the missionaries. It is in this last-mentioned respect that their presence and influence are exceedingly desirable. Being on the spot, and acquainted with every event which occurs, they not only become greatly interested in the salvation of the heathen, but are prepared to improve every opportunity for its promotion. For my own part, I cannot doubt that Christian communities among the heathen would produce the most desirable effects. Such a community, by necessarily employing a number of natives, would be placing them in the best situation for the reception of Christian instruction; by merely relieving the missionary from secular cares, they would be setting at liberty a considerable proportion of his time and powers for spiritual duties; by Christian tuition, visiting, conversation, and the distribution of religious books, they would greatly multiply his means of usefulness; and by embodying and exhibiting before the heathen, as a Christian Church, the benign and elevating influence of the gospel, they would be constraining observers to glorify their Father who is in heaven."

The same excellent missionary bears testimony to the invaluable influence of Christian female teachers in heathen lands. But to form an idea of their usefulness, he observes, "it is necessary to be a witness to their habitual engagements;" and expresses it as his opinion, formed from extensive intercourse with missionaries, that woman is as indispensable to the successful operation of missions, as she is to the well-being of society in Christian lands.

Now, let the wealthy Christian bear in mind that by going and personally coöperating with the Christian missionary, the cause of Christ among the heathen might receive not merely the advantage of his own time, and wealth, and influence—he might be honored of God in filling a wide sphere with the agency of Christian women also, and might, in various ways, eminently promote the interests of Christian colonization.

No good or useful act terminates in itself; and his example could not fail, by the Divine blessing, "to provoke very many." Why, then, should he decline this proof of his devotedness to Christ? It cannot be because it is impracticable; for the Christian missionary has gone before him, and is calling him to follow. He would not plead that it is because he has wealth, for that increases his responsibility; so that, instead of acting as a golden chain to bind him here, it should be rather converted into wings to bear him " far hence among the Gentiles." Had he never possessed that wealth, he himself might possibly have been a laborious missionary; and surely he does not imagine that his wealth was meant to diminish his usefulness by detaining him in self-enjoyment at home. He cannot plead that the state of the heathen does not require it; for let him know that if he will " retire to enjoy life," he retires amidst the cries and shrieks of a world perishing in its guilt. He will not say that his obligations to Christ do not demand it; for he daily acknowledges they might at any time justly require the sacrifice of life itself. Nor can he urge that it is not necessary, in order to demonstrate his devotedness to Christ; for the question is, whether his disinclination to take this step does not arise from his very want of devotedness! The sum which he contributes may be only serving to conceal his want of zeal for the active service of Christ; so that his personal consecration to Christ as a missionary layman may be just the very kind of evidence yet wanting, and indispensably necessary to establish the fact of his love to Christ.

11. Now, from the wants already named, it is evident that, as a missionary Church, we preëminently need *an increase of energy and zeal.* He must be ignorant indeed who does not know that rashness often passes for zeal, and that the path of wisdom lies between a blind impetuosity, on the one hand, and a cold, calculating policy, on the other. But blind must he be, also, not to perceive that much in the Christian Church, at present, which assumes the name of prudence, is timidity and unbelief in disguise. In reference to its financial affairs,

for instance, were all the maxims of worldly caution to be adduced in connection with all the promises of God addressed to a generous, enterprising, and open-handed faith, how much easier it would be to harmonize them with those maxims than with these promises! The spirit of commercial enterprise, the ardor of scientific pursuit, or the heroism of adventurous research, takes men annually by hundreds into the regions of pestilence, or storm, or eternal ice; but no sooner does a Christian minister leave home for a foreign field of labor, than, as if a miracle of self-sacrifice had taken place, a claim is set up in his behalf for the universal sympathy of the Church. Judging from the history of the Church, we have every thing to hope from bold measures; but judging from our own conduct, we have every thing to fear from them. "Prove me now," saith God, "whether I will not open the windows of heaven to bless you;" but who thinks of accepting the gracious challenge? Does not our conduct, in effect, reproach the first missionaries, and charge the confessors and reformers of later days with guilty rashness? If we are only prudent, what were they? And yet we profess to admire their deeds; boast of being their spiritual descendants; and acknowledge that we owe every thing, under God, to their boldness, fidelity, and zeal. Does not the conduct of the great majority of Christians at home reproach even the laborers who are at present in the missionary field? For, if those are right, must not these be wrong? If the reasons which those assign in justification of their course are to be held decisive, then have these laid themselves open to the charge of rash and inconsiderate zeal.

And yet who does not feel that theirs is the zeal we want? the zeal of a Paul and the first disciples; of a Luther and the early reformers; of an Eliot and our first missionaries; a zeal which would startle the Church, and even be stigmatized by thousands of its members—for what zeal has not been? zeal that would be content to be appreciated by the Christians of another generation. The zeal wanted is that which, while it invites prudence to be of its council, would not allow her to reign; and which, while it would economize its means and provide for real evils, would gather incitement to increased activity from the obstacles lying in its way—the zeal of our momentary but strongest impulses made perpetual. The energy we want is that which springs from sympathy with the grandeur of our theme, the dignity of our office, and the magnificence of the missionary enterprise. O, where is the spiritual perception that looks forth on the world as the great scene of a moral conflict, and beholds it under the stirring aspect which it presents to the beings of other worlds? Where are the kindled eye, and the beaming countenance, and the heart bursting with the momentous import of the gospel message? Where the fearlessness and confidence whose very tones inspire conviction, and carry with them all the force of certainty and the weight of an oath? Where the zeal which burns with its subject, as if it had just come from witnessing the crucifixion, and feels its theme with all the freshness and force of a new revelation? The zeal which, during its intervals of labor, repairs to the mount of vision to see the funeral procession of six hundred millions of souls? to the mouth of perdition, to hear the voices of all these, saying, as the voice of one man, "Send to our brethren, lest they also come into this place of torment?" to Calvary, to renew its vigor by touching the cross? Enthusiasm is sobriety here. In this cause, the zeal of Christ consumed him; his holiest ministers have become flames of fire; and, as if all created ardor were insufficient, here infinite zeal finds scope to burn; "for the zeal of the Lord of hosts shall perform it."

12. And where is this flame to be kindled—*where is the live coal to be obtained, but from off the altar?* It was there that the servants of God in every age found it, and there they kept it bright and burning. It was there that Christ himself sustained that zeal, in the flames of which he at last ascended as a sacrifice to God. And it is only in proportion as we are found at the same altar of devotion, that we can hope to imbibe his spirit, or to enjoy the honor of advancing his cause.

But it may be asked, Has not a spirit of supplication, of late years, distinguished the Churches of Christ? Notwithstanding what we have said of a congratulatory nature on missionary meetings for prayer, in a preceding page, we feel bound to reply, Only very partially—whereas the prayer wanted is universal; only very feebly—whereas the prayer wanted is the effectual, fervent prayer, which availeth much; only by uncertain fits—whereas the prayer needed is the continuous, unbroken, persevering cry of importunity; only the prayer of party, (effects prove it,)—whereas the prayer required is the prayer of "all, with one accord."

Prayer, indeed, is always indispensable. It brings us to the one spot, and keeps us in the only place in the universe which properly belongs to us—at the feet of God. It tends to annihilate self; amounts to a confession of our utter dependence upon God; renders appropriate homage to his greatness; and thus keeps us in constant and active communication with the Fountain of grace.

There are times, however, when the duty of prayer becomes unusually urgent. If, for instance, a period should arrive in which the philosophy and the philanthropy of this world should profess to be aiming at human happiness, in common with the gospel, and should consequently appear to be almost identified with it, how important that the Church should affirm the essential difference between these agencies—the one expecting the renovation of society from human means alone, the other relying supremely on the power of God as indispensable to success! But how can Christians visibly and directly vindicate the Divine honor in this respect, except as they are known to be in the habit of appealing to that power, and importunately invoking the Divine interposition? Now, such a period is the present. The world is teeming with projects for the amelioration of the race, and is full of expectation from the future. But though it is thus looking, at length, in the same direction as the Church, far different are the specific objects at which they aim, and the principal means they employ. "Our hope is in God." But this we can make apparent only by evincing our dependence on him in prayer. We are to show that in this vital respect we are at issue with a skeptical philosophy at the very outset; that while prayer is the last instrument which the world would employ, we not only employ, but rely on it; and that we place it, in the order of means, as first and best. It is in this way alone that we can practically rebuke the pride of man; proclaim the utter insufficiency of mere human means to renovate the world; and claim for God the glory due unto his name.

If, again, a period should come in which the Church should be quickened into general activity for the good of the world, the only way in which the great mass of the partially enlightened could be preserved from the danger of relying unduly on that activity would be by their being kept in the posture of humble acknowledgment and earnest prayer. Now, such a season of growing activity has arrived; and such a danger has doubtless come with it; and the more that activity increases, the greater our liability to rest in it, to the guilty exclusion of Him who alone can render it useful. This, indeed, does not imply that we are to do less, but to pray more. The greater the sacrifice laid on the altar, the stronger the flame necessary to consume it. We are to remember that He whom we serve is jealous for his honor; that he regards every power in the universe as more or less opposed to him, but the power of prayer, and the means which prayer has sanctified; that he views it as an attempt to do without him; as a hostile endeavor to contravene the great principle of the gospel of Christ—"that not by might, nor by power, but by his Spirit alone," the maladies of the world shall be healed. If we look into the censer of the "angel standing at the golden altar which is before the throne," and if we there mark what it is of all human instrumentality which ascends to heaven, we shall find that it is only that which is sanctified by prayer. When the clamors of a prayerless zeal have subsided, and the undevout deeds which have dazzled and astounded men have spent their force, let us mark what is left in the censer—only that which partook of the nature of prayer. This is all that lives to reach the skies; all that heaven receives from earth; all that is ever permitted to ascend before God. And when the history of the world shall finally be summed up, nothing which had not been in that censer will be named except to be condemned. Preaching itself—benevolent activity in all its forms—except so far as it is associated with devotion—will be passed over to record the triumphs of prayer. Many a Christian, who once filled the public eye with his active deeds and burning zeal, will be comparatively unnoticed; and the man of prayer—the wrestler with God—will be drawn out from his closet obscurity, and proclaimed in his stead; and it will then appear that while the one was only moving earth, the other was moving heaven.

If the activity of the period referred to aimed supremely at spiritual results, the necessity for prayer would be still further increased; for it is expressly in order to the production of such results that the agency of the Holy Spirit has been appointed and promised; and it is only in proportion as we implore his presence and influence that we honor that appointment, or can obtain the fulfilment of that promise. But such is the special aim of all the Christian activity of the present period. Without despising or overlooking any of the real interests of humanity, the great and ultimate object of our endeavors is purely spiritual — the regeneration of the world. Here, then, we are brought into the special province of the Spirit — a region in which our only robe should be humility, our only posture that of dependence, our only language prayer. Here, as the great missionary Spirit, he looks on all the ordinances of the Church as the instruments with which he works, and on all its members as the organs through whom he speaks, and on the entire dispensation as emphatically his own. Now, how can we place ourselves in harmony with such an arrangement, without earnest, united, persevering supplication for his gracious influence?

The first prayer of Christ himself on his ascension to heaven was for the effusion of the Spirit; and the first prayer of the Church should be for the same blessing. Why is it — let there be great searchings of heart — why is it that the promised impartation of the Spirit is withheld? Why is it that we enjoy only a few drops of that mighty influence of which, at this moment, the heavens are full? Only one explanation can be given: "We have not, because we ask not; or because we ask amiss." Individual Christians have not, particular churches have not, the Church collectively has not duly felt its need of that influence, nor sent up the prayer which is equal to bring it down. If, then, we would not grieve the Holy Spirit of God — if we would do homage to the office which he holds in the plan of the world's redemption — if we would do honor to the mediation of Christ on account of which his gracious influences are imparted — in all our entreaties for the conversion of the world, our loudest supplications must ascend for the advent of the Holy Spirit.

Besides, it is only as our endeavors for the salvation of the world are accompanied by prayer, that we are acting in harmony with the pervading spirit of the gospel constitution. According to that spirit, every thing is made dependent on prayer, and may be effected by it. What is the sacrifice of Christ himself, in practical effect, but prayer in its most concentrated, intense, and prevailing form—the prayer of blood: a prayer so ardent that he consumed himself in the utterance: a prayer which is ascending still, and still filling the ear of God with its entreaties: a prayer from which all other prayers derive their prevailing power? Hence it is said, "He is able to save unto the uttermost all them that come unto God by him, seeing he ever liveth to make intercession for them." He has turned the merit of his sacrifice into prayer. Intercession, in his hands, is a chain fastened to the throne of God—the support and stay of a sinking world. Yes, even Jesus prays, and by prayer succeeds. If he would have the heathen to be his for an inheritance, he is directed to ask to that effect. And accordingly he does ask: "For Zion's sake," saith he, "I will not hold my peace; and for Jerusalem's sake I will not rest, until the righteousness thereof go forth as brightness, and the salvation thereof as a lamp that burneth." And shall he pray for this object alone? He summons his Church to join him: "Ye that make mention of the Lord," saith he, "keep not silence, and give him no rest." He places them at his side by the altar: puts into their hand a censer filled with incense like his own; and thus seeks to multiply the voice and effect of his own intercession.

Wise and gracious arrangement! For owing to this it is that every believer—even the poorest and the obscurest—is afforded an opportunity of indulging his supreme love to Christ by aiding the advancement of his kingdom. Let him not waste his moments in fruitlessly deploring how truly small the largest gifts which he can lay on the altar of Christ; how little the time which he can give to his service; or how circumscribed the influence which his lowness of station permits him to exert for his glory. The throne of grace is open—open to him—open to all. "Here," he may say, "here I can gratify my love to Christ, and give a loose to all the ardor of my soul. Poor I may be in the world's account; but here I can pour out at his feet the wealth of my affections. Busy I may be in the service of man; but here I can repair, in thought and desire, and serve him continually. And let my influence with man be as limited as it may, here I can come and have power with God. While others are engaged in pleading for the cause of Christ with men, here I can come and plead for it with God: here I can vie with an apostle. While a Paul is planting, and an Apollos watering, here I can aid them both by bringing down the increase."

If, indeed, the salvation of the world be our aim, whatever may be instrumentally necessary to that salvation should be made the subject of prayer. Especially should the spiritual prosperity of the Christian Church excite our earnest desire. Is it inquired, What should be the special object of supplication for the Church? It wants more spirituality and distinctness from the world: it wants a higher appreciation of its office as the instrument of Christ for saving the world: more of the spirit of liberality to sacrifice for Christ; of union in accordance with the prayer of Christ; of zeal which shall burn for the universal triumphs of Christ. But one want there is which comprehends the whole,—the impartation of the Spirit of Christ. Could a convocation be held of all the churches upon earth, the object of their one united cry should be for that promised Spirit. Let that be secured, and in obtaining that we shall obtain the supply of every other want: we should find that we had acquired the same mind which was also in Christ: a benevolence which would yearn over the whole human race: a brotherly love which would combine with the whole body of Christians for the recovery of the world: a zeal which would be ever devising fresh methods of usefulness, practicing self-denial, and laying itself out in the service of Christ; and a perseverance which would never rest till the whole family of man should be seated together at the banquet of salvation.

But if, by thus imploring an effusion of the Spirit on the Church, we are, in effect, interceding for the world, since it is through the instrumentality of the Church that the world is to be converted to Christ, how important that we should realize in thought the dignity and responsibility of our office! We go to God as the earthly representatives of mankind. We pass to the throne of grace through multitudes, myriads of human beings. May we not hear them, as we go, imploring a place in our supplications? May we not see all Africa assembled in our path, urging us to go to God for them, to describe their wrongs, to ask for the blessings of the reign of Christ for them? And before we have done pleading for Africa, China comes with its untold myriads, entreating us to intercede for them. And while yet we are pleading for China, India comes with its tale of lamentation and woe, and entreats us to speak for it; and can we refrain? And when we grow faint, they all combine their entreaties that we cry to God for them louder still; that we call in help—more intercessors, and more still—till all the Church be prostrate in prayer. And when we move to quit the throne of grace, they all, in effect, entreat us not to leave them unrepresented before God. "If there be a God," they say, "and if prayer can reach him, do not leave us thus, or we perish. Our only hope is in the God you worship, the Saviour you proclaim. Pray that the blessings of his grace may be extended to us." Did we habitually realize our office thus, our prayers would rise to a degree of importunity to which nothing could be denied essential to the success of our missionary endeavors.

And be it remarked that prayer is not only desirable, obligatory, urgent,—the time has come when, in an unusual sense, it is inevitable. We read of the Church of old being shut up unto the faith which should afterwards be revealed. The Church at present is shut up unto prayer. It must submit to deep disgrace in heathen lands, or call down unusual measures of help from heaven. It is so completely ensnared by success, that it must sound a retreat, or betake itself to God in unwonted prayer. Happy necessity, which shall drive it to this resource! Blessed exigence, which shall bring the whole Church on its knees before God! The time to favor her, yea, the set time will then have come. "God, even our own God, will bless us." Gazing from his throne upon his Church suppliant at his feet, he will say, "Behold, she prayeth: let the windows of heaven be opened, and the blessing be poured out."

Again, then, we return to the position with which we commenced this part of our subject,—and our survey of the necessities of the Church has only deepened our conviction of its truth,—that its great practical want as a missionary Church is a spirit of entire devotedness to its office. He who knows any thing of the human mind, knows that its full energies are never put forth unless its object be single. He who knows any thing of the relative design of the Christian

Church, knows that it deserves the undivided attention and entire consecration of the whole Christian. And he who knows any thing of the history of that Church, is aware that those who have effected the greatest good in their own age, and who are producing the greatest impression on posterity, were distinguished for the entireness with which they gave themselves up to the service of Christ. Not that they occupied a public sphere, perhaps, nor that they were distinguished by any one peculiar mode of doing good; but, whatever their station, and however diversified their Christian activity, they could each say, like the apostle, though in another sense, "One thing I do." One all-pervading passion, one all-controlling purpose, bound their various and versatile efforts together, causing the whole to result, like the intricate motions of a complicated machine, in one entire effect. Their talents, which, without this spirit of devotedness, would have been comparatively wasted, or have ranked as insignificant, by it acquired a concentration and a power which arrested attention, and moved society. Feeble rays of knowledge which, without this, would have been useless to all but the possessors themselves, by it were collected into a focus, and made to illuminate and burn. Powers of persuasion and reasoning, which, without it, would seldom have moved or convinced, by it acquired an impassioned earnestness which *would* be heard, and could not fail to be felt. Each appeal which they made for God, however simple the terms in which it was couched, was charged high with feeling and fervor: each sentence an arrow with barbed and sharpened point: each attempt to reason for God, "logic set on fire." Opportunities of usefulness which, without it, would have passed by them unseen and neglected, were, by it, anticipated, waited for, met, seized, improved, multiplied. Characters which, without it, would have been unnoticed, by it acquired an air of originality and greatness, and even obtained a widespread ascendency over other characters.

There are men now occupied in the field of missionary labor whose names, but for this, would never have been heard of beyond their own immediate circle; but whose praise is now in all the churches, and will be to the end of time. Not a man of this kind ever lives without leaving on society permanent traces that he has been among them. And why? Partly for this reason: that the undivided and devoted man of God will be ever and anon impelled, by the very law of his devotedness, to advance a step, at least, beyond his contemporaries; to carry out into vigorous action some principle which they are content to retain slumbering in their creeds; to give himself up to the power of his principles. True, by so doing he may often attempt more than he can effect; but what then? He will effect more than most men attempt.

And is not the devoted Christian the only one likely to develop and draw out into benevolent activity the resources of those around him, and of the Church in general? No one else will feel sufficiently concerned to attempt it; or if he did, the attempt, counteracted as it would be by his own example, would prove nugatory on others, and recoil with shame on his own head. But the Christian whose heart is wholly devoted to Christ, cannot see the paucity of his own means in contrast with the magnitude of the work to be performed, and then look around on the unemployed and ample resources of the Church, all of which are due to the service of Christ, but nearly the whole of which are lying open to the incursions of the world, without attempting to reclaim them for Christ. He cannot recollect that each member of that vast body of the faithful has his post assigned in the cause of human salvation; that in that post all his Christian influence should be put into constant requisition; and that every thing dear to God is suspended and suffering, owing to the general neglect of this truth, without feeling impelled to warn his fellow-Christians. He believes, and, therefore, speaks; while his example, louder than words, reminds them that they are not their own: that they are exclusively the property of Christ.

And is not the Christian whose devotedness is such that he cannot be satisfied with giving himself less than wholly to the service of Christ, and who would fain see all the resources of the Christian Church pressed into the same service, and all its members coöperating with him to the utmost; is not he, for the very same reasons, likely to be the most earnest in his entreaties for the indispensable influences of the Holy Spirit? Yes: whatever else may be essential in order to the conversion of the world, he will insist first and last on the agency of the Holy Spirit. Remembering that the present is emphatically the dispensation of the Spirit, that to convince men of sin is the office of the Spirit, that the ordinances of tne Church are the instruments of the Spirit, and that every Christian member is at once the mouth of the Church and the organ of the Spirit, in their united appeals to the world; he feels as if he could not move without the Spirit; but remembering, also, that his influence is promised to prayer, he cannot do less than cry earnestly for his aid. Thus earnestly sought, and appropriately honored, the presence of the Spirit will be felt, nourishing and enlarging his piety into an element; not affecting a part of his character merely, but pervading the whole; consecrating his knowledge, and turning it into heavenly wisdom; keeping him on his watch-tower, looking out for the signs of the times, and the means of improving them to the glory of God; inspiring him with a growing confidence in God, in the sufficiency of the gospel to meet the wants of the Church and of the world; concentrating his powers to the one great object of human salvation; impelling him, under a sense of the magnitude of the work to be accomplished, to excite and engage the agencies of all around him; and yet deepening his conviction that, could all these agencies be put into full activity, the power of the Spirit alone could crown that activity with success. As certainly as he believes this he will pray: as certainly as he prays he will obtain the Holy Spirit; and as certainly as he is actuated by the Spirit of God, his will be a devoted and efficient instrumentality.

Now, such entireness of consecration is, not among other things, but above all other things, in the order of means, indispensable. Always obligatory, it has now more than ever assumed a character of pressing, crying urgency. The spiritual wants of the heathen become apparent faster than we can supply them. Cries for missionary help thicken around us more rapidly than we can meet and appease them. The Church is distracted by the multiplicity of demands made on it, compared with the scantiness of means at present at its disposal. Entire devotedness would remedy the evil; not so much by adding to those resources the thousand means of influence which are now wasted in the world, as by certainly securing an unmeasured blessing from on high. God would arise out of his place; and then, although our means were much scantier than they now are, the work would rapidly proceed to a glorious consummation.

Christians, then, must live to Christ for the conversion of the world. The individual believer must come to feel that his very *business* as a Christian, his *calling*, is to propagate his religion. Instead of waiting for great conjunctures to arise before he begins to serve the missionary cause, or delaying until he has been transported to some distinguished field of usefulness at a distance, he must remember that, wherever he is, the sphere of his duty is always lying around him. Instead of waiting for others to move, each one must act under a sense of his individual responsibility to Christ, and as if he heard the Saviour's voice singling him out to tax his powers to the utmost in his service. Instead of taking example from the generality of those around him, he must take his standard from the word of God, and he will be furnishing a model for them, giving a pattern to the future, becoming the founder, not of a new doctrinal sect, but of a body of Christians distinguished by simply harmonizing their life with their professions. Instead of admiring the devotedness of Christ at a distance, he must feel that, like Christ, he has a work given him to do—the extension, or prolongation, in a sense, of the very same work: that as the course of Christ led direct to the cross, his life is to be a continuation of the same course, from the cross to the sinner whom it concerns; so that the same object for which his Lord came into the world and died, he is to live for till he quits the world.

Heads of families must remember that parental influence and domestic relationships are to be consecrated to the same object. Not only must they train their children to habits of benevolence, early impressing them that the principal value of money consists in its subserviency to the cause of Christ: they must look higher and farther even than this. They must themselves feel that the chief value even of their children, consists in their consecration to the same glorious cause. And, therefore, they must early begin to train them to take part in it; instructing them in the nature and progress of Christian missions; impressing it on them that the conversion of the world to Christianity is the noblest enterprise in which they can engage; inspiring them, if consistent with other claims, with zeal to embark in it; and in the event of their so doing, preparing, as far as possible, to support them in it.

Christian ministers must not regard the fact that they are occupying spheres of usefulness at home, as a sufficient reason for declining to enter the missionary field. They are to consider that as long as the demand for laborers is so much greater among the heathen than it is here, there is a standing call in Providence to exercise their ministry among them; and that unless they can show the best reasons for non-compliance, they are bound to listen and obey. Should such reasons, however, exist, they must be missionaries at home. Their ministry, to be effective, must develop all the resources of the Church, and bring them forth into actual operation. The holder of the five talents was to increase them, not by acting without them, but with them; and the man of God, when put in trust with the ministry of a particular church, is to look on each of its members as a talent concerning which the Divine Proprietor is saying, "Occupy till I come: employ every member—every moment and faculty of every member—to the best advantage, that each may be the means of winning another, and that my church of five hundred may be the means of gaining other five hundred more." With this solemn charge resting on his spirit, he will feel that his first object is to make the most of that church with whose instrumentality his Lord has intrusted him. Its members may not be educated, wealthy, numerous, nor, in a worldly sense, influential. But they are such as God hath collected and formed into a church, to take part in his sublime purpose of saving the world. One thing is certain, therefore, that they are all to be employed. In this sense, there are to be no "private Christians" among them. Every believer is a public man, taken up into the universal designs of the God of grace. In whatever sense they are private, then, like the ranks of an army, all are to take the field: the only concern of the minister must be how to dispose of his forces so as to render them most effective in the cause of God. A ministry which begins and ends with itself—however pious, intelligent, and eloquent it may be—is only the ministry of one man; and even that counteracted, neutralized, and often rendered worse than useless, by the slumbering and selfish inactivity of the people. But a ministry which sets and keeps in motion an entire church, however destitute it may be of other qualifications, becomes, in effect, the ministry of all its members, and thus proves an instrumentality of the widest influence and of the greatest efficiency. And never, till the entire Church is thus moved, and all its resources put into actual requisition, will the full value of the Christian ministry be seen; for never till then will it fully answer the high object of its Divine appointment in the conversion of mankind.

Why should not each church, or Christian community, take into sober consideration what is its proportion of the agency necessary to evangelize the world? Every church has its few active and its many indolent members; or, at least, those who are kept from indolence chiefly to avoid the shame and the remonstrances to which it would lead; and well do the few know that if the many were as active as themselves, their collective usefulness might be greatly increased. And well does each of our great missionary societies know that if all the unemployed resources of the community to which it belongs were but brought out from the napkin in which they are shrouded, and from under the bushel where they are hid, and placed at its disposal, soon might the sphere of its operations be enlarged to an almost indefinite extent. Now, this must be done. The Lord of the Church has made it the duty of his people statedly to pray that more laborers may be sent forth into the moral harvest. But this supposes that we are all anxious to furnish the requisite number, and that as soon as any who are eligible for the work appear in the Church, we regard it as an answer to our prayers, and take the necessary steps for sending them forth. Accordingly, instead of contenting itself with an annual contribution merely, each church must become, in a sense, a complete missionary society. If suitable agents, or those who may be made such, exist within its bosom, it must seek them out, and press them into the service. If the minister himself should express a desire to dedicate himself to the work, let the people generously sacrifice their own wishes for the good of the heathen. If the missionary preacher cannot be found among them, the missionary layman may. If the wealthy Christian has no higher reason for remaining at home than that which arises from his comfort and convenience, he must be affectionately admonished that the least he can do is to send and support a missionary in his stead. The churches severally must feel a distinct responsibility: each must perform a portion of duty: the whole work must be taken up more in detail; and each individual Christian must have the appeal carried home to his conscience as to the manner and the extent in which he will obey the last command of Christ, till he feels that it is a question which he must personally, and in the presence of God, decide.

The Church universal must unite. Not only must denominations of Christians verbally acknowledge the common guilt of their existing dissensions—they must be seen practically repenting, sympathizing, coöperating, and even emulating with each other in the sublime struggle of saving a world of souls from death. "The plague is begun." For ages the plague has prevailed. Countless myriads of immortal beings have, in consequence, perished. And still its desolating influence sweeps over the nations. The recovery or destruction of unknown multitudes depends on the instant application of the Divine remedy. That remedy is in the hands of the Church; and it is there that she may rush with it "between the dead and the living." And what she may do, she must do; nor must she expect to achieve "any deliverance in the earth," any signal or final triumph, until she has laid herself out to the utmost with a view to it. "When Zion travailed, she brought forth," and not till then. "A woman when she is in travail hath sorrow;" and so has a Church laboring, and in pangs for the regeneration of the world. The only question with such a Church will be, and the only consideration for us must be, Is it within the compass of our power to send the gospel through the world? Not whether we can send it with a small effort, or in a way which shall not materially interfere with our favorite plans of ease and habits of personal gratification. But can we, by "strong crying and tears," by the practical activity of a bold and vigorous faith, by the most strenuous and persevering exertions, furnish a dying world, the Saviour's world, with the means of salvation? The question must be answered by the actual experiment of unreserved devotedness.

PART VI.

MOTIVES TO ENFORCE THE ENTIRE CONSECRATION OF CHRISTIANS TO THE GREAT OBJECTS OF THE MISSIONARY ENTERPRISE.

It now remains that we exhibit and enforce some of the motives which exist for entire consecration to the great objects of the missionary enterprise. And remembering how much may depend, under God, on their right selection and earnest inculcation, the writer cannot but humbly and earnestly implore the gracious aid of the Holy Spirit, that none of the precious and momentous interests involved may suffer in his hands. As if all the heathen world were present as his clients, and he were pleading for them in the audience of the entire Church assembled on their behalf, and within hearing of the reproaches of the myriads whom the Church has suffered to go down unwarned to perdition, and within sight of the great tribunal, and of Him who sits on it, he would faithfully, affectionately, solemnly urge the duty of unreserved devotedness as the only hope, from the Church, for the heathen world. Let Christians, then, devoutly consider the grounds on which we urge this, and the reasons which bind them to comply—reasons so affecting and weighty that, although the wisest and the holiest men have in all ages united to enforce them with tears and entreaties, and though some of these men of God appeared to have been continued on earth chiefly to enforce them, devoting their whole lives to the work, yet they never have, never can have, full justice done to them; reasons so vast, that in order to comprehend them, we must compute the worth of all the souls perishing in ignorance of Christ through the want of it, and of all the glory which through eternity would redound to God from their conversion; and reasons so deeply laid in the Divine purposes, that the great object of the advent itself—the salvation of the world—is suspended on their taking effect.

Some of those reasons we have enforced already; not waiting till we approached the close of the subject, but urging them as they arose successively out of the various Parts. Indeed, the whole of the First Part may be considered as an exposition of the scriptural obligations to the duty; while the Second Part, on the benefits of the missionary enterprise, afforded us an opportunity of showing that the nearer we have approached to entire devotedness, the greater have been the advantages to ourselves and others: the Third Part, on missionary encouragements, showed that nothing but such devotedness is requisite in order to give the gospel to all mankind: even the objections to the missionary object, enumerated in the Fourth Part, were shown to be either utterly unfounded, or easily convertible into motives to the most self-denying zeal for its advancement; and the Fifth Part professed to show that such consecration forms the moral fitness which the Church wants, and to specify the various respects in which, under God, it would tend to supply our missionary defects.

I. We would now entreat the reader to consider that this entire devotedness is called for, if only *to retrieve, as far as possible, the evil effects of our past conduct,* both as individual Christians, and as members of the visible and universal Church. As converted men, we can probably look back to a period when we lived exclusively to ourselves. During the whole of that time, we are to remember, our life was planted in battery against Christ. Through that entire period, our character was full of influence—daily and hourly increasing the power of old trains of evil influence, or originating new ones. Each of these trains is still in existence: all of them are at this moment in operation somewhere: some of them doubtless in eternity—in hell. Tremendous reflection! they have entered into the character of some of the lost—become elements of damnation; and are now, while we are here at ease, imparting a darker shade of malignity to their thoughts, and deeper, coarser accents to their blasphemies. And on they will go, extending and multiplying their fearful effects, till all of them have worked out and discharged their proper results in the same appalling issue. And is it for us to be now satisfied with the consecration of less than the whole of our remaining influence to counteract the evil? Even if Christ did not expressly require it—if he were even to give us a dispensation from it—would our sense of obligation, our agony of solicitude to retrieve the past, allow us to accept it? If tears could wash away the evil of the past, could we do less than wish that our head were a fountain of waters, that we might weep night and day? But tears cannot: to remove its guilt there must be blood of infinite value; and to counteract its depraving influence, a Spirit of almighty power; while all that we can do—and surely we shall not plead for doing less—is to be the devoted, unintermitting channel for the communication of both to the world.

Besides which, we now stand related to the Christian Church; and this entire devotedness is called for to retrieve the effects, not only of our own conduct, but also of those who for ages have been the professed representatives of dishonored Christianity to the world. Let us think what that conduct, age after age, has been. From the moment the command went forth, "Preach the gospel to every creature," the world was divided into two classes. Those who possessed the gospel were to view themselves as standing to the rest of mankind in the relation of guardians—agents of mercy—instruments of salvation. What they ought to have been we have seen!—alas! how perfect the contrast to what they have been! It is fearful to think that, since then, forty thousand millions of human beings should have been allowed to pass through this world of guilt and woe on their way to a dark and dreadful eternity, without having heard from the Church a single accent of mercy and salvation. It is startling and alarming to reflect that there should be a greater number of heathen in the world at this moment than at any previous period since the gospel dispensation commenced: greater even than about fifty years ago, when the modern missionary effort began; for while, owing to our languid measures, we are proselyting them only at the rate of some hundreds or thousands annually, they are yearly adding to their ranks, by mere increase of population, about three millions and a half.

But we speak not of mere neglect. Simply to have disregarded the command of Christ to evangelize them, would have been harmless, perfect innocence, compared with what men called Christians have done under the pretence of obeying it. Simply to have left the heathen to perish in ignorance and idolatry, would have been mercy, benevolence, compared with the cruelties they practiced under the name of conversion. As they ascended, generation after generation, to the bar of God, and were asked the solemn question, "Where is thy heathen brother?" to have been able to reply, "Gone down unwarned to perdition," would have been comparative merit. But his blood was on their hands—they were there reeking from his slaughter—his injured spirit was there to accuse them. Let us track their progress among the heathen; and, if we can find it by no other marks, we have only to select the path most strewed with the wrecks of humanity—it is sure to be theirs. What was Southern America a century after the first nominal Christians landed there? the vast and crowded sepulchre of her murdered sons. Ask Northern America, Where are thy children of a thousand tribes? and the hill and the valley which knew them once can only echo, Where?—for men called Christians have been among them. A voice is heard in the South, "lamentation and bitter weeping, [Africa] weeping for her children, refuses to be comforted because they are not. Thus saith the Lord, Refrain thy voice from weeping, and thine eyes from tears; for thy work shall be rewarded, saith the Lord; and they shall come again from the land of the enemy. And there is hope in thine end, saith the Lord, that thy children shall come again to thine own border." But whose is that land of the enemy? and why were they taken there? Whose can it be but the land of Christians? and what could they aim at but their conversion? Unexampled infatuation! In each of the instances we have named, the system of fiendish iniquity was commenced in the dishonored name of Christ, and for the professed extension of the faith. And yet—unparalleled inconsistency!—the only men they martyred were those who attempted scripturally to extend that faith!*

But speak we of the past? Still the evil rages and extends. At this moment, men called Christians are the main props of

---

[* See Introduction.—T. O. S.]

idolatry in India—more useful to Juggernaut than his own hereditary priests. They aspire not to serve at his altar: they are content to hold up his train. Jesus and Juggernaut are alike to them; and they lend the sacred shield of the one, to guard the blood-stained and worn-out throne of the other. Slavery, under another name, driven from disembowelled Africa, is coasting other shores, seeking whom it may devour. The monster has tasted blood, and will not soon be driven from human flesh. Colonization and commerce still advance, with murder in their van. Those ships, whose holds are filled with distilled poison; those decks, piled with the instruments of destruction; that large fleet, freighted with opium— all proclaim their sleepless activity and their chosen means. Go, mark the thousand shores and islands of the Pacific, and say, with what are their tribes maddened, but with the liquid fires which *they* have imported? with what are they slaughtering each other, but with the weapons which *their* hands have supplied? with what are they pining and wasting away, but with the loathsome diseases which *their* vices have left behind? Missionaries of Christ! is there a single coast, a solitary island, whose virgin soil has not yet been defiled by their touch? Hasten away, or they will be there before you: there, to propagate an influence which ages of Christian effort will not be able to efface—there, to render the Christian name a name for avarice and treachery, licentiousness and blood.

True, there are exceptions to these statements; but rare exceptions they are. True, most of the actors in these tragic scenes have been Christians only in name; but in name they have been, and therein lies the evil. True, we are not directly answerable for the evil; but deeply *implicated* we are. When Christians should have been protesting, counteracting, moving heaven and earth against it, they all slumbered and slept. Were they not then implicated in the guilt? And the only condition on which *we* can escape the same implication is, by doing what they neglected. Let us omit a single prayer; withhold a single mite; send out a single missionary less than we could; delay a single moment to do any thing short of all we can do; and, during that moment, and to the full amount of that neglected means, we are implicated in the guilt, and are abetting the destructive influences which for ages have been turning the Christian name among the heathen into a curse.

Even if it were possible for Christians instrumentally to arrest and annihilate at a blow all the wide-spread machinery of evil which they have allowed to cover the earth in their name, ages would elapse, time itself must expire, before the pernicious influence of what has been done would cease to work against them. But, till that blow be struck, not only will those evil influences already in action continue to extend— new ones will be daily originated and augmenting their force. For the sake of the Christian name, then, in which the foulest atrocities have been committed; for the sake of the Church which has guiltily allowed it; for the sake of that world which has meantime suffered the dreadful effects, and which often thrusts away the cup of salvation because proffered by Christian hands, let no one bearing the Christian name live to himself. Could each one multiply himself and his means a thousand-fold, all would be necessary, if only to retrieve the guilt of the past.

II. Entire devotedness to the cause of Christ is necessary, *not only to retrieve the past, but as the only alternative of partial hostility against him at present.* He that is not with me, saith Christ—and therefore during every moment in which he is not with me—is against me. Lax views on this subject are the origin of much of that inferior piety by which the Church is enfeebled, and its usefulness impaired. Christians generally appear to proceed on the supposition that there is a sense in which they are still partially their own; that there are considerable portions of their time in which they are at perfect liberty to relax as they please; that at such times their conduct is quite neutral in its influence; that any thing short of positive hostility against Christ, is to be put down to the account of so much service done for him. Now, were this supposition as true as it is false—were it quite possible for the Christian to withhold from Christ a portion of his resources, without rendering by such an act the least advantage to the foe, it would still be highly inconsistent and unjust. For at the very moment we are relaxing in his service, unnumbered agencies of his are at work for us. At the moment we are self-indulging, we are doing it with his money, in his time, at his expense, by the light of his sun. But when we remember that every particle of influence withheld from Christ, is so much employed against him—that neutrality here is impossible, the consequences of such conduct are alarming. Were it possible for us to ascend some mount of vision whence we could look down upon the consequences of our conduct, we should see that at the moment when we thought ourselves most perfectly detached from all around us, there is a sense in which we were then standing in the midst of the universe with lines of relation uniting us with all its multitudes. We should see that often, when we thought our character most unobserved and at rest, it was giving out moral influences without intermission; that the moment they ceased to be good, they began to be evil; that, however apparently unimportant, they have ever since been swelling that tide of evil by which myriads are borne on to perdition. We should see that the world is the scene of a moral conflict; that in that conflict we hold an appointed post; that at that post every thing we possess is a weapon of war; that never have we ceased to wield it either for evil or for good; for the moment in which we thought we were only pausing, a shout of joy ran through the ranks of the invisible foe, who beheld in that pause a proof of our weakness, and the sign and means of their own strength; so that when we thought we were only doing nothing for Christ, they hailed us as an accession to their own ranks acting against him; and thus we should see why it is that Meroz was cursed because they came *not out* to the help of the Lord, and why it is that, in the final judgment, those who did nothing will find themselves standing side by side with them that did evil, and involved in the same condemnation.

It follows, then, that if we are doing a particle less than all we can do for the kingdom of Christ, we are incurring a proportion of the guilt of those who are doing nothing, and for the very same reason. The obligation which binds us to take any part in the grand conflict which is waging, not only holds us responsible for doing every thing in our utmost power, but actually regards whatever is short of this as so much opposition, with our cognizance, against him. Let us not suppose, then, that because we are doing something, we are sufficiently demonstrating our fidelity to his cause: if we are only doing one-third, so to speak, of what we could do, the other two-thirds are operating, *as ours*, in hostility against him, as truly as that one-third is operating, as ours, in his behalf. If there be, for instance, somewhere in the heathen world a certain amount or form of evil which *my* agency, armed with power from Heaven, might entirely subdue, and I have aimed at the destruction of only one-half of it, the other half must be regarded as my agency for upholding the cause of idolatry. If a Church, or an individual, support—as some do—a native teacher of Christianity in India, on the condition that he be called by the name of the Christian contributor, and if, while supporting only one, he could support two, he must be regarded as working there by two representatives—one for Christ, the other against him. True, the second or evil agent has not been named after him, is not supported by him; but inasmuch as he could, by the Divine blessing, be counteracting double the amount of evil influence which he is, that portion of it against which he proclaims no war, and makes no effort, is to be held as working against Christ, with his connivance, and in his name. Precious influence! each grain of which exceeds all calculable value. Well might our Lord be jealous for every particle; since there are but two treasuries in the universe, one for him, and the other for Satan; so that every grain withheld from his, falls into and enriches the other. And well may the Christian regard himself with all the sacredness of a temple, since he cannot yield himself to any other claimant than Christ, even for a moment, without yielding himself, during that moment, to a hostile party. So that, in truth, our only escape from partial hostility to Christ, is that of unreserved devotedness to his service.

III. The reference we have made to the great moral conflict which is pending, reminds us next, that *the state of the heathen is such as to require the entire amount of Christian influence for its amelioration.* It is affecting to think that while we are sitting, perhaps in our home, comparatively unmoved, there are, elsewhere, above six hundred millions of our race under the almost undisturbed domination of Satan; that these myriads are the wretched survivors of untold generations, who have lived and died under the same vassalage; that, as if they were born and were living in hell instead of on earth, the destroyer is living and walking amongst them; and that almost all the influences under which they pass across the stage of life, and which are perpetually darting and acting upon them from all sides round, are the influences of a system which he has been thousands of years constructing and maturing; to which he has been constantly adding something, and the sole merit of which, in his eyes, consists in the efficacy and certainty with which it invades and destroys them. Such, we may suppose, was the sight which Jesus beheld, when from the mountain's top the tempter meant that he should see only "the kingdoms of the world *and the glory* of them." And is it true that, after the gospel has been amongst us nearly two thousand years, *that* spectacle is to be seen still? Ascend, in thought, the same mount—we might say to the inquirer—and you behold substantially the same vision. Take a hasty glance at them, at least; more you cannot; for were they to assume the most dense and compacted form, days must elapse before they would all have passed. Look down upon them—if the thick darkness which hangs over them will permit—look down and mark their condition. Listen to the din of the great Babel: do you hear any voice of prayer? do you see any hopeful sign? It is true they have priests—but they are impostors and murderers; and altars—but they are stained with human blood; and objects of worship—but they "sacrifice to devils, and not to God." Look closer still; and as you look, think of all the elements of influence—ancestry, wealth, numbers—you cannot name one which is not made to minister to their destruction. Enumerate the vices—avarice, sensuality, revenge—you cannot specify one which is not, not merely embodied, but adored; for these are their gods, under other names. You cannot point out a single object in the air, the earth, or the waters, which might be pressed into the service of sin, and which is not actually so employed. You cannot discover a single individual who is not acting on every other being in all that countless mass in confirmation of their common depravity. You cannot name a sense of the body, a faculty of the soul, an evil propensity of our nature, which is not seized and held fast by as many hands as some of their false divinities possess, and which does not lend its willing aid in return. You cannot name a single moment, from birth to death, in which the whole of this infernal machinery is not everywhere in destructive activity, shedding poison and raining death; an activity, compared with which the utmost mechanical velocity, or the still greater activity of the material elements themselves, are mere quiet and repose.

And having surveyed this dense array of evil—having explored this living continent of depravity—do you wonder that God does not burn it from the earth? does not forthwith sweep the whole of these myriads away with the besom of destruction? *Them!* Destroy them! Their guilt is, in one respect, venial, compared with the sin of the Christian Church. Their state, fearful as it is, is explicable, compared with the conduct of those who hold in their hands the known means of their rescue, but refuse to employ them.

Look, we entreat you, look at those myriads again. You think, perhaps, that you do see them; many, at least, may flatter themselves that they do; but no, they have not yet—their conduct proves it. See, the countless mass is at worship —before the throne of Satan, glowing as with the heat of an infernal furnace—with rage, lust, and cruelty for their religious emotions. Look at them again—their demon-worship is over; but are they satisfied? How eager their looks! how objectless and restless their movements! how the living mass of misery heaves, and surges, and groans, and travails in pain together!

Look at them once more: they are travellers into eternity: mark how vast the procession they form, how close their ranks, how continuous the line, how constant and steady the advance! Do you see them now? Then you see that angry cloud which hangs over their ranks—which moves as they move—and which ever and anon emits a lurid flash: it is stored with the materials of judicial wrath. Do you mark them still? Then you see that thousands of them have reached the edge of a tremendous gulf—it is the gulf of perdition, and they are standing on the very brink. Are you sure that you see them? God of mercy! They are falling over—they are gone! And we never, never tried to save them! Father, forgive us: we know not what we do. Saviour of sinners, spare us yet another year. We know they are lost—lost to happiness and lost to thee! We could have told them of thee—shown them thy cross—given them thy gospel—pointed them the way to heaven. But they are lost!

Talk not of enthusiasm! He who has felt most has not yet felt enough. We are speaking of scenes of misery over which a Paul wept with anguish! We are living in the very world for which Christ bled in agony! Those very scenes which hardly raise an emotion in us, are the scenes which moved the heart of God—which produced the cross of Christ. So that were every Christian to tremble with emotion—were the members of every Church to meet on the subject, to start from their supineness as one man, and to utter a loud cry of lamentation—were the whole Church to be seized as in travail for souls, it would be only what sympathy with Christ requires, and what the state of a perishing world demands.

IV. The duty of intense devotedness to the work of imparting the gospel is greatly increased *by the remarkable manner in which Providence has brought and placed the world at our feet in order to receive it.*

There might have been but one unenlightened district left on the face of the earth—but one unconverted man; and he a miserable object, the lone inhabitant of some distant and desert isle. Yet such is the human soul; so incomparably superior, owing to its spiritual nature, its endless duration, and its vast capabilities, to the whole material universe, and so momentous an object is its recovery in the estimation of Christ, that, if necessary, it would be the duty of all the other inhabitants of the earth to have embarked their treasures, joined their supplications, combined and taxed their utmost resources, for the conversion of that solitary man. But if all this would be justified for the salvation of one man—if a particle less than all this would be a betrayal of our trust, an insult to all immortal natures, and treason against the throne of Christ, when only one soul was concerned, what must be the guilt of less than entire devotedness when the unconverted are so many that they are crowded in cities, swarming on islands, overflowing continents, teeming everywhere? If, when the Church had so far "multiplied, and replenished the earth," as to have left but a single district unenlightened, it would yet be bound, if necessary, to devote all its united energies to the recovery of that solitary region, where could we find language strong enough to describe the inconsistency of that region, if on the contrary supposition that it alone possessed the gospel, and all the rest of the earth were perishing, it yet contented itself with a few cheap and easy expressions of concern for their salvation?

But though this supposition partially represents our actual

position and conduct in relation to the heathen world, our opportunities of saving them might have been such as to render the attempt all but hopeless. We might have been held in cruel slavery, unable to move without a chain; or the scattered inhabitants of some arctic region, comparatively cut off from intercourse with the rest of the world; or imprisoned, for every missionary purpose, in the heart of a vast continent; or the idolatrous nations generally might be so averse to Christianity, as rigorously to inflict death on any of its agents, who might dare to approach them. And yet if, even then, less than entire devotedness to the world's salvation would have been the highest guilt, by what plea can we now excuse ourselves for less, when the world, in a sense, is given into our hands? We might have been originally an island of barbarians, the prey of every roving pirate, and the trembling victims of civilized oppression. And if then the dayspring from on high had visited us, and prepared us for all our subsequent improvement—if, as our ancient oppressors declined, and were recalled from the stage of action, *we* gradually emerged, and rose into national importance—if, when the ark of the truth was in danger, we were honored by God to act as its defenders—if, as often as our foes combined to destroy us, they were not only defeated, but doomed to the mortification of seeing us rise to greater prominence than before—if a name and a character became ours which operated universally in our favor as a moral charm—if our commerce were welcomed in almost every port—if our political influence were felt in every cabinet—if surrounding powers were dispossessed of their foreign dependencies that we might enjoy them—and if other vast and populous regions of the earth came unexpectedly into our possession, till a considerable portion of the race were sitting at our feet—should we not feel that each stage of our course had brought with it an increase of responsibility, till our position had become one which left us no alternative but that of entire consecration to its duties? But who does not know that this is far below the reality of our history?

What was our political condition only a century ago? The great powers which divided the empire of the world did not reckon us among them. The total number of British subjects, including those of all our dependencies, did not exceed 13,000,000. What is their number now? Upwards of 152,000,000, which is more than a sixth portion of the human race; considerably more than the population of the ancient Roman empire; nearly double that of the nations now subject to Mohammedan rulers; and greatly exceeding the number of those who acknowledge the supremacy of the Pope. In order to this, we have been permitted to succeed to the possessions of Holland and of Portugal in India—to the empire of the Mohammedan sovereigns of India—to the commercial ascendency of the Venetians in the Levant—to a political and moral ascendency more nearly approaching to universal empire than probably any other nation of which we read in the pages of history. But why? The believer in revelation has but one reply. Why was each of the great nations of antiquity made in succession the leader of the world? why, but that it might answer some specific moral purpose, corresponding with its advantages and obligations? But failing to fulfil its high vocation, there came forth the likeness of a man's hand, and wrote the doom of each, and gave its power to another.

"When do you expect that your nation will recover its power in India?" said an Englishman to a Portuguese priest of Goa, soon after the power of Portugal in India had been overthrown. The priest replied, "As soon as the wickedness of your nation shall exceed that of ours." We hold India by the imperative condition that we subserve the designs of Providence respecting it: let that condition be violated, and the possession ceases with the infraction. Our ascendency and advantages are so many talents of mighty worth; and He who has conferred them has done so with deep calculation and for a special end. They constitute Britain the centre around which at this time revolve the hopes and destinies of man. But whatever the *nation* is, it is for the *Church*. The military conquests of the former have been permitted only for the peaceful achievements of the latter. Territorial enlargements and political influence have been given us only to prepare the way and create a sphere for our missionary efforts. But who can measure the largeness of that sphere, count up the population which it contains, and remember that our opportunity for giving them the gospel is only for an appointed time, without feeling that for the

Church to lose a moment, or to neglect an effort for saving them, is treachery to itself, murderous cruelty to them, and trifling with God? And the call for this unremitting concern becomes more urgent from the fact that, as a nation, we have obtained much of our political influence over them by an energy of application to our object in which treasures and lives, by hundreds and thousands, have been treated as the small dust of the balance. Shall less energy be exhibited by the Church militant, in claiming them as the subjects of Him who is King of kings and Lord of lords?

And still further is this demand on our devotedness increased by the fact that a very large proportion of the heathen of whom we speak, not only ascribe our mutual position to an invisible hand, but are actually ready to place themselves as disciples at our feet. Hundreds of thousands of them may be said to be standing at this moment on the threshold of the temple of idolatry, ready to quit it for ever. Shall we call them into the Church of Christ, or shall we remand them back to rekindle the fires of their Molech, and to rebuild the altars of their demon-worship? Multitudes of them are standing at the gates of the Christian Church—the hand of Providence has directed them there—they bring with them signs from heaven that he has sent them, and that he expects us to receive and instruct them. Are we ready to make the sacrifices which the occasion requires? At all events, if we will persist in neglecting them, let us plainly avow the reason. Before we finally dismiss them to destruction, let us, by public manifesto, or otherwise, exculpate Christianity, and blame the only guilty cause by telling them, "Your conversion to the Christian faith is an object of the highest importance. To effect it would greatly augment our heavenly happiness, secure infinite blessedness to you, and bring to God everlasting glory. As far as our instrumentality is necessary, the means are all in our possession. But we cannot furnish them without abridging our self-indulgence; and as this requires more love for your souls and regard for the authority of Christ than we possess, we see no alternative but that of leaving you to perish." Now, startling as such language may seem, by what other terms can we excuse ourselves from entire devotedness to their salvation?

V. Some *have exhibited this devotedness;* and here is another inducement to our consecration. For though our obligation is quite independent of what others may do, yet the fact that some have entirely surrendered themselves to that obligation, furnishes us with an additional motive to do likewise, and will render us the more inexcusable if we do not. Are we asked the names of such men, and who they were? Ask—we reply—ask inspiration the names of the men who first filled the world with the news of salvation, from the burning Paul to the humblest evangelist of his day. Ask Protestant Christendom the names of her reformers and confessors; and she will tell you of a Wycliffe and a Zuingle, a Luther, a Melancthon, and a Huss—men of whom the world was not worthy. Ask our missionary societies the names of their honored founders, and they will tell you of men who travelled, pleaded, wept, while the world around them slept. Ask them the names of the missionaries they most delight to honor, and they will give you a long list of worthies, from an Eliot of the seventeenth century, penetrating the depths of the American wilderness, to the Moravian heroes of the eighteenth century, braving the snows of Greenland, down to the man of "Missionary Enterprises," just gone to explore the Southern Pacific for fresh fields of gospel triumph.* And what shall we more say? for the time would fail us to tell of a Brainerd and a Stach, a Swartz and a Coke, a Martyn and a Morrison, a Carey and a Marshman, who through faith subdued kingdoms to the obedience of Christ, turned spears into pruning-hooks, civilized savage tribes, smote off the fetters of the slave—gave the Bible to the nations—and went everywhere claiming those nations for God. Had the Grecian soldier a loftier character to sustain after Thermopylae and Marathon? What a character have we to sustain since such men trod the earth! Yet ask them the secret of their success; ask *them*, we say—for they are near us—do we not feel their presence? are we not sensible of a great cloud of witnesses? Ask them the secret of their success—and, while they point to Him at whose feet they cast their crowns as the efficient cause, they will tell you that, instrumentally, they owe it to the singleness of their aim, the unity of their purpose, the utter devotedness of their lives to their great object. And yet

---

* Now gone to his reward, as the "Martyr of Erromanga."

ardent, devoted as they were, in what respect did they exceed their duty?

Holy, honored, illustrious men, what are we that we should be admitted to your glorious fellowship! Had *you* not lived, we should have applauded deeds which now we must pass unnamed! We cannot talk of what we give in your presence—you gave yourselves. We cannot boast of our enthusiasm in your hearing—your zeal consumed you. We dare not speak of our sacrifices before you—you would remind us that the world has had but one sacrifice, and never can have another—and yet you gave your lives, your all. How have you raised the standard of Christian action! What new responsibilities have you devolved! Never can we vindicate our title as your successors, nor complete what you began, but by binding ourselves up with it, as you did, for life and for death.

VI. The importance of a devoted Church will appear, if we reflect that *the distinguishing characteristic of the age is that of change and transition, and that only such a Church is prepared to turn this peculiarity to the proper, the highest account.* Never, since time began, was the human mind in such close, quick, constant, sympathetic, universal communication as now. And, consequently, never was there so general and thorough an awakening of mind as now. Look where we will, it is quivering with impulses, thrilling with excitement, restless for change, panting for a good which it has not. This state of things has been brought about, partly *by* Christian activity—entirely *for* that activity. The world could not take the proper advantage of it, if it would, for it has not the means; nor would it, if it could, for it has not the motives; nor might it, under any circumstances, for the great changes and improvements of society are evidently reserved by God to be effected by his Church. Hence, all the great and beneficial movements of the day—the liberation of the slave, the religious education of the young, the advancement of civilization—have, in fact, originated with Christians; and for this obvious reason, that the glory might be exclusively his own. But for the same reason that these great movements have not originated with a worldly philosophy, the greater and more spiritual changes yet to take place will not originate with a worldly Church. We want one of the primary means.

which is visible union. And this makes it evident—evident to the world—that we want one of the primary motives—*that zeal for Christ, and love for souls, which would impel us to unite.* And hence it is obvious that, in the eyes of the world, we must be wanting in weight of character. For, in order to obtain the direction of public opinion at home, and to take advantage of changes abroad, we must be in advance of the world—in advance of its intelligence in every thing relating to human welfare—in advance of its benevolent activity—but, above all, in immeasurable advance of its character. Rather, we should have said, we must have a character of our own to which the world would never venture to make a pretension: a character for disinterestedness, liberality, self-denial, and united supplications to God: a character for being always ready—ready with our plans, and ready with our means, for seizing every opening of usefulness: a character for denying ourselves that we might be thus ready, and yet not being sensible that we denied ourselves at all: a character for living only for one object—to establish the reign of Christ upon earth. Such a character, indeed, the world might not admire, but could not resist.

But *is* this our character? Are we thus ready? Are not a thousand doors of usefulness standing open at this moment, in India alone, which we are not prepared to enter? Are we not distracted between the scantiness of our present available resources, and the number and diversity of the demands made on them? Yet the world knows full well, and we know too, that, were we truly in earnest, we could multiply these resources a thousand-fold. The world knows, and we know too, that the tax paid by the country on a single article of luxury exceeds all that Christians contribute to religious objects; and that, of that tax on self-indulgence, Christians pay a large proportion, despite the cries of a perishing world. Now, what is all this but a want of character—a want of weight with the world—a want of readiness to take the direction of its movements—a want of fitness to be honored and employed by God in that capacity—a want of that which nothing else could supply, but which itself could supply the want of every thing else; for a Christian Church thoroughly imbued with the Spirit of Christ, and devoted to the great object of its existence, would find in its character an amount of wealth, influence, and moral power, to which the world would render involuntary homage, and which God would crown with distinguished success.

VII. Connected with this view is another consideration. If the present be an age of transition and change, it is, on that very account, *the commencement of a new era:* on us it devolves to give the first impulse to that era; but that first impulse is likely to impart more or less of its own character to the whole era of which it is the commencement—likely to propagate its influence on to the end of time: how unspeakably important, then, that the impulse should be of the most holy, ardent, and scriptural kind! in a word, that it should be given by men living to Christ!

It is the undying, self-propagating nature of our moral influence which invests every thing we do with so much importance: its immediate effect may be trivial, but who shall calculate consequences never ending, ever expanding? Christian parents, the scale on which you give is likely to affect the liberality of your children's children to the remotest generation. Christians, you are living for futurity. The character you impress on the age is not to die with you—it is the legacy you will bequeath to posterity. The influence you are now putting into circulation is not to be limited to the present: it will reach to those you never saw, and descend to other times. Churches of Christ, reflect! traces of your character will reappear ages hence, in the Churches of India and Africa, China and Japan—of shores yet undiscovered, and nations yet unformed. You are giving Christianity to posterity: what kind of a Christianity are you giving it? A languid, feeble, spiritless thing, or a system instinct with life? Shall it go forth to the world, and down to the future, covered with the honors and repeating the achievements of its first days? or a half-hearted, torpid, self-indulging system, living on the world's sufferance, and struggling on for a bare existence? Remote generations summon us to duty, and adjure us, by the responsibility of our present position—by the bright hopes we cherish of millennial bliss—and by the certainty that the impulses we are now giving to religion will impart a character to that bliss, a lustre or a shade—that we give them the Christianity of apostolic times, fresh from the cross, and glowing with the fire of a Paul.

VIII. But from all this it follows that *nothing done for Christ is lost;* and that as the whole, with all its immediate and remote results, will eventually form a subject of interesting retrospection, it supplies us with a powerful motive to present devotedness. We mean not to intimate that the costliest service we can render has any inherent worth, or any independent influence, to produce the smallest spiritual results. But we *do* mean to say, that nothing scripturally done for Christ is lost; that of every such act he graciously takes the charge—appoints it a place in his system of means—and causes it to move in a line parallel with the great laws of his government.

Say, what of all the past is lost? The mites of the widow? True, the gift in itself was small, the act trivial; but she has, in high moral effect, been giving them daily, ever since. They have multiplied into millions. Those mites have formed an inexhaustible fund, and to the end of time will constitute for the Church an ever-augmenting treasury of wealth. What is lost? The labors of those who first took the mission field, and who have already fallen? True, they failed in some of their immediate ends, and fell comparatively unwept. But, holy, honored men, your day of moral power is yet to come. Already your names are our titles: your memory is our inspiration: your noble deeds are our heraldry: your example, a precious part of our inheritance. By the perusal of your tale shall many a youthful bosom swell with the sacred ambition of living to Christ in heathen lands; and, as he hears your name pronounced with benedictions, or touches the soil which contains your hallowed dust, or opens the sacred page which you first laboriously unlocked to wandering eyes—your memory shall fire his zeal, and in his labors shall you live again. What is lost? The blood of the martyrs? True, they fell. The car of the demon to which they were sacrificed, rolled over them and on: "their ashes flew, no marble tells us whither:" the voices which bewailed them sank into silence: the tyranny which crushed them waxed stronger and stronger; and age followed age apparently only to blacken their names, or to proclaim that they had lived and died in vain. But did they? Let the history of truth struggling with error ever since testify. Never have their sufferings ceased to thrill the general heart. Long have some of their softest whispers at the stake been oracles to support the suffering, and watchwords to animate the valiant for the truth.

And such shall be your honored destiny, martyrs of Madagascar! Precious were your deaths in the eyes of your Lord. Precious in our eyes is every drop of your blood. And the time shall come when precious shall be the spot where you were speared in the eyes of your own people. At present they deem you vanquished. But *they* never fail who die for Christ. That land belongs to him. And, when he assumes his right, your wounds shall plead for him: the spear that pierced you shall blossom and bud: your martyrdom, subservient to a higher influence, shall give a resistless impulse to the cause of truth.

That time will come—the time when Christ will have taken, not that island only, but the earth for his possession. The price has been paid—the transfer made—the time for actual possession appointed—the approach of that time Divinely indicated. Let us imagine that future period to have come. There is Christendom purged of its corruptions: India without its caste: China without its wall of selfishness: Africa without its chains: earth without its curse. All its kingdoms, consolidated into one vast spiritual empire, are happy in the reign of Christ, and prostrate at his feet. And. will it form no part of the employment of that blessed time, to trace back that grand consummation to all the trains of instrumentality which led to it? It will, doubtless, form a part of the occupation of heaven itself. And in the prosecution of that inquiry, will there be one period whose annals shall be referred to with surpassing interest? one, from which that great ocean of results will be found to have derived many of its most important springs and streams of Christian influence? That period will doubtless prove our own. And will not *he* be among the happiest Christians *then* who perceives that, by embarking his all in the cause of Christ, he has an ample revenue of glory to lay at his Saviour's feet?

Young men, remember this. The morning of your life, and the morning of a glorious day, are dawning together. Would you inscribe your names on a page which will be read with interest by a renovated world? In the great audit, would you stand for more than a unit? Then must you spring to action at once. Delay a while—and, go where you will, no country will be left for you to be the *first* to claim for Christ: no language remain for you to consecrate by *first* pronouncing in it the name of Christ: no single tribe to whom you can present the *first* Bible! Happy deprivation! and is nothing left—no lofty mark for Christian ambition to aim at? Yes, the Church has left you one, at least—and that the loftiest of all. There is yet left to you the high distinction of not living to yourselves. Aim at and exhibit that distinction; and, at the period of retrospection of which we speak, it shall be found that if others began an era of activity, it was yours to eclipse them by commencing an era of devotedness.

IX. But we ascend to higher reasons still. *All things belong to Christ by original, mediatorial right, and were constructed by him expressly with a view to subserve his mediatorial plan.* "All things were created *by* him, and *for* him." "He is both the First and the Last," the efficient and the final cause of all things. The creation of the universe is not to be regarded as an act terminating in itself; or as performed merely for the purpose of exhibiting as much of the Divine glory as, taken by itself, it was calculated to display. Nor is the mediatorial office of Christ to be regarded as an afterthought—a supplementary appointment in consequence of the unexpected derangement and failure of a previous design. The constitution of a Mediator is to be viewed as having been the primary step toward the creation of the universe. Nor is the introduction of sin to be regarded as having been originated or necessitated by this original arrangement. On the contrary, it implies that the evil having been infallibly foreseen, the entire plan of the Divine procedure was laid with a view to an adequate remedy. Creation itself, therefore, was a mediatorial act; and every thing made was expressly intended to answer to the great remedial design, and was so made as to be best adapted for the purpose.

It follows, then, that no part of creation answers its highest end until it becomes subservient to the designs of Christ. Numerous other ends it may answer; many of them may be important ends; and all of them may be allowable; but failing of subserviency to the mediatorial government of Christ, it fails of the chief end for which it was brought into existence. It was not till the earth echoed the first promise, and became a theatre for unfolding the scheme of mercy which that promise enclosed, that it was promoted to the grand office of its creation. It was not till the objects and elements of nature became recognized images and emblems of that great scheme, that the true reason of their existence and particular construction was made known. The offices of prophet, priest, and king—of father, husband, and friend, found not their true distinction till they became known types of the mediatorial relations of Christ. Till Christ assumed our nature, the great reason for the existence of humanity itself remained undeveloped; and, until he died, the temple of the universe may be said to have been destitute, except in the Divine intention, of altar, sacrifice, and priest. The cross was the true centre of the world made visible. And hereafter it will be clearly seen that all nations, objects, and events, answered their real design only as they revolved in subordination around it: that it never moved, but all things were meant to fall into its train: never stood, but all things were called to bow down before it: never spoke, but they were all expected to echo its voice. It will, as we have shown, be distinctly seen, that wealth attained its true destination only when it fell into the treasury of Christ: that speech realized its grand design only when it became "a means of grace:" that all the relationships of life, and all the mutual influences with which those relationships invest us, found their proper end only when they harmonized with the central influence streaming from the cross.

But what powerful motives does this view of the mediatorial lordship of Christ supply to our entire consecration to his service! For until the great design of the office be fulfilled in the spiritual recovery of the world, the unnecessary diversion of a single particle of influence from his cause is an act of rebellion against his authority. Had such a diversion been the first and solitary instance of the kind ever known, it could not have occurred without exciting a burst of loyal indignation from every part of the Divine dominions. How much greater the guilt, then, of such an alienation now, when the rebellion is so general that nearly "all things" on earth, "created by him and for him," are turned and pointed against him! Had an angel been sent down to stand between us and every such act, it should not have deterred us so powerfully as this consideration. Wherever we look, we may rest assured that his eye is resting at the same moment on all within the circle, with a look of sovereign and jealous appropriation. On whatever we may lay our hand, his hand has been there before us, and left a sign which marks it entirely for his own. Wherever we may go—into the bosom of the family, the place of business, the seat of power and national government—he is there before us to assert his original claim, and to impress on every thing the solemn sentence, "*by* me, and *for* me."

Little, indeed, do the rulers of the earth think of any higher end than that of national prosperity and aggrandizement; and matter of high scorn would it be to them to be told that, in the true system of things, they come after the Christian missionary, and are appointed to minister in his train. Little do the men of science, commerce, and power, concern themselves to inquire why "the sea and the dry land" were originally distributed into their present geographical form; why an insignificant island should hold distant and populous nations in dependency; and why tides and oceans roll between. They need to be reminded, however, that in the government of Christ there is a reason for all this, and that that reason is worthy of Him for whom the whole exists: that it is something higher and greater than that of merely supplying their tables with luxuries, or even their coffers with funds. They are to be told that, could they be taken to the summit of that lofty reason, they would be able to command a view of both eternities: that on looking down upon the movements of time, in vain would they look for the signs of their own existence, unless they are living for Christ: that, from that height, the light of heaven falls on nothing which is not directly or indirectly advancing his great design: that it is reflected from the path of the Christian preacher with a strength which throws the track of an army into the shade, and from the vessel conveying a herald of salvation to some heathen shore with a lustre which leaves a warlike navy involved in midnight darkness.

But if all things are *for* him, why are they not *with* him? Why will they not find the perfection of their nature, and the reason of their existence, in his service? It is not that they are not needed. So vast and full of grace is the design of the mediatorial economy, that it wants them all—has work for them all. It cannot do without them—consistently, that is, with existing appointments—it cannot do without them. They are the only instruments which it chooses to work with. It seeks to enlist into its service all the relations which bind us together, and all the natural means by which we influence each other. It claims the infant heart, by looking at it through the eyes and caressing it in the tones of maternal love. The father's authority, the sister's entreaty, the brother's warning, the servant's fidelity, the tradesman's integrity and weight of character, the persuasions of friendship, the active attention of neighborly kindness, the disinterested benevolence of public life, the powerful influence of righteous government—it wants them all, has work for them all. And even if it had them, the kindest tones cannot equal the tenderness of its entreaties: the hottest tears cannot express its anguish over human misery: the most throbbing heart cannot beat quick enough to satisfy its eager longing for human salvation: all the influence which collective man could wield in its behalf, could not do justice to its free, and full, and gushing benevolence—could not furnish channels wide and deep enough to pour forth the ocean-fulness of its grace.

X. But the great gospel argument for such consecration is one superinduced on that of the original right of Christ, and is known and felt by the Christian alone—*the claim of redemption.* "What! know ye not that ye are not your own? for ye are bought with a price!" The fact that Christ is our Creator and Proprietor, gives him, as we have seen, a right in us which nothing can ever alienate; but on this right, original and unalienable as it is, he does not often insist. The fact that we have ever been cared for by his providence, that we have never been out of the arms of infinite tenderness, gives him a claim on us which nothing can ever cancel; but on this claim, strong and subduing as it is, he does not ordinarily insist. He has a claim more powerful and affecting still—the fact that he has bought us, bought us with a price! He comparatively waives every other ground of claim, and trusts to this alone. He knows that all other claims are included in it or connected with it: that this may be felt after the heart has become insensible to every other claim: that it is the last and strongest plea which infinite love itself can employ.

And what a claim it is—the claim of redemption! Alas, that our familiarity with it should ever diminish its freshness and force: that we do not always feel as if the price had only just been paid—the mystery of the cross just transpired! To think that there should have been a period in our history when we were lost; lost to ourselves—all our capacity for enjoyment being turned by sin into a felt capacity for suffering; lost to the design of our creation—all our powers of serving Christ being perverted into instruments of hostility against him; lost to the society of heaven—the place which awaited us there to remain eternally vacant; the part we should have taken in the chorus of the blessed to remain for ever unfilled; heaven itself, as far as in us lay, turned into a place of mourning and desolation; lost to God—to the right of beholding, approaching, and adoring the vision of his eternal glory! To think that, in point of law, we were thus lost as truly as if the hand of justice had seized us, had led us down to our place in woe, drawn on us the bolts of the dreadful prison, and as if years of wretchedness and ages of darkness had rolled over us there. Well may we ask ourselves again and again, How is it we are here? here in the blessed light of day? here, in the still more blessed light of God's countenance? here, like children sitting in their father's smiles? Why is this, and how has it come to pass? Has justice relaxed its demands? or have the penal flames become extinct? What, know ye not that ye are bought with a price? It is the theme of the universe. Look on that glorious being descending from heaven in the form of God: know ye not "the grace of our Lord Jesus Christ"—that he sought no resting-place between his throne and the cross? Behold that cross: know ye not that "he loved us and gave himself for us?" that "he bare our sins in his own body on the tree?" Approach nearer, and look on that streaming blood: know ye not "the precious blood of Christ," and that that blood is the price of your redemption? Hear you not the voice from heaven which now says, "Deliver them from going down to the pit, for I have found a ransom?" Feel you not the Spirit of God drawing you, with gentle solicitations and gracious importunities, to the feet of Christ? See you not that he who was delivered for your offences, hath been raised again for your justification, and is now waiting to receive the homage of your love? How much owest thou unto thy Lord? Try to compute it. He asks only his due. So that if there be any part of your nature which he has not redeemed, or any thing in your possession for which you are not indebted to him, keep it back, and apply it to some other purpose. But does not the bare suggestion do violence to your new nature? does not every part of that nature resent the very idea, and find a voice to exclaim, "O Lord, I am thy servant, I am thy servant, thou hast loosed my bonds?"

And while standing in the presence of this matchless display of grace, and subdued by its influence, does the eager inquiry spring to your lips, "Lord, what wilt thou have me to do?" Do? what *can* you do but make known that grace to others: what can you do but let the stream of gratitude, which his great love has drawn from your heart, pour itself forth into that channel in which a tide of mercy is rolling through the world, and bearing blessings to the nations? What did the apostles do under similar circumstances? So powerfully were they constrained by the love of Christ, that they thus judged that instead of living as if they were under little or no obligations to him, they should henceforth act as if the duty of living to him were the only obligation they were under; and that the best way of doing that would be by conveying the knowledge of his redemption to others, and thus working out the grand purposes of his atoning death. What can you do but let your love to Christ take the same form as his love to you? and what was that but compassion for the guilty, and active, devoted, unsparing efforts to save the perishing? He, indeed, could save, and did save in a way in which he can never be copied; but so much the greater our obligation to imitate him where imitation is possible; especially, too, as the only walk of benevolence which his all-performing compassion has left open to us, is that which leads from his cross to the sinner; and the only labor left us, that of endeavoring to draw all men unto him.

XI. And this reminds us that not only are we his by original right and his by redemption, but *that the great object for* which, relatively, he has brought us under such obligations, and for which he has, in addition, formed us into a Church, is, that he might engage and engross our instrumentality for the salvation of others. If "he gave himself for us," it was "that he might purify unto himself a peculiar people zealous of good works." If we "are created in Christ Jesus," we are created "unto good works." "What! know ye not that your body is the temple of the Holy Ghost, which is in you, which ye have of God, and ye are not your own? for ye are bought with a price; therefore glorify God in your body and in your spirit, which are his." What! can you have allowed an analogy so obvious as that which exists between a temple and a believer, to escape your notice? Angels mark it; and that is one reason why they rejoice over the sinner when he repents: they know that God is consecrating another living temple, is advancing another step towards the completion of that universal temple destined to resound through eternity with the echoes of his praise. God himself designs it—designs that the consecrated character of the temple on Zion shall be copied and repeated in the devoted character of every living temple.

If, then, we would see the pattern of our Christian devotedness, let us go, in imagination, and survey the temple and its service. Are we not conscious of a holy awe stealing over our minds as we approach it? Such should be the feeling which the presence of the Christian inspires—that he is a man set apart for God. Let us enter the sacred precincts, cross the threshold, and look around: all its priests are the anointed servants of God—all its vessels holiness to the Lord—all its parts sprinkled with blood. Can we imagine any thing which we see in it, taken and applied to any other than temple purposes, without a sense of profanation? that priest, for instance, just offering the victim, polluted with licentiousness? that sacred vessel taken away and turned into a cup of intemperance? that altar transferred for a time to the temple of Molech? or the temple itself, lent, during the interval of God's worship, to celebrate the orgies of some idol god? The very thought seems profanation, blasphemy! and why, but because we feel that the place is sacred to God throughout, and should be entirely and exclusively devoted to his service? Well, know ye not that the Christian is now the temple of

God? and that he has claims on our devotedness which he could never have on a material temple—the claim that every thing we are and have belongs by purchase to the God of the temple? and that, by voluntarily and cordially devoting the whole to him, he counts himself glorified? "Thou that abhorrest idols, dost thou commit sacrilege?"

And not only every individual believer, but every particular church, is a living temple. Its members, "as living stones, are built up a spiritual house, a holy priesthood, to offer up spiritual sacrifices, acceptable to God by Jesus Christ." And may we not suppose, must we not believe, that, as often as we meet in this capacity, the Lord of the temple himself comes amongst us? Must we not conclude, that as he walks in the midst of the churches, marking the character of their services and the degree of their devotedness, his eyes are as a flame of fire? Is the particular church, then, to which we belong prepared for the searching inspection? Does he find our knowledge of his salvation—the first Christian talent with which he intrusts us—kept, like a vessel of the sanctuary, bright and burnished by constant use? Our speech—do "the lips of the priest keep knowledge," and the people "order their conversation aright?" Are our tongues like living censers for offering up the incense of praise? The influence arising from our relationship—are we employing it as a golden cord for drawing others with us into the Divine presence? Does he find none of his property abstracted from the treasury, and lavished on worldly objects? or is it all ready to meet his claims? Is self-denial among us, bearing its cross, and presenting its precious oblations? And Christian activity and zeal, flaming like an altar of sacrifice, and ready to say, "The zeal of thine house hath consumed me?" and prayer, interceding for the world; wrestling with God for a universal blessing? Souls are perishing—souls have been perishing during the whole time of our connection with the Church, and that Church has been appointed instrumentally to save them: amidst the wide-wasting ruin of immortal spirits perpetually going on around us, have we, by prayers, by entreaties, by the Spirit of God, saved one? We stand related to the whole Church—to the entire world—and the present is a time in which that relation is daily becoming more visible, and entailing increased responsibility. Louder voices, and loftier claims, are summoning us to action, than any which the Churches of former times have ever heard. Do we mark the Divine indications in this respect, and sympathize with the cries of the world, and with the office of the Church, as a great missionary society to answer those cries? Are we exciting each other to come to the help of the Lord; and aspiring to lead the van of the Christian enterprise? Is the influence of our Christian activity made to be felt around? Are other churches glorifying God in us? Has the world reason to bless God for our existence?

But, if each particular church, still more is the Church universal to be regarded in the light of a temple devoted to the service of Christ. Shall the Lord of the temple claim its entire consecration in person? Why may we not suppose him to descend, and appear in the midst of his people, to enforce the claim? But how should we prepare for his reception? and what will he expect at our hands? "Blow ye the trumpet; sanctify a fast; call a solemn assembly." Every Christian of every denomination, "holding the Head," should be summoned—for the occasion equally concerns us all. All we have must be brought into his presence: our children must be sent for, our property, our means of every description—whatever can be employed in his service. Nothing must be forgotten—nothing kept back. Thus prepared for his arrival, behold him come! *him*—the victim of Calvary—the Head of the Church—the Saviour of the world—clothed, as when John beheld him, in priestly attire; and, in his countenance, majesty blended with tenderness and rebuke. Looking around on the hushed and breathless assembly, he may be supposed to say, in accents which thrill through every soul, "Ye are not your own; ye are bought with a price." Your bodies, your spirits, your children, your property, your churches—all these are mine. For this cause I died and rose again, that I might be Lord of the whole. I come to claim it. If you can name any faculty of your nature which I have not ransomed; any moment of your time which I do not confer; any thing here in your possession which might not be employed in my service, it is yours to use at pleasure. Recall the past; if you can name any effort, however feeble, made in harmony with my will, but made in vain, with such efforts I dispense. Survey the world! If you can point to a spot where the destroyer of souls is not working the great system of destruction, that spot I allow you to pass by. Call for your race; let them pass before you in their nations and tribes; if you can point out one soul which is not in danger of perdition; one which my blood cannot cleanse; one which does not belong to me—him I allow you to neglect. Hearken, and you may hear the loud and piercing cry of souls perishing; if you can ever listen attentively without hearing it; if you can discover a pause in that fearful cry even for a moment, during that moment I allow you to relax. But no, it is incessant. How long shall it continue? Shall not India have a cross? Shall not Africa have a gospel? the world their Saviour? True, you have begun to lift the cross before the eyes of the nations; and wherever you have done so, angels have had to celebrate its triumphs. But your talents unemployed, your resources unexplored, your opportunities unimproved, evince how small the sympathy you have hitherto felt with it. Lift it higher, that more may see it; and higher still, that all the ends of the earth may behold it. I died for the world. Go, and proclaim it to every creature. The resources necessary are in your possession. I see them around me; and I accept the surrender. For this alone have I waited. All things now are ready. The fulness of time for the world's recovery has at length arrived. Nothing shall now delay the great consummation. The Sabbath of time has come—the jubilee of the world. I hear its gathering sounds of joy. I see its myriads flocking—all flesh coming to pray before the Lord—my righteousness their only robe, my name their only plea. My people, my own, my blood-bought Church, if ye know the grace of your Lord Jesus Christ, if his love can move your hearts, if his glory be dear in your eyes, be faithful to your trust; unite your resources; devote your energies; live for me. God himself from his throne shall rejoice over you, the eternal Spirit shall give efficacy to your every act; and then, soon shall you see a converted world, and I shall see of the travail of my soul and be satisfied; while Earth with all her tongues, and Heaven with all her harps, shall together roll the triumphant song, 'Alleluia, the Lord God omnipotent reigneth.'"

But this is the identical strain in which our Lord is to be regarded as constantly addressing us. In what other terms can we reply but by saying, Blessed Saviour, we are here before thee; we are thine. Do with us as seemeth good in thy sight. Only forgive the past. Breathe on us thine own Holy Spirit. Accept now our entire dedication; and, henceforth, by thy grace, we will *live* to reclaim the world which thou hast *died* to redeem.

XII. Only let these sentiments of devotedness be embodied by the Christian Church, and *the honor and triumph of the gospel will be complete*. And never till then will even *the evidences* of Christianity be complete. The logical argument for its truth, indeed, is perfect; no chain of reasoning can be more entire. But were its miracles to be all repeated again, and its prophecies to be multiplied a hundred-fold, some signal display of the power and excellence of its motives would still be wanting as the practical result of the whole. That signal proof is simply Christian consistency—*the consistency of a devoted Church*. In lieu of this, the world will accept nothing—not even the most convincing arguments and cogent appeals: "give us," they say, "a practical proof that you yourselves believe and are in earnest." Christ will accept nothing—not even the loudest professions; "if ye love me," saith he, "keep my commandments:" we ourselves can accept nothing—not even the activity of the missionary enterprise; our consciences testify against us, and say, "All this activity is far less than you can do; and you are pledged to do all that is possible for the recovery of the world. But where is your self-denial? As yet, you have given only the crumbs that fall from your table: where is your consecration? At present, you act only from occasional impulse, or compunction, or the lowest degree of principle: where is the weight of your character? Not merely is it wanting—well would it be if this were all—but it is against you; in exact proportion as it is absent from the cause of Christ, it is present to assist and promote the cause of his foes—to prolong the ruin of immortal souls. Until this evil be remedied, therefore, expect to be kept low, humbled, and disgraced, before the world; to be strangers to every thing like pentecostal visitations from on high; to be fearful, uncertain, and unhappy in yourselves But only remedy the evil—only be consistent—and then "arise and shine, for thy light will have come, and the glory of the Lord will have arisen upon thee."

What could stand before the gospel of Christ, were all the spirituality of its doctrines, the holiness of its precepts, and the earnest and compassionate benevolence of its aims, embodied and made visible in the living character of its disciples? Who could doubt the reality of its miracles, when the Church was seen standing upon them, so to speak, as on the mount of God, herself the crowning miracle—the great moral miracle of a vast community living, not unto themselves, but unto Him that died for them, and rose again? Who could question the truth of prophecy, when the fulfilment of a thousand prophecies was realized in that sublime spectacle itself; when the Church herself became a standing prophecy; her every act a presage of success; her every conflict a prediction of victory; her consecrated character, as the representative of her Lord's character, prophesying to the world, in mute but mighty eloquence, that to him every knee must bow? Who could doubt the reality, the superiority, the divinity of the gospel, when it had thus transferred the whole might of its own character to the character of the Church? We ourselves could not—though now, as the necessary result of our superficial acquaintance with that power, we often do; but then, in the largeness of its views, we should acquire such an expansion of soul, and in the execution of its lofty purpose such a sympathy with true greatness, as would make the weak like David, and David like an angel of the Lord. The world around us could not: as in primitive times, "fear would come upon every soul;" God would give us "favor with all the people," and would add "to the Church daily such as should be saved." Nor could the heathen themselves: their great argument against Christianity would be gone; the main objection with which our comparative apathy arms them, would, by the very change of our conduct, be converted into an irresistible plea in its behalf.

Who, that is acquainted with history, does not know the powerful influence of superior character? The world has nothing to compare with it. Laws, armies, revolutions, are only its creatures, or visible expressions. What deep homage the world has often paid to it! Royalty has trembled before it, till throne and sceptre shook. A nation, in the crisis of its existence, has passed by the palace, and gone in full confidence of aid to the cottage—the aid of character. An army in its peril has sued to it, as in the instance of Swartz, and been saved by it. The history of Christian missions proves that whole tribes of heathen have been moved and subdued by it, even when years of preaching had apparently failed. And often has a corrupt Church owed its toleration and continuance to the profound respect which the world felt for the character of a few of its members. But in all these instances, be it remarked, the character which has exercised the greatest influence is that which approached nearest to a union of integrity and disinterestedness—in other words, a character formed of *holy benevolence*. Now, what is this but the identical character which the gospel concentrates all its power to produce? What was the character of Paul but this? and what could wealth, rank, the world, have added to his influence for good? His disinterested, self-denying devotedness to the service of Christ, armed him with a power which will continue to be felt to the end of time, and which will probably be felt incomparably more then than now. But if the character of a single Christian can exercise such a sway, what would be the influence of a society of such men? Not living to themselves; not meeting for purposes of gain, but freely sacrificing it all; not prosecuting the Christian cause slowly and timidly, but, from enlightened conviction, precipitating themselves into it; abandoning themselves to it; showing themselves ready to sacrifice life for it! And if the influence of a single society of such men would be great, who can calculate the results which would ensue, were such the character of the entire Church? Were all the influences of which we spoke in the opening chapter—the influences arising from knowledge, speech, relationships, property, compassion, self-denial, perseverance, union, prayer—were all these developed in the Church to their utmost, and placed under holy principle, so as to become the sacred influence of Christian character, what a halo of glory would be shed over the whole of its earthly course! Were our conscientiousness in the service of Christ such, that we welcomed every duty, however trying; and such our courage in his cause, that we shrank from no danger; and such our sympathy with the travail of his soul, that our toils and travail for the same object knew no limits— what a kind of emblazonment would be thrown over the very *name* of Christianity! If we had simply acquired the char acter of not living to ourselves; of sincerely commiserating the miseries of the world, and of practically devoting ourselves to their removal—how impossible it would be to pronounce that *name*, without calling up in the heart feelings of homage and love! The character of the Church would give it the mastery of the world, and invest it with glory in the eyes of God; "and upon all the glory there should be a defence."

Now, what was the character of Christ but this? And what is our character to be but a copy of his? As his representatives, Christianity is to possess us, to live over again the life of Christ in us—speaking through us, breathing in us, acting by us. And it is this identity of character with the character of Christ which is to invest our every movement with so much influence. It is not to arise, as we have intimated already, from the increase of property and resources which such a self-denying character would necessarily place at our disposal—though that is to be taken into the account—but from its placing our character in harmony with perfection. The influence of Christ himself arises from his having placed himself, in an infinitely higher sense, indeed, in perfect harmony with the will and character of the Father. Sin had introduced apparent disorder into the Divine government, arraying law against law, and justice against mercy. Every principle of that government—every law in the universe—was calling, crying, for vindication in the punishment of man; while love, in apparent opposition to them all, was calling for his deliverance. Christ met them all with the cross; appeased them all, harmonized them all, and set them all again at liberty. His cross owes its influence entirely to the fact that he thus placed it, as the means of atonement, in harmony with all the great laws of the Divine government. By abandoning himself entirely to these, he moved the universe. All moving powers, all spiritual influences, the Holy Spirit himself, have thus become his.

And as he acquired his infinite influence in the mediatorial government by placing himself, as the great sacrifice for sin, entirely at the Divine disposal, and by identifying himself with the cause of holiness and mercy, the subordinate influence of our character is to arise entirely from our identity with his. But moving only in a line with him, taking law from no lips but his, copying no example but his life, and living instrumentally for no end but that for which he efficaciously died, our character would be in effect the prolongation of his own, and our influence his influence. The world could not doubt our identity with Christ; for they could not hear us speak, in our Christian capacity, but they would hear the compassionate voice of Christ; nor could they look on our conduct without being reminded of his example. They could not doubt of the power of Christian principle; for they would see that it secured the self-denying energy of the whole man, the whole Church. They could not question the distinctiveness of the Christian character; they would feel that the world had nothing like it; that the entire Church was an organization as distinct from every other society as if it had come down direct from heaven; and yet that it stood apart from the world and above it, only that it might draw them more effectually to Christ. They could not doubt our belief of their danger, or the depth of our concern for their deliverance, for they would see it in the unremitting earnestness of our efforts to save them. Nor could they doubt any longer the power of the gospel to transform the world; for every day would bring them the report of fresh accessions made to the kingdom of Christ. Only let the Church be itself; only let it become the devoted agency which it was meant to be; and the world should soon be given into its hands. Who could see it move in its missionary path without being ready to precede it as its eager herald, shouting, " Prepare ye the way of the Lord?" for Christ himself would be with it. Who could look down on the idolatrous regions which lay in its route without summoning them to surrender in the name of the Lord, and feeling the certainty of their speedy subjection to Christ? Who could look into the roll of prophecy without the full conviction that all those predictions which paint the universality and glory of Messiah's reign had reached the eve of their fulfilment? The honor and triumph of the gospel would be completed.

XIII. Our *regard for the glory of God requires this consecration.* This motive alone should be sufficient to engage the entire Church in one unsparing effort for the world's conversion. Darkness still covers the earth. Satan is still the god of this world. Idolatry continues to defy the heavens. Alas! what a debased and maddened world turns round to the eye of God! What shouts of hostility arise from it! What spectacles of shame, what enormities of guilt, are exhibited upon it! Now, can we remember whose character it is which is most insulted by this fearful state of things, and whose interest it is which is most wronged, without feeling "grieved at heart?" Can we imagine him "looking down from heaven," as of old, "upon the children of men, to see if there are any that understand and seek after him," and then picture to our minds the scenes which present themselves to his holy eye—the polytheism and practical atheism, the sottish ignorance, the horrid rites and ceremonies, the depraved passions, unnatural cruelties, and revolting immoralities—without feeling a holy zeal for God kindling within us? Can we imagine him listening to the sounds at this moment ascending from the vast regions of Asia, and think of "the lords many and gods many" whose names he hears invoked, while his own is comparatively unpronounced, without feeling even an anguish of concern for the vindication of his righteous claims? Can we remember that the Being who is thus robbed of the homage of his creatures is "God over all blessed for ever?" and that the being who appropriates that homage is the enemy of God, and the destroyer of souls, without feeling "very jealous for the Lord God of Israel?" Or can we remember, that while much of the great array of evil of which this world is the scene, is maintained in open defiance of his reign, as if he were the Tyrant instead of the God of the universe, many of the prevailing atrocities are perpetrated in his name, and as acceptable homage to his throne, as if he were the great Patron of iniquity— can we think of this without lifting up our eyes to heaven, as Jesus did, and exclaiming, "O righteous Father, the world hath not known thee!"

But might they not have known him? And, if so, must not the guilt of their ignorance, at present, rest on those who might have made him known? And can we remember what it is that we have to make known concerning him, without feeling that every moment during which we continue to withhold the gospel from the nations, we are virtually withholding from God his highest glory; that we are concealing from them a scheme of mercy from which he is expecting to derive his richest revenue of praise for ever? The knowledge of the arts, the discoveries of science, the treasures of philosophy—all these might be kept from them with comparative impunity; but that we should keep back from them, age after age, knowledge so important that prophets have been sent to impart it, angels have been the bearers of it, the Spirit himself has uttered it, till, in these last days, God has actually spoken to us by his Son; knowledge which so deeply concerns his own character, that it cannot be withheld without the most fatal results, nor imparted without reflecting on his name eternal glory—this should surely cover us with shame as it does with guilt. What if no news had come from heaven since the voice of inspiration died for a time on the lips of Malachi; what if no voice had ever cried in the wilderness, "Prepare ye the way of the Lord;" and no intimation been afforded that "God is love"—what at this moment would have been the state of the world but that of universal gloom and desolation? its only light streaming from the fires of demon-worship, its only sounds yells of defiance against Heaven? Yet such, in effect, is the lamentable condition in which we are voluntarily allowing large portions of the earth to lie. As if God had never spoken to *us*, we have never spoken to *them*. As if he were the cruel Moloch they suppose him to be, we have never told them the glorious fact that He is love—that he hath "so loved the world as to give his only-begotten Son, that whosoever believeth in him should not perish, but have everlasting life." As if he were quite as much in love with obscenity, revenge, and blood, as they choose to believe him, we have not chosen to warn them to the contrary. As if he had taken no steps whatever to correct the fatal error, had evinced no concern at the stain which thus blots out his glory—though in every age, and through every moment of the time that he has been suffering the foul and enormous wrong, he has been reminding us that he is filled with jealousy for his name's sake, and urging us to preach the gospel to every creature, as the only way of putting an end to the great lie which is everywhere told and believed against him—we have taken no steps to vindicate his blessed name. And the consequence is, that the glory of the incorruptible God is still represented by the most degraded and loathsome forms, and "the truth of God is changed into a lie." And yet we profess to feel for the dishonor put on him! Where, considering our means—where is our consistency?

But grievous as this dishonor is when considered simply by itself, there is a consideration which, in the eye of God, aggravates it without measure—the fact that it should be inflicted on him at the expense of his only-begotten and well-beloved Son. To have kept back the disclosures concerning himself made by his mere human messengers, would have been highly dishonoring to God; but that we should keep back from the dark world, not only his glory, but the very "brightness of his glory;" that we should conceal from a world filled with the most revolting and hideous images of Deity, "the Express Image of his person"—this is to put a slight on the character and work of Christ, which he cannot away with. That we should have seen the cross of Christ, and should yet have allowed the world to go on offering its human and other sacrifices, as if he had not "died once for all;" that we should have held this gospel in our hands, and yet have allowed a thousand impostors and demons to publish their Shastres and Korans instead; that we should "know the grace of our Lord Jesus Christ," grace so amazing that it is ever receiving ineffable expressions of the Father's complacency, and filling all heaven with praise, and yet that we should account it hardly worth reporting—this is to "wound the Father through the Son;" and that we should act thus, knowing as we do know how the heart of God is set on the glory of Christ, the height to which he has exalted him, and the promises of universal dominion and homage he has made to him—this is not merely to dishonor Infinite Majesty, but, what is incomparably worse, to inflict a wound on the very heart of Infinite Love.

Or can we, finally, remember what is to be the end of the whole mediatorial economy—that it is to redound "to the praise of the glory of his grace"—without feeling that to do any thing less than the utmost in our power to hasten the great consummation, is to publish our guilty indifference concerning it? It is impossible, even now, for the true Christian to hear of a single rebel submitting to God, and being brought back into harmony with the holy universe, without rejoicing in the honor which it brings to God. The very angels rejoice on account of it, in the presence of God. They see so many laws harmonized by it, so many claims satisfied, so much glory reflected on every attribute of the Triune God, that they rehearse for the last great chorus of the universe. But if the recovery to God of a single sinner redounds so greatly to his praise, what will be the glory accruing to him from a recovered world? In some respects he will be honored more by the obedience of earth than by the homage of heaven. There his glory has never been obscured; here it has suffered a long and dreadful eclipse; when, therefore, it shall again irradiate the world, well may the unfallen before the throne exclaim, "Holy, holy, holy is the Lord God of hosts; the whole *earth* is full of his glory!" When, in defiance of the machinations of the prince of darkness, and the mighty depravity of man, the empire of grace shall be everywhere triumphant, what honors will be recovered to the blessed God of which he has long been defrauded! When all things shall be sacred to his name, and all hearts reflecting his image, what expressions of his purity and love will be poured over the earth as the waters cover the sea! How will the mountains echo it to the valleys, and the valleys roll it back again to the mountains, that *even here*, at length, "the Lord God Omnipotent *reigneth!*" How will one continent proclaim it to another, and the ocean waft it to the main, that "the kingdoms of *this world* have become the kingdoms of our Lord and his Christ!" And when it shall be distinctly seen that, from first to last, the recovery of the world was entirely owing, through every stage and every step, to his boundless grace, what ascriptions of honor will the assembled and admiring universe pour forth, like the sound of many waters, to God and to the Lamb!

Now, is it possible for us to know that for that glory he is waiting; that his Church is constituted expressly to promote it; and that he is looking to every member of that Church to hasten its arrival, without feeling ourselves called on individually to put forth all our energies for its speedy consummation? Can any object in the universe be so momentous as the vindication of the Divine character, and the completion of the Divine glory? All other interests, compared with it, are lighter than nothing, and vanity. Compared with this, no thing is sacred, great, or precious. At the least signal, all heaven would rush together for its vindication; every holy intelligence become a champion in its behalf. And is it possible, that though the vindication of his glory has in an important sense been given into our charge, and though all the world is denying his existence, aspersing his name, or usurping his rights, yet, on turning his eyes from that great spectacle of blasphemy, to see what his Church is doing for its abatement, he should find us conniving at it, and, by our conduct, confirming it? Is it possible that the least stain cast upon our own name should arm our every power for its vindication, while the sight of hundreds of millions trampling his honor in the dust, and laboring in mad enmity to extinguish the last ray of his glory, should yet leave us calmly to give nearly all our time and attention to "what we shall eat, and what we shall drink, and wherewithal we shall be clothed?" "Father, forgive us, we know not what we do."

But not long can this state of things continue. The great cause of the Divine glory has come on in the heathen world. Ages have elapsed since the Christian Church was commissioned to plead that cause in all the earth. Still, however, the momentous controversy remains undecided. But God is giving indubitable signs that he will now bring it to an issue. Every minor interest must stand by. The theatre of the world is clearing for the decision. The Church is imperatively summoned to appear and give witness for God. To us he is saying, as he did to the members of his ancient Church, "Ye are my witnesses, that I, even I, am God, and besides me there is no Saviour." Christians, the world is waiting to receive your evidence. "By the mercies of God," will you not go and testify in his behalf? Satan is witnessing against him, and millions are crediting the revolting testimony: will you not hasten or send to testify for him? Atheism and Buddhism are denying his existence; and China, one-third of the human race, believe it; will you not go and proclaim, "This is the true God, and eternal life?" His ancient people are scattered over all the earth, each of them still with a veil over his heart, and stained with the blood of the Just One: will you not beseech them to "look upon him whom they have pierced," and urge on them his claims as their own Messiah? Popery is concealing, imprisoning, destroying his word as a dangerous book, and embracing an image or an amulet instead: will you not enable and urge its votaries to "search the Scriptures," to consult them as the "oracles of God?" Mohammedanism is denying the Divinity of his Son, and honoring an impostor in his stead: will you not attest that there is none other name under heaven given among men, whereby we can be saved, but the name of his Son our Saviour? Hindooism is affirming that his name is Kalee, and that he has given one half of the human race to be slaughtered for his honor; that it is Juggernaut, and that his worshippers must be covered with the scars of self-torture, and his chariot grind its way through a path strewn with their prostrate bodies: will you not arouse, will you not impel others to join you, and will you not speed to tell them all that "God is love?" universal and infinite love? Shall his cause have only a few friends to espouse it? Shall "the Church of God, which he hath purchased with his own blood," find few tongues to proclaim that that "blood cleanseth from all sin?"

Followers of God, his cause, your cause, the cause of a deluded and dying world, is before you. In every part of the world he has obtained for you a hearing, and is awaiting your arrival. At this moment he is saying to his Church, to every individual member, to the Christian reader of this book—and saying it, not for the third, but the thousandth time—"Lovest thou me?" Then, by the tender and melting considerations which led you at first to surrender yourself to my claims; by the weight of all the obligations under which my grace has laid you; if there be any thing in my gift of Christ to excite your love, any thing in his blood to benefit the world, any thing in my glory to engage your concern, awake to your high prerogative and office, call down the aid of the Holy Spirit, and let every creature hear you "testify that the Father sent the Son to be the Saviour of the world." Soon should "my name be great among the heathen; and in every place incense and a pure offering would be offered on my altar." No longer should my character be defamed, my government impugned, my designs impeached and opposed, nor my honors usurped; but everywhere would my claims be brought forward to the public view, and everywhere should I be acknowledged as "God over all, blessed for ever." The earth should be "filled with my glory, and all flesh see it together."

XIV. Then such a consummation of the Divine glory would be equally *the completion of human happiness.* Indeed, what but this constitutes the happiness of heaven? Conceive of the will of God "done on earth as it is in heaven," and you conceive of "the days of heaven upon earth." The last idol would have been cast away, and the last rod of the last oppressor broken. Every government would but execute the law of God, and every subject would but obey the gospel. The activities of mind, the discoveries of enterprise, the accumulations of wealth, the changes of empire, the revolutions of time—all would be seen laid at his feet, and falling into his plan. Every habitation would be a house of God; every occupation a holy exercise; every day a return of the Sabbath; for whatever was done " would be done to the glory of God." Like what a sea of glass would the universal mind of man become; everywhere pure and unruffled, and reflecting only the colors of the rainbow round about the throne! What a world! when, compared with its all-pervading peace, and loveliness, and light, "the former heavens and the former earth shall not be remembered nor come into mind."

And is there ground to conclude that this sublime result shall be realized? "The mouth of the Lord hath spoken it." "I have sworn by myself, the word hath gone out of my mouth in righteousness, and shall not return, that unto me every knee shall bow, and every tongue shall swear." At what precise period, or to what exact point of perfection the result may be realized, we cannot say, and are not anxious to know. Sufficient is it for us to know that the time shall come when the world shall be seen prostrate before God in worship. And then will it be clearly perceived that this has been brought to pass as the result of all that God has planned, and Christ has suffered, and the Spirit has effected. The very mention of his name then will be sufficient to bring the world into a posture of adoration. They will come before him hungry for his blessing, languishing for his Spirit, coveting, craving the gifts of his grace. "O Thou that hearest prayer, to thee shall all flesh come!" They shall not be satisfied to enjoy thee alone; they shall go out, and with a friendly violence compel others to come in, and share thy favors with them. "It shall come to pass, that there shall come people and the inhabitants of many cities; and the inhabitants of one city shall go to another, saying, Let us go speedily to pray before the Lord, and to seek the Lord of hosts; I will go also. Yea, many people and strong nations shall come to seek the Lord, and to pray before the Lord." Churches shall come to adore him, cities to consult him, nations to surrender to him, all the kindreds of the earth to fall down before him. They shall not be content to praise him alone; they shall feel as if they wanted help—the help of the world—to raise a song adequate to his praise, and a prayer equal to the ardor of their desires. "And it shall come to pass that from one new moon to another, and from one Sabbath to another, shall all flesh come to worship before me, saith the Lord."

Then man will have found his only proper place; will have returned to the only spot in the universe which becomes him—at the feet of God. And, having found his proper place, his ultimate end, there will he rest; going out of himself, and losing himself in God. Then God will have recovered his proper glory; every idol will be abolished, every rival power cast out, the eyes of all will wait upon him, all flesh will be seen staying themselves upon him; he will be seen by the universe as the centre of a lapsing creation, the support and stay of a sinking world. Then the design of the whole gospel constitution will be completed—"that no flesh should glory in his presence;" every thing will have redounded to the glory of his grace. And when all flesh shall thus be seen, in effect, prostrate before God in prayer, what will it be but a prelude to the worship of heaven? What will remain but that the whole should be transferred to the employment of praise above! Infinite love, ascending the throne, and putting on the crown, shall sit down and enjoy an eternal Sabbath of love! while the myriads of the redeemed and glorified, casting their crowns before him, shall ascribe their happiness to him, and the jubilee of eternity shall begin.

And is such to be the end of the missionary enterprise? And is this the object at which it calls us to aim? Christian, where else are interests like these at stake? Where else, amidst all the enterprises of time, does so wide a field stretch before the view, or such momentous consequences await the result? To overrate such an object is impossible; to stand aloof from it, or even to regard it coldly, is enormous guilt. What, then, is the amount of practical interest which you are taking in it? Ask yourself—is it at all commensurate with its mighty claims?

The policy of statesmen, and the projects of national ambition, may lay wide their schemes over other realms, and subordinate passing events, and entail the fulfilment of their designs on their successors to a distant posterity; but here is a scheme so vast in its sweep, as to subordinate all other plans to its design; so varied in its workings, as to demand the strenuous activity of every agent in the universe; and yet so self-sufficient as absolutely to stand in need of none. Need you be reminded that in the arrangements of that plan a post of activity is assigned to you; and that in that post the whole of your sanctified influence is laid under tribute through every moment of life? Great, indeed, is your guilt if you are acting on any independent plans of your own; if you are planning for any thing but how best you may blend with its working, and aid in its accomplishment.

A mere worldly philanthropy may boast of its generous doings, and point to its schools, and hospitals, and humanizing institutions—though even these were originated indirectly by the influence of Christianity; but here is a cause which, having done all this, would yet hardly count its work begun; which scatters these minor blessings as it advances to accomplish a good infinitely greater; which can point to ignorance sitting at the feet of Christ, hordes of the wilderness converted into Christian Churches; the worshippers of demons made kings and priests unto God, and actually mingling in the adorations of the temple above. But how much of all this, and what particular part of it, were you the means of originating or effecting? And what are you now doing to augment these happy results? What source of tears are you now laboring to dry up? What particular form of evil is now engaging your attention and filling you with concern? What object engaging your special and earnest supplication?

Science may talk of the future, may promise largely, and be sanguine of its useful results; but here is a cause which makes all the wants and woes of the world its own, and will never count its work complete till they have all been removed and forgotten. On this cause, all the treasures of the universe have been lavished, all creation is groaning and travailing in pain together for want of it, and all the voices of heaven and earth are urging you to take part in it. What are you doing for its promotion? Is the utmost extent of your instrumentality in its behalf a small donation in money, and occasionally a languid prayer?

History may record her eventful eras, when all the powers of earth were drawn up in hostile array, and all its interests suspended on a single conflict. Such may be regarded to have been the case when the great question was to be decided by a single blow between Greece and Persia, whether freedom or slavery should be the future inheritance of mankind; when the victory of Constantine determined whether paganism or Christianity should hold the throne of the Roman empire; when, on the plain of Tours, it was decided whether the Crescent should prevail over the Cross in the west as it had in the east—whether Imposture should drive the Truth from the earth; and when, on the event of the Armada, it was to be decided whether Popery or Protestantism should prevail, whether the earth should belong to Christ or to Antichrist. But here, all that is left of these ancient elements of conflict is marshalled anew; every thing depraved and malignant is here found in conflict with every thing benevolent and holy, and the issue is to involve the final destiny of immortal myriads. Are you conscious of having caught the spirit of the contest? of feeling how much may depend, under God, on your single arm? and are you, accordingly, to be found at your post, and acquitting yourself as a good soldier of Jesus Christ?

Eventful times and great enterprises may have produced extraordinary men—men whose memory biography may have embalmed; whose honors heraldry may have emblazoned; whose likeness art and genius may have taxed their powers to multiply; whose fame is accounted so precious, that nations may have charged themselves with the office of guarding it; and the youth of each succeeding generation may be taken to their tomb as to a shrine, and be taught to regard them as filling the place of a glorious ancestry, urging them by their example to an emulation of their noble deeds. But here is a cause which has ever been producing men "of whom the world was not worthy;" men "whose names are in the book of life;" men "whose praise is in all the churches," kindling holy enthusiasm, and who, by their influence, are reproducing themselves in the useful lives of others: men who, "though dead, are yet speaking," speaking together, and saying, "Be ye followers of us, as we followed Christ." Are you heeding the exhortation? Might it be fairly inferred from any thing visible in your conduct that you are living for the great object for which many of them cheerfully died? that you sympathize with them in the intensity of their concern for the salvation of the world? Philosophy may boast of her martyrs, and tell her disciples what severity of discipline, and what untiring patience and perseverance, the prosecution of her claims and projects requires; but here is an object which demanded the actual sacrifice of the Son of God, and which is ever demanding the unrelaxing and unqualified devotedness of all his followers in all succeeding times. What sacrifices are you making in its behalf? and in what do those sacrifices consist? Here is an object which brings you into contact with more than prophets and apostles, and which requires you to imitate a higher example than that even of confessors and martyrs. By summoning you "to the help of the Lord," it calls you to act at his side, places you under the notice of his eye, and requires you to "follow his steps." Have you ever been seized with the hallowed ambition of copying his example? Are you aspiring to win from his lips the "Well done, good and faithful servant," which awaits each of his devoted followers, on their arrival in his presence above?

Others may boast of comprehensive designs, and talk of final causes; but here is the final cause itself—an end so great, that all other ends stand to it only in the relation of means—so lofty, that there is nothing higher—so glorious, that every thing in the universe is honored by serving it. The one point, the sole end, to which every thing in the government of God is tending, is, "to the praise of the glory of his grace;" and to this point it is tending with the directness and force of a universal law. Every mite given, every Bible distributed, every missionary sent forth, every Church planted, falls in with that stream of events, and forms a part of that vast combination of means by which God is reducing and restoring all things unto himself. Even now, the agencies of Providence are urged into unusual activity—all things are rushing to that final issue. Delay to join in the march of mercy, and you will lose opportunities of honoring God, and of serving your race, such as never occurred to the Church before, and can never be enjoyed by you again. Be indolent, covetous, self-indulgent now, and the very stones will cry out. Continue to live for yourself, and the universe will upbraid you—the perishing will point at and reproach you as accessory to their destruction—the Judge himself will say, "I never knew you." On the contrary, be faithful now, and the very trees of the field will clap their hands: live unto the Lord, and all things shall live for you, and be ready to serve you in his cause: be entirely devoted to his claims, and others shall be moved by your example, and the world blessed by your influence, and Christ himself shall rejoice over you. Less than entire consecration has been tried for ages; and the fatal result is to be seen in the thousands perpetually passing—passing at this moment—to the bar of God from regions where the sound of salvation has never been heard. If you sympathize with Christ, then, in the travail of his soul, you will from this time see what entire devotedness can do for their recovery. Moved by his example, you will look through your tears on a world perishing in its guilt; and you will feel that you are never imitating him so much as by self-denying, painstaking endeavors for its salvation. Subdued by the tenderness of his claims, you will freely acknowledge that you are not your own : that the same reasons which bind you to do any thing for Christ, bind you to do every thing in your power, and to do it in the best possible manner : that you are bought with a price which might well purchase the entire dedication of a whole universe of intelligent beings to all eternity. Affected and engrossed by the magnitude of his cause—the cause of the world's recovery—you will feel that to throw less than all your energies into its promotion is an insult to all the momentous interests which it involves. Not only, therefore, will you task your own powers in its behalf—you will task them partly in an earnest endeavor to move heaven and earth to join you. In a word, constrained by his love, you will "thus judge"—and never can you be said to be moved by his love except as you are thus judging, and laboriously acting on the judgment— "that if one died for all, then were all dead; and that he died for all, that they who live should not henceforth live unto themselves, but unto him who died for them and rose again." Hasten, then, into his presence, fall down at his feet, and surrender yourself, and every thing you have, to his service. He will graciously accept the dedication; and ten thousand ages hence you will be still praising him that you did so; and an unknown number will join in blessing him on your account.

INDEX.

	PAGE
Abraham, holy agency of	62
Activity, a means of usefulness	56
Christian, final success of	262, 367
Agency, Christian, Divine origin of	69
true character of	21
America, aborigines of	246
resources and responsibility of	249
American Baptist Board of Missions, origin of	148, 151
Board of For. Miss., origin of	148, 151
Methodist Episcopal Missionary Society	149, 151
Protestant Episcopal Missionary Society	149, 151
Angels, agency of	129
holy activity of	88
interest of, in Christ's mediation	88
sympathy of, in man's salvation	80
Antioch, conduct of the church at	81
Apostles, conduct of, in the diffusion of the gospel	77
manner in which they understood prophecy	123
qualified and authorized to diffuse the gospel	67
travels of	81
Apostolic epistles, illustrative of the spirit of missions	84
Arts, promoted by missionary efforts	158
Asiatic churches, injunctions to	140
Association, principle of moral	33
Baptist Miss. Society, origin of	147, 151
Basle, missionary seminary at	148
Bible Society, origin of the	149
Biography, right influence of, on Christians	332
Boyle, Hon. R., Christian zeal of	145
Brahminism, decline of	169
Britain, extensive influence of	249
political state of	359
temporal benefits of, from gospel	157
British churches, influence of missions on	192
Britons abroad, influence of missions on	211
Central Africa, present state of	245
Character, Christian, elevated by missions	201
weight of	379
China, present state of	169
Christ, anticipation of his glory	34
character of	381

	PAGE
Christ, devotedness of, to his engagements	65, 96
influence of his advent on man	29
intercessory prayer of	126
irresistible claims of, on the devotedness of his people	97
jealousy of, in addressing his Church	136
kingdom of, gradually set up	126
mediatorial right of	368
pity of, for the lost world	125
promise of his presence	127
satisfaction of, in his conquest of the world	132
Christian, closeness of his identity with Christ	71
fitness of, for usefulness	43
motives for his activity	133
object of Christ in redeeming	373
prayer of, for the world	72
Christians, expectations of Christ from	67
past conduct of, to be retrieved	353
present responsibility of	99
their means of usefulness	48
union of, for the diffusion of the gospel	74
Christendom, the divisions of	246
Christianity, influence of, on individual man	37
means of its early extension	141
temporal benefits afforded by	153
tendency of, to form society	45
Christian influence, prominence of, in the New Testament	60
instrumentality, theory of	33
labor, impossibility of being lost	366
Church Missionary Society, origin of	147, 151
the completion of its triumphs	378
decline of its devotedness and prosperity	139
Divine displeasure with the supineness of	387
duty of individual members of	388
increase of its influence	93
influence of unity in	48
missionary constitution of	311
present transition state of	364
prosperity, arising from activity	138
separation of, from the world	45
usefulness of	46

(397)

INDEX

Church, views of, enlarged by missions 196
Churches, the reformed 247
Civilization, how produced by Christianity 158
Clean water, how sprinkled on the Church 121
Colonization, peculiar to Christianity 257
Coming of Christ, scriptural import of the phrase 106
Commerce, promoted by missions...... 189
Compassion, a mean of usefulness.... 57
Consecration, Christian, importance of 306, 342
  required by our regard for the glory of God 382
Consistency, Christian, influence of.. 378
Conversion, triumphs of 189
Covenant, new, character of 120
Creation, anticipation of the deliverance of 35
Cross of Christ, influence of 35, 127
David, tabernacle of, its reference to the Church 119
Dependence and influence, universal law of 21
Devotedness, Christian, examples of, 302
  importance of 357
Disunion among Christians, evils of.. 302
Dry bones, valley of 119
Dutch missions 145
Edinburgh Missionary Society, origin of 147
Education, promoted by missions 161, 178
Emulation, Christian, promoted by missions 194
Era, commencement of a new 365
European character, raised by missions 188
Evil, moral influence of the introduction of 26
Foulahs, civilization of the 282
France, naturalism of 247
French Protestant Missionary Society, origin of 148
Friends' mode of civilizing Indians.. 283
Future, disclosures of the, made to the Church 91
General Baptist Missionary Society, origin of 148, 151
Geneva missions 154
Gentiles, why first preached to by the apostles 123
German Missionary Society, origin of 148, 151
Germany, rationalism of 247
Glasgow Missionary Society, origin of 148
God, character of, pledged for the success of the gospel 108
  eminently glorified by missions. 212
  promises of, as to the success of his word 108

Gospel, adaptation of, to the mind.... 38
  influence of its success 107
  perpetuity of the preaching of... 124
  power of, illustrated by missions 209
  published by an angel 128
  result of its publication 319
  withholding of, dishonor done to Christ 385
Greek Church, present state of 246
Happiness, human, completion of..... 389
Harvest, influence of Christians on the moral 73
  of the world, how reaped by Christians 125
Heathen, awfully dangerous state of 271, 357
  not to be neglected on account of the state of home 236
  readiness of, to receive the gospel 361
Heaven, how fully prepared for the redeemed 90
  the heathen prepared for by missions 182
History, encouragement given by, to Christian agency 231
  eventful eras of 392
Holy Spirit, agency of, in the Church 68
  given for the diffusion of the gospel 74
  glory of his dispensation 111
  influence of, on man 30
  influence of, essential to usefulness 49
  promise of his influence 68
  promise of, in connection with injunctions to duty 107
  work of, to glorify Christ 70
Hope, influence of, on Christian activity 105
Horsley, Bishop, quoted on the rule of prophecy 107
Humanity promoted by Christian missions 162
Humility, Christian, vast importance of 308
Idolatry abolished by missions 173
Impending judgments, usefulness of 122
India, early missions in 143
  present state of 230, 256
Indians, missions to 145
Infanticide abolished by missions.... 109
Infidelity lessened by missions..... 205
Influence, moral power of 22
  Christian, constantly accumulating 92
  mighty power of 224
  prominence of, in the New Testament 69
  moral, stimulated by sin 29
Instrumentality, Christian, theory of 36
  holy, employed by the patriarchs 61
Jehovah, love of, to man 66

Jerusalem, conduct of the church at 80
Jewish economy, adaptation of, to
   bless the world 63
   Church, a type of the Christian . 64
   influence of......................... 93
   separation of, from the world 64
Jews, awakening among.................. 248
   conversion of, by the gospel....... 118
   society for the conversion of, origin of 143
Johnson, Dr. S., extract from........... 93
Judgments, great, overruled for the salvation of the world............. 114
Karaite Jews, claims of................. 248
Kingdom, establishment of Christ's.. 150
   of Christ, certain progress of the 122
   gradually set up 126
Knowledge, a means of usefulness... 50
Laws, institution of, promoted by Christian missions 102
Laymen, necessity of the missionary agency of............................ 329
Liberality, necessity of increased pecuniary 324
Literature promoted by missions...... 184
London Missionary Society, origin of............................. 147, 151
Man, dependence of, on others......... 22
   knowledge of, promoted by missions................................ 187
Mediation effected by missionaries ... 105
Methodist Missionary Societies,
                            147, 149, 151
Millenarianism opposed to Scripture 106, 112
Millenarians, mistakes of............... 104
   objections of, to missions, refuted 294
Millennium, Christian expectation of 102
Ministers, necessity of their increased attention to missions 320
Missionaries, earliest, sent from Britain 142
Missionary activity, origin and history of 141
   efforts, success equal to........ 217, 258
   enterprise, summary of............ 151
   temporal benefits of............. 153
   information, importance of the diffusion of...................... 314
   societies, tabular statement of.... 151
   influence of their origin....... 147
   spirit, existence of, in early ages 141
   existence and progress of, in the churches. 250
Missions, benefits of, beyond calculation 170
   Christian, history of................. 138
   Church constituted for 264
   conviction of the Church as to its duty towards 209
   evidence furnished by, of the truth of Christianity 207

Missions, importance of the due appreciation of......................... 309
   influence of, on the increase of the Romish Church............... 140
   influence of science on........... 254
   motives to engage in 348
   must precede civilization 276
   not impracticable................... 273
   objections to, answered............. 269
   obligations not lessened by want of funds or union............ 291-293
   peculiar advantages derived from 223
   Protestant, origin of................ 141
   providential facilities for......... 254
Morality promoted by missions 103
Moravian missions, origin of...... 146, 151
Mosaic dispensation, agency of........ 62
Nations, existence of, preserved by missions 164
Native agency, success of.............. 226
Netherlands Miss. Society, origin of.. 148
New creation, the....................... 131
New England, Christianity planted in 145
Opposition to the gospel, destruction of 129
Parental influence, corruption of..... 26
Paul, conduct of, in reference to the gospel............................... 77
   self-denial of......................... 78
Peace, promoted by missions 179
Persevering activity, a means of usefulness................................. 57
Philanthropy, worldly, inefficiency of 301
Piety, importance of an increase of.. 315
Prayer, a means of usefulness....... 58
   increase of, for missions...... 259, 266
   need of a larger increase of 234
   spirit of, prompted by missions.. 259
Preaching, importance of, in the conversion of the world............. 123
Property, a means of usefulness....... 54
   consecrated to missions............ 199
Prophecy, favorable influence of, on missions 201
   influence of, on the Church 102
   wise reserve of 109
Providence, dispensations of, favorable to missions...................... 358
Rationalism among Christians and Jews 247, 248
Redemption, claim of 371
   harmony of, with the Divine mind................................ 32
   its Divine origin.................... 29
Relationship, a means of usefulness 31, 52
Religion, cause of, but one............ 195
Remedy for selfishness, how provided 28
Renovation of the world, an object of ancient expectation 124
Responsibility, extent of moral....... 25

INDEX.

Rhenish Missionary Society, origin of 148, 151
Roman greatness, its character 92
Romish Church, influence of missions on the increase of 140
 present state of 247
Russia, early establishment of Christianity in 142
 education in 246
Sabbath, observance of, promoted by missions 180
Satan, conquest of, over man 27
 subdued by Messiah 30
Schlegel, extract from 92
Science, inefficiency of 391
 promoted by missions 184
Self-denial, a means of usefulness..... 55
Self-examination, importance of 301
Selfishness, its origin 25
 remedy for 28
Shipping interest, promoted by missions 190
Smith, Dr. J. P., extract from 102
Society for Promoting Christian Knowledge, origin of 145
 for Propagating Christian Knowledge, origin of 146
 for Propagation of the Gospel in Foreign Parts 146
 for Propagation of the Gospel in New England 145
Speech, a means of usefulness........... 50
Stone, progress of the living 129
Suttees abolished by missions 169
Swartz, character of... 188
Swedish missions 145

Swiss missions................................... 145
Swiss, the, originators of Protestant missions 144
Tapu, abolished by missions 108
Temple, erection of the spiritual....... 130
 the ancient, type of the Christian and the Church 375
Tract Society, origin of the 149
Truth, evils of partial views of.......... 298
 moral influence of 34
Union, a means of usefulness 59
 Christian, importance of............. 321
 Christian, promoted by missions 107
Universe, dependence and influence, the law of 21
Watson, Richard, quoted 166
Wesleyan Missionary Society 147, 151
Western Africa, mission of Friends to 148
Wisdom, holy, increase of................. 316
Woman, rank of, elevated by missions 109
Work of Christ, relation of, to man... 29
World, entire conquest of................. 393
 effect produced by surveying it.. 376
 moral aspect of, favorable to missions 252, 265
 moral state of...................... 381, 387
 pernicious influence of, on man .. 39
 political state of, favorable to missions 235
 present awful state of 355
 result of the conversion of 385
Young men, appeal to...................... 367
Zeal, Christian, necessity for an increase of 332

THE END.

www.ingramcontent.com/pod-product-compliance
Lightning Source LLC
Chambersburg PA
CBHW032011220426
43664CB00006B/206